THEORIES OF AFRICANS

Black Literature and Culture
A series edited by Houston A. Baker, Jr.

THEORIES OF AFRICANS

Francophone Literature and Anthropology in Africa

Christopher L. Miller

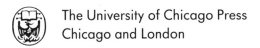

The University of Chicago Press
Chicago and London

The University of Chicago Press, Chicago 60637
The University of Chicago Press, Ltd., London
© 1990 by The University of Chicago
All rights reserved. Published 1990
Printed in the United States of America
99 98 97 96 95 94 93   5 4 3 2

Library of Congress Cataloging-in-Publication Data

Miller, Christopher L., 1953–
    Theories of Africans: Francophone literature and anthropology in
Africa / Christopher L. Miller.
        p.   cm.—(Black literature and culture)
    Includes bibliographical references and index.
    ISBN 0-226-52801-4 (cloth). ISBN 0-226-52802-2 (pbk.)
    1. African literature (French)—History and criticism—Theory,
etc.   2. Literature and anthropology—Africa. French-speaking West.
3. Africa, French-speaking West—Intellectual life.   4. Mandingo
(African people)—Intellectual life.   5. Africa, French-speaking
West, in literature.   6. Mandingo (African people) in literature.
I. Title. II. Series.
PQ3980.M55   1990
840.9'96—dc20   90-36154
                                              CIP

For Christopher Rivers

La transparence n'apparaît plus comme le fond du miroir où l'humanisme occidental reflétait le monde à son image; au fond du miroir, il y a maintenant de l'opacité, tout un limon déposé par des peuples surgis de la face cachée de la terre, limon fertile mais à vrai dire incertain, le plus souvent nié ou dominé.

—Edouard Glissant, in *La Quinzaine littéraire*

Contents

Acknowledgments

My work on this project has benefited from a great deal of support, both intellectual and material. My graduate and undergraduate students at Yale have been a constant aid, as interlocutors and sounding boards; many of the ideas expressed here only took form in the process of class-room dialogue. For various kinds of intellectual support, I would like to thank Henry Louis Gates, Jr., Anthony Appiah, Sara Suleri, Fredric Jameson, Joan DeJean and Nancy Miller, and Howard Bloch. Manthia Diawara and Anne McClintock deserve special thanks. Peter Brooks's help has been indispensible to me. I am also grateful to Mogens Trolle Larsen and Michael Harbsmeier of the Center for Sammenlignende Kulturforskning in Copenhagan, who organized a colloquium entitled "From Orality to Literacy and Back," for their invitation and support. In Dakar, I was particularly aided by Madame Dramé of the Présence Africaine office, Helen Picard, Alioune Tine, Cheik Aliou Ndao, Madické Diop, Jean-Pierre Makouta-M'Boukou, Aminata Maïga Ka, and Papa Gueye Ndiaye of Nouvelles Editions Africaines; in Bamako by Alpha Konaré, Barbara Hoffmann, Ismaila Samba Traoré, Moussa Sow, and the late Massa Makan Diabaté; and in Abidjan, by Amadou Koné, Christopher Fitzgerald, Kodjo Léonard, and Niangoran Bouah.

Research for this project was greatly aided by a National Endowment for the Humanities summer stipend; a Morse Fellowship in the Humanities from Yale University; and a Fulbright grant, which permitted me an extended trip to Senegal, Mali, and Côte d'Ivoire in 1987.

Most of all, I am grateful to Christopher Rivers for making the work worthwhile.

Earlier versions of three chapters appeared in journals, to which I am grateful for permission to reprint. Chapter 1 appeared as "Theories of Africans: The Question of Literary Anthropology," in *Critical Inquiry* 13, no. 1 (Autumn 1986), © 1986 by The University of Chicago. All rights reserved. Chapter 2 appeared as "Ethnicity and Ethics in the Criticism of Black African Literature," in *The South Atlantic Quarterly* 87, no. 1 (Winter 1988). Versions of chapter 3 appeared in *The Southern Review* 23, no. 1 (January 1987) and in *Culture and History* 3 (1988). I am also grateful to Alpha Oumar Konaré, editor of *Jamana,* for permission to reproduce the cartoon from that journal. In all cases, the present chapters supersede previously published versions.

1

Une caravane traverse l'étendue infinie et morne de ces plaines, caravane de négriers, le plus souvent poussant devant eux de lamentables théories d'hommes, de femmes, d'enfants couverts d'ulcères, étranglés par le carcan, mains ensanglantées par les liens.

A caravan traversed those dismal and endless plains: slave traders driving wretched files ["theories"] of men, women, and children, covered with open sores, choked in iron collars, their wrists shackled and bleeding.

—Yambo Ouologuem, *Le Devoir de violence*

Introduction: Reading through Western Eyes

Caveat Lector

At the moment when this study was first conceived, American literary criticism was beginning to open its doors once again to the outside world. Edward Said wrote in 1983 that "contemporary critical discourse is worldless;"[1] today, it is somewhat less so. For the reader of black African literature in French, the dethroning of rigid theoretical criticism and the questioning of the Western canon (which was the material base of that criticism), have come none too soon. The approach to a reading of Camara Laye, Ahmadou Kourouma, or Mariama Bâ should never have been the program prescribed for Rousseau, Wordsworth, or Blanchot. If one is willing to read a literature that might not be a rewriting of Hegel (or even of Kant), and if the negative knowledge of recent theoretical criticism is questioned in the universality of its applications, then what options are really open to a Western reader of non-Western literature? Claiming a break with his/her own culture and critical upbringing, can he/she read the other, the African, as if from an authentically African point of view, interpreting Africa in African terms, perceiving rather than projecting?

1. Edward W. Said, *The World, the Text and the Critic* (Cambridge: Harvard University Press, 1983): 151.

1

A consideration of the Western reading of African literature should begin with what African critics have written on the subject. Their comments are sobering. J. P. Makouta-M'Boukou, a francophone critic and novelist, rightly scolds Western critics who refuse to take into account the distance between themselves and African culture, and who read African literature only in function of their own cultural context.[2] The Nobel laureate Wole Soyinka, more forbiddingly, complains : "We black Africans have been blandly invited to submit ourselves to a second epoch of colonisation—this time by a universal-humanoid abstraction defined and conducted by individuals whose theories and prescriptions are derived from the apprehension of *their* world and *their* history, *their* social neuroses and *their* value systems." Elsewhere, Soyinka refers to Westerners hovering over African literature like vultures.[3] Chinua Achebe denounces Western critics who arrogantly claim to understand Africa better than African writers do, and he invites Westerners to adopt a new humility "appropriate to [their] limited experience of the African world;" he also urges that "the word *universal* [be] banned altogether from discussions of African literature until such time as people cease to use it as a synonym for the narrow, self-serving parochialism of Europe."[4] (For all practical purposes, the United States may be considered part of "Europe" here; in francophone Africa, Americans are included among *Européens*.)

The most powerful analysis of the system that gives rise to these complaints comes from the francophone African philosopher Paulin Hountondji. In a critique of the market dynamics that control the relation between Western academies and the African world, Hountondji shows how the division of labor has been unequal, with the highly valued role of *theorizer* belonging almost exclusively to Westerners, while Africans are confined to the gathering of raw information. Africa provides materials (like palm oil or literary texts), which European institutes process into finished commodities (like Palmolive soap or works of criticism of African literature). The "brain drain" of intellectuals from the South into the academies of the North is just a symptom of a large centripetal machine which sweeps "all intellectual and scientific expertise . . . toward

2. *Introduction à l'étude du roman négro-africain de langue française* (Abidjan: Les Nouvelles Editions Africaines, 1980): 9.

3. *Myth, Literature and the African World* (Cambridge: Cambridge University Press, 1976): x; on vultures, quoted in Omafume F. Onoge, "The Crisis of Consciousness in Modern African Literature," in Georg M. Gugelberger, ed., *Marxism and African Literature* (Trenton, N.J.: Africa World Press, 1985): 41.

4. Chinua Achebe, "Colonialist Criticism," in *Morning Yet on Creation Day* (London: Heinemann, 1975): 6, 9. See also D. Ibe Nwoga, "The Limitations of Universal Critical Criteria," in Rowland Smith, ed., *Exile and Tradition: Studies in African and Caribbean Literature* (New York: African Publishing Co., 1976): 8–30.

the center," that is, toward Europe and the United States.[5] According to Hountondji's analysis, no individual can escape from this system (but I take him to mean that everyone must try). For an American scholar, positioned at the extreme margin in relation to Africa, yet living and working in the country that Hountondji calls the very "center of the center" of the knowledge industry, the contradiction could not be greater.

This series of quotations from African critics would appear to leave little hope of a positive role for the Western critic. The most salutary contribution might be to fall silent and wait for the balance of power to change. In my opinion, however, the change is already taking place, and the solutions to European hegemony are implicit in the critiques I have cited. Hountondji's work—to which I will return later in this chapter—already constitutes a step toward altering the system he describes. Along with V. Y. Mudimbe, Hountondji makes it possible for readers to conceptualize Africa and its cultures using models that are proposed by Africans; these scholars are breaking down the wall between "theory" as exclusively Western and "information" as all that Africa can provide. So the intellectual landscape is already different from the one lamented by Makouta-M'Boukou, Soyinka, and Achebe, or at least *it should be.* In order for anything to change, the Western reader must now contextualize African texts within an increasingly African framework. All of the disciplines of the humanities are in the process of decolonization, and as the process moves forward, it becomes both possible and imperative for readers to supplant Eurocentrism with Afrocentrism, while remaining attentive to *eccentric* strategies that operate in new, overdetermined spaces. Thus, for example, the publication of UNESCO's multivolume history of Africa has made it possible to see history written from the point of view of the colonized and to end the monopoly of history told from the European perspective; thus the publication of Mudimbe's *The Invention of*

5. Paulin Hountondji, "Reprendre," in V. Y. Mudimbe, ed., *The Surreptitious Speech: "Présence Africaine" and the Politics of Otherness 1947–1987,* forthcoming. For historical perspective on the division of labor in African studies, see Robert Thornton, "Narrative Ethnography in Africa, 1850–1920: The Creation and Capture of an Appropriate Domain for Anthropology," *Man* n.s. 18, no. 3 (September 1983): "There is a clear division of labor between the producers of information and the theory-smiths of the universities in Europe, Britain and America" (516); see also Michael Crowder, " 'Us' and 'Them': The International African Institute and the Current Crisis of Identity in African Studies," *Africa* 57, no. 1 (1987): 109–22. For a radical critique of the American African-Studies establishment, motivated by anti-Vietnam war sentiments, see Africa Research Group, "Les études africaines en Amérique: la famille étendue," in Jean Copans, ed., *Anthropologie et impérialisme* (Paris: Maspero, 1975): 155–212.

6. Portions of this paragraph are taken from my essay, "Alioune Diop and the Unfinished Temple of Knowledge," in *The Surreptitious Speech,* ed. Z. Y. Mudimbe (forthcoming).

Africa makes manifest a sea change in African discourse: as Mudimbe puts it, the African "subject-object" now has "the freedom of thinking of himself or herself as the starting point of an absolute discourse."[7]

In the wake and in the midst of these changes, African literature can no longer be seen as the passive client of Western readership and criticism; Africa can no longer be treated (and never should have been treated) as a "void" or a "blank." Responsible critics will no longer be able to ignore the mediation and authority of African commentaries, critiques, and theoretical models, no more than in the past they seemed able to ignore the so-called universal standards of Western judgment. Only in *dialogue* with these new voices can Western reading and criticism of African literature continue with any claim to legitimacy. The spirit and practice of dialogue thus provide a temporary answer to the initial question of how Western reading might dare to proceed in the wake of colonial history. But dialogism is itself a problem that will warrant further consideration, in a later movement of this chapter.

Thinking programmatically about Western approaches to African literature leads me to one major hypothesis, around which the rest of this book will turn: that a fair Western reading of African literatures demands engagement with, and even dependence on, anthropology. The demonstration of this point begins from the premise that good reading does not result from ignorance and that Westerners simply do not know enough about Africa. Much of what I will be arguing here grows out of my basic belief that no responsible Western reading of African literature can take place in the vacuum of a "direct" and unmediated relationship with the text. What the literary text says is necessary but not sufficient; other texts must be brought into the dialogical exercise of a good reading. Taken at face value, my hypothesis means simply that any non-African reader (or even an African reader from a different cultural area) seeking to cross the information gap between himself or herself and an African text will very probably be obliged to look in books that are classified as anthropology. The history of the academic separation of disciplines has made this a fact. But it is a fact that is both surrounded by controversy (due to the colonial history of anthropology) and largely ignored: critics have pored over numerous African texts, texts that deal with culturally encoded and culture-specific issues, without bothering to look at the ethnographic works that form an implicit dialogue with their literary counterparts.[8] In this study,

---

7. V. Y. Mudimbe, *The Invention of Africa: Gnosis, Philosophy and the Order of Knowledge* (Bloomington: Indiana University Press, 1988): 200.

8. There are exceptions to this rule, such as Jacques Bourgeacq's *"L'Enfant noir" de Camara Laye: Sous le signe de l'éternel retour* (Sherbrooke, Québec: Naaman, 1984), and

I will therefore be trying to fill a gap, to perform an obvious task that has mostly been neglected. The task is to seek a better understanding of francophone African literature by placing it within its historical, political, but especially anthropological context. This is not intended to place anthropology in a position of dominance or to let it block out other concerns, which I hope will find adequate attention here. Rather my desire is to blend disciplines together in a hybrid approach befitting the complexity of cultural questions in Africa and their translation into Western understanding.[9]

If the task has been neglected, it is perhaps due to the controversy

---

Robert Philipson's article "Literature and Ethnography: Two Views of Manding Initiation Rites," in Kofi Anyidoho, ed., *Interdisciplinary Dimensions of African Literature*, Annual Selected Papers of the African Literature Association, no. 8 (1982): 171–82; I will refer to both of these works in chapter 4. See also Bernard Mouralis's discussion of anthropology in *Littérature et développement: Essai sur le statut, la fonction et la représentation de la littérature négro-africaine d'expression française* (Paris: Silex/ACCT, 1984): 44–57. The practice of a self-reflexive Western reading is not totally without precedent: Daniel Delas, in his *Léopold Sédar Senghor: Lecture blanche d'un texte noir ("L'Absente")* (Paris: Temps Actuels, 1982), stages a deliberately "unauthorized" reading. He consciously *applies* Western methods (8), while remaining attentive to their limitations, and he concludes that there is a fundamental "conflict" between "white reading" and "black reading" (113).

9. I have been influenced in this undertaking by James Clifford's "On Ethnographic Authority," *Representations* 1, No. 2 (Spring 1983), 118–146 (reprinted in his *The Predicament of Culture: Twentieth-Century Ethnography, Literature, and Art* [Cambridge: Harvard University Press, 1988]: 21–54), by V. Y. Mudimbe's *L'Odeur du père: Essai sur les limites de la science et de la vie en Afrique noire* (Paris: Présence Africaine, 1982), and by Michèle Duchet's *Anthropologie et histoire au siècle des lumières* (Paris: Maspero, 1971). One of the most important precursors to this study is Sunday O. Anozie's *Structural Models and African Poetics: Towards a Pragmatic Theory of Literature* (London: Routledge & Kegan Paul, 1981), which the author describes as an attempt to impose "a more rigorous ordering of sense" within the criticism of African literature (viii). Anozie takes as given the universalism of structuralism and its focus on the "immanence of language." His analysis of Negritude thus addresses questions of grammar and semiology rather than, for example, politics. The role Anozie accords to Western theory is exemplified in the following statement: "It is therefore hard to vizualize the constitution of a viable African theory of poetics outside the framework of semiology" (159–60). Anozie nonetheless struggles, within the frame provided by Lévi-Strauss, Jakobson, and Barthes, toward a description of African difference. *Structural Models and African Poetics* stands as a sign of its times—at the high water mark of "theory"—and as a brilliant exercise in applied theory. For a harsh critique, see Anthony Appiah, "Strictures on Structures: The Prospects for a Structuralist Poetics of African Fiction," in Henry Louis Gates, Jr., ed., *Black Literature and Literary Theory* (New York: Methuen, 1984): 127–50. Other works relevant to the present context include: Dan Sperber, *Le Savoir des anthropologues* (Paris: Hermann, 1982), Clifford Geertz, *The Interpretation of Cultures* (New York: Basic Books, 1973), and Paul Désalmand, *Sciences humaines et philosophie en Afrique: la différence culturelle* (Paris: Hatier, 1978).

surrounding the very mention of "anthropology" in Africa, with its imperialist connotations and its threat to "tact." [10] To make use of anthropology is to borrow trouble, for reasons that I will explore. But while
still on the threshold, I would like to outline the basic links between
francophone African literature and anthropology, those ties that cannot
be ignored. The first link is a matter of history: the French-language literature of sub-Saharan Africa emerged at the same time as the new body
of ethnography on Africa; the two bodies of writing produced versions
of Africa in tandem, and, as we will see, they were inextricably interwoven. This is connected to a more general point made by Jonathon Ngate:
that "francophone African literature has been, in effect, a continuous
attempt at fleeing from its Western models." [11] Particularly in the early,
pre-Independence years, from 1920 to 1960, francophone African discourse was one part of a larger phenomenon, colonial discourse as a
whole; and in the politics of the time, anthropology was the most powerful mode of colonial discourse.

The second link between anthropology and this literature is a matter
of rhetoric. If the term "anthropological rhetoric" can be used as a description of the devices by which cultures are represented to each
other—through modes of address to a reader who is presumed to be alien
to the culture in the text—then francophone African literature has always practiced some form of anthropological rhetoric. From its first
through its most recent text, this literature continually uses devices such
as footnotes, parentheses, and character-to-character explanations in order to provide the reader with necessary cultural information. Due to the
conditions in which this literature arises—notably the limited literacy
and knowledge of French throughout "francophone" Africa—readers of
a francophone text cannot be presumed to be local. Every time an author
uses a phrase like "here in Africa," a *non-Africa* is revealed to be at play
in the writing and reading process. A degree of "otherness" is inscribed
in any text which addresses itself to a world that is construed as outside.
This means that the controversial "otherness" associated with anthropology is not wholly absent from the literature in question here, and that
the relationship between the two bodies of texts must be approached with
an open mind.

These assertions have raised more questions than they have answered,

10. See Kwame Anthony Appiah, "Out of Africa: Topologies of Nativism," *Yale Journal of Criticism* 2, no. 1 (Fall 1988): 165.

11. Jonathon Ngate, *Francophone African Literature: Reading a Literary Tradition*
(Trenton, N.J.: Africa World Press, 1988): 18. In this useful study, Ngate explores modes
of engagement and resistance to such Western models.

and I would now like to turn to a more detailed consideration of the fundamental issues.

Theory and Difference

What is designated as "theory" in Western academies is the most prestigious and valued mode of production. If you are a theorist, you have been promoted above the sphere of material information; you operate in the realm of pure thought. But if we begin from a *material* understanding of theory and see it in the global context analyzed by Hountondji, a great deal of mystification will be dispelled: theory is simply that which is labelled as theory by the institutions that empower themselves to do so. "Theory" therefore stands as a figure for the role that Westerners have assigned themselves in their relation to Africa—detached, objective, universal, synthesizing, and, most of all, powerful. My contention is that certain forms of theory, prevalent in American criticism since the mid-1970s, have posed a tremendous problem for the Western reader of African literatures. That problem is associated first with the word "theory" and the division of labor I have referred to, but also with the word "difference." Deconstructive theory in particular has problematized the thinking of difference in a way that has opened many doors, while insisting that others remain shut.

The opposition between theory and difference should be a false one: from Blanchot and Bataille to Derrida and De Man, concepts such as alterity, deferral, adjournment, and difference itself occupy a privileged position. Paul De Man's formula for describing allegory, to take one example (in "The Rhetoric of Temporality") as "renouncing the nostalgia and the desire for totalization"[12] seems to be the very model of a non-imperialistic *tolerance* of difference. The subject renounces any claim to possession or totalization, permitting the other to be itself. Yet in that phrase we see the roots of an intellectual problem: renouncing the claim to *have coincided* with the other allows the other to be different and apart from the subject, but when the subject renounces even the *desire* to coincide, the question of *knowing* the other becomes problematic. Can knowledge be knowledge without coinciding, without on some level claiming or stumbling into appropriation and possession? The deconstructive theory of "difference" relegated difference to the realm of the purely theoretical. When, in the context of De Man's article on "Semi-

12. "The Rhetoric of Temporality," in *On Interpretation*, ed. Charles S. Singleton (Baltimore: Johns Hopkins Univ. Press, 1969): 191.

ology and Rhetoric," the television character Archie Bunker asks Edith, "What's the difference?" (between lacing his bowling shoes "over" or "under"), the question is purely rhetorical. As De Man comments, "'What's the difference?' *did not ask for difference* but means instead '*I don't give a damn what the difference is*'. . . . Grammar allows us to ask the question, but the sentence by means of which we ask it may deny the very possibility of asking."[13] In this episode of "All in the Family," Archie Bunker went on to say the following (which De Man did not quote): "I didn't say 'What's the difference—explain it to me', I said 'What's the difference—who the hell cares?'"

But suppose we *had* to care what the difference is, even faced with all the "vertiginous possibilities of referential aberration" associated with literature? Suppose that we could no longer afford the mandarin detachment from messy differences in the plural; that the matter of difference were simply too urgent to be glorified and homogenized as differance-with-an-A. Such is the question confronting the Western reader of African literatures. How can we proceed from a rhetorical "What's the difference?" to an *anthropological* "What is different?" without jettisoning the wisdom of the former for the benefits of the latter? The challenge now is to practice a kind of knowledge that, while remaining conscious of the lessons of rhetorical theory, recognizes European theory as a *local phenomenon* and attempts dialogue with other localized systems of discourse.

Deconstructive theory offers important lessons about the relation between discourse and its object, lessons that should be kept in mind especially by Westerners approaching African literatures. Readers with strong theoretical backgrounds recognize that knowledge—particularly Western knowledge of Africa—far from being simply *lux et veritas*, can most often be revealed as a corrosive project of appropriation wherein the Western reader projects desires onto the other. Once the African text has surrendered its meaning, a treaty is signed, written by the Western critic who thereby influences not only reception of the present work but also publication of future African works, still largely published in Paris. The interpretive tie between reader and text is also a bond of enslavement. This perception is valid and finds explicit confirmation in the African critiques of Western criticism seen earlier in this chapter.

But problems can arise when this negative model of interpretation

13. "Semiology and Rhetoric," in *Allegories of Reading* (New Haven: Yale Univ. Press, 1979): 10; emphasis mine. Barbara Johnson has referred to this passage from De Man in her "Gender Theory and the Yale School," in *Rhetoric and Form: Deconstruction at Yale*, edited by Robert Con Davis and Ronald Schleifer (Norman: The University of Oklahoma Press, 1985): 101–12.

takes on a life of its own, enjoining the Western reader to assess only that of which he/she can be sure—his/her own reading processes. Readings are only readings of readings; the observer cannot talk with authority about the observed; knowledge is fiction. Paradoxically, the only positive object of knowledge left to be trusted is not an object at all but the solitary subject, paralyzed by its own power. When this point has been reached, a kind of blindness results.

An illustrative example comes from classroom experience, from a discussion of Cheikh Hamidou Kane's novel *L'Aventure ambiguë*. The culture depicted by Kane, that of the Diallobé of Senegal, has been Islamic for centuries; the novel is concerned with the ambiguities involved in choosing between adherence to the old culture and surrender to the new one, that of French colonialism. But the third part of Africa's "triple heritage"—indigenous, pre-Islamic culture—remains an issue. The portrait of one of the principal characters, La Grande Royale, is itself already a "reading" of her face as a text:

> On la nommait la Grande Royale. . . . On ne voyait d'elle que le visage . . . qui était comme une page vivante de l'histoire du pays des Diallobé. Tout ce que le pays compte de tradition épique s'y lisait. Les traits étaient tout en longueur. . . . Tout le reste disparaissait sous la gaze qui, davantage qu'une coiffure, prenait ici une signification de symbole. L'Islam refrénait la redoutable turbulence de ces traits, de la même façon que la voilette les enserrait. Autour des yeux et sur les pommettes, sur tout ce visage, il y avait comme le souvenir d'une jeunesse et d'une force sur lesquelles se serait apposé brutalement le rigide éclat d'un souffle ardent.

> They called her the Most Royal Lady. . . . She was sixty years old, and she would have been taken for scarcely forty. Nothing was to be seen of her except her face . . . [which] was like a living page from the history of the Diallobé country. Everything that the country treasured of epic tradition could be read there. All the features were in long lines. . . . All the rest disappeared under the gauze, which, more than a coiffure would have done, took on here a symbolic meaning. Islam restrained the formidable turbulence of those features, in the same way that the little veil hemmed them in. Around the eyes and on the cheeks, over all this countenance, there was, as it were, the memory of a youth and a force upon which the rigid blast of an ardent breath was later brutally to blow.[14]

The passage leaves no doubt that it is concerned with the violent silencing of one culture by another. That which represses is named as Islam; "all the rest," hidden behind the veil, is identified two pages later as "un fond de paganisme," a pagan substratum, the pre-Islamic culture of the Diallobé which has not been completely erased after centuries of inculcation.

---

14. *L'Aventure ambiguë* (Paris: Union Générale d'Editions, 1961): 30–31; English translation by Katherine Woods, *Ambiguous Adventure* (New York: Walker and Company, 1963): 20–21. I have altered the translation.

A student well-trained in theory objected, however, to this interpretation of the blank face behind the veil on the grounds that such an interpretation was a mere "inscription" of outside information onto the text. Such inscription or projection is indeed to be guarded against. But then this text is not a blank, nor does it allow a blank to exist in tranquility; the text itself inscribes a certain historical and cultural message onto the emptiness of La Grande Royale's face. My student's reluctance to go beyond the veil was motivated by laudable impulses—the desire to leave the other alone, a refusal to reduce the text to a mere illustration—but her reading of the veil as only a veil, a trope about tropes, excluded the possibility of perceiving the traits that are there behind the veil, the traits which make up a portrait of *difference* and tell a story of violence. We cannot forget that texts are nothing if not "inscribed"; they are inevitably affected by their historical and cultural situation.

What becomes of difference in a methodology that trusts only self-reflexivity? The impulse to leave the other alone rejoins the impulse to obliterate the other on the ground they have in common: the inability to describe something outside the self, to see, in Clifford Geertz's words, "ourselves among others, as a local example of the forms human life has locally taken." This is an ability without which Geertz says "objectivity is self-congratulation and tolerance a sham."[15] The justification for taking the risk of describing cultures is thus *ethical*, and the question of ethics is one to which I will return in chapter 2. It is also evident that much of what I am saying here amounts to a defense of difference and otherness as inescapable armatures of reading and writing.

Anthropology and Negritude

The reader of African literature seeking a happy model of knowledge, turning to anthropology for transparent translations of the African difference, finds a field preoccupied with—guess what?—the imperialism of knowledge and the recourse to self-reflexivity. In order to see how this came about, we must first ascertain what anthropology is supposed to be. The etymological meaning of the word barely begins to tell the story: "the science of man" sounds like the self studying the self. The *International Encyclopedia of the Social Sciences* begins its article on anthropology with the claim that this science is "the most comprehensive of the academic disciplines dealing with mankind," but the author goes on to issue this significant restriction: "Although in principle anthropology has always had an equal interest in societies of all types, in practice it has

15. *Local Knowledge* (New York: Basic Books, 1983): 16.

involved a concentration on primitive, or preliterate, peoples, most frequently defined as those that did not have writing at the time of first contact with the West."[16] The watershed between anthropology and its first-world (or urban) counterpart, sociology, seems to adhere to the distinction between oral and literate cultures; but that division is the locus of unfathomable myths and delusions which reinforce the barriers between "us" and "them."

In fact, the history of anthropology has appeared to adhere more to the *Oxford English Dictionary*'s third definition: "the study of man *as an animal*," implying both difference and inequality. Man as an animal is primitive man, man excluded from progress and development, stuck in time at the zero point where time begins and has no meaning. Man as an animal represents a general threat or challenge not only to the meaning of time but to meaning in general. Studying man as an animal is an act of redemption, of elevation, by which "the primitive" is translated out of a static, amorphous, oral condition into books and articles that make sense.

The problem is that books that make sense out of African cultures have not generally been African books, and the European mind "discovering" Africa has desired symmetrical counterparts to the codifications of culture represented by, for example, the Bible and the Koran. Like the proverbial group of blind men describing the elephant, Westerners have tried to produce global descriptions that will make Africans fit into the Western categories of "religion," "psychology," and "literature." Titles such as *La Bible noire* and *La Philosophie bantoue*, even *Oedipe noir* and *The Black Decameron*, reveal an impulse to assimilate and westernize in the process of explaining and making known. No one would call *La Chanson de Roland The White Sunjata*.

Unlike a "literary anthropology" of the Middle Ages, in which the term "anthropology" serves as a purely retrospective approach,[17] an inquiry into the relation of literature to anthropology in francophone Africa must face up to the substantial interference that has taken place between that literature and the institutionalized discipline of anthropology. It has been a complex, often messy relationship. A few cautionary tales are therefore in order concerning the history of academic questions with ramifications in the everyday life of colonialism.

Placide Tempels's *Bantu Philosophy* is an example of a text that would no longer be considered real anthropology but had status and

16. Joseph H. Greenberg, "Anthropology: The Field," in *International Encyclopedia of the Social Sciences* (New York: Free Press, 1968): vol. I, 304–5.

17. See R. Howard Bloch, *Etymologies and Genealogies: A Literary Anthropology of the French Middle Ages* (Chicago: The University of Chicago Press, 1983).

influence in its time, and whose ghostly presence keeps returning in debates over African philosophy and literature. *Bantu Philosophy* is a telling illustration of how the desire to explain African culture can lead the well-meaning Western writer to obliterate Africa with kindness. Father Tempels was a Belgian missionary in the Belgian Congo. He begins his work by blaming the misunderstanding between Europe and Africa on a European failure to recognize the African world view as a valid philosophy. We must, he writes, "understand their metaphysic"; "the gulf between Africans and Whites will remain and widen so long as *we* do not meet them in the wholesome aspirations of their own ontology."[18] All questions of behavior and belief in Africa can be answered by "a single principle, knowledge of the Inmost Nature of beings, that is to say, . . . their Ontological Principle" (23). That ontological principle is identified later as a "single value: vital force." African life can be explicated in terms of a balance of forces; African cultural formations as mechanisms for maintaining that balance. It is by this world view that Tempels's Bantu differs in *essence* from the European, and I would not like to comment on the truth value of his analysis but rather on the uses to which he quickly puts it, that of better controlling Bantu behavior.

Tempels allows that there is a negative in all this: "This explains what has, indeed, been true, that the thing which most inhibits pagans from conversion to Christianity and from giving up magical rites is the fear of attentuating this vital energy through ceasing to have recourse to the natural powers which sustain it" (32). The good news is that the Bantu is basically monotheistic, believing in a single creator god (among others), and that "metaphysics is within the capacity of every Bantu" (49). But now faced with an essentially different civilization, what becomes of the *mission civilisatrice* and the project of assimilation? How can the missionary urge to convert natives and obliterate difference be reconciled with the unalterable philosophical truth that Tempels has discovered? It is here that *Bantu Philosophy* becomes a telling case study in the manipulation of difference.

Tempels advocates that the colonial project be redirected, "to educate them to discover the ancient elements of truth ever present in their traditions" (114), because "European civilization imparted to the Bantu is a mere superficial garb which has no deep impact upon their souls." Tempels therefore proposes a new *philosophical* colonialism based on a profound understanding of Bantu essence, readily available in his book of 120 pages:

18. Placide Tempels, *Bantu Philosophy*, trans. Colin King (Paris: Présence Africaine, 1959): 16, 18.

The Bantu can be educated if we take as a starting point their imperishable aspiration towards the strengthening of life. If not, they will not be civilized. Their masses will founder, in even greater numbers, in *false applications of their philosophy*; that is to say, in degrading 'magical' practices; and meanwhile the others, the évolués, will make up a class of pseudo-Europeans, without principles, character, purpose, or sense. . . . It is in Christianity alone that the Bantu will find relief for their secular yearning and a complete satisfaction of their deepest aspirations. . . . *Christianity . . . is the only possible consummation of the Bantu ideal.* [120−21; emphasis mine. The translator points out in a footnote: "Fr. 'idéal,' but Du. 'heimwee': homesickness, nostalgia!"]

Once the essence is identified, the missionary/anthropologist/philosopher can determine the truth or falsehood of its application and judge the native's art of living: "It is we who will be able to tell them, in precise terms, what their inmost concept of being is" (25). The new colonialism is thus far more insidious than the old slash-and-burn variety. "Tolerance" of difference is at its most pernicious here: I understand your essential difference from me, and will make you live up to it with an imposed program of separate development. Apartheid, it should be pointed out, is of course "nothing" but a theory of *separate*, i. e. differentiated development and of "tolerance" of an enforced difference.[19] As Césaire writes of *La Philosophie bantoue*, "Everyone wins: big corporations, colonial settlers, the government, excepting the Bantu, of course."[20] Tempels's text is the most striking example of miscarried anthropology and philosophy since Gérard de Nerval's conclusion that Islam is "une sorte de secte chrétienne."[21] His version of respect for difference is a sham, a fiction that ultimately justifies conquest and subjugation.

Bantu Philosophy stands as a cautionary tale about the pitfalls of dif-

19. Cf. Vincent Crapanzano, "Waiting," *The New Yorker*, March 18, 1985, 97: "apartheid . . . is an extreme case of the Western predisposition to classify and categorize just about everything in essentialist terms."

20. Aimé Césaire, *Discours sur le colonialisme* (Paris: Présence Africaine, 1955): 37; for sustained critiques of Tempels, see F. Eboussi Boulaga, "Le Bantou problématique," *Présence Africaine* 66 (2d Quarterly, 1968): 5, "voici vingt ans, un livre révélait au monde que le bantou était le Monsieur Jourdain de la philosophie: il en faisait sans le savoir"; and Paulin Hountondji, *Sur la "philosophie africaine"* (Paris: F. Maspero, 1977): 46: "*La Philosophie bantoue* [fit] feu de tout bois, en projetant massivement dans l'âme bantu ses propres rêveries métaphysiques, quitte à les renforcer par quelques descriptions ethnographiques sommaires propres à faire illusion." See also V. Y. Mudimbe, "Niam M'Paya: aux sources d'une pensée africaine," in *L'Odeur du père*, 125−34. For a defense of Tempels, see Meinrad P. Hebga, "Eloge de l' 'ethnophilosophie'", *Présence Africaine* 123 (3d Quarterly, 1982): 20−41.

21. "Il faut conclure . . . que l'islamisme ne repousse aucun des sentiments élevés attribués généralement à la société chrétienne. Les différences ont existé jusqu'ici beaucoup plus dans la forme que dans le fond des idées; les musulmans ne constituent en réalité qu'une

ference. It provides an extreme example of what can go wrong in the practice of describing other cultures. Why, then, take the risk? Why bother with Western interpretations and codifications of African culture at all? Why not read Africa *on its own terms*, unshackled from oppressive notions of difference and otherness? There are two responses to this question.

The first is simply that the terms in which African literature in French was initially conceived were French terms, and that literary history thus makes attention to difference a necessity. Everyone may agree that Africa *should* never have been treated as a void or a blank, but the study of colonialism shows that *it was*. The processes of projection (which I analyzed in an earlier study),[22] by which the identity and desires of the colonizer reproduce and satisfy themselves, are directly related to colonial policy. Projection translated into political terms becomes what I would call colonial *inscription*, the imposition onto Africa of French systems (like money, schools, streets, and place names), making Africa "French." This is what Said calls "manifest Orientalism."[23] The fact of colonialism and its interference in African systems breaks down any absolute barrier between Africa and the West; contemporary African discourse in all the disciplines of the humanities seeks to address this problem.[24]

A ground-breaking analysis of our area of concern within this entangled history is Guy Ossito Midiohouan's *L'Idéologie dans la littérature négro-africaine d'expression française*, which carefully traces the origins of the francophone tradition and deflates the myth of "militant unanism."[25] He demonstrates the extent to which, in the early years of the tradition, involvement or "collaboration" with the French was the rule rather than

---

sorte de *secte chrétienne*." Gérard de Nerval, *Voyage en Orient*, in *Oeuvres* "Bibliothèque de la Pléiade, (Paris: Gallimard, 1961): vol. 2, 628.

22. Christopher L. Miller, *Blank Darkness: Africanist Discourse in French* (Chicago: University of Chicago Press, 1985).

23. Edward W. Said, *Orientalism* (New York: Random House, 1979): 206.

24. See Isaac James Mowoe and Richard Bjornson, eds., *Africa and the West: Legacies of Empire* (New York: Greenwood Press, 1986).

25. Guy Ossito Midiohouan, *L'Idéologie dans la littérature négro-africaine d'expression française* (Paris: L'Harmattan, 1986): 11. This work is the most succinct and persuasive history of this literature, with a concentration on its ties to France. Midiohouan's intention, stated in an article published earlier, is nothing less than to rewrite the historical understanding of the francophone tradition: "*Il est désormais nécessaire de réécrire l'histoire de la littérature négro-africaine d'expression française en remettant le système colonial (néo-colonial) français à sa place et dans son rôle; en accordant toute leur importance aux rapports qu'entretenait (entretient) ce phénomène littéraire avec la littérature coloniale (française).*" "Exotique? Coloniale? Ou quand la littérature africaine était la littérature des Français d'Afrique," *Peuples noirs, peuples africains* 29 (1982): 119–20.

the exception (even if the exceptions, such as the newspapers *La Race nègre* and *Le Cri des nègres*, were notable).[26] This is not shocking if one stops to consider that the tradition in question is a *francophone* one, involving knowledge of the French language: where else would it have come from but "working with" (collaborating with), literally, the French colonizers? The first "writers" were not *littérateurs* but clerks and typists, who formed "the bridge between the colonizer (whose equal partner they could never be) and the colonized people (from whom they were supposed to be separate)" (Kuoh J. Moukouri, quoted in Brunschwig, 122). They were part of the "politically reliable, grateful, and acculturated elite" that the French tried to create throughout their colonial empire.[27] The first "literary" (that is, fictional) work in the tradition, Ahmadou Mapaté Diagne's *Les Trois volontés de Malic*, was a propagandistic fable designed to promote French colonial education; the earliest recognized literary writers—René Maran, Bakary Diallo, Paul Hazoumé—were profoundly indebted to the colonial system for their livelihood, their education and, of course, the language in which they wrote.[28] Maran was a

26. On the meaning of collaboration in this context, see Henri Brunschwig, *Noirs et blancs dans l'Afrique noire française* (Paris: Flammarion, 1983): "Ce terme [*collaborant*], évidemment, ne doit pas être pris dans le sens du collaborateur en Europe au cours de la Seconde Guerre Mondiale. Le collaborant est celui qui assiste le colonisateur, blanc ou noir, sans pour autant renoncer à son identité" (96). Brunschwig refers to those who did renounce their identity as *evolués, assimilés,* or *lettrés*; these are all terms that were in colonial usage. As a work of history, this book invites some scepticism in that it has nothing at all to say about African resistance to colonialism, but explains the French enterprise as a form of "anarchy" (151), systematized on paper only (209), in which blacks and whites were equally implicated. Brunschwig's interpretation, supported by statistics, states that, for lack of French settlers to run their colonies, the French were forced to get Africans to colonize each other ("L'indigène colonisé se mua lentement, au cours de deux ou trois générations, en indigène colonisateur" [163]). This thesis can only be appraised when compared to the extensive accounts of resistance found in, for example, the UNESCO *General History of Africa*, vol. 7, *Africa Under Colonial Domination 1880–1935*, ed. A. Adu Boahen (London: Heinemann, 1985). The UNESCO history, however, has nothing to say about collaboration. For a general introductory history, see Patrick Manning, *Francophone Sub-Saharan Africa 1880–1985* (Cambridge: Cambridge University Press, 1988).

27. Benedict Anderson, *Imagined Communities: Reflections on the Origin and Spread of Nationalism* (London: Verso, 1983): 115.

28. See Ahmadou Mapaté Diagne, *Les Trois volontés de Malic*, first published in 1920 (Nendeln: Kraus Reprints, 1973); René Maran, *Batouala: véritable roman nègre*, first published 1921 (Paris: Albin Michel, 1965)—it should be noted that although Maran was born in Martinique, he served in the French colonial service in Africa, and his novel is often considered to be "African"; Bakary Diallo, *Force-Bonté*, first published 1926 (Nendeln: Kraus Reprints, 1973); Paul Hazoumé, *Doguicimi* (Paris: Larose, 1938). See Ossito Midiohouan's chapter on "Le roman colonial négro-africain," 60–78. See also John D. Erickson, *Nommo: African Fiction in French South of the Sahara* (York, S.C.: French Literature Publications Co., 1979): 91–130.

Martinican black working in the French colonial service in central Africa; Diallo was a colonial soldier; Hazoumé was an ethnographer.

So the first consideration to keep in mind is the historical origins of the francophone literature in a class of Africans who were deeply involved with the colonial system. The colonial school is the material cause of this literature. No wonder that even the second generation of black francophone writers, the first to formulate a theory of African difference in French, also showed a complex involvement in the issues of French culture. The inventors of Negritude ideology—Léopold Sédar Senghor, Aimé Césaire, and Léon Damas—were educated in the French colonial system and were more accustomed to expressing themselves in French than in Martinican Creole or Senegalese Wolof. The birthplace of black francophone literature is more Paris than Fort-de-France or Dakar, and it is now easy to recognize in Negritude—the concept and the literary movement—the signs of alienation from the author's native past: nostalgia, and so to speak, the desire to coincide again, to bring the past back. This perception is a consequence of hindsight and need not be seen to diminish the historically contingent validity of Negritude.

We know as a fact of literary history that Negritude was informed by a particular anthropology, and by one very particular anthropologist, Leo Frobenius (a German active in the first half of this century). Senghor writes in his preface to a Frobenius anthology in French "no one better than Frobenius revealed Africa to the world *and Africans to themselves*[29]—creating a strange echo with Césaire's heroic figure of Patrice Lumumba in *Une saison au Congo*, who proclaims "I speak and restore Africa to herself" ("je parle et je rends l'Afrique à elle-même").[30]

Senghor writes of Frobenius:

> Je ne saurais mieux faire que de dire ici, les leçons que nous avons tirées de la lecture de Frobenius, et surtout de ses deux ouvrages fondamentaux, traduits en français: *Histoire de la Civilisation africaine* et *Le Destin des Civilisations*. Quand je dis 'nous', il s'agit de la poignée d'étudiants noirs qui, dans les années 1930, au Quartier Latin, à Paris, lancèrent, . . . le mouvement de la Négritude.[31]
>
> Frobenius fut véritablement le moteur spirituel de l'émancipation de l'Afrique noire: sa vision idéaliste d'une Afrique encore pure, non contaminée par les influences extérieures, était pour nous . . . un aliment qui attisait notre ferveur.[32]

29. Léopold Sédar Senghor, "Les Leçons de Leo Frobenius," in *Leo Frobenius 1873/ 1973: Une Anthologie*, ed. Eike Haberland (Wiesbaden: Franz Steiner Verlag, 1973): vii. This work will henceforth be referred to as *Anthologie*.

30. Aimé Césaire, *Une Saison au Congo* (Paris: Seuil, 1973): 94.

31. Senghor, in *Anthologie*, vii; he refers to the two works by Frobenius elsewhere as "sacred books" and compares his reaction to that of St. Paul on the road to Damascus (*Liberté 3: Négritude et civilisation de l'universel* [Paris: Seuil, 1977]: 13; 340).

32. "Les Leçons de Léo Frobenius" (a different article from the preface to the *Anthologie*, but bearing the same title), *Présence Africaine* 111, no. 3 (1978): 147–48.

I can do no better than to state here the lessons that we drew from our reading of Frobenius, and especially from his two basic works, translated into French as *Histoire de la civilisation africaine* and *Le destin des civilisations*. When I say "we" I mean the handful of black students who, in the 1930's, in the Latin Quarter, launched the Negritude movement.

Frobenius was truly the moving spiritual force in the emancipation of black Africa: his idealistic vision of a still-pure Africa, not yet contaminated by outside influences, nourished our fervor.

What, then, is Frobenius's uncontaminated Africa? It is a place of "perfect order," which, at the time of the European discoveries, echoed a strangely European sense of *Gemütlichkeit*: "carefully designed streets, lined with trees for mile after mile as far as the eye can see . . . nothing but magnificent fields . . . crowds of people dressed in silk and velvet; great States, *where the smallest detail bears witness to a perfect order*" (*Anthologie*, 66). Visiting the Kasai region of the Congo in 1906, Frobenius finds something like an "esthetocracy" in which "each cup, each pipe, each spoon is a work of art." My point is of course not that Frobenius was inaccurate in his physical description of African civilization, rather that his writing *rewards* Africa for conforming to a European image of civilization, for acting as a mirror in which a European can contemplate his own idea of beauty. The totality of African art is the cornerstone of Frobenius's anthropology—art is everything and everything is art; therefore art is *functional* and wastes no time or energy on false seductiveness: "There is nothing that tries to seduce through softness and sensitivity . . . everything is functional, rough, austere, tectonic [Teutonic?]" (69).[33] This is *the* essence of African art and African being for Frobenius: the essence preexists the art in which it is found; it *governs* ("il *régit* toute l'Afrique"), it manifests itself, it releases itself. [34] His verb *beherrschen*, which may be accurately translated as "command" or "govern," cannot help but recall Hegel's famous chapter on the Master (*Herr*) and the Slave (*Knecht*): the master is "consciousness that exists for itself," but can only exist "through an other"; the other, the slave, is "consciousness repressed within itself." [35] Note that it is a style posited as a totality by Frobenius's discourse that rules over Africa; as with Tempels's philosophy, Africans themselves are *subject* to, even subjugated by, an essence discovered by an outsider, of which, like Monsieur Jourdain and

33. The original German reads: "Alles ist zweckmäßig, herb, streng, tektonisch!" ("Die Kunst Afrikas," *Der Erdball* no. 3 [1931]: 90).

34. "Wer sich ihm bis zum vollen Verständnis genähert hat, der wird bald erkennen, daß er als Ausdruck des Wesens ganz Afrika *beherrscht*." ("Die Kunst Afrikas," 90; emphasis mine).

35. G. W. F. Hegel, *Phänomenologie des Geistes* (Frankfurt/M: Ullstein Verlag, 1970): 113–20.

his "prose," they may be wholly unaware: this is Hegel's "consciousness repressed." [36]

Frobenius goes on to say, "It [this style] must have been born and must have crystallized itself a very long time ago, and it has preserved itself ever since in *all its originality*. " This analysis leaves him "strengthened with this intimate knowledge of the African essence" (69). That perfect preservation or mummification of an essentialized style—a style that is an essence—makes it a perfect primitivism. Nothing has changed of this essence, nor can it ever change; it can still be discovered, studied, and mastered. Frobenius uncovers the essence not as would Gobineau, to denigrate, but rather to assimilate and redeem. It becomes the basis of a theory whereby a *Euro-African* civilization can be posited in Southeast Europe and Northeast Africa, a theory based on comparisons of cave paintings. Europe and Africa share common roots; it is just that "the vital sentiment . . . has become completely foreign to us, whereas it continues to inspire vast ethnic groups of Africa" (75).

One would like to avoid a facile interpretive hindsight or retrospective indignation; one should admit that when Frobenius wrote "the idea of the barbarous Negro is a European invention" (*Anthologie*, vii), the idea was brave and revolutionary. But one is compelled to look into the ideology and cultural baggage that Senghor in particular took on when he was seduced by Frobenius's positive valorization of African civilization.

Léopold Sédar Senghor, one of the three founders of the Negritude movement, president of Senegal from 1960 to 1981, and the first black elected to the French Academy, is one of the mainstays of francophone culture in Africa. I will refer to his views regularly in the course of this study. For Senghor, any bridge between two civilizations is one more contribution to "la civilisation de l'universel" and is therefore to be encouraged. But Senghor reads Frobenius not on an intercontinental or global level but as a particular link between Negritude and *Germanity*. In two articles, one from 1961 and the other from 1972, Senghor expands on a theory that was Frobenius's, that of the fundamental unity and affinity between black African and German thought. Frobenius wrote: "The West created English realism and French rationalism; the East, German mysticism. . . . The accord, with corresponding civilizations in black Africa, is complete" (*Anthologie*, xi).

36. It is this notion of African philosophy as a *mentality*, as "une vision du monde spontanée, collective et implicite," that Paulin Hountondji attacks in Tempels's work, to replace it with "l'analyse explicite, personelle, laborieuse qui prend cette vision du monde pour objet" (*Sur la "philosophie africaine,"* 65). Hountondji himself describes this transition as one out of a state of *enslavement*, "ce renoncement tragique à penser par nous-mêmes et pour nous-mêmes: l'esclavage" (44).

Senghor speaks of his childhood fascination with things German ("I was seduced by the numerous acts of bravery, of nobility of the soul, which were emphasized at the time of their actions in battle . . ." [*Liberté* 3, 339], and tells of his exposure to the Romantic poets, the philosophers and ethnographers, and principally to Frobenius. What did Germanity offer to an African intellectual? "Une saisie en profondeur des choses . . . la faculté de répondre à l'appel du réel, de vibrer aux ondes de l'Autre, du Toi." ("A grasp of things in their depths . . . the ability to answer the call of the real, to echo the vibrations of the Other, of the intimate Thou" [*Liberté* 3, 13, 14]). German and African civilizations are those "which have not yet lost the equilibrium between the soul and reason" (*Liberté* 3, 340). Senghor writes that after his demobilization in 1942: "I immersed myself, again, in German philosophy, starting with Marx and Engels, winding up where I should have started: with Hegel, to which I added Husserl and Heidegger" (*Liberté* 3, 342).[37]

If I began by promising to engage with a literature that is not a rewriting of Hegel, something has obviously gone wrong; "difference" has all but disappeared. For the younger generation of post-Independence African writers, Senghor's reliance on Frobenius's anthropology could *only* have led to cultural assimilation and the erasure of difference, for it was a sign of alienation in the first place. A particularly harsh and quotable critique is Stanislas Adotevi's *Négritude et négrologues*:

La négritude est une donnée de la conscience réfléchie, c'est l'aliénation intellectuelle du nègre . . . On ne peut se mettre à la fenêtre et se voir passer dans la rue . . . La négritude c'est la dernière-née d'une idéologie de domination . . . C'est la manière noire d'être blanc . . . C'est l'aboutissement de plusieurs décades d'*ethnologie*. . . . La négritude est sur le plan politique ce que La Philosophie Bantoue est idéologiquement pour l'Afrique. Senghor c'est le Père Tempels mis en mouvement, pour la même cause et dans la même mésaventure.[38]

Negritude is a notion of reflexive consciousness, the intellectual alienation of the Negro. . . . You can't stand at the window and watch yourself go by in the street. . . . Negritude is the last-born child of an ideology of domination. . . . It is the black way of being white . . . It is the end product of many decades of ethnology. . . . Negritude is to politics what *Bantu Philosphy* is to ideology for Af-

---

37. I am not aware of any comment by Senghor on the following passage from Hegel: "Africa proper, as far as History goes back, has remained—for all purposes of connection with the rest of the World—shut up; it is the Gold-land compressed within itself—the land of childhood, which lying beyond the day of self-conscious history, is enveloped in the dark mantle of Night. . . . In Negro life the characteristic point is the fact that consciousness has not yet attained to the realization of any substantial objective existence—as for example, God, or Law" (*The Philosophy of History*, trans. J. Sibree [New York: Dover, 1956]: 91, 93).

38. (Paris: Union Générale d'Editions, 1972): 101, 207, 153, 54.

rica. Senghor is Father Tempels on the field of action, for the same cause and in the same misadventure.

For Adotevi, "Eurocentrism commands all anthropological discourse," and anthropology is a fifth column within Negritude.

A newer generation of Africanist anthropology has confronted the problem of Eurocentrism, and one would like to know what Adotevi's attitude would be toward, for example, the theories of Clifford Geertz or James Clifford, the new ethnographies of Jean-Loup Amselle or Jean Bazin, work by Victor Turner or Robert Farris Thompson, James Fernandez's "an-trope-ology," and the self-reflexive "ethnopsychoanalytic" work of Paul Parin, Fritz Morgenthaler, and Goldy Parin-Matthèy, to name a few examples.[39] I will address new versions of anthropology in a discussion of dialogism, below. But for our immediate purposes, we must ask where Adotevi's moment of total rejection leaves us in relation to the body of francophone black African literature.

First, as I have indicated, it leaves us with an important project of tracing the influence and infiltration of European aesthetics and ideology within particularly the early productions of African literature in French. But that first project engenders a second, equally important one, that of reading the post-Independence literary productions which themselves critique the anthropological bias of their precursors. Such a text, for example, as Yambo Ouologuem's *Le Devoir de violence*, a novel in which we find "Fritz Schrobenius," "explorer, tourist and ethnographer," a lampoon of Frobenius :

[Schrobenius voulait] ressuciter, sous couleur d'autonomie culturelle, un univers africain qui ne correspondait à plus rien de vivant . . . il voulait trouver un sens métaphysique à tout . . . Gesticulant à tout propos, il étalait son "amitié" pour l'Afrique et son savoir orageux avec une assurance de bachelier repêché. Il considérait que la vie africaine était art pur.

[Schrobenius had] a groping mania for resuscitating an African universe— cultural autonomy, he called it—which had lost all living reality. . . . He was

39. See Clifford Geertz, *The Interpretation of Cultures* (New York: Basic Books, 1973); James Clifford, *The Predicament of Culture* (see note 9 above); Jean-Loup Amselle, "Ethnies et espaces: pour une anthropologie topologique," in Jean-Loup Amselle and Elikia M'Bokolo, eds., *Au Coeur de l'ethnie: ethnies, tribalisme et état en Afrique* (Paris: La Découverte, 1985): 11–48; Jean Bazin, "A chacun son Bambara," in *Au Coeur de l'ethnie*, 87–127; Victor Turner, *The Forest of Symbols* (Ithaca, N.Y.: Cornell University Press, 1967); Robert Farris Thompson, *The Flash of the Spirit* (New York: Random House, 1983); James Fernandez, *Persuasions and Performances: The Play of Tropes in Culture* (Bloomington: Indiana University Press, 1986): xv; Paul Parin, Fritz Morgenthaler, and Goldy Parin-Matthèy, *Fear Thy Neighbor as Thyself*, trans. Patricia Klamerth (Chicago: The University of Chicago Press, 1980).

determined to find a metaphysical meaning in everything . . . Gesticulating at every word, he displayed his love of Africa and his tempestuous knowledge with the assurance of a high school student who had slipped through his final examinations by the skin of his teeth. African life, he held, was pure art.[40]

Ouologuem's response to false images of cultural identity is to undermine the notion of identity itself, to construct a universe in which all bonds of unity are bonds of enslavement, including the bond between Ouologuem's writing and the European texts that he plagiarized.[41] Reading *Le Devoir de violence* contributes to the articulation between literature and anthropology only by showing how it has gone wrong in the past.

Under the weight of this ambiguous tradition, what, then is to be done? I have outlined responses to the involvement of this literary tradition with anthropologies of the past; but my aim in this book is not limited to a critique of outdated models. If anthropology has anything to offer the reader of African literatures, it is not just ethnographic "facts" but also access to modes of understanding that emanate from other cultures. This is a far more ambitious and tantalizing prospect. The formulation of any literary-anthropolgical approach would involve recourse to African systems of knowledge that owe nothing to the Western world. The grandest promise of anthropology is of gaining access to such systems through the supposedly transparent mediation of ethnographic texts. The inescapable epistemological paradox here is of course that access to non-Western systems is mediated through a discipline that has been invented and controlled by the West. My contention is that without a surrender to that paradox, without some reliance on anthropological texts, Westerners will not be able to read African literatures in any adequate way. This is where the risk of "difference" must be either taken or refused; in this book I choose to take the risk, as an experiment, while attempting to remain aware of its pitfalls.

African Philosophy and Ethnic Tradition

Once the risk is accepted, the terms under which the African world is to be described must be negotiated. For example, the use of anthropological sources in conjunction with literary texts may be necessitated as a form of access to what is called "tradition" or "ethnicity." Targetting these categories would be one aim of a literary-anthropological inquiry, for it would allow the reader to explore the elements in a text that do not

40. *Le Devoir de violence*, 102; *Bound to Violence*, 87.
41. See my "Trait d'union: Injunction and Dismemberment in Yambo Ouologuem's *Le Devoir de violence*," *L'Esprit créateur* 23, no. 4 (Winter 1983): 62–73.

derive from French forms such as genre, style, etc. But what is implied by
these terms? To begin the process of negotiation, it may be helpful to
survey a debate on ethnicity and tradition that has taken place within
African intellectual circles, a debate whose points are instructive and
whose references will already be familiar.

I am referring to the debate on the question of "African philosophy,"
which represents an attempt to cope with the aftermath of Tempels and
other colonials. On one side of this dispute are the "ethnophilosophers"
associated with Tempels and those who do not reject him, devoted to
describing an African world view that is first and foremost *different* from
that of Europe. The difference of Africa is founded on the study of "ethnic
realities"; the status of its intellectual product derives from its independence. For "ethnophilosophers" (the name is obviously not of their own
design), "pure" philosophy (as practiced by their adversaries) can be described like this: "to apply to our African societies pure forms of universal thought providentially and definitively revealed by philosophers of
Books." [42] Those philosophers of the Books (European books), critics
of ethnophilosophy, most importantly Paulin Hountondji and Marcien
Towa, advocate a radical departure from the "ghetto" of ethnic difference, a *prise de conscience* by the African of contemporary rather than
traditional reality: "We must at all costs liberate our thought from the
Africanist ghetto where some have sought to lock it up" (Hountondji,
"Philosophie," 49); "We must affirm ourselves in the world as it is. . . .
Such a decision . . . if it is to lead anywhere, requires a radical break with
our past (Towa, *Essai*, 41). A counterpart in the world of the novel is
Ousmane Sembene, whose radical heroes in such works of socialist realism as *O pays, mon beau peuple!* and *L'Harmattan*, as we will see in
chapter 2, advocate a sharp awareness of global political reality, along
with a harsh scepticism directed at "retrograde" traditions. [43]

For this school, Africa's failure to resist European conquest is a sign
of almost ontological, certainly philosophical, weakness: the backward
gaze of the ethnophilosopher (or the Negritude poet), by concentrating
on the specificity of Africa's cultural difference, "runs the risk of saving
precisely that which caused our defeat" (Towa, *Essai*, 41). Only one path
remains open, that of surrendering identity and difference as a price to be
paid for gaining power and equality:

La volonté d'être nous-mêmes . . . nous accule finalement à la nécessité de nous
transformer en profondeur, de nier notre être intime pour devenir l'autre. Pour

42. Hebga, "Eloge de l'‘ethnophilosophie,'" 32.
43. Cf. Kwasi Wiredu, *Philosophy and an African Culture* (Cambridge: Cambridge
University Press, 1980): "There is an urgent need . . . for the kind of analysis that would
identify and separate the backward aspects of our culture from those worth keeping" (41).

nous approprier le secret de l'Europe, savoir un esprit nouveau et étranger, nous devons révolutionner le nôtre de fond en comble, ce faisant nous devenons assurément semblables à l'Européen. (48)

The will to be ourselves . . . brings us face to face with the necessity to transform ourselves profoundly, to negate our inner being in order to become the other. In order to appropriate for ourselves Europe's secret, that is, this new and foreign spirit, we must revolutionize our own spirit completely; in so doing we will assuredly become like the European.

For Towa, to be different, to have an identity, is to be a slave: "In regard to all worship of difference and identity, we must cultivate a systematic scepticism, without which we run the risk of confirming our own servitude" (*L'Idée*, 67). In order to gain the "secret of the West," one renounces the secrets of Africa. The antiethnophilosophers ask rhetorically, "What is African?" (reminiscent of the deconstructive question posed by De Man/Archie Bunker, "What's the difference?")—meaning that an essentialized, *metaphysical* Africanity is a trap;[44] to which the ethnophilosopher responds rhetorically, "What is rational?"—meaning that even "pure" European philosophy (in which the "secret" resides) is riddled with myth, ethnography, theology, and biology, and is no guarantor of anything.[45]

Hountondji and Towa's philosophy, which refuses the name "African," may be compared to "theory" as I have discussed it here. Both are rigorous systems based on Western books; both provide the certainty of a preordained system; both risk the loss of identity and difference, the assimilation of Africa into the categories of the West. The "radical praxis" of the African philosopher is aimed at a gain of power for Africa, but it assumes that the West does indeed have a philosophical "secret" that permitted it to conquer the world, rather than seeing that conquest as a historical flash in the pan, the result of a temporary accident rather than a recuperable secret. Of course it must also be argued that, secret or not, European imperialism has changed the terms of any African discourse forever and must be dealt with. But why should it be that the West, by virtue of its sheer power, has the only secret worth preserving? Surely traditional Africa had and has its own. Whatever radical praxis the present may require, the imprint of the past—of identity, of difference, of the hundreds of African ethnic cultures—should not be ignored. I will extend this argument in chapter 2.

No one would want literary theory to occupy a similar position in the

---

44. Hountondji, 72: "Nous ruinons, en somme, la conception mythologique dominante de l'africanité et revenons à l'évidence toute simple, toute banale, que l'Afrique est avant tout un continent, et le concept d'Afrique un concept géographique, empirique, non un concept métaphysique."

45. See Hebga, "Eloge de l' 'ethnophilosophie,'" 28.

interpretation of African literature, as a body of texts and knowledge that wholly displaces local concerns. The anthropologically-informed reading I have called for here is of course related to the project of ethnophilosophy, if only in the sense that any attention paid to "tradition" leads one back to the time before the European conquests, before the "secret" got out, into a world of multiple identities, orality, and folklore. For some this may represent a ghetto, a jail of difference, a relegation to quaintness, and a lapse into exoticism. At its extreme, this is the danger: interpreting any African text only in terms of its author's ancestors' beliefs and customs. Clearly, an anthropologically-oriented approach is more applicable to some authors than to others.

No attempt to describe Africa's difference—as "primitive," "animist," "prelogical," "collective," "rhythmic," or whatever—seems immune from connotations and taints of ethnocentrism when seen in retrospect. By defining the other's difference, one is forced to take into account, or to ignore at one's peril, the shadow cast by the self. But without some attention to the "difference" of the African past, how can we accurately read the African present? There are in fact two ways to lose identity, be it one's own or someone else's: as Césaire wrote, "There are two ways to lose oneself: by segregation in the particular or by dilution in the 'universal'" ("Il y a deux manières de se perdre: par ségrégation murée dans le particulier ou par dilution dans l'‘universel'").[46]

The study of black African literature in French requires an approach that is sensitive both to local, ethnic differences and to the homogenizing effects of the French language. The part that "theory" has to play therein should be cautiously determined by asking to what degree it is appropriate. The epigraph at the beginning of this chapter, from *Le Devoir de violence,* serves as an emblem of the cautionary tales I have been telling. Ouologuem uses the word *théorie* in an ancient sense that remains current in French: "groupe de personnes qui s'avancent les unes derrière les autres; [in Antiquity], Députation envoyée par une ville à une fête solonelle" (*Petit Robert* ; the *Oxford English Dictionary* lists this as a "specialized usage:" "a body of *Theors* sent by a state to perform some religious rite or duty"). Ouologuem's "theory" of Africans is a vision of the African holocaust, Africans being led in bondage toward a new world, a reminder that any link can be a link in a chain of enslavement.

Europeans have been making "theories" of Africans for centuries. My feeling is that the most fruitful path for the Western critic of African literature—the "Theor"—is not to play it safe and "stay home," nor to pretend to "leave home without it" and approach African literature with

---

46. *Lettre à Maurice Thorez* (Paris: Présence Africaine, 1956): 15.

a virgin mind, but to balance one impulse against the other: to reconsider with scepticism the applicability of all Western critical terms and to look to traditional African cultures for terms they might offer.

Dialogism and Representation

In response to the messy history of hegemony and conflict, recent trends in anthropology seem to offer a far more congenial model of interpretive practice: I am referring to dialogue and dialogism. As the trademark and battle cry of a reform movement within the field of anthropology, dialogism seems to promise a great deal of help to the process of negotiating the terms of description. It in fact represents a renegotiation of the contract between anthropology and the world. Furthermore, dialogue as a theory (and, more obviously, as a practice) emerges at a crossroads between literary studies and anthropology and is therefore of real concern in the context I have evoked here. Dialogue is, however, not a panacea; its force as an imperative turns out to have consequences that must be examined. I would like to expose a few theoretical considerations about dialogism while adjourning a fuller, contextual analysis to a later chapter.

Contemporary revisionist anthropology began as a critique of its classical precursor, represented not so much by Frobenius or Tempels (who are marginal, if symptomatic, figures) as by Evans-Pritchard, Malinowski, Lucien Lévy-Bruhl, Marcel Griaule, Maurice Delafosse, and others. While certain of the early anthropologists had a habit of blowing up partial, contingent experiences into totalized "world views," the recent critiques have turned attention toward the impact of the observer on the observed, the social and historical context, and ideological interferences. They have also advocated *heteroglossia* and *dialogue* as anthropological practice. Situating themselves within what they call the "crisis of representation . . . within most disciplines of the humanities and the social sciences," George Marcus and Michael Fischer, coauthors of *Anthropology as Cultural Critique*, observe that "In these fields, long-standing commitments to general, totalizing systems of theory are suspended for the sake of intimately representing, and valorizing, difference and diversity in the face of widespread perceptions of an increasingly homogenized world."[47] This statement is emblematic of a wide movement of reaction against the discursive power of the West; Marcus and Fischer speak for

47. George E. Marcus and Michael M. J. Fischer, *Anthropology as Cultural Critique: An Experimental Moment in the Human Sciences* (Chicago: University of Chicago Press, 1986): 112. For a similar call for dialogism, articulated on a more technical and practical basis, see Tatiana Yannopoulos and Denis Martin, "De la question au dialogue . . . A propos des enquêtes en Afrique noire," *Cahiers d'études africaines* 71, vol. 18 (1978): 421–42.

all those who would like to escape into some more congenial mode of representation.

The discursive power that these critical anthropologists need in order to advance their cause is largely mustered through an applied reading of Mikhail Bakhtin. James Clifford, in his seminal essay "On Ethnographic Authority," shows what a use of Bakhtin's terms has to offer. Clifford writes: "Ethnography is invaded by heteroglossia. This possibility suggests an alternate textual strategy, a utopia of plural authorship that accords to collaborators not merely the status of independent enunciators but that of writers" (51). Heteroglossia is the polyvocality of discourse; it is according to Bakhtin the "base condition governing the operation of meaning."[48] Dialogism and heteroglossia define each other; dialogism is "the characteristic epistemological mode of a world dominated by heteroglossia." So what does it mean for ethnography to be "invaded" by heteroglossia?

First, it simply suggests the cross-fertilization from the literary theory of Bakhtin to the new anthropology or meta-anthropology of Clifford, Marcus, Fischer, and others. But more importantly, this talk of an "invasion" describes a paradoxical movement by which the antiauthoritarian discourse of Bakhtin enables a revolt within anthropology and the establishment of a new theoretical regime. Clifford and Marcus, in the introduction to their volume *Writing Culture*, quote Bakhtin on dialogue in order to reveal and deflate the authoritarianism of traditional ethnographies. They claim: "Once dialogism and polyphony are recognized as modes of textual production, monophonic authority is questioned, revealed to be characteristic of a science that has claimed to *represent* cultures."[49] They italicize the verb "represent," casting a questioning glance on the problem of speaking for or writing for an other—which is, after all, the foundation of the anthropological enterprise. Representation can no longer be assumed to be transparent and monological; a new image of authentic representation, based on polyvocality, is suggested. Furthermore, simplistic versions of authenticity itself are thrown into doubt, and a more reflexive (and literary) vocabulary is pressed into service: in Clifford Geertz's phrasing, "Fiction, not falsehood, lies at the heart of successful anthropological field research." This fiction can never be completely convincing but will remain "continuously ironic."[50]

48. Michael Holquist, glossary in Mikhail M. Bakhtin, *The Dialogic Imagination* (Austin: University of Texas Press, 1981): 428.

49. James Clifford and George E. Marcus, eds., introduction to *Writing Culture: The Poetics and Politics of Ethnography* (Berkeley: University of California Press, 1986): 15.

50. Clifford Geertz, "Thinking as a Moral Act: Ethical Dimensions of Anthropological Fieldwork in the New States," *Antioch Review* 28, no. 2 (1968): 155. See Steven Webster, "Dialogue and Fiction in Ethnography," *Dialectical Anthropology* 7 (1982): 91–114.

Imagining for a moment that this utopian vision had been conceived and miraculously realized a long time ago, even at the beginning of the twentieth century, we could fantasize about the problems that we would *not* now have to face. Anthropology would have been a very different science; Tempels and Frobenius might not have existed. Representations of others and self-representations would have circulated freely without ever drowning each other out. Knowledge would, in Steven Webster's beautiful phrase, "arise in the unforeseen dialogue between [subject and object], not the closure of some illusory resolution in behalf of one or the other" ("Dialogue and Fiction," 111). If the rules of discourse had been decentered and pluralized, any francophone African literature would not have had to explain itself to France, and the Western reader would be in a far less uneasy position today. Even though this is only a fantasy, Bakhtinian criticism shows how dialogue and polyvocality can be uncovered within apparent hegemonies, and this opens doors toward a better understanding of colonial and postcolonial literatures.

Such a fantasy obviously depends on a complete rewriting (or ignorance) of the material conditions of history: colonialism, the centralization of power in European capitals, the consequent emergence of a colonial literature subject to censorship and promotion by imperial authorities. All of these are factors that vitiate dialogism within the substance of history.

I would also like to mention one theoretical problem that arises in the conversion of discourse from totalization to dialogism; it is a problem we already saw in the context of deconstructive literary theory. If anthropology becomes dialogical, infused with the complexities and contradictions of interacting systems of thought, it seems that everyone will gain. The demise of false transparency may make it more difficult to "look up" the meaning of a "symbol," but the meanings we do construct will consequently be more valuable. But if description and representation themselves are renounced, if the focus of ethnography shifts completely from observed to observer, then its use value as an interlocutor for the criticism of African literatures will have been lost. I do not know if Stephen Tyler is joking when he writes in *Writing Culture*, "Ethnography [is] defined neither by form nor by relation to external objects; it *describes* no knowledge and *produces* no action."[51] This nonrelation to a world of objects is analogous to De Man's renunciation of "the desire to coincide"; both statements leave the subject in a position of radical self-reflexivity. Tyler seems to represent the extreme edge of a movement in anthropology that is collectively tempted to go as far as he does but scrupulously holds back

51. Stephen A. Tyler, "Post-Modern Ethnography: From Document of the Occult to Occult Document," in *Writing Culture*, 122–23.

lest their discipline self-destruct. Stephen Webster astutely observes: "Escape from ethnocentrism is our business, but a definitive escape puts us out of business altogether" (101).

Within the zone of operations occupied by the "ethnography-as-text" movement, all is not harmonious. It is given that knowledge and understanding are dialogical, but *being* dialogical proves to be more difficult than one might expect. Some suggest that, "since the ethnographer ultimately holds the pen, true dialogue is not represented in recent modernist experiments, and cannot be in any fundamentally authentic way" (*Anthropology as Cultural Critique*, 69, paraphrasing Stephen Tyler). Paul Rabinow, in *Writing Culture*, chastises Clifford for talking "a great deal about the ineluctability of dialogue (thereby establishing his authority as an 'open' one), but his texts are not themselves dialogic." According to Rabinow, "both Clifford and Geertz fail to use self-referentiality as anything more than a device for establishing authority" (244). In the context of this study, Rabinow's comments serve as a warning: dialogism as a mere *style* of representation must not be mistaken for genuine dialogue itself.

In fact, the problem of maintaining dialogism as a reliable figure of interpretation or mode of writing is inscribed deep within Bakhtin's thought itself; it is not a simple matter of correctly "applying" Bakhtin in order to be dialogical. Any use of Bakhtin within an African context would have to come to terms with his distinction between epic and the novel. His vision of the epic world as "single and unified," lacking in "any relativity," as "walled off absolutely," "impossible to change, to re-think, to re-evaluate," adds up to an oppressive anthropological interpretation of preliterate culture as Oriental despotism.[52] There are many ironies produced when Bakhtin is, incongruously, "applied" to Africa: the first is that the novel, which for him represents freedom, dialogue, and development, arrives at the end of a gun barrel. The "freedom" of representing consciousness, through the borrowed conventions of the novel, is an *imposed* freedom. Monologue seems to keep reasserting itself in the heart of dialogical projects. In chapter 3, I will explore the complex relations of freedom and power involved in the transition from orality to literacy, which is what Bakhtin's discussion of epic and novel is actually all about.

Dialogue and freedom, even if they prove difficult or unattainable in the final analysis, remain the most compelling *ethical models* for the representation of cultures. It seems dubious that heteroglossia can be given the status of a "base condition" to which all language returns, since

52. Bakhtin, "Epic and Novel," in *The Dialogic Imagination*, 15, 17, 35.

monologue also keeps reappearing. The two imperatives need to be recognized as at once incompatible and necessary to each other. Neither monologue nor dialogue can be limited to any specific time, place, or genre; nor can they be appropriated by any ideology (try as they might).[53] The distinction between them, however, remains essential and indissociable from an ethical value judgment: dialogue is simply "better" than monologue. How ethics fits into an anthropological framework is the subject of the next chapter.

The new critical anthropology has, if nothing else, dispelled a notion that sometimes troubles the invocation of ethnography within literary circles: the idea that anthropology and ethnography are purely referential sciences, piles of data, tools of the referential fallacy. The work of James Clifford in particular has built a bridge between literary studies and anthropology as equally complex discourses about culture.

The chapters that follow represent a partial and incomplete trajectory among questions of anthropology, African literature, and the ethics of representation. The most significant armature is geographical and cultural: the principal works discussed here all come from a culturally coherent zone within West Africa. The ethnic group I concentrate on here is the Mande, composed of descendants of the medieval Mali empire, famous for their *griots*' oral traditions and producers of some the francophone Africa's finest writers. While this choice is certainly no more "narrow" than confining oneself to, say, the American South, it makes this book an exception in its field, where most book-length studies range broadly through the whole of francophone Africa. My hope is that the accumulation of information about this one culture will translate into lucid readings of the texts in question.

Each chapter of this study will interrogate a specific theoretical model and examine its claims to competence about Africa. Due to the historical fact of the division of labor discussed earlier, these models will more often than not be Western in origin. My overall intention is not to "apply" Western theory to African literature nor to present an argument "against theory" but to articulate problems associated with the meeting and mixing of these two discourses and to weigh the relevance of "theory" itself. Chapter 2 continues the treatment of theoretical questions raised in this introduction, analyzing them within the principal co-

53. See, for example, the battle between Ken Hirschkop ("A Response to the Forum on Mikhail Bakhtin") and Gary Saul Morson ("Dialogue, Monologue, and the Social: A Reply to Ken Hirschkop," in *Critical Inquiry* 11, no. 4 [June 1985]: 672–86). Their attempts to use Bakhtin for opposing "liberal" and "Marxist" agendas are amusingly and mutually contradictory.

nundrum in the criticism of African literature, the opposition between "ethnicity" and "ethics"; the chapter concludes with reflections on my own critical position. Chapter 3 begins the specific study of Mande literature by tracing its origins in orality and the process of its translation into francophone-literate modes. The remaining chapters each deal with a major novel, which I analyze in relation to a problem in anthropology or literary theory: Camara Laye's world-famous *L'Enfant noir* in relation to totemism, Ahmadou Kourouma's *Les Soleils des indépendances* in relation to political and literary-theoretical dialogism, and Mariama Bâ's *Une si longue lettre* in relation to canonicity and gender theory.

2

In every age, among the people, truth is the property of the national cause. No absolute verity, no discourse on the purity of the soul, can shake this position.

—Frantz Fanon, *The Wretched of the Earth*

Ethnicity and Ethics

Ethnicity, Ethics, and Ethos

There are sound reasons for which the African writer or critic might want to abandon all notions of difference or otherness. Marcien Towa's position—that it is impossible to have identity and equality at the same time, that one must abandon identity in order to be equal, because difference is always a prison—dramatically illustrates the problems associated with "otherness." I have argued that Western readers are in a different position, laboring under an ethical imperative to be attentive to difference, and that anthropological (along with political and historical) awareness is a necessary precaution to be taken against blindly appropriative reading. The problem is that Towa's rejection of difference is but the tip of an iceberg of resistance to anthropology in Africa and in the West: to think anthropologically is to validate *ethnicity* as a category, and this has become a problematic idea.[1]

Unexamined premises thus underpin the conceptual structure here, namely ideas of what is "ethnic" and what is "ethical." I argue that the ignorance of difference is unethical, but in this I am swimming against the strong current of opinion represented by Towa. Disputes concerning ethnicity and ethics in fact constitute the central topos in the criticism of African literature; these theoretical categories are of course at the heart

1. For another example, see Locha Mateso's critique of Lilyan Kesteloot; he takes her to task for her "célébration de la différence," which he sees as part of "une critique 'différentielle' sur la base de l'appartenance raciale des écrivains. Elle donne parfois lieu à une vision manichéenne et à des simplifications abusives" (*La Littérature africaine et sa critique* [Paris: ACCT/Karthala, 1986]: 182, 205).

of politics in Africa as well. Conflicts between an ethic of national unity and ethnic entropy have animated the history of postindependence Africa. The aim of this chapter is to describe the debate on ethnicity and ethics among Africans and Westerners and to show how theoretical and literary concepts are acted out in politics. All too often, literary and social criticism establishes thought patterns that become difficult to call into question, patterns that impose themselves on reality; the supposed opposition between ethnicity and ethics is the most prevalent of these self-perpetuating models.

Advocates of difference are of course not hard to find in African literary culture. They give various names to their object, such as Negritude, Africanity, and African personality; each of these labels represents an African ethnic or cultural aesthetic, and sometimes an irreducible essence. On the other hand, there are those who would replace "the notion of ethnicity with clear class consciousness,"[2] ethnicity with ethics. Africanists in political science, sociology, and cultural studies tend to agree that there is a fundamental tension or binary pairing between ethnicity and the ethics of modernization; Ali Mazrui writes, "Ethnic consciousness in Africa has often militated against class consciousness."[3] The claim to occupy the ethical high ground and to possess the only fully integrated political and aesthetic vision—a claim made by certain Marxist critics—deserves scrutiny, and this is one of my goals in this chapter. To the discomfort of those who focus on ethnicity, Marxists look upon anthropological concerns as misguided attempts to isolate Africa within a fortress of cultural specificity, as a refusal to see broad patterns. But from the perspective of anthropologically oriented criticism, the Marxist approach tends too much toward projection of a Eurocentric paradigm onto Africa, a continent in reference to which terms such as "class struggle" and "proletariat" need to be rethought. Reviewing a Marxist study of African literature, the Nigerian critic Chinweizu writes: "African Marxist critics often display towards African writers the frustrations of a sergeant-major. . . . Marxism has had little influence on contemporary African literature, for only a handful of literary works satisfy Marxist criteria for socialist art."[4] The ethnic approach, while ignoring prescriptive visions, claims cultural specificity and seems in a better po-

2. Georg M. Gugelberger, introduction to his edited volume, *Marxism and African Literature* (Trenton, N.J.: Africa World Press, 1985): v. Further references to this work, abbreviated *MAL*, will be included in the text.

3. Ali Mazrui, "Cultural Forces in African Politics: In Search of a Synthesis," in Isaac James Mowoe and Richard Bjornson, eds., *Africa and the West: Legacies of Empire* (New York: Greenwood Press, 1986): 50.

4. Chinweizu, review of Emmanuel Ngara's *Art and Ideology in the African Novel*, *Times Literary Supplement*, June 13, 1986.

sition to find out what is actually *different* about Africa and its literature. Ethnic models include Senghor's Negritude, Jahnheinz Jahn's *Muntu*, Wole Soyinka's *Myth, Literature and the African World*, and the "Afrocentric liberationist" approach of Chinweizu and his coauthors in *The Decolonization of African Literature*. Each of these represents a pursuit and defense of difference. The diametrical opposition between these two schools, like all mutually exclusive oppositions, invites :eappraisal.[5]

Let me begin with a false solution. Stephen A. Tyler, in his contribution to *Writing Culture*, erases the etymological and discursive boundary between ethnicity and ethics in order to reinvent a "post-modern," "occult" ethnography. The solution is based on a flawed etymology: Tyler writes, " The rhetoric of ethnography is neither scientific nor political, but is, as the prefix *ethno-* implies, ethical."[6] Writing in an evocative, almost occult style, his text divided into different "voices" that dialogue with each other, Tyler describes an ethnography "defined neither by form nor by relation to an external object," which "*describes* no knowledge and *produces* no action," but "transcends instead by *evoking* what cannot be known discursively or performed perfectly" (122–23). His etymology of the word "ethnography" as coming from "ethics" is certainly less than perfect. Ethics, from the Greek *ethika*, "character or manners," is related to the notion of *ethos*, the characteristic spirit of a people, but is not the same as ethnic, from the Greek *ethnos*, nation or race, especially "Gentile, heathen, pagan." Ethnicity is otherness; to be ethnic is to be a *goy*, a heathen (the *Oxford English Dictionary* remarks: "hence the confused forms *hethnic, heathenic*"). Ethics, the science of morals, bears on the moral character of individuals or collectivities, and is therefore similar to but not identical to ethnography, the "description of nations or races . . . with their customs, habits [i.e. "character or manners"] and points of difference."[7]

Ethos is thus a bridge between ethics and ethnicity, showing wide

---

5. It is also important to keep in mind that Marxism is not alone among powerful ideologies in its mistrust of ethnicity; as Crawford Young points out, "The most prestigious ideologies in the contemporary world—socialism, in its diverse forms, *and liberalism*—tend to place a negative valuation on cultural pluralism, and in different ways validate class-oriented perceptions of society" ("Patterns of Social Conflict: State, Class, and Ethnicity," *Dædalus* 111, no. 2 [Spring 1982]: 93, my emphasis).

6. James Clifford and George E. Marcus, eds., *Writing Culture: The Poetics and Politics of Ethnography* (Berkeley: The University of California Press, 1986): 122.

7. The etymologies of "ethics" and "ethnography" are from the *Oxford English Dictionary*. Cf. Werner Sollors's gloss on the *OED*: "To say it in the simplest and clearest terms, an ethnic, etymologically speaking, is a *goy*. In English usage, . . . the word retained its quality of defining another people contrastively, and often negatively" (*Beyond Ethnicity: Consent and Descent in American Culture* [New York: Oxford University Press, 1986]: 25).

areas of common enterprise: to describe a people is to describe not only their customs and manners but also their moral character. But once the *ethos* differs, ethnicity and ethics begin to go their separate ways. Few undertakings have proven more prone to ethical pitfalls than the description of other peoples: Clifford Geertz states that the ethnographic encounter has "an inherent moral asymmetry;"[8] the science of ethnography, as numerous recent critiques have shown, worked hand in hand with the forces of colonialism, providing a theoretical framework and a practical justification for conquest and control.[9]

In addition, recent work has shown that colonizers often invented ethnic traditions for "their" natives in order to control them and to simplify thinking about them; Terence Ranger's fascinating study of this phenomenon shows how "everyone sought to tidy up and make more comprehensible the infinitely complex situation" of cultures in Africa.[10] Jean-Loup Amselle's "deconstruction" of ethnicity goes so far as to suggest that there were no *ethnies* whatsoever in precolonial Africa; all were constructed by the colonizers in order to divide and conquer.[11] Does this mean that ethnicity itself is an illusion, a useless category of interpretation?

It does not, for several reasons. First, the kind of ethnicity that Amselle deconstructs is an ancient Western myth of tribalism, a metaphysical, essentialized means of segmentation. According to such a notion of ethnicity, any person is in his or her essence a member of one and only one ethnic group, which is wholly distinct from all other groups. The fallacy is obvious, even if this myth enjoyed a long life. The new, critical anthropologists have attacked manipulations of "tribal authenticity" based on this essentialized idea of ethnicity, particularly within the museum establishment.[12] In place of this, Amselle proposes a welcome corrective:

8. Geertz, "Thinking as a Moral Act: Ethical Dimensions of Anthropological Fieldwork in the New States," *The Antioch Review* 28, no. 2 (Summer 1968): 151.

9. See Gérard Leclerc, *Anthropologie et colonialisme: essai sur l'histoire de l'africanisme* (Paris: Fayard, 1972); Alf Schwartz, *Colonialistes, africanistes et Africains* (N.p.: Nouvelle Optique, 1979); Talal Asad, ed., *Anthropology and the Colonial Encounter* (New York: Humanities Press, 1973); Daniel Nordman and Jean-Pierre Raison, eds., *Sciences de l'homme et conquête coloniale: constitution et usages des sciences humaines en Afrique* (Paris: Presses de l'Ecole Normale Supérieure, 1980).

10. Terence Ranger, "The Invention of Tradition in Colonial Africa," in Eric Hobsbawm and Terence Ranger, eds., *The Invention of Tradition* (Cambridge: Cambridge University Press, 1983): 249.

11. Jean-Loup Amselle, "Ethnies et espaces: Pour une anthropologie topologique," in Jean-Loup Amselle and Elikia M'Bokolo, eds., *Au coeur de l'ethnie: Ethnies, tribalisme et état en Afrique* (Paris: La Découverte, 1985): 23.

12. See James Clifford, part 3, "Collections," of *The Predicament of Culture: Twentieth-Century Ethnography, Literature, and Art* (Cambridge: Harvard University Press, 1988): 187–251.

that we think instead in terms of *spaces*. Ethnic groups are "relations of forces" (21) within spaces, organized by exchange, language, state power, and religious culture. Ethnicity thus becomes a fluid *process* of "composition, decomposition and recomposition" (29).

But the most important point that Amselle makes is that within this sea of instability, two factors make it impossible to throw out ethnicity with the bathwater of colonialism. One factor is that ethnonyms acquire a *performative* power that transcends their initial inaccuracy: the "application of a signifier to a social group itself creates that social group" (37). This is one way in which identities are acquired, borrowed, and exchanged. The other factor is the existence of ideologies of ethnicity within social groups, making the study of "ethnicity"—now understood as a *discourse*—imperative. Amselle cites the example of the Mande (the "ethnic" sphere within which most of this study will operate) as a society that makes use of a genealogical fiction in order to foster social coherence (35). That fiction, the Sunjata epic, will be the subject of the next chapter.

Amselle's lessons on ethnicity are well taken. Ethnicity cannot be taken for granted; ethnonyms must be deciphered within their time and place, observed as they mutate. For the moment I will define ethnicity as a sense of identity and difference among peoples, founded on a fiction of origin and descent and subject to forces of politics, commerce, language, and religious culture. "Ethnicity" will thus not stand for a conceptual prison but for an inquiry into notions of identity and difference.

We have already seen that such inquiries raise political and ethical questions. We must therefore distinguish between ethnographies that are "ethical" and those that are in need of ethical critique. This means we must decide what is ethical, and different answers to this question frame the debate that I want to analyze here. I propose the following itinerary: to investigate first the ethical claims of Marxist critics of African literature, along with their critique of ethnicity, in a recent volume of criticism edited by Georg M. Gugelberger, *Marxism and African Literature*; and then to examine the antinomies of ethnicity and ethics in a closely related nexus of African texts and historical events. This will include the works and political fate of the late Guinean poet and politician Kéita Fodéba, known to posterity through the important place a poem of his occupies in Frantz Fanon's essay on national culture; Fanon and Fodéba are further linked by their textual and extratextual relations with the late dictator of Guinea, Sékou Touré.

The Marxist Critique of Ethnicity

My observations on Marxist critiques of African literature will respond to chapters in Gugelberger's volume, which includes work by both African and Western critics. In his preface, Gugelberger confesses that he was initially disappointed by African literature :

As a comparatist interested in literary theory and related isssues, I had expected from African literature, and more so from African literary criticism, what so many writers and critics had merely taken for granted: a specific political relevance. I expected to find, with the transition from colonialism to 'independance,' the kind of increased politicization we unfortunately find less and less in experimental and avant-garde modernist and post-modernist Western literature. I quickly learned that a geographic definition of Third World literature does not necessarily imply a politically progressive attitude. (*MAL*, v)

The attitude with which Gugelberger turns toward Africa is a familiar one: his own intellectual and cultural background have given him certain needs and expectations; he knows in advance what the nature of African literature should be. He doesn't need to have read African literature in order to know what problems it should address, what answers it should provide: African literature should be the antidote to Western lassitude and stagnancy. The "specific political relevance" he seeks is determined by global factors, such as colonialism, which encompass but also transcend Africa; but the politics of the texts he reads are not entirely to his suiting—they lack "relevance." Gugelberger is not alone in his experience of disappointment; I have found it fairly common for American students to have their expectations confounded by the actual texts of francophone Africa, particularly those of the early period. Too often we Westerners expect third world literatures to respond to our hopes and concerns, to liberate *us*, when in fact they may be answering their own questions instead of ours. The problem is, how do we know the difference?

Among Westerners who are confronted with the incongruency between their theoretical expectations and the "reality" of Africa, there are two broad patterns of response: either to explain it as due to something specifically African, and then almost inevitably to isolate it as material for the Western "knowledge industry," or to assimilate the difference to some known paradigm or methodology that has universal applicability. Gugelberger, confronted with this choice, can only opt for the universal approach. In order for a Marxist analysis to proceed, there can be no African absolute that makes all outside terminology and methodology irrelevant. This is to say that ethnicity must be contained, discounted, even made into a shibboleth for the opposing side, and that is exactly what Gugelberger proceeds to do. He quotes Peter Nazareth in order to derive a class-based definition of political progressiveness. The quotation from Nazareth points in a textual direction that we will follow here, toward Fanon; Nazareth writes: "To belong to the Third World is therefore to accept an identity, an identity with the wretched of the earth spoken for by Frantz Fanon, to determine to end all exploitation and oppression" (*MAL*, v). Gugelberger adds: "This definition—if adhered to—clearly replaces not only the old geographic definition but at the same time the notion of ethnicity (race/Africaneity) with clear class consciousness."

Ethnicity is therefore the principal obstacle to a Marxist analysis of African literature, and Gugelberger makes this clear:

We have to look at things dialectically. What at first appears progressive (ethnicity, populism) can easily turn into something less progressive, something which actually enforces the status quo. (*MAL*, xiii)

The 'ethnic imperative' most likely has been the strongest in post-independence Africa's search for a viable and non-Eurocentric aesthetics. . . . [Naming various approaches, including Jahn's, Soyinka's, and Chinweizu's, Gugelberger states:] Most of these are basically 'formalist' concepts of a dangerous intrinsic orientation, historically understandable, but not therefore less regrettable. . . . In the long run they have to be subordinated to the *ethic imperative* if African literature and criticism are to be spared the pitfalls of Western art and literature. (*MAL*, 1)

At the same time that African literature is somehow to be tutored, raised, and educated in a way that makes it purer than European literature, that purity or absence of pitfalls will not be based on or lead to any notion of Afrocentrism: "it is doubtful that we can ever arrive at . . . a criticism based on the rejection of European critical concepts" (3); "with due respect for the search for a national literature (as an educative tool) [apparently a nod to Fanon] it will be patently impossible to arrive at a separate African aesthetics" (13–14). With this statement, difference disappears. There simply is no room in this Marxist perspective for a notion of "authentic" identity rooted in tradition or history. If Africans are to follow an ethical imperative in their lives and their literatures, they must not worry about the European provenance of that imperative. To quote from another postcolonial context, that of Vietnam, "There is no shame in using a science even if it was developed by men from another continent. . . . The methods of thought and action that inspired Lenin and Mao Tse-Tung have a universal value . . . ; it is thus not surprising that knowledge of the fundamental laws of history came to us from Europe."[13] This is held to be true even if the views that Marx and Engels themselves expressed on Middle East and African societies "have often

13. Nguyen Nghe, "Frantz Fanon et les problèmes de l'indépendance," *La Pensée* 107 (January-February, 1963): 35–36.

been interpreted as a justification for colonialism" and have proved to be "something of an ideological embarrassment for Marxists." [14]

The choice that is forced upon the colonized self is thus a stark opposition between equality and identity; ethics dictates equality, which in turn seems to sacrifice ethnic identity. We are back to Towa's position: "In order to affirm and assure itself, the self must be negated, must negate its own essence *and its past*; the self must expressly aim to become like the other, similar to the other, and thereby *uncolonizable* by the other." [15] Without equivocation, Towa sees what this suggests: that the African become just like the European. But Towa's harsh prescription (which is largely a reaction against Negritude) is perhaps more realistic and less mystified than the standard Marxist notion of a universal identity. Nazareth, referring to Fanon, speaks of an identity with all the wretched of the earth. While this is an ideal of incontestable value, I think that, in the light of history, it nonetheless needs to be recognized as an ideal; but I will return to this question of unity and ideal solidarity in discussing Fanon below. My point here is that the rejection of ethnic identity leads into either Towa's Europeanism or a universalism that needs to be analyzed in its application.

I would like to focus for a moment on an important problem that arises in the Marxist critique of ethnicity in general. Any approach calling itself Marxist must have some historical dimension. Yet one finds in some Marxist appraisals of African literature and culture not only a critique of the past but almost a denigration of it and a failure to take it into account in analyzing the present. The prescriptive occludes the descrip-

14. Bryan S. Turner, *Marx and the End of Orientalism* (London: George Allen & Unwin, 1978): 3. For Stephen Katz, however, Marx's and Engels's articles on colonialism—in which European intervention is seen as aid to development—are a false impediment to real class analysis of Africa; for Katz, these writings "are not a significant contribution to Marxism in general, and . . . our Marxist ideas on the exploitation of the Third World should have as little to do with them as possible." I am not sure the problem can be so easily dismissed. Stephen Katz, *Marxism, Africa and Social Class: A Critique of Relevant Theories* (Montreal: McGill University Centre for Developing-Area Studies, 1980): 5. For an African Marxist critique of Eurocentrism in European Marxism, see Amady Aly Dieng, *Hegel, Marx, Engels et le problèmes de l'Afrique noire* (Dakar: Sankoré, 1978), esp. chapter 1, "Le Marxisme et les problèmes de l'Afrique noire," 9–41. Dieng's second chapter, on Marx, confronts and deals with the issues that Katz brackets; for a similar approach, see Sine Babacar, *Le Marxisme devant les sociétés africaines contemporaines* (Paris: Présence Africaine, 1983), chapter 1, "Spécificités africaines et marxisme simplifié," 13–70. A different kind of African critique of Eurocentric Marxism comes from the novelist Ayi Kwei Armah, in "Masks and Marx: The Marxist Ethos vis-à-vis African Revolutionary Theory and Praxis," *Présence Africaine* 131, no. 3 (1984): 35–65.

15. Marcien Towa, *Essai sur la problématique philosophique dans l'Afrique actuelle* (Yaoundé, Cameroun: Editions CLE, 1971): 42, emphasis mine.

tive and the analytic. Thus what begins as an understandably iconoclastic attitude toward tradition can become an ahistoricism, Eurocentrically discounting and devalorizing everything that preceded colonization; hence it would be a failure of Marxist objectives: to analyze thought as it reflects its "concrete social situation" and to "always historicize."[16]

Omafume F. Onoge, a contributor to Gugelberger's volume, is an articulate example of this. With considerable justification, Onoge attacks Western critics who prescribe a heavy dose of traditionalism, animism, and "telluric sentiment" for an African literature of an "authentic exoticism."[17] Such critics, among whom he includes Dorothy Blair and Lilyan Kesteloot, place themselves in a position to "induce" African authors to "be true to themselves,"[18] like Tempels in his *Bantu Philosophy*. Onoge sees this colonialistic version of ethnicity as a form of bourgeois individualism. He compares Aimé Césaire's version of Negritude to Léopold Sédar Senghor's, calling the former "revolutionary affirmation" and the latter "mystical affirmation." Césaire's *Cahier d'un retour au pays natal* is infused with a "revolutionary affirmative consciousness" and denies "any further legitimacy to the prevailing ideological charters of colonial constrictions," but its assault on colonialism "still lacked rigour" (*MAL*, 24–27). Onoge reproaches Césaire for defining Negritude elliptically ("my negritude is neither tower nor cathedral/it takes root in the red flesh of the soil").[19] The poetic discourse is simply not positive enough, and Césairean Negritude is left in limbo between public and private, revolutionary and quietistic. Senghor, by contrast, is hopelessly trapped in the ideology of ethnicity : "Vital forces, religious preoccupations, innate rhythms, congenital emotionality, a-logicality, and a non-analytic participation with the physical environment in a perennial orgy of tom toms . . . " (*MAL*, 29). Onoge asserts that Senghor's Negritude is in fact "unhistoric," meaning that the timelessness of Senghor's traditional Af-

---

16. Fredric Jameson, *Marxism and Form* (Princeton, N.J.: Princeton University Press, 1971): xviii; Frederic Jameson, *The Political Unconscious: Narrative as a Socially Symbolic Act* (Ithaca, N.Y.: Cornell University Press, 1981): 9.

17. Dorothy Blair, quoted in Onoge's essay, "The Crisis of Consciousness in Modern African Literature: A Survey (1974)," *MAL*, 32.

18. "Once a critic has noticed this inconsistency . . . he should try to get in touch with the writer concerned, either directly or by inducing him to tell the *truth* as he sees it." Kesteloot, quoted in Onoge, *MAL*, 31. This quotation is from an essay, "Problems of the Literary Critic in Africa," which is included in Kesteloot's major opus (which still serves as the first historical reference point in this field), *Black Writers in French: A Literary History of Negritude*, trans. Ellen Conroy Kennedy (Philadelphia: Temple University Press, 1974): 349–66.

19. Aimé Césaire, *The Collected Poetry*, trans. Clayton Eshleman and Annette Smith (Berkeley: University of California Press, 1983): 68.

rica shows it to be an essentialized, mystified, pseudohistorical vision. In response to these limited and perhaps dated models, Onoge applies Gorky's distinction between two versions of realism: on the one hand, critical realism, which is *"engaged* with the contemporary reality in a critical way" but has no positive vision of its own to offer, and on the other hand socialist realism, which for Onoge is the answer to "the revolutionary aspirations of the exploited classes" (36).[20]

What becomes of the concern for the traditional past in the perspective of socialist realism? Onoge's position is ambivalent. Attention to the past was a phase that African literature had to go through, but "what was wrong was a retrospective fixation" (37). He quotes the Kenyan novelist Ngũgĩ wa Thiong'o: "It is only in a socialist context that a look at yesterday can be meaningful in illuminating today and tomorrow." It should be noted that Ngũgĩ's position on language makes him a strange and pivotal figure in this debate. Having called for the abandonment of colonial languages, Ngũgĩ now writes his original works in Gĩkũyũ, the language of his ethnic group; he does this, however, not out of nostalgia for ethnic roots but rather as a "conscious deliberate rejection" of the class that aspires to English-language prestige and as a "total identification with the position of peasants and workers in their struggle." The literature produced in European languages "is *not* African literature at all"; it is *"Afro-European* literature," to be distinguished from Kenyan national literature, which "can only grow and thrive if it reaches for its roots in the rich languages, cultures and history of the Kenyan peasant masses who are the majority class in each of the Kenya's several nationalities."[21] Even this class-based use of ethnicity, however, invites critique, for among Kenya's "several nationalities" some are politically dominant, and some are dominated. Ngũgĩ's Gĩkũyũ, as it happens, is the language of the dominant group in Kenya; his choice of Gĩkũyũ may represent liberation in a Gĩkũyũ context, but to others it may have a different implication. The look back into the past that is implied by writing in an African language may remain at odds with the forging of a national culture (as Ngũgĩ uses the term, in the singular). This is a question I will discuss further in reference to Fanon.

20. Emmanuel Ngara, finding the term socialist realism too "shrouded in controversy," uses "socialist art," defined as "works that depict reality from a Marxist point of view, works which reflect the class structure of society and which present social struggles from the point of view of class and promote the ideals of socialism" (*Art and Ideology in the African Novel: A Study of the Influence of Marxism on African Writing* [London: Heinemann, 1985]: 16).

21. "Return to the Roots: National Languages as the Basis of a Kenya National Literature and Culture," in *Writers in Politics* (London: Heinemann, 1981): 58–59.

The socialist look at yesterday as described by Onoge is however a very particular one: its most striking feature is its orientation of the past toward the future, the drawing of description toward prescription, history toward History. In Onoge's description, socialist analysis has the ethical advantage of exposing the roots of Africa's current woes in the nature of capitalism, and the roots of contemporary capitalism in colonialism. But he says nothing about the advantages of socialist analysis of precolonial Africa. Anything prior to the European appropriation of the continent is of much less interest and relevance because precolonial systems and thought patterns, as recent as they are and as much as they have managed to survive, present a challenge to socialist analysis. This challenge, as far as I can see, has not been met. Practicioners and prescribers of socialist realism have been too content to dismiss the African past with a wave of the pen. Thus precolonial societies are referred to as "feudal," assimilating the African past to the European past; this is symptomatic of the imposition of an outside paradigm on a situation that may or may not conform. Thus Onoge, in a discussion of the obstacles faced by socialist realism in Africa, briefly mentions the lack of mass support from an "educated audience": "Yet to break with this [elite] audience, as he [the potentially revolutionary writer] must, in order to adopt the *people* as his constituency, poses communication problems which have no easy solution at the moment. For the African case, it is not just the colonial tongue which isolates the writer from the people. There is also the question of mass illiteracy even in our own languages!" (*MAL*, 40).

Consider the implications of the word "illiteracy" (a point on which I will expand in the next chapter). This term assumes the point of view of literacy to be the legitimate one; societies without European writing systems are described as deviant from this norm. This ignores the possibility of describing positively—or at least neutrally—cultures without writing in the Western sense of the term: where mass "illiteracy" is said to reign, *orality* has in fact been the motor of cultural and political expression since long before European and Moslem incursions. One chapter in Gugelberger's volume is concerned with an oral art form, Urhobo song-poetry of Nigeria, and Godini G. Darah's critical work therein stands as a corrective to Onoge's use of the term "illiteracy." This shows that a Marxist perspective need not, should not preclude understanding of African tradition: this is where work needs to be done. But Darah's analysis does not really bear on precolonial history, so we do not know what he would do when the terms of modernity were no longer applicable. What is needed is a nonexclusionary form of cultural Marxist analysis, which treats class and ethnicity in Africa with an open mind; since the work of Claude Meillassoux, there has been a Marxist anthropology of Africa, but mainly limited to economics;[22] in cultural, and especially literary interpretation, the opposition between ethnicity and ethics is maintained.

Particularly in earlier years, the choices available in the ideological marketplace of at least the literary sector seemed to be either a timeless image of ethnicity, as offered by Negritude, or an ethical concern for the present and the future, coming from the left. The prominent Senegalese writer Ousmane Sembène, in his novel *O pays, mon beau peuple!*, published in 1957, described a corrupt traditional king in graphic terms:

Le lendemain, il fut conduit devant Sa Majesté. C'était un homme qui devait vivre perpétuellement assis. Ses reins étaient cachés par la masse de chair qui débordait de chaque flanc; pour comble d'horreur, son cou disparaissait entre une tête minuscule et un ventre énorme orné en son milieu d'une hernie ombilicale. A bien le regarder, Oumar se demandait si cet homme était en mesure de réfléchir. . . . A deux ou trois pas de lui, un valet, éventail en main, balayait sa face monstrueuse.[23]

The next day he was brought before His Majesty, a man who must have lived perpetually seated. His loins were hidden by the mass of flesh that spilled down his sides; most horrible of all, his neck disappeared between a miniscule head and an enormous stomach, decorated in the middle by an umbilical hernia. Taking a good look at him, Oumar wondered if this man was capable of thinking. . . . Two or three paces away, a valet fanned his monstrous face.

This Orientalist caricature should not be taken as a complete representation of Sembène's view of tradition. But the attitude evident here is symptomatic of socialist realism, of which *O pays* is a fine example. The hero of *O pays* is what is known in Anglophone Africa as a "been-to," having fought in World War II and having spent four more years in Europe, where he:

avait parfaitement assimilé les modes de pensée, les réactions des blancs, tout en ayant conservé au plus profond de lui l'héritage de son peuple. Il avait beaucoup vu, beaucoup appris pendant ses années d'Europe; d'importants bouleversements s'étaient produits en lui, il en était même venu à juger sans indulgence ses frères de race: leur sectarisme, leurs préjugés de castes qui *semblaient rendre illusoire toute possibilité de progrès social*, leur particularisme et jusqu'à la puerilité de certaines de leurs réactions "anti-blancs." (14–15, emphasis mine)

had totally assimilated the modes of thought, the reactions of the whites, while at the same time preserving deep within himself the heritage of his people. He had seen much, learned much during his years in Europe; important changes had happened to him. He had even gotten to the point of judging his racial brothers

22. See Claude Meillassoux, *L'Anthropologie économique des Gouro de Côte d'Ivoire* (Paris: Mouton, 1964); Emmanuel Terray, "Historical Materialism and Segmentary Lineage-Based Societies," in his *Marxism and "Primitive" Societies*, trans. Mary Klopper (New York: Monthly Review Press, 1972): 93–186.

23. Sembène Ousmane, *O pays, mon beau peuple!* (Paris: Presses Pocket, 1957): 105.

with indulgence: their sectarianism, their caste prejudice, which *seemed to make any possibility of social progress illusory*, their particularism, and even the childishness of some of their "antiwhite" reactions.

The difficulty here, as Sembène's novel shows, is in reconciling heritage and progress: the passage I have just quoted asserts the possibility of a benign coexistence between conservation and rejection, but it denies the violence that is evident in the hero's judgment and rejection of his heritage, of which the caste system, for example, is an integral part. The violence that is latent here is explicit in the caricature of the traditional king, whose head is literally belittled and with it his status as a valid political entity and person. Whether this violence is of a "liberating" Fanonian type is a question to which I will return. For the moment it is important to recognize the tension between tradition and the developmentalist point of view, a tension that is sometimes—as here in Sembène's description of the returning hero—glossed over.

Another aspect of O *Pays, mon beau peuple!* demonstrates the correlative of what we have just seen, the necessity of a visionary leader. Progress and justice depend on his reading of the people's needs: Sembène shows Oumar walking through the fields alone, hearing his people's voice "in his imagination, aided by the silence and the solitude."[24] But what if his imagination is deluded? This kind of leader's vision is conditioned by his solitude, which is to say his alienation from the people, whose voice is a mere metaphor.[25]

Sembène is not a doctrinaire Marxist. Jack Woddis, author of *New Theories of Revolution*, is, and in a chapter critiquing Fanon's theory of the revolutionary peasant, Woddis writes: "Most peasants are illiterate, ignorant and a prey to religious dogma and superstition. They are dominated economically by the chiefs and feudal landlords who exercise considerable ideological influence over them."[26] Illiterate compared to what? Ignorant of what? The political enlightenment and uplifting that Woddis wants for the peasants would come only at the cost of some cultural,

---

24. "Seul devant son peuple *qu'il voyait en imagination, aidé par le silence et la solitude,* l'émotion le prenait, il parlait et il entendait la voix de son peuple qui lui répondait" (121, emphasis mine).

25. Oumar's dialogue with his people is thus actually a form of false dialogue, a monologue with himself. This form of discourse is anything but typical of Sembène's writings, particularly his novels published after O *pays*. For an appreciation of Sembène's "radically 'democratic' narrative formations," namely irony and parenthetical statements that contest dominant "textual institutions," see Mary N. Layoun, "Fictional Formations and Deformations of National Culture," *The South Atlantic Quarterly* 87, no. 1 (Winter 1988): 53–73.

26. Jack Woddis, *New Theories of Revolution: A Commentary on the Views of Frantz Fanon, Régis Debray and Herbert Marcuse* (London: Lawrence and Wishart, 1972): 60. Further references to this work, abbreviated *NTR*, will be included in the text.

perhaps even physical violence. The Marxist perspective places in the central, dominant position values that may be universal but may also be Eurocentric; values that may mask or destroy that of which the Western outsider can never be completely sure: cultural difference. Any revolution in Africa must have the support of the so-called peasants, who make up the vast majority of the population, yet the peasants do not lead but must be led. The Guinea-Cape Verdean revolutionary Amilcar Cabral wrote: "[The peasantry] is almost the whole of the population, it controls the nation's wealth, it is the peasantry which produces; *but we know from experience what trouble we had convincing the peasantry to fight.*"[27] The Marxist leader must stand in a transcendent relation between the peasant and History. The peasant's destiny will be revealed to him by the leader, in a relation of active to "passive," literate to "illiterate," progress to tradition, knowledge to "ignorance."[28] This relationship may be absolutely necessary in order for social progress to take place, but it is similar to the relationship that obtained between the colonizer and the colonized. Implicit in this ideology is the belief that there may be truth in Africa, but Africans, especially the peasants, need the intervention of an outsider who will make their own truth known to them. The rhetorical relationship between the Marxist leader and the African peasant thus seems to have the same structure as the relationship between Lilyan Kesteloot and the author she will "induce to tell the *truth* as he sees it." This is the role that Placide Tempels assigned to another transcendent belief system, when he asserted that Christianity is "the only possible consummation of the Bantu ideal."[29]

To look at this situation in the extremity of its implications, ethnicity and ethics are simply and diametrically opposed. There is no advance in ethics without cost in ethnicity, and vice versa; ethical statements are intrinsically universal and must ignore localized differences, but localized belief systems resist the interference of outside "universals," which to them appear as other localized beliefs in disguise. In the context we have seen, the ethical concern for progress leads to an ethically dubious assault on tradition and ethnicity. Setting out to improve the *ethika*, the character or manners of Africans, Marxism must uproot the African *ethos*. In

27. Quoted in Woddis, NTR, 65.

28. "*For the moment*, [the peasant world] constitutes a mass of passive support for the power of the privileged groups, thanks in part to the influence of religious and feudal chiefs" (Romano Ledda, quoted in Woddis, NTR, 57). Woddis also quotes from Nguyen Nghe, "Frantz Fanon": "The peasant, by himself, can never acquire a revolutionary consciousness: it is the militant from the towns who must patiently seek out the most gifted elements of the poor peasantry, educate them and organise them; and it is only after a long period of political work that one can mobilise the peasantry" (NTR, 57).

29. Placide Tempels, *Bantu Philosophy*, trans. Colin King (Paris: Présence Africaine, 1959): 121.

this process, Africa remains an *ethnos* in the etymological sense: heathen or pagan, in need of conversion and redemption. Socialist realism in literature and politics may finish off the job that Fanon says colonialism began:

> La mise en place du régime coloniale n'entraîne pas pour autant la mort de la culture autochtone. Il ressort au contraire de l'observation historique que le but recherché est davantage une *agonie continuée* qu'une disparition totale de la culture pré-existante.[30]

> The setting up of the colonial system does not of itself bring about the death of the native culture. Historic observation reveals, on the contrary, that the aim sought is rather a *continued agony* than a total disappearance of the pre-existing culture. (*TAR*, 34; emphasis mine)

As they say about death after a long and painful illness, perhaps it is the best thing. If the alternative is the artificial preservation of culture through the "extraordinary means" of a state ideology like Negritude (or like Mobutu's pseudorevolution of "African authenticity" in Zaïre), then the opposition between ethnicity and ethics is indeed manichean.

I have outlined the situation in these stark terms for two reasons: first in order to prepare for the example that I have in mind, which deals with matters of literal life and death, and second because the discourse of criticism in Gugelberger's volume and in the field as a whole would lead one to believe that ethnicity and ethics are indeed incompatible. Are we faced here with an opposition that is absolute only on the level of theory, an incompatibility that is merely an aberration of polemical discourse to which reality need not or cannot conform? Is pragmatism the solution? Only through the analysis of a real literary situation, in its context, will we be able to answer such questions.

Death Sentences

The problem that concerns us here is that a claim to an ethical imperative in an anticolonial context may serve as a justification for another silencing of culture, eradication of difference, the very oppression that decolonization was supposed to relieve. My assumption is that in the black African context, "national liberation" should provide something better than the cultural imperialism practiced by the European colonial powers, for it was in the very name of culture and of difference that the battle for

---

30. "Racisme et culture," in *Pour la révolution africaine* (Paris: Maspero, 1964): 41, emphasis mine. Further references to this work, abbreviated *PRA*, will be included in the text, followed by references to the English translation *Toward the African Revolution*, trans. Haakon Chevalier (New York: Grove Press, 1967), abbreviated *TAR*. Translations that I have altered will be marked "AT."

independence was fought. Ousmane Sembène himself has stated, "To confront the colonial system and its corollaries, there is only one weapon: culture."[31] What happens, then, when a notion of culture is incorporated into a progressive ethical vision? Does the very concept of culture—a term used by thinkers from all points of the ideological spectrum—provide a solution to the opposition we have seen? Two figures in particular need to be introduced here: Amilcar Cabral and Frantz Fanon.

Cabral, the leader of the liberation stuggle in Guinea-Bissau, in an important essay called "National Liberation and Culture," recognizes the importance of culture no matter what its ideological character might be:

A nation which frees itself from foreign rule will only be culturally free if . . . it recaptures the commanding heights of its own culture, which derives sustenance from the living reality of its environment and equally rejects the harmful influences which any kind of subjection to foreign cultures involves. Thus one sees that if imperialist domination necessarily practices cultural oppression, national liberation is necessarily an act of culture.[32]

Cabral makes reference to the resilience of African culture, which "has survived all the storms, by seeking refuge in villages, in forests and in the spirit of generations of victims of colonialism." But while he admits there are "several African cultures" and not just one, Cabral states that the liberation movement must bring about "a convergence" toward "a single national culture," which itself is but a step toward "a universal culture." This means that, "in the face of the vital necessity of progress," certain tribal "acts and practices" will have to be left behind, those with "negative, reactionary or retrogressive aspects." These would certainly include the belief in and practice of "witchcraft," which came close to destroying his insurgency. Local cultures will be studied and judged by the members of the liberation movement, "to discern the essential from the secondary, the positive from the negative, the progressive from the retrogressive," all according to the standard of what Cabral calls "universal civilization" (15–17).[33] The latter is a phrase that sounds much like the Senghor's

31. *Man is Culture/L'Homme est culture*, The Sixth Annual Hans Wolff Memorial Lecture (Bloomington: African Studies Program, Indiana University, 1979): 19. Sembène goes on to ask, "Which culture? The old one?" and to make clear that whatever culture is "resuscitated" will have been profoundly altered by colonialism. There will be a process of "levelling" and of "fusion" in which castes, clans, collaborators, and resistors—the "contradictions" of the precolonial and colonial predicament—will be overcome.

32. Amilcar Cabral, "National Liberation and Culture," *Transition* 45, vol. 9, ii (1974): 13.

33. For Cabral, it is a functional rather than a moral judgment that the cadres must bring to bear on local cultures: "to compare this value with that of other cultures, not with a view to deciding which is superior or inferior, but to determine within the general framework of the struggle for development what help it can or must receive" ("National Liberation and Culture," 16).

civilisation de l'universel (and Senghor is anything but a Marxist revolutionary). Cabral is thus caught between two imperatives: on the one hand his own ethics and political beliefs, which lead to a universal standard, and on the other, his desire to respect local, ethnic cultures within the larger plan. As it actually happened, in 1963, the power of ancient, ethnic belief came "within a hair's-breadth" of causing disaster for Cabral's liberation movement in Guinea-Bissau, the PAIGC. Tribalism, witch-hunting, and belief in "bullet-immunizing charms" came close to destroying the struggle for national liberation, which was saved only by the "unquestioned authority" of Cabral himself (and "only" two executions).[34]

The most powerful discussion of culture within a progressive, revolutionary scheme is undoubtedly Fanon's chapter on "national culture" in *Les Damnés de la terre* (*The Wretched of the Earth*). Fanon shares with Cabral a belief in the necessity of moving from the particular to the universal; the chapter on national culture assumes a context in which the confines of a nation are not problematic and in which everything is subordinate to national liberation. There are three phases in the cultural development of colonized peoples: 1) assimilation, in which the artist proves that he/she has mastered the language and culture of the colonizer and can imitate received forms perfectly, but without originality; this corresponds more or less to the origins of the francophone African tradition as I discussed it in the introduction; 2) recollection, in which the artist "becomes unsettled and decides to remember," but is not involved with his/her own people; this sounds like the Mandarin side of Negritude: elite and removed from the masses; and 3) combat, revolution, national culture, in which the artist awakens the people from their lethargy. After independence, the artist's "concern to rejoin the people will confine him to *the point-by-point representation of national reality*."[35] The great novels of resistance written in the 1950s—Ferdinand Oyono's *Une vie de boy*, Sembène Ousmane's *Les Bouts de bois de Dieu*, Mongo Béti's *Le Pauvre Christ de Bomba*—come closest to this description.

It has been observed, especially by Jack Woddis, that Fanon is not very good about particulars: when he talks about classes, it is without precision; all is reduced to the simple opposition between colonizer and colo-

---

34. Basil Davidson, *Let Freedom Come: Africa in Modern History* (Boston: Little, Brown, 1978): 343–50.

35. Frantz Fanon, *Les Damnés de la terre* (Paris: Maspero, 1978 [first published in 1961]): 153–56, emphasis mine; *The Wretched of the Earth*, trans. Constance Farrington (New York: Grove Press, 1963): 225, AT. Further references to this work, abbreviated *DT*, will be included in the text, followed by reference to the translation, abbreviated *WE*. Translations that I have altered will be marked "AT."

nized.[36] But there is one major problem that Woddis does not sufficiently explore: the question of what is a nation.

Briefly, I would submit that Fanon's use of the word "nation" covers over important unresolved tensions between ethnicity and ethics: by placing the word at the center of his concern for evolution, without questioning the complexities of its application to different geographical and cultural environments, Fanon winds up imposing his own idea of nation in places where it may need reappraising. As David Caute has accurately pointed out, "It is curious that Fanon, who wanted to snap the bonds of European culture, should have transformed arbitrary European structures into the natural units of African progress."[37] Far from being "natural national entities" or cohesive nation-states, the modern nations of black Africa must make do with borders created to satisfy European power brokering in the "scramble for Africa," borders that often violate rather than reinforce units of culture. They are, for the most part, communities that were "imagined" on the conference tables of Europe, inherited by Africans, who must deal with their contradictions.[38] In Fanon's essay on national culture, there is no analysis of what a nation might be, whether it is the same in reference to Algeria as it in reference to Guinea, Sénégal or, most notoriously, the Congo (now Zaïre). The single most important fact of political existence in black Africa, the artificiality of the national borders and the consequent problem of cultural and linguistic disunity, receives no attention. Precolonial groupings are referred to as "tribes."

More specifically, when Fanon says "nation," I think he means Algeria. When he says "Africa," he also seems to mean Algeria. Discussing the coming of independence to black Africa, Fanon states:

Si on ne se réfère pas constamment à la lutte du peuple algérien on risque de ne pas comprendre précisément l'évolution des rapports entre les colonies et la domination française. (*PRA*, 166)

If one does not constantly refer to the struggle of the Algerian people, one runs the risk of not exactly understanding of the evolution of relations between the colonies and French domination. (*TAR*, 142)

36. Woddis complains: "Fanon is not concerned with the facts, with reality, only with his own generalised assertions" (*NTR*, 50).

37. David Caute, *Frantz Fanon* (New York: Viking Press, 1970): 87.

38. The best understanding of how the idea of "nation" imposed itself in colonial societies comes from Benedict Anderson's *Imagined Communities: Reflections on the Origin and Spread of Nationalism* (London: Verso, 1983). Anderson makes the crucial observation that "Print-language [that is, literacy] is what invents nationalism, not a particular language *per se*" (122); in French colonial Africa, "print-language" and French were of course the same. On nationalism in Africa, see also Nsame Mbongo, "Problèmes théoriques de la question nationale en Afrique," *Présence Africaine* 136, no. 4 (1985): 31–67.

The goal is independence on a national scale, leading toward independence on a global scale and a humanism "built to the dimensions of the universe" (*TAR*, 114). But the universality comes from Algeria, the "guide territory" (146), "brother country, country that calls, country that hopes" (179). Fanon describes his vision of the "African revolution" as the opening of a "South front" in Algeria in order to "carry Algeria to the four corners of Africa:"

Partons. Notre mission: ouvrir le front Sud. De Bamako acheminer armes et munitions. Soulever la population sahelienne, s'infiltrer jusqu'aux hauts plateaux algériens. Après avoir *porté l'Algérie aux quatre coins de l'Afrique*, remonter avec toute l'Afrique vers l'Algérie africaine, vers le Nord, vers Alger, ville continentale. (*PRA*, 206, emphasis mine)

We are off. Our mission: to open the southern front. To transport arms and munitions from Bamako. Stir up the Saharan population, infiltrate to the Algerian high plateau. After *carrying Algeria to the four corners of Africa*, move up with all Africa to African Algeria, toward the North, toward Algiers, the continental city. (*TAR*, 180, emphasis mine)

The relation between North and South, between "African Algeria" and "all of Africa," is a relation of uplifting, tutelage, and assimilation. The loss of ethnic identity does not trouble Fanon, for the fragmentation of "tribalism" must be transcended, as it was, according to him, in Slovakia, Estonia and Albania (*PRA*, 212; *TAR*, 186). Neither Fanon nor Cabral addresses the question of ethnicity as anything other than a primitive stage to be transcended, or, in Fanon's vocabulary, "liquidated." (Meanwhile, Fanon's "Algerocentrism" did not prevent him from becoming an outsider—at least posthumously—in an increasingly Arab, that is, *ethnic*, Algeria.)[39]

For Fanon, violence has a transcendental power to liberate and cure the psychological ills of the colonized; violence "illuminates," "deintoxicates," and "unifies the people" (*DT*, 51–52; *WE*, 94: AT) Unity will either come spontaneously or will be imposed violently:

La violence dans sa pratique est totalisante, nationale. De ce fait, elle comporte dans son intimité la liquidation du régionalisme et du tribalisme. Aussi les partis nationalistes se montrent-ils particulièrement impitoyables avec les caïds et les chefs coutumiers. La liquidation des caïds et des chefs est un préalable à l'unification du peuple. (*DT*, 51)

Violence in its practice is totalizing, national. It follows that it is closely involved in the liquidation of regionalism and of tribalism. Thus nationalist parties show

39. According to Irene Gendzier, Fanon's posthumous influence on the Algerian revolution was undone by an increasingly ethnic, rather than ethical, conception of national culture; Fanon, as a non-Arab, was marginalized (*Frantz Fanon: A Critical Study* [New York: Pantheon Books, 1973]: 243–49).

no pity at all toward the caids and the customary chiefs. Their liquidation is the preliminary to the unification of the people. (*WE*, 94: AT)

Fanon's response to local resistance is to call out the firing squad. I will not rehearse at length his reasons for advocating the liquidation of ethnic chiefs and rulers. In fact, under both French and British rule, local ethnic chiefs—the *chefs coutumiers*—were sometimes tools of the colonial endeavor. But not entirely, and now that the story of colonialism is being heard from the point of view of the colonized, in volumes like the UNESCO *General History of Africa*, there is cause for reconsideration.[40] Still, for Fanon, ethnicity is unethical: ethnic forces are consistently reactionary, dupes of the colonizer. The peasant masses are stuck in time, outside of history, "plunged . . . in the repetition *without history* of an immobile existence."[41] Fanon's view of precolonial history as no history at all is massively ethnocentric, reminiscent of Hegel's assertion that Africa is "the land of childhood, . . . lying beyond the day of self-conscious history,"[42] and of Hugh Trevor-Roper's characterization of African history as the "unrewarding gyrations of barbarous tribes in picturesque but irrelevant corners of the globe."[43] The radical vision of history as subordinated to History, particular to universal, local to global—whether it comes from the right, the left or the idiosyncratic Fanon—leaves no room for local knowledge.[44]

What matters most, what is most impressive in reading Fanon, is the sheer power of a theoretical *truth* to dictate who shall live and who shall

40. See *General History of Africa*, vol. 7: *Africa under Colonial Domination 1880–1935*, ed. A. Adu Boahen (London: Heinemann, 1985).

41. "Les masses paysannes plongées, nous l'avons vu, dans la répétition sans histoire d'une existence immobile continuent à vénérer les chefs religieux, les descendants des vieilles familles. La tribu, comme un seul homme, s'engage dans la voie qui lui est désignée par le chef traditionnel. À coups de prébendes, à prix d'or, le colonialisme s'attachera les services de ces hommes de confiance" (*DT*, 85).

42. *The Philosophy of History*, trans. J. Sibree (New York: Dover, 1956): 91.

43. Quoted in Philip D. Curtin, "Africa in World History," in Mowoe and Bjornson, eds., *Africa and the West*, 14.

44. My interpretation of *Les Damnés de la terre* would appear to be at odds with Patrick Taylor's version of Fanon in his eloquent and superbly documented study *The Narrative of Liberation: Perspectives on Afro-Caribbean Literature, Popular Culture, and Politics* (Ithaca, N.Y.: Cornell University Press, 1989). Starting from the premise that Fanon's works are *narratives*, Taylor interprets Fanon's texts as "totalizations that bring order to the circumstances and events of colonialism so as to present a historical process in which human actors can find themselves" (11). Taylor's emphasis is consistently on the prescriptive, visionary, performative side of Fanon's writing. But while Taylor convinces me of his own ethical vision of liberation as a rigorous and consistent system of thought, he does not convince me that this system comes from Fanon. He does not present an adequate reading of the complexities within, for example, the chapter on national culture, before he states:

be liquidated. In the first chapter of *The Wretched of the Earth*, "On Violence," Fanon makes the very idea of truth subordinate to the immediate colonial situation, in which "there is no truthful behavior" (*WE*, 50): "Truth is that which hurries on the break-up of the colonialist regime; it is that which promotes the emergence of the nation. . . . The good is quite simply that which is evil for 'them'." If the concept of truth is subordinate to the immediate political situation, then the analysis of that situation is all the more crucial; questions must be asked. Who decides what favors the emergence, and for that matter, who has decided what kind of "nation" shall emerge? According to Fanon, this must be up to a leader whose will is "the authentic mouthpiece of the colonial masses" (*DT*, 34n; *WE*, 72n). I am interested here in exploring the consequences and the *future* of Fanon's discourse of violent totalization by reading his references to two Guinean writers and political figures, Ahmed Sékou Touré and Kéita Fodéba. This may provide an object lesson in the tensions between a transcendent, totalized, ethical truth on the one hand, and on the other, political and literary practice in black Africa, which tends to be very close to ethnic issues. The story that emerges will also serve as useful historical background for the remaining chapters of this book.

The Prison-House of Guinea

There is reason to think that Fanon saw Sékou Touré, the late president of Guinea, as a leader who was the "authentic expression of the colonial masses" (this concerns Guinea-Conakry, the former French colony, not to be confused with Guinea-Bissau, the former Portuguese colony led into independence by Amilcar Cabral). Sékou Touré is quoted favorably several times in *Les Damnés*, including the prominent epigraph at the beginning of the famous chapter on national culture:

Il ne suffit pas d'écrire un chant révolutionnaire pour participer à la révolution africaine, il faut faire cette révolution avec le peuple. Avec le peuple et ces chants viendront seuls et d'eux-mêmes. (*DT*, 141)

"National culture is not given as a finite symbolic structure in the way that nationalism is. It *remains eternally open* to the process of human liberation" (187, emphasis mine). Taylor shares with Chester J. Fontenot, Jr. (whom he criticizes) a desire to see Fanon as "open," in spite of textual evidence to the contrary (see note 70 below). The "open" interpretation of Fanon can be inferred from reading the national culture chapter, but the problem is that other, less appealing things can be inferred as well, and those are the problems that concern me here. Fanon's works may indeed be "the historical points of departure for a liberating consciousness" (44)—that is certainly the purpose I would like them to serve—but they have engendered other questions as well.

To take part in the African revolution it is not enough to write a revolutionary song; you must fashion the revolution with the people. And if you fashion it with the people, the songs will come by themselves, and of themselves. (*WE*, 206)

With this characteristic flair for rhetoric and doctrine, Sékou Touré's utterances fit into various places in Fanon's essays, Touré apparently serving as a practitioner of what Fanon preaches. This pronouncement is of particular interest here, because it specifies exactly what the role of art should be in Africa at the moment of independence. "Authentic action," Sékou Touré states, comes from being "a living part of Africa and of its thought"; there will be "no place for the artist or the intellectual" outside of the struggle with the people. This certainly agrees with what Fanon goes on to say in the body of the essay. The artist of the third stage, the forger of national culture, is the "mouthpiece of a new reality *in action*" (*DT*, 154; *WE*, 223, emphasis mine). It thus comes as a significant moment when Fanon incorporates a very long poem into his essay, offered as "a true invitation to thought, to demystification, and to battle" (*DT*, 157; *WE*, 227). The poem, entitled "Aube africaine" (African Dawn), is presented as a model of national culture. Here is Fanon's introduction:

Kéita Fodéba, aujourd'hui ministre de l'intérieur de la République de Guinée, lorsqu'il était directeur des Ballets africains n'a pas rusé avec la réalité que lui offrait le peuple de Guinée. Dans une perspective révolutionnaire, il a réinterprété toutes les images rythmiques de son pays. Mais il a fait davantage. Dans son oeuvre poétique, peu connue, on trouve un constant souci de préciser le moment historique de la lutte, de délimiter le champ où se déroulera l'action, les idées autour desquelles se cristallisera la volonté populaire. (*DT*, 157)

Kéita Fodéba, today Minister of Internal Affairs in the Republic of Guinea, when he was director of the "African Ballet" did not play any tricks with the reality which the people of Guinea offered him. He reinterpreted all the rhythmic images of his country from a revolutionary standpoint. But he did more. In his poetic works, which are not well known, we find a constant desire to define accurately the historic moment of the struggle and to mark off the field in which actions will unfold, the ideas around which the will of the people will crystallize. [*WE*, 227, AT)

Having started the essay on national culture with a quotation from Sékou Touré that defines revolutionary poetry, Fanon now calls on Touré's minister of the interior for an exemplary text. I would like to examine in some detail the recontextualization of Kéita Fodéba's works by Fanon.

There is not an abundance of information available on the late Kéita Fodéba. He is remembered among West African intellectuals today as a brilliant artist. Born in 1921 in the Mande area of upper Guinea, Fodéba was educated at the élite Ecole William Ponty in Dakar and studied law in Paris starting in 1948. He apparently began writing in order to make money, but his writings were banned throughout French Africa in 1951; his poems were seen to be "strongly Marxist and nationalist."[45] He consequently turned to ballet as his means of expression and founded the Ballets africains, which became famous for its presentations of what Fodéba called "modern folklore," that is, traditional Mande music and dance adapted to Western means of presentation. According to the critic writing in *Présence Africaine*, the Ballet was a wonderful show, presenting "*authentic* African music," but it opened no "new perspectives" and was not without traces of "exoticism."[46] Léopold Sédar Senghor, writing in 1959, gave the Ballet high praise but warned against a creeping "American flavor" that could ruin the perfect and complete "symbolic naturalism" of the spectacle.[47] Could the "revolutionary perspective" of the ballet that Fanon refers to consist entirely in the accurate presentation of *ethnic* reality? Documentation on the Ballets Africains is not sufficient, but in the context of the French colonial policy of assimilation, any survival of local culture could be seen as an act of resistance.

Kéita Fodéba's published works include three volumes of poetry, but the total number of poems appears to be only eight.[48] The first volume, *Poèmes africains*, published in 1950, is thus almost his complete works. The poem that Fanon uses in his essay, and Fodéba's entire oeuvre, are not startlingly militant; in fact, it is surprising that the French colonial government, Fanon, and critics as well have seen his works as Marxist in tendancy or highly nationalistic in a Fanonian sense.

The ethnicity of the Mande is a constant theme in his works; in an article on African dance, Fodéba stated outright what is implied in this

45. Donald E. Herdeck, et al., *African Authors: A Companion to Black African Writing* (Washington, D.C.: Black Orpheus Press, 1973): 181; Janheinz Jahn, Ulla Schild, Almut Nordman, *Who's Who in African Literature* (Tübingen: Horst Erdmann Verlag, 1972): 131.

46. G. Rouget, "La Musique: Les Ballets africains de Kéita Fodéba," *Présence africaine* 7 (April-May, 1956): 138–140. Cf. Lansiné Kaba, "The Cultural Revolution," 202–3: "The group performed African songs and dances from Senegal to the Congo, with special emphasis on the Mandinka folklore of Guinea and Casamance. First it performed mainly for African circles in Paris, then it attracted the attention of critics because of its authenticity, the sophistication of its staging, and the literary and ideological quality of its scenario."

47. Léopold Sédar Senghor, "Les ballets africains de Fodéba Kéita," in his *Liberté 1* (Paris: Seuil, 1964): 290, 289.

48. The first volume was *Poèmes africains* (Paris: Pierre Seghers, 1950), including 7 poems (further references to this work, abbreviated *PA*, will be included in the text); the second was *Le Maître d'école, suivi de Minuit* (Paris: Pierre Seghers, 1953), comprised of two poems, one of which had appeared in the first book; the third volume was *Aube africaine* (Paris: Pierre Seghers, 1965), which reprinted modified versions of 6 poems that had appeared earlier. Herdeck lists *Le Théâtre africain* ("no date") under poetry in his *African Authors*, but I have found no further reference to this work.

context: "As far as we Blacks of Africa are concerned, it is obvious . . . that it is still historically [too] early for us to lose all our African *ethnic* characteristics."[49] An ethical protest against French colonialism is present, but so is a strange homage to the French. The first poem is a perfect blend of ethical protest and ethnic tradition: "Minuit" is written in dramatic form, with the stage set as a Mande village, a *griot* bard playing his "guitar," another griot telling the story. We are thus presented with a setting that could not be more traditional, dating back centuries in Mande history to the time of the emperor Sunjata, who united much of West Africa under Mande hegemony in the early 13th century. In a note that precedes the *Poèmes africains*, the publisher explains that Kéita Fodéba has "transcribed into French legends that have up to now been recounted, danced, mimed, and chanted by griots in the villages." The act of pure transcription is what may be called the degree zero of francophone African literature, the point at which the author is merely a transcriber and translator of oral texts; this degree zero describes large numbers of texts from the early francophone tradition. Fodéba is presented here as just such an author, whose concern is more with the local *ethos* of his people than with ethical protest.

The "legend" that is told in "Minuit" does not, however, come from a mythical past. It begins with an explicit political reference:

C'était en 1892, dans le cercle de Siguiri [where Kéita Fodéba was born] au coeur du vieux Manding, Samory était repoussé vers le Sud et les Blancs venaient de construire le petit fort Galliéni. L'administrateur qui dirigeait alors le cercle, commandait toutes les régions des deux rives du Niger et les cantons aurifères du Bouré. Cette année-là, les récoltes étaient particulièrement abondantes et les fêtes se multipliaient dans les villages; tout chantait la vie. (*PA*, 10–11)

It was in 1892, in the *cercle* [administrative zone] of Siguiri [where Kéita Fodéba was born] in the heart of the old Mande kingdom; Samory had been repulsed to the South, and the Whites had just built the small Fort Galliéni. The administrator who was running the *cercle* commanded all regions on both banks of the Niger and the gold-mining cantons of Bouré. That year the harvests were particularly abundant and there were numerous fêtes in the villages; everything sang of life.

What was introduced as legend thus takes place in a setting that is very precise and fully a part of history in the Western sense of the term (something with names, dates, and facts), without leaving behind history in a Mande sense (which we will examine in the next chapter), involving the praise of ancestors and kings. This story is part of the history of African

49. Kéita Fodéba, "La Danse africaine et la scène," *Présence Africaine* 14–15 (June-September, 1957): 202.

resistance to colonialism: Samory, who is identified in a footnote as "Grand chef Noir," was perhaps the most successful of African kings and emperors who fought French incursions into their territory.[50] The hero of the poem is introduced as "a handsome young man named Balaké, of the great family of Kéitas." This places the hero in his clan, that of the Kéitas, descendents of the emperor Sunjata, founder of the Mali Empire, and in his "caste," that of the nobles. Notions of caste and clan are fundamental to Mande ethnography, and I will discuss them in the next chapter. The point that needs to be recognized here is that Kéita Fodéba *engaged* with his ethnic tradition in his works. By writing this poem, he involved himself with the most traditional Mande art form, praise of ancestors.[51]

In this case, traditional art and contemporary protest are one: the story told here is of a hero who is persecuted by the French because he was loved by a young woman who was also the object of attention from the French adminstrator and his African interpreter. A French officer is killed one night near Balaké's house, and Balaké is unjustly accused, tried, condemned, and then executed by firing squad twenty-four hours later. The ethical protest of Kéita Fodéba's poem centers on this unjust execution. The implications for an overall judgment of French colonialism are obvious, and the ban begins to become "understandable."

"Aube africaine," the poem that Fanon uses as an "authentic invitation to reflection, demystification, and struggle," is the story of one African's experience in World War II, but told from the point of view of his traditional village. The poem opens in a pastoral setting, at dawn, which is described symbolically as the "struggle between day and night." Iterative verbs referring to the activities of daily life seem to evoke timeless, endlessly cyclical tradition. But the repetition of tradition is broken by

50. See Yves Person, *Samori: Une Révolution dyula*, 3 vols. (Paris: IFAN, 1968–75).
51. Kéita Fodéba's name poses some questions in this regard. The author shares the name Kéita with the hero of the poem, but this does not actually suggest any relation. If Kéita Fodéba were a descendant of the Kéita family, and therefore noble, his life's work as a poet and musician would have been anomalous, for, as we will see in the next chapter, nobles cannot do the work of griots. Kéita Fodéba is a puzzling case in that he bears the noble Kéita name but was reported to have had a "griot background" (Herdeck, *African Authors*, 181); this is a virtual impossibility. Especially in the 1950s, it would have been inconceivable for a Mande nobleman to organize or perform music and dance (still today, the old "caste" divisions carry over into modern music and other art forms). Inquiries in West Africa from January to March of 1987 revealed that Kéita Fodéba was born out of a mixed marriage: interviewed by telephone in the Ivory Coast, Kéita Fodéba's daughter, Mlle Mariam Fodéba, informed me that his mother was a Diabaté and his father a Kéita. Since the Diabaté were traditionally griots to the Kéita, this marriage was forbidden. The usage of the name Fodéba as a family name (*jamu*) by Kéita Fodéba and his surviving family would tend to indicate that the name Kéita in his name implies no genealogical (patrilineal) link to that clan.

the arrival of news that the white colonizers have required the village elders to select one man to serve in World War II. The elders choose Naman, "the most representative young man of our race," understanding that what he will prove will be the courage and glory of the Mande people. Many months after his departure, his wife receives the first message from him, which she cannot read and which he might have had written by an intermediary scribe. Naman has been in North Africa; he is headed for Corsica, Italy, and Germany, where he will be wounded and taken prisoner by the Germans. At this point in the village, Naman is promoted to the rank of "Douga," the order of the vulture, making him a hero associated with the emperors of Mali. But the tragedy happens on his return to Senegal. A letter is received from Naman's friend, announcing that, ironically, Naman survived the war but not the peace; he was killed in the dispute between African soldiers and their white "chiefs." Fodéba ties the poem to a brutal historical event, the massacre of Senegalese soldiers returning from combat in Europe, by French soldiers, at Thiaroye, Senegal on December 1, 1944: [52]

"C'était l'aube. Nous étions à Thiaroye-sur-Mer. Au cours d'une grande querelle qui nous opposait à nos chefs blancs de Dakar, une balle a trahi Naman. Il repose en terre Sénégalaise." (PA, 25)

"It was dawn. We were at Thiaroye-sur-Mer. During a great dispute between us and our White chiefs from Dakar, a bullet betrayed Naman. He lies at rest in Senegalese soil."

The poem ends with an allegorical punch, as a vulture, symbol of the heroic order of Douga, circles over Naman's body, "seeming to say to him:"

"Naman! Tu n'as pas dansé cette danse sacrée qui porte mon nom. D'AUTRES LA DANSERONT."

"Naman! You have not danced the sacred dance that bears my name. OTHERS WILL DANCE IT."

What others? The possibilities of meaning shift as this poem is taken out of its original context and transplanted into the Fanon essay; it is important to analyze that shift.

The original context is obviously not one of pure Mande ethnicity; the

52. See Mamadou Traoré Diop, "Colonial Spasms: The Martyrs of Thiaroye," *West Africa* 3546 (12 August 1985): p. 1647. Diop points out that this event, which in many postcolonial societies would be the object of a national memorial, was instead "covered up" and neglected by Senghor's government. See also Jonathon Ngaté, *Francophone African Literature: Reading a Literary Tradition* (Trenton, N.J.: Africa World Press, 1988): 167, n. 4. The events at Thiaroye are also the subject of the latest film by Sembene Ousmane, "Camp de Thiaroye."

whole point is the disruption of that world by colonialism. But taken as it comes in the *Poèmes africains*, it is scarcely conceivable that "others" could refer to anyone outside the Mande "race." The dance of the vulture, as described by Fodéba elsewhere, belongs exclusively to a Mande elite: "In our times, Mande tradition has adopted this 'Dance of the Vultures' as an honorific distinction and no one has the right to dance it if he has not made himself worthy of it through some brilliant achievement and if he has not been authorized by the Counsel of Elders."[53] The Douga is thus a reflection of the hierarchical, casted order of traditional Mande society. Any "others" who will dance the Douga will come as links in a chain going back to the founding emperor Sunjata; the only part of that chain that is visible in "Aube africaine" is the part that is directly linked to ethnic tradition.

Before looking at the altered condition of "Aube africaine" in the context of Fanon's essay, I would like to point out that there are other poems in *Poèmes africains* that reflect strangely on the protest value of "Aube africaine." "La légende de Toubab Bailleux" ("The Legend of White Man Bailleux") is the story of an early white settler who "incarnates the ideal of Union," that is, a "sincere union" between France and Africa.[54] The last poem in the volume, "Noël de mon enfance" ("A Christmas from my Childhood"), is precisely the kind of look back into the past that Fanon would not approve of: the narrator, remembering the good feeling between his people and the French colonizers, says, "I participated in the most alive of all communions between the races" ("Je participais à la plus vivante des communions des races"):

"Blancs! Aujourd'hui est votre fête; soyez les bienvenus chez nous! Notre maison est la vôtre. Entrez-y, et que la Paix soit avec vous. Galliéni, en abordant les rives du DJOLIBA, notre fleuve Niger, ne parlait-il pas de Paix? . . . Ensemble, dans cette belle maison, nous cultiverons le plus doux et le plus précieux les aliments, celui dont se nourrissent les peuples vraiment forts: LA PAIX." (*PA*, 45–46)

"White people, today is your holiday; you are welcome among us! Our house is yours. Come inside, and may Peace be with you. Did not Galliéni, as he ap-

---

53. Kéita Fodéba, preface to Michel Huet, *Les Hommes de la danse* (Lausanne: La Guilde du Livre, 1954): 10–11. He repeats this statement in "La danse africaine et la scène," 204–5.

54. "Quel Malinké oserait aujourd'hui oublier Toubab Bailleux, le Blanc qui s'était fait Noir dans le petit village de Damissa? Le pays le renierait aussitôt, car, de jour en jour, le sacrifice de Bailleux est davantage en relief. [He committed suicide after accidently killing a Malinké hunting companion.] Chaque Malinké de la région doit au fond de son coeur, célébrer Toubab Bailleux, au risque de commettre le plus grossier sacrilège et surtout d'avoir le nom mêlé à l'air des parjures et des déshérités. . . . Toubab Bailleux, hors de lui-même, s'enferma dans son échoppe, et en silence, se suicida après avoir écrit: 'Je meurs en aimant la FRANCE, je meurs en aimant les Noirs'" (*PA*, 34, 38).

proached the banks of the DJOLIBA, our River Niger, speak of peace? . . . Together in this fine house, we will cultivate the sweetest and most precious of
foods, that which feeds the strongest people: PEACE."

The presence of these texts raises issues I cannot fully explore here, questions of irony ("it means the opposite of what it says") and of history (the
nostalgia for a perfected, peaceable colonialism was common among
francophone African intellectuals in the 1940s and 50s). The French
could have excised a few lines from two poems and distributed *Poèmes
africains* as their own propaganda, espousing their favorite theme: that
colonialism is justified by the desire of the natives; that the colonizer
brings peace and freedom. One critic claims, in contradiction to all others, that far from being banned, Fodéba's poems were "adopted in the
school curriculum as part of the 'Africanisation' programme";[55] a poem
like "Noël de mon enfance" makes such a claim conceivable. Whether
these collaborationist texts were put to such use or not, their very existence makes it problematic to characterize Fodéba's entire oeuvre as
"strongly Marxist and nationalist."

But I would like to return to "Aube africaine," taken more or less in
isolation. Now, one might ask, if the chain of Douga dancers goes back
to Sunjata, to what does it go forward? "Aube africaine" already shows
the traditional world being broken; when Fanon uproots this poem and
places it in a context of revolution, the future tense of "D'autres la danseront" takes on meanings that were only latent before: reflection, demystification, struggle. The chain may be unbroken into the future, but
the restriction of its reference to Mande ethnicity alone cannot hold.
Faced with a unified colonizing force, Africans must throw off their tribal
past in order to gain power and self-determination.[56] Fanon writes in his
commentary on the poem: "*All* those niggers and *all* those wogs who
fought to defend the liberty of France or for British civilization recognize
themselves in this poem by Kéita Fodéba" (*DT*, 162; *WE*, 232, emphasis
mine). The cost of this universality is a bit of the cultural specificity:
Fanon, in reproducing the text, suppressed ethnic details such as the spe-

55. "Excerpts from those essays ["Minuit" and "Aube africaine"], lacking explicit political references [*sic*], were adopted in the school curriculum as part of the 'Africanisation'
programme. By 1955 Fodéba was acclaimed as the most popular writer and artist in the
whole of French-speaking West Africa" (Lansiné Kaba, "The Cultural Revolution," 203).
Although, as we have seen, Fodéba's works contained elements that readily lend themselves
to a colonial curriculum, it is difficult to give weight to Kaba when he says that the poems
lacked "explicit political references." One has to wonder if Kaba, Herdeck, et al., or Jahn,
et al. have actually seen a copy of *Poèmes africains*.

56. "Il n'y a pas de communauté de destin des cultures nationales sénégalaise et guinéenne mais communauté de destin des nations guinéenne et sénégalaise dominées par le
même colonialisme français" (*DT*, 163).

cific names of guitar and *cora* melodies that accompany the recitation, as well as the footnotes explaining the terms *cora* and *garde-cercle* (see *PA*, 21). And in the translation of the poem in *The Wretched of the Earth* (231), the word "sacred" is missing from the description of the "Douga."[57]

I do not propose to divide the meaning of the poem between an authentic/original and a revolutionary context, as if the two were divorced and incompatible. Both must be read. But my general point is that the revolutionary meaning that is present in Kéita Fodéba's poem depends on the traditional past in order to produce itself; *the ethical is indebted to the ethnic.* The others who will dance may be Mande, Dogon, Baluba, or Zulu, but the heroic level of their struggle is defined by the strictly Mande imperial past. The ethical and the ethnic are one and the same in the context of the *Poèmes africains* of Kéita Fodéba. To a certain extent, this is a reflection of the period. It is hard now to imagine a time when the assertion of African ethnicity was a revolutionary stance, and yet even the ideology of Negritude had that potential, and in some contexts is still claimed to have it.[58] But the ethnic and the ethical become opposed in Fanon because the ethnic must be transcended in favor of the ethical. Fanon allows the look backward into tradition, but only to the extent that it is "in the intention of *opening the future*, as an invitation to action and as a basis of hope" (*DT*, 162; *WE*, 232, emphasis mine). But if the *future* is the point, if Fanon's use of the word *avenir* actually has to do with that which was "to come," then it is incumbent on us to take advantage of hindsight and see what Fanon could not have seen: the fate of his discourse. This will involve a shift of registers, a fall from the mesmerizing heights of Fanon's rhetoric, not out of rhetoric itself but into another rhetoric, that of plots and executions.

In his commentary on "Aube africaine," Fanon refers to the role that Kéita Fodéba assumed in the newly independent Republic of Guinea

57. It is interesting to note that the version of "Aube africain" published after Independence contains new verses that accentuate the more Fanonian side. The new phrases are in italics here: "En effet, c'était l'aube ... *aube de la Liberté africaine*. ... 'Naman, tu n'as pas dansé cette danse sacrée qui porte mon nom! / *En libérant la Patrie africaine*, l'autres la danseront'" (*Aube africaine*, 79–80). But it is ironic that the call to liberation is issued in print only in retrospect, after Independence.

58. See, for example, Chinweizu's surprising interpretation of Negritude as revolutionary resistance to colonialism: he claims that the Anglophone world was browbeaten by Wole Soyinka into rejecting the resistant, decolonizing power of Negritude. This is far from current interpretations of Negritude among francophone intellectuals, who tend to see in it an apologetic address to French readers (Chinweizu, Onwuchekwa Jemie, Ihechukwu Madubuike, "The Leeds-Ibadan Connection: The Scandal of Modern African Literature," *Okike* 13 [January, 1979]: 37–46). Cf. Marcien Towa, *Léopold Sédar Senghor: Négritude ou servitude?* (Yaoundé, Cameroun: Editions CLE, 1971).

ruled by Sékou Touré: "The poet Kéita Fodéba was training the Minister of Internal Affairs of the Republic of Guinea to frustrate the plots organized by French colonialism" (*WE*, 232; *DT*, 162). Fodéba, like many of his educated contemporaries, was called upon to serve his new country. His future was tied to the future of Fanonian discourse as put into practice by Sékou Touré. These two Guineans, whose words form pillars of support for Fanon in the essay on national culture, were to act out a drama of violence within a few years of Fanon's death; whether the violence of their drama was of a "liberating" sort is far from clear. It is certain that the French left Guinea in a huff, destroying equipment and suspending almost all financial support, and that their attitude continued to be spiteful. All of this because the Guineans, following Touré's leadership, voted "non" to a continuing union with France in the referendum of 1958. Furthermore, it is likely that the French government plotted against Sékou Touré and his rule. But Touré is also said to have "relied . . . upon pseudo-plots as a pretext for ridding himself of his opponents."[59] To this end he invented the concept of the "permanent plot," "le complot permanent," which he described elaborately in print.[60] Through it all Touré remained a master of discourse, quoting Fanon, forging slogans, writing "militant poems," wrapping himself in a socialist, ethical garb.[61] His voice so dominated the scene that, for a period, "no major works [were] published in Conakry except the President's books and poems, and these [had to] be abundantly quoted by members of the élite to secure their positions."[62] (Sékou Touré's personal dominance of Guinean discourse is an interesting case of the political "monologism" we will study in relation to dialogue in chapter 5.) His ostensibly socialist ideology became, according to critics, purely a matter of words, of the jargon he employed. He made "pragmatic," local use of Marxist ideology in the cynical sense that he used it solely to preserve his own state power. In

59. Claude Rivière, *Guinea: The Mobilization of a People*, trans. Virginia Thompson and Richard Adloff (Ithaca, N.Y.: Cornell University Press, 1977): 83–84; 123.

60. Sékou Touré, et al., *Révolution démocratique africaine no. 38: Le Complot permanent* (Conakry: Imprimerie Nationale Patrice Lumumba, 1970).

61. It should also be noted that his claim to authority was enriched from the traditional side by his claim of descendance from Samory. A work that appears to be more or less an authorized biography states that Samory is "the renowned great-grandfather of Ahmed Sékou Touré through his maternal grandmother, Bagbé Ramata Touré, a daughter of the Almamy [Samory]" (*Sékou Touré* [London: Panaf Books, 1978]: 18). No author is listed for this work, but Sékou Touré, his party and government are recognized in the acknowledgments for their "encouragement."

62. Lansiné Kaba, "The Cultural Revolution," 214. On Sékou Touré's writings, see Bernard Mouralis, "Sékou Touré et l'écriture: réflexions sur un cas de scribomanie," *Notre Librairie* 88–89 (July-September 1987): 76–85.

reality, it is alleged, his Guinea was always dominated by multinational corporations, in "one of the strongest capitalist and neo-colonialist footholds in West Africa."[63] Yves Bénot describes the process as "an evolution towards the right," whereby Sékou Touré switched alliances and returned to private enterprise, while still giving lip service to "the hegemony of the working classes."[64]

But the notion of the permanent plot was capable of—and perhaps designed to—destroy those closest to the leader. When Kéita Fodéba's time came, in 1969, the "plot" began, appropriately, with words alone:

Des propos à caractère subversif tenus par les trois parachutistes, ponctués souvent de menaces contre les voyageurs civils, . . . et d'injures proférées a l'adresse des responsables de la Nation, avec la nette détermination de ne jamais livrer les noms des meneurs du complot.[65]

[There were] remarks of a subversive nature made by the three parachutists, often punctuated by threats made against the civilian passengers [during a flight across Guinea that was to bring the three in on suspicion of disloyalty] . . . and by insults directed at the responsible authorities of the Nation, with the clear determination never to reveal the names of the leaders of the plot.

The accusation that Sékou Touré made against Kéita Fodéba, which stated principally that Fodéba was plotting a coup d'état, includes possession of subversive newspapers and tape recordings: *words*. Touré concludes: "We know that his salon had become a veritable nucleus for the systematic denigration of the regime and its leaders."[66] Fodéba's alleged crime consisted entirely of words and thoughts, but these were enough for him to be arrested, along with a thousand others. He was executed on May 27, 1969.[67] The poet whose works were banned because they protested against unjust executions, who had dared to defy colonial authority by asserting his African ethnicity, thus finds himself—on the other side of the mirror that is Independence—fighting and losing a similar battle. Fodéba was not accused of partisan ethnicity that we know of,

63. Claude Abou Diakité, *Guinée enchaînée ou le livre noir de Sékou Touré* (Paris: D.A.C., 1972): 80. Cf. Rivière, *Guinea*, 94: "In regard to most of the specified rights [in the Guinean constitution of 1958], except those relating to social assistance, education, and nondiscrimination, one has only to assume the exact opposite of the constitution's provisions in order to grasp the reality." See also Catherine Peyrega, *Sékou Touré est-il marxiste?* (Bordeaux: Publications d'Etudes et de Recherches Socio-Economiques, 1977).

64. Yves Bénot, *Idéologies des indépendances africaines* (Paris: Maspero, 1972): 265–80.

65. Sékou Touré, et al., *Le Complot permanent*, 47–48.

66. *Le Complot permanent*, 54–55.

67. Herdeck, et al., *African Authors*, 131; Lansiné Kaba states that Fodéba was condemned to death in 1971 ("The Cultural Revolution," 213).

except in the etymological sense, in that Sékou Touré made him into a heathen, a pagan, an exile from a kingdom in which one discourse reigned. Sékou Touré's supposedly ethical stance becomes a grotesque of itself. And the greatest irony in this may be that, far from being a martyr for freedom of expression, Kéita Fodéba may have built his own gallows: it is alleged that, in his role as Minister of the Interior he "created the repressive system" of Guinea and "put it at Sékou Touré's disposal." [68]

Sékou Touré's epigraph to Fanon's essay asserted that chants will come of their own accord once the artist is one with the people; but if the poets are all dead, or sent into exile like Camara Laye, or imprisoned like the historian D. T. Niane, then where will the chants come from? Perhaps from a "people" that only the leader can define, hear, and represent.

Ethics and the Bind of Relativism

The sequence of events I have described remains open to a variety of interpretations, and I do not offer Kéita Fodéba's fate as a necessary outgrowth of either Marxism or Fanon's theories, or as a tale whose moral is that nothing can ever change. We should resist the temptation to make Kéita Fodéba into a martyr, since it is far from clear in what cause he died. There are many troubling questions that remain.

First among them would be the question of responsibility. Does the fact that Sékou Touré wrapped himself in Marxist and Fanonian discourse make Fanon responsible for the reign of terror in Guinea? The question is reminiscent of debates on the relation of Nietzsche to Nazism: to what extent is an author responsible for readings and misreadings of his or her texts? [69] A full and sensitive reading of Fanon's texts might reveal an "open" system that has been wrongly "closed" by critics; but the problem that concerns me is precisely how the textual paradoxes in Fanon's writing were translated into unambiguous political oppression by a "misreader" like Sékou Touré. [70] Fanon's discourse of mystified violence was seen even at the time to have the potential for abuse: the Vietnamese communist Nguyen Nghe found that "by centering his theses on

68. Kaba, "The Cultural Revolution," 213.

69. See Christopher Norris, "Deconstruction Against Itself: Derrida and Nietzsche," *Diacritics* 16, No. 4 (Winter 1986): 61–69.

70. Chester J. Fontenot, Jr. offers such a reading. Fontenot gives detailed and insightful attention to the complexities of Fanon's writings, interpreting them as "literary artifacts which have an integrity of their own" (60); but his concern for appreciating the "openness" of Fanon should not obscure the problems that arise within certain moments of temporary closure, such as when he advocates "liquidating" native chiefs. See Fontenot, *Frantz Fanon: Language as the God Gone Astray in the Flesh* (University of Nebraska Studies, n.s. 60 [Lincoln: University of Nebraska Press, 1979]: 9).

violence, Fanon gives a simplifying vision of the struggle for the liberation of colonized countries, a vision that risks leading to authoritarian
solutions."[71] Violence was a theoretical abstraction for Fanon, who, according to one source, "never became part of the armed struggle [in Al-
geria], nor saw the violence of which he speaks" (Fontenot, 39). He
nonetheless lived within the climate of revolutionary violence, and his
work treated its victims.[72]

So the sequence of texts I have covered here leads from Fanon's discourse on liberating violence inevitably to thoughts on the violence of
discourse. The words that Sékou Touré used, the socialist ideology that
he either reproduced or travestied, the volumes of poetry and prose that
he published up to his death in 1984, were conditions of possibility for
his actions. At all times, Touré claimed an ethical stance. The totalized
ideas of Revolution, of Nation, and of violence itself allowed Sékou
Touré—like any ruler—to relativize and liquidate the other: confident
that he hears the people's will, the ruler is free to dispose of individual
persons at will. (*Jeune Afrique* has even alleged that Sékou Touré was
involved in the assassination of Amilcar Cabral.)[73] Fanon's essays had a
part to play both in Touré's discourse and in his actions, providing a
theoretical basis for relativizing truth and ethics.

What, then, is ethical? Claims of access to a transcendental truth alone
cannot guarantee ethics since transcendental truths, "absolute verities,"
are only figures of discourse. Thus while Fanon is often cited piously
these days as the patron saint of decolonization, as a prophet, his transcendental truths—bearing the same names, speaking the same language—are made completely unethical by Sékou Touré. What *is* ethical
would be a dialectical relationship between a transcendental truth and
respect for the other, for difference. A self relating to itself has few ethical
problems. In this sense, *there is no real ethics without ethnicity*, without
the disquieting, untidy presence of the other.[74] The relation to the other
is the relation of ethnicity; it is also the relation between any theoretical

71. Nguyen Nghe, "Frantz Fanon," 28. For a full discussion of Fanon's theory of violence, see Emmanuel Hansen, *Frantz Fanon: Social and Political Thought* (Nairobi: Oxford
University Press, 1978), chapter 5, "Paths to Freedom: Revolutionary Violence," 90–139.

72. He was also the target of several apparent assassination attempts. See Hansen,
Frantz Fanon, 28–37. Hansen confirms that Fanon "did not play any combat role in the
Algerian revolution" (98). For Hansen, Fanon was able to achieve "total fusion of the role
of the intellectual and that of the political activist" (34), but this was *in Tunis*, not Algeria.

73. Sophie Bessis, "Qui a tué Amilcar Cabral?," *Jeune Afrique* 1193 (November 16,
1983): 53–61.

74. This statement is related to a moment in Jacques Derrida's critique of Lévi-Strauss,
on which I will comment in the next chapter: "Il n'y a pas d'éthique sans présence *de
l'autre* . . ." (*De la grammatologie* [Paris: Minuit, 1967]: 202).

discourse and Africa; claiming an ethical imperative does not exempt the Western critic from a relation of difference.[75] Ethnography is conscious thought bearing on those whose *ethos* is different, perhaps not conforming to one's particular transcendental truth. The totalizing unity that Marxism aims for as an ethical concern runs into ethical problems precisely because it tends to overlook or "liquidate" that which deviates from unity. It lacks relativism.

Everyone gives lip service to dialectics. Gugelberger claims to be looking at things dialectically when he states that ethnicity used to be progressive but now "enforces the status quo" (*MAL*, xiii). But this is a dialectic in which the elements are static: history may change, but ethnicity and ethics are discrete and mutually exclusive at any given moment. Each should rather be seen in terms of the other; the *content* of these terms clearly changes according to changing situations. The poems of Kéita Fodéba analyzed here are in many ways typical of the situation

75. The relation I am proposing here between ethnicity and ethics has little in common with J. Hillis Miller's *The Ethics of Reading* (New York: Columbia University Press, 1987), which I find to be largely hostile to the notions of plural difference that are necessary for venturing outside the Western canon. Miller's title should be *The Ethics of "Reading,"* because he uses word "reading" as if it were the private property of deconstructionist critics alone; he suggests that his and their approach is the only one that leads to "reading." ("Reading itself is extraordinarily hard work. It does not occur all that often" [3]; "Deconstruction is nothing more or less than good reading as such" [10]—in other words, good reading is deconstruction.) The ethical study of political and historical contexts (which are only figures, that is, texts), "requires . . . a mastery of the varieties of figure inhabiting this region of linguistic transaction" (7); in other words, all real "reading" will remain dependent on the discoveries made by deconstruction in the 1970s—nothing need change. Of course, he indicates, reading has social and ethical *consequences*, but "reading" (in his sense) will not be affected by any new attention to these *secondary* issues; good "readers" will still need to be deconstructors. Miller is at pains to maintain the primacy of the literary code, its "freedom" and "performative power" (8). His insistence on language as the most comprehensive medium, as the unsurpassable limit, ultimately makes abstract any notion of ethics: "For De Man [and, apparently, for Miller] the ethical is one (necessary and necessarily potentially aberrent) act of language among others. . . . It is impossible to get outside the limits of language by means of language" (58–59). While I have no intrinsic objection to deconstruction as a partial and limited approach among others, I object to Miller's claim to its supremacy, and I remain troubled by the glib bracketing of ethical questions within the safe confines of "language"—particularly in light of De Man's passing association with fascism (which came to light after the publication of *The Ethics of Reading*). Robert Bernasconi, in his "Deconstruction and the Possibility of Ethics" (in John Sallis, ed., *Deconstruction and Philosophy: The Texts of Jacques Derrida* [Chicago: University of Chicago Press, 1987]), moves in tandem with Hillis Miller, following Heidegger instead of De Man on a path that "instructs"—that is, deconstructs—the demand for an ethics, which is "referred to . . . its *impossibility*" (135). How can one not be troubled by the coincidence (which does not bother Bernasconi at all) between the bracketing or "impossibility" of any ethics on the one hand, and on the other, complicity with fascism on Heidegger's part and on De Man's?

of francophone African literature: caught—productively so—between local and global, tradition and progress. I believe that his work and his fate demonstrate the need for a more fluid dialectic between ethics and difference, between the widest global implications of culture and the most obstreperous local resistance. That dialectic is the process of *politics*: the political is the medium in which ethnicity and ethics interact. The political is thus not a third term that can explode or transcend the opposition between these two imperatives; it is rather the means by which these seemingly exclusive terms can (and must) be worked out and brought into dialogue.

To say, as some do, that ethnicity and ethics are mutually exclusive and irreconcilable is thus "true": true between quotation marks because it is true in theory and in the discourse of a naive or oppressive politics. But walled within the discourse of theory, we can make anything we want appear to be true (which is itself a theoretical statement).

The most difficult implication of the position I have taken here is that it seems to place me within the bind of relativism: claiming to transcend one's own beliefs, which is a dubious claim. The relativist is accused of thinking he or she can "shop" freely among all beliefs and truths, of "imagining [wrongly] a position from which we can see our beliefs without really believing them"; this would be a claim to "knowing without believing" (anything).[76] The possibility of doing so is contradicted by the critical study of, for example, the history of anthropology, which reveals that thinkers do not often transcend their own social and political background, or their "beliefs." Tempels is the most egregious example.

My argument in this chapter has, however, tended toward the following conclusion: that the *failure to relativize* one's own beliefs is more dangerous than the failure to stay within them. Unless the Western critic attempts to suspend—to hold in at least temporary abeyance—the systematic criteria and judgments that emanate from Western culture, ethnocentrism will persist forever. There is no way to break down intellectual imperialism if Western disciplines are not reconceived as "local knowledge." The Western critic must, of course, avoid the converse error, that of being deluded into thinking his/her beliefs have been completely suspended and that his/her analysis is transcendentally "free." But we should bear in mind that it was Auguste Comte, the founder of *positivism*, who disputed the intellectual foundations of relativism: "The thinking individual cannot cut himself in two—one of the parts reasoning,

---

76. These quotations are from Steven Knapp and Walter Benn Michaels's critique of Stanley Fish, in W. J. T. Mitchell, ed., *Against Theory: Literary Studies and the New Pragmatism* (Chicago: University of Chicago Press, 1985): 27.

while the other is looking on."[77] Perhaps thought cannot be the object of thought; but even Comte had to make his definition of "positivism" dependent on the *relations*, the relativity, of "one's real needs" within a wider world.[78] He thereby admits that one must reflect on one's "real needs," and, in some sense, "stand at the window and watch yourself go by in the street." In this context, those needs include seeing oneself—as best one can—as an object among others. Stanley Fish, reviewing the discontents of interdisciplinary studies, rightly points out that our inability fully to assess our categories of thought while inhabiting them does not disallow thought itself, but only makes it impossible for us to be "gods."[79] We must make peace with the bind of relativism, for it is here to stay.

Relativism, retooled as contemporary critical anthropology, thus becomes indispensible as a mode of intercultural critique; Marcus and Fischer write:

Contemporary interpretive anthropology . . . is the essence of cultural relativism properly conceived as a mode of inquiry about communication within and between cultures. In the face of undeniably global structures of political and economic power, ethnography, as the practical embodiment of relativism and interpretive anthropology, challenges all those views of reality in social thought which prematurely overlook or reduce cultural diversity for the sake of the capacity to generalize or to affirm universal values. . . . Thus, contemporary interpretive anthropology is nothing other than relativism rearmed and strengthened for an era of intellectual ferment.[80]

77. "L'individu pensant ne saurait se partager en deux, dont l'un raisonnerait, tandis que l'autre regarderait raisonner" (Auguste Comte, "Cours de philosophie positive, première leçon," in *Oeuvres choisis* [Paris: Editions Montaigne, n. d.]: 83; trans. Paul Descours and H. Gordon Jones, *The Fundamental Principles of the Positive Philosophy* [London: Watts & Co., 1905]: 34). In the introduction, above (p. 19), we saw Stanislas Adotevi's paraphrase of Comte: "On ne peut se mettre à la fenêtre et se voir passer dans la rue," in *Négritude et négrologues* (Paris: Union Générale d'Editions, 1972): 100. The quotation from Comte should be considered in relation to the dominant method of twentieth-century ethnography, participant-observation, which demands precisely that the field worker "cut himself in two."

78. Comte espoused a form of "positive relativism": "C'est la relation qui détermine exactement chaque terme. . . . La précision n'est elle-même précise qu'une fois réduite à celle qui est 'compatible avec la nature des phénomènes et conforme à l'exigence de nos vrais besoins' [the quotation is from Comte]. . . . Ainsi, chaque notion constituant la positivité reçoit sa qualité positiviste en participant, selon la formule platonicienne, à la relativité." Henri Gouhier, introduction to *Oeuvres choisies* of Comte, 31.

79. Stanley Fish, "Being Interdisciplinary Is So Very Hard to Do," *Profession* 89 (1989): 21.

80. See George E. Marcus and Michael M. J. Fischer, *Anthropology as Cultural Critique: An Experimental Moment in the Human Sciences* (Chicago: University of Chicago Press, 1986): 32–33.

In the remainder of this study, my response to the bind of relativism is neither to seek some miraculous solution to it nor to ignore the real problems it poses; relativism both underpins and undercuts an intellectual endeavor like this one. The mélange of questions, approaches, and sources that will fuel the readings that follow is a reflection of who I am (an American who has spent time living, teaching, researching, and travelling in Africa and who has been trained in the United States in the analysis of literary texts) and of what I have been able to see, read, and understand. It will display a continuing, if skeptical, interest in Western theoretical issues, especially when they claim competence in regard to Africa; this is to some extent a reflection of my milieu, but equally a reflection of the discursive field that exists in African studies. I will therefore not pretend to transcend or abandon the American academic scene, but from within it I will attempt a dialogue with another scene, whose issues and language are partially, *problematically*, different: francophone Africa. The result will be anything but a "pure product."[81]

81. See Clifford's introduction to *The Predicament of Culture*, "The Pure Products Go Crazy," 1–17.

3

On a toujours pensé que l'Afrique était la civilisation de la parole. Je constate tout le contraire: nous sommes vraiment la civilisation du silence.
Un silence métissé.
[Africa has always been thought to be the civilization of the spoken word.
I maintain quite the opposite: we are actually the civilization of silence.
A half-caste silence.]
—Sony Labou Tansi [1]

What one learns to read is always another language.
—John Guillory [2]

Orality through Literacy: Mande Verbal Art after the Letter

From "Illiteracy" to "Orality"

Literacy: This subject was introduced 3/8/83. For works catalogued before that date see Illiteracy.
—Card Catalogue of Sterling Memorial Library, Yale University

Recent reports in the press have uncovered an alarmingly high rate of illiteracy in the United States. In the "overdeveloped" countries of the West, where the written word is the key to economic survival, it is normal to refer to illiteracy as a "disease" to be eradicated. In developing nations, that economic imperative is even more pressing. But the term "illiteracy" imposes a negative judgment and prevents one from thinking, in positive or at least neutral terms, of *orality*: those nonliterate verbal arts and forms of expression that sustained cultures for centuries before writing came along. "Illiteracy" is a "scriptocentric" term—it presupposes writ-

1. Sony Labou Tansi, *Les Sept solitudes de Lorsa Lopes* (Paris: Seuil, 1985): 9.
2. John Guillory, "Canonical and Non-Canonical: A Critique of the Current Debate," *ELH* 54, no. 3 (Fall 1987): 501.

ing as the norm, and the absence of writing as a flaw. The shift in terminology from "illiteracy" to "orality" has important implications for the
relations between the modern West and the third world. Those implications, as seen in the context of one African culture, are the object of this
chapter. Distinctions between the oral and the written underpin the entire relationship between sub-Saharan Africa and the West; as we saw in
the introduction, this problem of difference also defines the field that has
been considered proper to anthropology. In addition, the proximity of
oral traditions is certainly one of the distinctive characteristics of African
literatures.

The question of orality and literacy in black Africa is not a matter of
ancient history or theoretical abstraction. The advent in Africa of writing
as we know it was the direct result of European conquest and colonization—processes that encompass the lifetimes of people who are still alive,
processes that are very much at issue in African life today. Orality and
literacy are two worlds that coexist in a state of tension, enriching and
contradicting each other in daily life. In the majority of cases in black
Africa, to write is to write in French, English, or Portuguese—or in Arabic, which has been in use in certain parts of black Africa for several
centuries; literacy in African languages—with notable exceptions such as
Swahili in Tanzania—is largely an adjunct to or a stepping-stone toward
competence in a European language. This is particularly true in the
francophone countries, where the groundwork for developing African-
language literacy is only now being laid. In Mali, the Bamana language
is taught, but it is referred to by some as a "Trojan horse" for French:
Bamanankan comes first in order to facilitate the teaching of French.
Many African intellectuals now support the concept of real national-
language literacy and literature, but they differ widely on questions of
feasibility and timing. Some francophone writers, adhering to an élite
standard, find the whole idea of writing in African languages absurd. It
is certain that a great many practical problems have to be solved before
viable national-language literatures emerge.

Throughout Africa, writing in European languages has proved endur-
ingly advantageous (or necessary), and the "neo-African" literatures that
have developed in those languages over the last century seem unlikely to
wither away. At the same time, writing and reading must be recognized
as privileges of a small élite: the sub-Saharan countries of the Sahel are
estimated to have an overall literacy rate of five percent.[3] Literacy must

3. Patrick Marnham, *Fantastic Invasion: Notes on Contemporary Africa* (New York:
Harcourt, Brace, Jovanovich, 1979): 106. UNESCO statistics on francophone countries
show literacy rates ranging from less than 1% in Niger to 6% in Senegal (in 1961), 19%
in Cameroun (in 1962), and 30% in Zaïre (in 1962). Literacy in all these cases means

be distinguished from oral knowledge of European languages, which may reach fifteen percent of the population of a city like Bamako, the capital of Mali; in Abidjan, the largest city in the Ivory Coast, almost everyone has some knowledge of French.

Everywhere, élitism vexes intellectual life. By speaking and writing in European languages, the African intellectual makes him/herself incomprehensible to the majority of the people, who become an object in the intellectual's discourse. European-language literacy is the most important element in a process of distancing, a displacement that removes the intellectual from the immediate sphere of traditional culture. That removal is a sensitive topic and is variously described as either alienation or the condition necessary for perspective and understanding. It certainly produces a counteractive desire for the rediscovery of tradition and orality through the discourses of art and the human sciences. The initial removal from tradition is the condition of possibility allowing the Westerner access to the African's patient, scientific rediscovery of his or her people, of him or herself. It is here that the African quest for identity and the Western quest for alterity meet.

If to write in Africa is usually to write a European language in a European alphabet and to show the signs, to recreate the traces of colonial domination, to speak is far more frequently to speak an African language; this language may have assimilated large numbers of European words, but its syntax and patterns remain African, relatively untouched by literacy.[4] Orality in its broadest sense thus has a clear political connotation in Africa, representing the authenticity of the precolonial world:

---

literacy in French; illiteracy is defined by UNESCO in these terms: "A person is illiterate who cannot with understanding both read and write a short simple sentence on his everyday life" (*Statistics of Educational Attainment and Illiteracy* [Paris: UNESCO,1977]: table 6). On the other hand, in certain small areas of certain countries, the rate of enrollment in school and therefore of literacy is significantly higher: of children 7 to 12 years old in the Ivory Coast, fifty percent are estimated to be in school (P. Thomas, "L'Alphabétisation en Côte d'Ivoire: Situation actuelle," *Cahiers Ivoiriens de Recherche Linguisitique* 1 [1977]: 53). Governments that have engaged in concerted literacy campaigns have made a difference: Tanzania is estimated to have a literacy rate of seventy-five percent (*The New York Times*, "News of the Week in Review," November 3, 1985, 3).

4. Many African languages have been heavily penetrated by European words. As a prestige-linked speech pattern, the use of French words in Bambara, for example, is so frequent in the Malian capital of Bamako that a radio personality has a contest once a year to see if anyone can speak Bambara for a few minutes without using a single French word. While there is hardly an African language that has not assimilated European vocabulary (Lingala *motuka* for motorcar, Tshiluba *franc* for money, Swahili *Kingareza* for English), such borrowings adapt European words to the African world, appropriating them, following Léopold Sédar Senghor's dictum "assimilate, don't be assimilated."

"tradition" and orality are synonymous. The traditional African verbal arts, however, while still extant, are fast disappearing or becoming something else. It is said that every time an old African dies, "another museum disappears." The current generation of "griot depositaries"—oral historians fully trained in the traditional way—may well be the last. Some of their descendants (such as Mory Kante and Kassé Mady Diabaté) have electrified their music and now participate in the global recording industry.

The opposition between orality and literacy in black Africa is not, however, a clear distinction between, on the one hand, a purely authentic precolonial mode of expression preserved intact and, on the other hand, a fully westernized mode undifferentiated from European culture. The heat with which orality is debated among African intellectuals is explained by the ambivalence they feel toward the prestigious but lost autonomy of precolonial African society. There are those who reject traditionalism in all its forms, favoring a radical praxis devoted to competition with the West on its own terms: history, philosophy, and literacy as defined by the West. For Marcien Towa (our continuing point of reference), the oral tradition is nothing but a "griotisme avilissant"—a debasing minstrelsy, imprisoning Africans in a nostalgic identity that prevents confrontation with global reality.[5] The alternative is a renunciation of tradition, which is to say the oral tradition, in favor of anything and everything written, which is to say Western. While for certain philosophers such a practice would westernize only in order to beat the West at its own game, the practice is the same as that of colonialism itself: to "literate," so to speak, and thereby to obliterate precolonial culture. One critic quotes an Ivory Coast primary school text book which has the following sentences in capitals:

IL AIME ECRIRE, DONC IL EST SAUVE.

[He likes to write, so he is saved.]

And, in a symptomatic switch of gender from masculine to feminine and of mode from active to passive:

ELLE AIME LIRE, DONC ELLE EST SAUVEE.

[She likes to read, so she is saved.][6]

---

5. Marcien Towa, *L'Idée d'une philosophie négro-africaine* (Yaoundé, Cameroun: Editions CLE, 1979): 24.

6. Abdou Touré, *La Civilisation quotidienne en Côte d'Ivoire* (Paris: Karthala, 1981): 92–93. For a critique of the ideology of literacy, see this work and Roy Preiswerk and Dominique Perrot, *Ethnocentrisme et histoire: L'Afrique, l'Amérique indienne et l'Asie dans les manuelles occidentales* (Paris: Anthropos, 1975): 149–57.

What is saved? The modern black African may well be saved from having no chance at a job and at economic advancement in the literate sectors of society, but writing and reading do not save the African past in its traditional, oral form. But neither, I would contend, is the past wholly obliterated by an all-powerful, wholly alien monster of alphabetization.

My object here will be to examine the degree to which an outsider can gain access to the African past—the world of orality—through the context of transcriptions and translations into French: to read orality *through* and in spite of the transcriber's literacy as well as my own. The realm I aim to explore is the complex zone of interferences between orality and literacy in francophone black Africa. Specifically, I want to describe the conflict between the stated aims of oral traditionalists and the stated aims of literate, francophone historians in the context of one ethnic group, the Mande of West Africa. All that I know about orality is what I have read in books and what I have learned by speaking with African intellectuals (scholars and writers). My area of interest is the translated orality-*sous-rature* that remains within and is displaced by "real" (written) francophone literature. This effort can be seen as part of the movement, advocated by Brian Street, toward analyzing particular "literacies" *ideologically*—in their institutional contexts—rather than seeing literacy as a monolithic, global determinant; I however will focus slightly more on the particularities of a certain "orality."[7]

A broad overview of African orality would not be possible here. The verbal arts of Africa are as numerous and as varied as the peoples and cultures of the continent, encompassing sign systems that stretch and violate the Western categories of writing and speech. Among the more intriguing problems, one would want to study the use of proverbs in certain cultures that rely on them heavily; sign systems such as the brass weights made by the Asante to represent a proverb, as a kind of written version of it; the representation of words by their tone alone in the art of "talking drums;" and precolonial ideographic systems such as that found among the Ejagham of Cameroun and Nigeria.[8] Systems of expression like these pose real challenges to Western categories of understanding, notably the

7. See Brian V. Street, *Literacy in Theory and Practice* (Cambridge: Cambridge University Press, 1984). An important and related theoretical statement is made by Karin Barber and Paulo Fernando de Moraes Farias in the introduction to a volume they edited, *Discourse and Its Disguises: The Interpretation of African Oral Texts*, Birmingham University African Studies Series 1 (Birmingham, England, 1989): 1–10. The essays in this volume, which appeared too late to be fully taken into account here, constitute a major advance in the field.

8. See Ruth Finnegan, *Oral Literature in Africa* (Nairobi: Oxford University Press, 1976), the most comprehensive general source on African oral traditions.

definition of what is "written." I will limit myself here to two working assertions: first, that the verbal arts in Africa tend to blur the distinction between absolute orality and absolute literacy; therefore the evolutionary model of transition from primitive orality to civilized writing is clearly inappropriate. Second, that African verbal arts, even in an unspoiled traditional context, raise questions concerning the structure of traditional societies and the manipulation of power in them. The traditional verbal arts of black Africa are not necessarily synonymous with populism, accessibility, and acephalous democracy. The problem of social differentiation and exclusion—as seen first in the formation of a class of *assimilés* indebted to the colonial power, then in the elitism that troubles African literatures written in European languages today—is not automatically solved by recourse to orality and the oral tradition. The political questions are only transposed from an intercontinental face-off between Westerners and Africans to an *intra*continental face-off between Africans of different classes, castes, and clans. In examining any oral tradition, one must ask to whom that tradition belongs: to what ethnic group, with what social organization, and to what subgroup within that culture. One must try to find out what attitude the society as a whole manifests toward the spoken word and toward those who are its caretakers. The thrust of my argument here will thus work to question the tendancy of Western interpreters to project onto oral cultures a pure unity of mentality and of art.

No culture better illustrates this problem, nor in a way more relevant to the new francophone literature, than the Mande of West Africa. Mande society is structured around a particular attitude toward certain "materials," of which the spoken word is the most striking example. The fact that the Mande epic *Sunjata* was one of the first transcribed into French, and that the Mande ethnic group has produced some of the most prominent francophone writers, only adds to its importance.

Mande Ethnography and the Spoken Word

Le mal, c'est la parole incontrôlée et qui s'en va, tel un serpent enivré de son propre vénin.

—Massa Makan Diabaté, *Comme une piqûre de guêpe*[9]

Rather than forcing "the Mande" into a predetermined mold of "ethnicity," we should let what the Mande is control our notion of the ethnic. The Mande is anything but one of those rigid, reified stereotypes of an African "tribe" invented to serve colonial power (quite the contrary, since

9. (Paris: Présence Africaine, 1980): 48.

one of the greatest efforts of resistance to the French came from a rebirth of the Mande empire, the "Dyula revolution" led by Samory Touré in the late nineteenth century).[10] The Mande should be considered as a fluid "federation" of culture and genealogy, held together by history, myth, and structure; it is a sphere, a space, an *aire culturelle*. Included under the general heading of the Mande are all those groups who trace their ancestry to the medieval empire of Mali, that is to say all those whose history is related in the Mande epic I will discuss here: the Maninka or Malinke, the Bamana (formerly known as the "Bambara," a problematic and particularly fluid term, varying with the position of the person using it),[11] the Dyula (also spelled Djula), the Soninke, and others. These groups speak dialects of Mandekan, the language of the Mande, and "all share socio-cultural values defining kinship, political organization and economic activities."[12] The most important Mande common denominator for us is the binding power of oral history: the unifying force of the epic of Sunjata, the founding emperor. This oral text—its performance and reception—is therefore central to the very question of what is "Mande."

The Mande covers a huge part of West Africa, intermingling with other groups but dominating wide areas. Mande languages (the group of which is referred to as Mandekan) are on a par with Swahili and Hausa for sheer geographical spread, extending from Senegal and Guinea on the Atlantic coast, through parts of Liberia and the Ivory Coast; the Mande heartland is in eastern Guinea (where Camara Laye came from) and western Mali. But, as we will see in the last chapter of this study, other groups such as the Wolof of Senegal, who were conquered and incorporated into the Mali Empire, have closely parallel social and cultural systems, so that it is easier for an individual to move (by marriage, for example) horizontally from one system to another than vertically within either system.

10. See Yves Person, *Samori: La renaissance de l'empire Mandingue* (Dakar: Nouvelles Editions Africaines, 1976).

11. See Jean Bazin, "A chacun son Bambara," in Jean-Loup Amselle and Elikia M'Bokolo, eds., *Au coeur de l'ethnie* (Paris: La Découverte, 1985): 87–127.

12. Charles S. Bird and Martha Kendall, "The Mande Hero: Text and Context," in Ivan Karp and Charles S. Bird, eds., *Explorations in African Systems of Thought* (Bloomington: Indiana University Press, 1980): 13. Bird and Kendall also state: "That which unifies the Mande peoples culturally, i.e., that which gives coherence to their social structures, is not simply recognition of common ancestry; it is, rather, a system of commonly held beliefs—a philosophy, ideology or cosmology—which defines appropriate behavior for individual actors and allows in turn the interpretation of the behavior of others." See also Charles Bird, "Oral Art in the Mande," in Carleton T. Hodge, ed., *Papers on the Mande* (Bloomington: Indiana University Press, 1971): 15; in the same volume see Nicolas S. Hopkins, "Maninka Social Organization," 115, n.1: "The Maninka are more frequently called Malinké in the French language literature. I regard the Maninka and the Bamana or Bambara as the same people, with local differences between the regions."

Djibril Tamsir Niane, whose work I will analyze in this chapter, is an interesting example of this cultural/ethnic shifting: born to Tukolor parents and subject to three or four different traditions, Niane came to be of the Mande by assimilation and education, in a kind of total immersion in the culture.[13]

Any sense of fluidity in one's conception of the Mande should be tempered by an awareness of its "national" unity. Every seven years, a ceremony takes place in the village of Kaaba, Mali; through a ceremonial reroofing of the sacred Mande hut, a sense of Mande identity is fostered and preserved. Representatives come from across the borders that have divided the Mande since the colonial conquest; the gathering testifies to the endurance of their culture. When the Sunjata epic is performed in this context, it illustrates most dramatically the "function of national unity."[14]

The ethnographic sources on the Mande—from the late nineteenth century through the late 1980s—are full of terminological squabbles and substantive disagreements. Not being an ethnographer myself, I must therefore thread my way through a number of controversies, attempting to weigh evidence according to reliability and significance. I will begin by reviewing two principles of organization of Mande society: "clan" and "caste," both of which are problematic, both of which will be essential to the readings that follow.[15]

The colonial ethnographer Charles Delafosse—one of the classical sources in this area—pointed out in 1920 that Mandekan has no word for "clan," even if Mande society seems to have clans based on patrilineal descent and name.[16] "Clan" therefore symbolizes a certain imposition of

13. See Ray Autra, preface to Djibril Tamsir Niane, *Sikasso ou la dernière citadelle, suivi de Chaka* (Honfleur: Pierre Jean Oswald, 1971): 6–8. On the mobility of ethnic affiliations in the Mande area, see Jean Gallais, "Signification du groupe ethnique au Mali," *L'Homme* 2, no. 2 (May-August 1962): 106–129. Gallais states: "L'Africain de ces régions ne comprend pas l'appartenance à une ethnie comme une donnée naturelle qu'il est obligé de subir au même titre que sa taille" (129). See also Isabelle Leymarie, "The Role and Function of the Griots among the Wolof of Senegal," Ph. D. dissertation, Columbia University, 1979: 10; and Germaine Dieterlen, "The Mande Creation Myth," *Africa* 27, no. 2 (April 1957): 125, n. 3, "When he goes to Mande, a Dogon [an ethnic designation] is called Kéita [a *jamu* or patronym] and a Mossi is called Traoré."

14. John William Johnson, *The Epic of Son-Jara: A West African Tradition* (Bloomington: Indiana University Press, 1986): 50. On the reroofing ceremony, see Dieterlen, "The Mande Creation Myth," and Claude Meillassoux, "Les Cérémonies septennales du Kamablo de Kaaba (Mali)," *Journal de la société des africanistes* 38, no. 2 (1968):173–83.

15. Since I am not attempting an "ethnography" here, I will not review other principles of organization; they would include such structures as age groups, initiation societies, villages, and districts.

16. Charles Delafosse, "Des soi-disant clans totémiques de l'Afrique Occidentale," *Revue d'Ethnographie et des traditions populaires* 1, no. 2 (1920): 100.

ethnographic authority in order to discuss what needs to be discussed: Mande social organization. Delafosse, long before antiethnocentrism was fashionable, advocated abandoning the Western category (of "totemic clan") in order to "listen to what the natives say" (97). What they say is *jamu*, which refers to family name or patronymic. When one extrapolates ethnographically, from "what the natives say" to what it is convenient to write, the Mande appears as a configuration of a certain number of genealogical "clans." A clan (and, having derived the term, I will dispense with the quotation marks) is defined as all those descended from a single ancestor and bearing his name. A clan may now include over 100,000 people (Hopkins, 101). It should be noted in passing that the act of extrapolation from "what the natives say" to the language of ethnography is a transition from orality to literacy.

A *jamu* is both patronymic and praise name; Delafosse translates: "*Dia-mou*, that which honors, makes great or carries far back, genealogy, *titre de noblesse*" (104). The *jamu* is paramount in the notion of identity; to call someone by his *jamu* is to honor his ancestors; the *jamu* is to be "endlessly valorized." More recent Mande and Western writers corroborate much of what Delafosse asserted. For Mande people, "name and being are indistinguishable."[17] Clans derive not only their names from the oral tradition but also their relationships with other clans: "Relations between clans are modelled after the relations between their ancestors in the time of Sunjata" (Hopkins, 101), the founder of the Mali Empire. The story of Sunjata's life is thus a paradigm and a justification for networks of social relations—which clan is close to which, who is indebted to whom, and, most importantly, who shall rule the kingdom. Mande society thus in a real sense defines its self-image and organization by referring to the Sunjata epic. In one of the French versions that I will be analyzing, the following passage illustrates the relationship between the Sunjata legend and contemporary social relations:

> Soundjata proclama tous les interdits qui président encore aux relations entre tribus, à chacun il assigna sa terre, il établit les droits de chaque peuple et il scella l'amitié des peuples.

> Sundiata pronounced all the prohibitions which still obtain in relations between the tribes. To each he assigned its land, he established the rights of each people and ratified their friendships.

> [The passage goes on to explain what clan will take their wives from what clan, and who will be "joking cousins" to whom].[18]

17. Diango Cissé, *Structures des Malinkés de Kita* (Bamako: Editions Populaires du Mali, 1970): 123.

18. Djibril Tamsir Niane, *Soundjata ou l'épopée mandingue* (Paris: Présence Africaine, 1960): 141; trans. G. D. Pickett, *Sundiata: An Epic of Old Mali* (London: Longman,

Another important principle of organization is the notion or ideology of "caste." This is somewhat controversial. Western anthropolgists have recently been shying away from this term because they feel that it implies a rigid, hierarchical stratification of society, often associated with a notion of pollution; in other words, that the term should not be "borrowed" from India. Patrick McNaughton, one of the leading American specialists of Mande art, while recognizing a tripartite division of the society, carefully appraises notions of caste and finds that the necessary "ranking" and "ideological rationale" are lacking.[19] But this is contradicted by African scholars from the Mande area, who are almost unanimous in using the term "caste," if only in a particular sense. One's attitidue toward this problem depends on which of two things one makes dependent on the other: the "universal" definition of a term or its contextual usage.

For my part, I will follow the example of scholars like Sory Camara, who comes from and works on Mande oral traditions, and Abdoulaye-Bara Diop, who has written a full ethnography of the Wolof. In his far-reaching analysis of Mande griots, Camara finds that the three traditional groups "incontestably form a caste system," which is a "type of hierarchical integration," even if the ranking is complex and full of ambivalence.[20] His study certainly reveals a highly ideological system of beliefs that determine caste roles, a system with deep historical roots, continuing to affect people's lives today. Diop defines caste as "hereditary, endogamous groups, specialized by profession, maintaining hierarchical relations."[21] For Diop, caste must be understood as a principle that coexists with "order"—political power; his distinction helps to clarify some of the complexities we will see.

1965): 78. "Joking cousins" refers to another important principle of organization in Mande society. When a joking relationship or *sanakuya* obtains between two clans, members of the respective clans must exchange gifts, help each other in adversity (even bearing false testimony to defend a relation against true charges), and, most curiously, tease and insult each other with rude and obscene references. These encounters must not provoke any seriously violent quarrel.

19. Patrick McNaughton, *The Mande Blacksmiths: Knowledge, Power, and Art in West Africa* (Bloomington: Indiana University Press, 1988): 159.

20. Sory Camara, *Gens de la parole: Essai sur la condition et le rôle des griots dans la société Malinké* (Paris: Mouton, 1976): 57–58. Cf. Majhemout Diop, *Histoire des classes sociales dans l'Afrique de l'ouest*, vol. 1, *Le Mali* (Paris: Maspero, 1971): "Il est certain que nous avons affaire à un système de castes." (45).

21. Abdoulaye-Bara Diop, *La Société wolof: Tradition et changement* (Paris: Karthala, 1981): 27. Cf. Claude Rivière's definition: "groupements héréditiares, relativement endogames et hermétiques, attribuant à l'individu un statut déterminé dans la structure sociale et une fonction assignable dans la division du travail. Traditions et normes réglementent les rapports intercastes et fixent la position socio-culturelle de l'individu casté" ("La difficile émergence d'un artisanat casté, *Cahiers d'études africaines* 36, no. 9 [1969]: 605).

I will therefore use the term "caste" here, but only in the sense that it acquires in the work of Camara, Diop, and their colleagues, and in light of the McNaughton's careful reflexions. That is to say, I will use the word as it is used in francophone West Africa, where the social structure of India is the farthest thing from anyone's mind. In this case as in many others, European-language terms have been appropriated and recontextualized in Africa: thus vocabulary considered politically incorrect in the West—words like "tribe," "hut," and "caste"—are used in parts of Africa without negative connotations.

This explanation is necessary because the notion of caste is fundamental to everything we will look at in the remainder of this study. Caste displays "remarkable persistance" in Mande (and Wolof) society (Diop, 27); it is "the very armature of the old traditions." [22] Caste is inscribed in the francophone literature of this area, constituting one of its most important themes (see appendix to this chapter, "Caste in the Novel"), but it goes almost unnoticed in the literary criticism. The role of this institution and everything it implies in the Mande is a classic example of the "anthropological" factors that Western readers have overlooked.

What, then, is the caste system of the Mande? Traditional Mande society is divided between three groups: first the mass of citizen farmers, also referred to as nobles, second the captives or slaves, and third the *nyamakala*, in French *les gens de caste*, the "people of caste." [23] The first group may be referred to as nobles, if we again readjust the word to mean "well-born, belonging only to oneself" and accepting certain strictures on behavior. [24] The Mande term for this group is *hòròn* (plural *hòrònw*); within this classification, certain lineages are designated as royalty, namely those bearing the *jamu* Kéita inherited from the emperor Sunjata Kéita. Slavery was legally abolished by French colonial rule, although awareness of a person's descent from slaves is said to still play a role in determining social status; the *ideology* of slavery as debasement remains in force. [25] *Nyamakala* means the branch of society that manipulates *nyama*, potentially dangerous forces released through the performance or violation of ritual. *Nyama* is often represented as a vital but malevolent force, and this explains the need for a caste of persons qualified to handle it with care. Another translation of *nyamakala* is "anti-

22. Bokar N'Diaye, *Les Castes au Mali* (Bamako: Editions Populaires, 1970): 42.

23. See Rivière's definition of caste, note 21 above.

24. Quoted from Massa Makan Diabaté, in his novel *L'Assemblée des djinns* (Paris: Présence Africaine, 1985): 79, "*Hòròn*: bien né qui n'appartient qu'à lui-même."

25. Hopkins, "Maninka Social Organization," 108: "People now remember in great detail whose ancestors were slaves at the turn of the century when French colonial control was established and slavery abolished."

dote of evil" (Rivière, 607). But *nyama* is not simply an evil genie: it is closely associated with *action* and has also been translated as the "energy of action"[26] and "the necessary power source behind every movement, every task" and "a rationale for . . . [the] most fundamental behavior patterns" of the Mande people (McNaughton, *Mande Blacksmiths*, 15– 16). For Sory Camara, *nyama* is "all-powerful spirit," "the definitive form of the double, rendered autonomous"; the "ultimate aim of all accomplishments."[27]

But *nyama* has also been translated as "filth" or "garbage" (N'Diaye, *Castes*, 14). The late Mande scholar and novelist Massa Makan Diabaté, himself a part of one of the great griot families of Mali, translated *nyama* as "maléfice," evil.[28] It is unclear whether this represents an ambivalence within the word itself, or simply a homonymous, different word.[29] This conflict in the translation of the Mande term *nyama* represents an important aporia in our ability to interpret the cultural significance of the oral tradition, and I will return to this question presently .

The *nyamakala* are "socially differentiated by prescribed behavior"— both restrictions and privileges—and by "genealogically inherited professional capacities" (McNaughton, 159). Their responsibility is to deal with the forces of *nyama*. Members of the *nyamakala* traditionally inherit their occupation, which may be that of smith, musician, leatherworker, or, most importantly for us, verbal artist. I will refer to the latter profession by the Mandekan *jeli* as well as by the French term *griot*. Whether these three groups constitute three castes or one caste along with two asymmetrical "orders" (the nobles and the slaves), is an interesting but moot question.[30]

Anthropological sources cannot seem to agree on the social status of the *jeliw*, and the *nyamakala* in general, within Mande society. On the one hand, they are respected for their handling of materials that the culture deems sacred, dangerous, and unclean: wood, leather, gold, iron, music, and the spoken word. On the other hand, their contact with these materials, their practice of "activities deemed unworthy of the nobles," leads Sory Camara, among others, to a positive conclusion, which he

26. Charles Bird, "Poetry in the Mande," *Poetics* 5 (1976): 98.

27. Sory Camara, *Paroles très anciennes ou le mythe de l'accomplissment de l'homme* (Paris: La Pensée Sauvage, 1982): 211

28. Massa Makan Diabaté, *Le Lion à l'arc* (Paris: Hatier, 1986): 25, 34.

29. Manthia Diawara states that "*nyaman* with a 'n' at the end means trash" ("Popular Culture and Oral Traditions in African Film," *Film Quarterly* 41, no. 3 [Spring 1988]: 13). But John William Johnson says that "the word for garbage [is] a synonym for the word for occult power" (*The Epic of Son-Jara*, 11).

30. For a discussion, see Camara, *Gens*, 58.

considers to be of "capital" importance, that the *nyamakala* are held in "contempt . . . within Malinké society" (*Gens*, 79).[31] Activities such as shaving the heads of nobles and preparing the dead for burial involve the release of *nyama*. The *nyamakala* are charged with performing dangerous but necessary manipulations of forces, forces such as death and the spoken word.

It is obviously impossible to go any further without explaining that last juxtaposition: why should the spoken word be seen as such a force of disorder? The Mande attitude toward the word—as described in a wide variety of sources—is complex and ambivalent; it can be explained in shorthand by saying that speech is dangerous because it releases *nyama* when it transforms silence into noise. The general term for the spoken word is *kouma*, but *kouma* is only that speech that is associated with the outermost organs of speech—the mouth, the tongue, and the throat; other, deeper types of the word correspond to other bodily organs, in a hierarchy that equates interiority and depth with truth and trustworthiness. The mouth is possessed of the spoken word as a means of intersubjective communication. Speech from the mouth can be sweet and seductive but also dangerous:

Smooth talkers are always mistrusted: the cleverness of an adorned tongue, the beauty of the word from a sweet mouth, while trying to flatter the imagination and to move the person, *alter the sense of the real* and lead the soul into the vanity of illusions, pride and passions. Whence the attitude of the Malinké toward the griots. (Camara, *Gens*, 239, emphasis mine)

It has been pointed out that in Mandekan, all expressions in which "mouth" means "spoken word" are negative and revelatory of a "profoundly distrustful attitude toward the mouth as a symbol of the word among the Malinké." The tongue also is not to be trusted, for it can render one thought in more than one fashion, introducing duplicity and the possibility of lying. A person who is two-faced, who will be kind to your face but stab you in the back, is said to have a "split tongue," which is a serious insult (Camara, *Gens*, 239, 242). The word for neck (*kan*) also means "language" (as in "Mande*kan*"—just as "tongue" means lan-

---

31. Bird criticizes Zahan for stating that one set of griots are despised while another is not, without identifying the two sets, and Bird states: "It may be that Zahan is confusing the function 'griot' with the caste of bards 'griot'. . . . There are too many pieces of evidence which point to the griot's position as far from being despised." Citing examples of ritual exchange between nobles and griots, Bird says, "One wonders who is paying homage to whom," but he adds: "There does seem to be some resentment of the priviliged position of the griot in contemporary Mande society" ("Oral Art," 17). Cf. Mamby Sidibé, "Les Gens de caste au Soudan français," *Notes africaines* 81 (1959): "On compare couramment les *nyamakala* à des femmes et à des marabouts qui ont tendance à suivre ceux qui leur font de beaux cadeaux; c'est pourquoi tout en les traitant avec déférence, on s'en méfie" (16).

guage in English and French). *Kan*, like *kouma*, is speech as communication, but it is more given to reconciliation and promise than to injury and treachery, and it can undo damage done by *kouma*. As one moves deeper into the body, one leaves the realm of outward, audible speech. The organs of the belly are not organs of speech but of silence, the other of speech and the source of speech, that which contains and controls it prior to release. The inner organs are the point of origin of the word and of thought itself.

Dominique Zahan, a French anthropologist, describes a complicated scheme by which the Bamana conceive of the origin of the spoken word: thought takes the form of an "air bubble" passing through the liver, where it is assessed and can be censored; from there it proceeds to the kidneys, where its meaning is either hardened into precision or left vague. The Bamana scheme—parts of which Zahan says they explain "badly"—then takes the word, surprisingly, through the intestines and into the bladder. Urine is thought to give the word its fluidity and to beautify it. The word is then ejected upwards to the mouth, the "enemy of man," where it enters the world, capable of insulting and deceiving. The journey of the word upward and out of the mouth describes a fall out of authenticity and truth, which, in and of themselves, are synonymous with *silence*.[32] Simultaneous with the appearance of the word in the world is the possibility of lying: in Mandekan someone who is thought incapable of lying is said to have *no mouth* (Camara, *Gens*, 248). True knowledge is held in silence, safe from the transformation into speech that releases *nyama*. The Mande attitude toward speech reveals a sign system that is both dualistic and laden with danger.

Since the social status and reputation of any subcaste within the *nyamakala* is determined by the material they work with, the *jeliw* or griots suffer from a less than sterling reputation. Griots are "the people of the spoken word" among the Mandekalu, and their fate is tied to the fortunes and reputation of orality.

Griots are spokespersons and ambassadors, matrimonial go-betweens, genealogists and historians, advisors and court jesters. While their main function, praising the powers that be, makes them indispensable to support the status quo and protect nobles from the contamination of having to use loud, imprudent language, the nobles' dependence on these professional spokesmen only increases their distrust of them. *Jeliw* are "agent[s] necessary to constituting the prestige of others" (Camara, *Gens*, 173); their clever manipulations of words are indispenable to instill bravery and a sense of honor in the nobles. By reciting the glorious lineage of some-

---

32. See Dominque Zahan, *La Dialectique du verbe chez les Bambara* (Paris: Mouton, 1963): 15–30.

one's ancestors, the *jeli* reminds the noble of what he has to live up to. During ceremonies, the *jeliw* provide music and speech. A nobleman would no more think of standing and giving a fine oration than he would of playing an instrument and singing. The speech of a nobleman must be quiet and prudent at all times; he has a "positive mind," not "chasing after fantasies," "not adding any *supplément* to his words" (Zahan, *Dialectique*, 141). Zahan points out that the spoken word as it exists among nobles in initiation societies is everything that the speech of griots is not: measured, discreet, controlled. Speech and nobility are incompatible; but, while a nobleman's speech may be closer to the truth of silence, silence itself is impotent in the world. Silence may be safe from *nyama*, but this means that silence cannot act, for *nyama*, contamination, is also the force of action. A nobleman needs speech in order to govern, but he also needs a spokesman to protect him from the polluting *nyama* unleashed by speech.

In exercising his office, the nobleman speaks a simple phrase in a low voice, directly to his *jeli* alone. The *jeli*'s job is to beautify the basic idea, to refine it, make it more ornate and seductive—in effect, to create an *illusion*:

The man [the nobleman] thus speaks in a low voice and with very simple words: "It is friendship that brings me here!" The griot [takes this basic message and beautifies it, saying] : "I Sékou say that the heavens and the earth were created by love. But I am neither powerful nor rich; it is only kola nuts that I bring to my friend." (Camara, *Gens*, 105)

The speech of griots may be represented in its most paradigmatic form by the utterance:

> I fa ka nyi! I ba ka nyi!
>
> Your father is good! Your mother is good!

Genealogy and praise. In a cartoon from the Malian cultural journal *Jamana* (see figure 1), we see a female griot exclaiming "Your father is good! Your mother is good!" while a river of material rewards flows her way. This satire alleges that some contemporary griots are artless and know little more than bald flattery. The cartoon also serves to illustrate the fact that in a city like Bamako, the oral tradition of the Mande is alive and remains highly lucrative, even if, in the view of some, it has been corrupted.[33]

The griot's ability to add tropes, to deviate from a kind of speech that is seen as pure and basic, is symptomatic of his "singular," perhaps "de-

---

33. To the scene depicted in the cartoon we could add that of a griot performance put on at the enormous modern Palais de la Culture in Bamako, at which the admission charge is so high that only a tiny audience can afford a ticket. A Malian scholar comments: "Si

Fig. 1. Cartoon showing a griot woman singing "Your father is good! Your mother is good!" A stream of material rewards comes back to her from the two richly-dressed men she is flattering. From the Malian cultural journal *Jamana*. Reprinted from the collections of the Library of Congress and by permission of *Jamana*.

viant" role within Mande society. In a culture that values silence as in every way superior to speech, and secrecy as the highest form of knowledge—questions to which I will return—the *jeliw* are a caste of professional loudmouths. In a society based on the ritual exchange of gifts, the griot only receives and never gives; for a noble, this would be a source of shame. The griot can enter your home and demand what he wants; you refuse at your peril, for his powers of speech, usually used to praise, can be turned from *chant* to *chantage*, from praisesong to bribery. Uninvited, a griot may begin singing your genealogy; if a sufficient gift is not forthcoming, he may begin weaving in sly references to skeletons in your closet such as ancestors who were slaves.[34]

dans les campagnes, l'épopée [Sunjata] est source de prise de conscience, source d'émulation saine, moyen de préserver le patrimoine culturel, dans les villes elle tend à devenir un appât entre les mains de quelques hommes d'affaires avides de gain culturel." (Abdoulaye Sall, *Epopée et actualité à la lumière de "Kala Jata" de Massa Makan Diabaté et de l'épopée mandingue de Djibril Tamsir Niane*, Mémoire de fin d'études, Ecole Normale Supérieure, Bamako, May 1977, 29).

34. "Chaque Malinké, si noble soit-il, a dans son ascendance quelque ancêtre esclave ou captif de guerre et il est toujours malséant de se l'entendre rappeler, surtout en public. . . . Le mot 'chantage n'est pas trop faible [sic?] pour désigner certaines de leurs [griots']

But in an age of things fallen apart, for the sake of accuracy we must distinguish griot from griot. Within the caste, one may find the *nyo* (a griot by birth who is untrained and unknowledgable), the *datigi* (a "beau parleur," smooth talker), and the *naara* (a "man of talent," who has been fully initiated to the science of oral history).[35] Invoking these distinctions, the griot Wa Kamissoko describes the economy of gift exchange in his "thoughts on the meaning of gifts offered to griots."[36] On the most debased level, there is exploitation of the noble by the griot; the third and highest level of gift reflects the privileged relationship that occurs when birth, training, and practice are all propitious. The point of view taken is that of the nobleman:

> So-and-So [Untel] is an incorrigible blabbermouth [*da-tigi*], and he stays around my house all day; if I didn't give him anything, he would go and "spoil" my name [*n'toko tinya*] by slandering me. It happens like this from the moment you first offer a gift to a person of caste. So-and-So lays siege to my house and never leaves it day or night; consequently I'll give him something so that he'll leave me in peace: this constitutes the second gift. Out of all the gifts that one can offer to men of caste, the most desirable one depends on the following conditions: the ancestor of So-and-So was my family's *nyamakala*; his father was my father's "property," just as his ancestor was my ancestor's. So-and-So, in his turn, was born for me and belongs to me. Consequently, if all the property I had in the world was one cola nut, I would take it and give it to my man of caste: this is an act that is called *sonni*, giving one's heart (in other words, something intimate and essential). (199–200)

Wa Kamissoko's conclusion is that griots of the Mande are not in love with gold or silver; what counts for them is dignity. By the frequency with which this argument is made one can tell how much weight there is against it: griots must prove their dignity, for society expects them to be inveterate money-grubbers who will do anything for financial reward.

It is therefore possible for the griot to become quite wealthy through his privilege to use and abuse language; but the price he pays is distrust

---

pratiques" (Emile Leynaud and Youssouf Cissé, *Paysans Malinké du Haut Niger* [Bamako: Imprimerie Populaire du Mali, 1978]: 103). M. G. Smith describes how, among the Hausa, rich merchants of low origin are easy targets for this kind of bribery. See "The Social Functions and Meaning of Hausa Praise-Singing," *Africa* 27 (1957): 31.

35. Wâ Kamissoko, in *Actes du Deuxième Colloque International de Bamako 10 février—22 février 1976* (Paris: Fondation SCOA pour la Recherche Scientifique en Afrique Noire, 1976), 8–9.

36. *L'Empire du Mali. Un Récit de Wâ Kamissoko de Krina, enregistré, transcrit, traduit et annoté par Youssouf Tata Cissé*, Deuxième Colloque International de Bamako, February 16–22, 1976 (Paris: Fondation SCOA pour la Recherche Scientifique en Afrique Noire, 1976), 197ff.

and debased social status. Griots' flamboyant public behavior has been a social problem, and African governments have at times sought to exercise control over them by passing ordinances (at one point, the government in Mali tried to ban the giving of gifts to *nyamakala*; see N'Diaye, 123). Says one Mandeka: "Griots are like women—they can never be completely trusted, and they tend to go where the money is."[37] The incidental gender-figuring and stereotyping of griots is a subject I will discuss in the last chapter of this book. Information presently available does not permit a comparison of male and female griots; but female griots appear to be totally excluded from the recitation, transcription, and publication of the most prestigious oral text, the Sunjata epic.

While debasement and transgression are unmistakably at the root of the Mande attitude toward griots and toward the *nyamakala* caste as a whole, to say that these groups are simple objects of contempt would be inaccurate. Griots, manipulating the word instead of gold or iron, are objects of resentment, fear, and mistrust, but because of their ability to manipulate the most powerful force in the world—that of the word— they must also be treated with deference, placated, and bought off.

Wholecloth and Truth

Souviens-toi que la belle parole n'est pas toujours la parole vraie.

—Massa Makan Diabaté, in *Le Lieutenant de Kouta*[38]

The question of the "accuracy" of griots is one that seems to preoccupy Western observers more than Mande people themselves. It is a question that goes to the heart of the conflict between tradition and modernity in today's Africa. Anthropological sources are unanimous in warning the reader/listener to beware, for griots are notorious liars, crafty word-smiths who can talk their way out of any corner by making things up. One Western historian introduces his volume of Mande oral texts from the Gambia with this caveat:

Griots . . . have a reputation for being a mercenary, wily lot. Because of their intense pride in their knowledge and because they are so accomplished at narrat-ing stories—any stories—I seldom found a *griot* who would admit that he did not know the answer to one of my questions or that the information he had on a subject was not what had been passed down to him from reliable, traditional sources. Consequently, I asked many a *griot* a specific question, to which I re-ceived an artfully narrated answer, only to find sometime later that the *griot* had

---

37. Quoted in Gordon Innes, *Sunjata: Three Mandinka Versions* (London: School of Oriental and African Studies, 1974): 105n.

38. *Le Lieutenant de Kouta* (Paris: Hatier, 1983): 94.

likely fabricated the answer out of whole cloth or had adapted several scraps of local folklore to meet his needs in a pressing situation.[39]

The same historian points out that the chronology one can piece together from oral literature is suspect because it has no "middle past," only memories going back a few generations, then a gap, then ancient legends. Yves Person, the eminent French Africanist, advocated the use of oral sources in studying African history, but warned that they "must be scrutinized . . . with suspicion, because of [their] fundamental subjectivity," especially in regard to chronology.[40]

As go-betweens and spokesmen, griots are involved in political questions; they are responsible for conserving and disseminating history, but "unfortunately, very often they invent [it] out of wholecloth or modify [it] in order to please the village they are in at the moment, the family they are currently exploiting."[41] True casted griots, according to A. Hampaté Ba, ignore "the discipline of truth"; a proverb states, "The griot is allowed to have two tongues," and another, "Such is the speech of the *jeli*! It isn't the real truth [la vérité vraie], but we accept it as such."[42] How can it be that this caste of flatterers, illusionists, and liars, with a license to distort and misrepresent the truth for its own purposes, is the memory of the entire society, charged with the preservation of genealogies, historical fact and social relations?

The problem is not just that the Western discipline of history is frustrated by the African oral tradition and its disregard for "positive fact"; the problem is also that the oral tradition makes claims for itself that sound like claims to positive factuality. Griots are described by Africans as "archivists" of their civilization, "great depositaries, who, it can be said, are the living memory of Africa"; "it used to be that the griots were the Counsellors of kings; they maintained the Constitutions of kingdoms by the labor of memory alone."[43] A fictive griot, in a novel by Massa

39. Donald R. Wright, *Oral Traditions from the Gambia*, vol. 1: *Mandinka Griots*, Papers in International Studies, no. 37 (Columbus: Ohio University Center for International Studies, 1979): 13–14.

40. Yves Person, "Tradition orale et chronologie," *Cahiers d'études africaines* 7, no. 2 (1962): 462. See also Leynaud and Cissé, *Paysans Malinké*: "Il n'entre pas dans notre propos de dégager la valeur historique des témoignages et des récits des griots. Il est certain que l'on peut douter en partie de leur sincerité et de leur souci d'authenticité historique" (105).

41. Dr. Toutain, "Notes sur les castes chez les Mandingues et en particulier chez les Banmanas," *Revue d'ethnographie* 3 (1885): 345.

42. Ahmadou Hampaté Ba, "La Tradition vivante," in Joseph Ki-Zerbo, ed., *Histoire générale de l'Afrique*, vol 1, *Méthodologie et préhistoire africaine* (Paris: UNESCO, 1980): 202, 215.

43. Ba, 215. Ba defends the veracity of oral history by specifying that it is not only casted griots who perform oral narrative texts: hearing a story, one might want to know whether it was a griot telling it, who was therefore not to be trusted, or a "traditionalist-

Makan Diabaté, assures us that the last word, on which all the others rest, is the truth; we only have to take the words as they come and wait patiently for the truth to be pronounced.[44]

Yet the griots' privilege, acknowledged by society, is that of an abusive freedom of speech. We are faced with a modified version of the paradox of the Cretan liar in which the man who comes from the village of liars says that he speaks only the truth.

But whose truth are we talking about? The question of the factual truth value or historicity of the oral tradition may itself be one of those prejudicial Western preoccupations that preordain a distorted answer. Gordon Innes, introducing three versions of the Mande *Sunjata* epic, points out that the Western reader "is likely to ask himself which one is 'correct,' which is the 'true' version," but that "this is an attitude of mind that is quite alien to the Mandinka listener," who listens to his or her national epic for feelings and for truth at a deeper level than that of mere fact" (Innes, *Sunjata*, 30). The question of accuracy goes to the heart of the quarrel between literate and oral societies.

Sunjata

In looking at the Mande national epic *Sunjata* I wish to use the question of historicity only to highlight the relationship between transcriber and griot, between writing historian and speaking historian. I also want to focus on the griots' representation of orality in their own texts—to the extent that these transcriptions can still be called their own. As it happens, historical accuracy is one of the claims they make.

First, it is important to situate the Sunjata text within Mande oral literature. There has been much discussion as to whether the Western term "epic" is applicable to African narratives (a discussion that runs parallel to those about "clan" and "caste"). Ruth Finnegan claims that epic as "a relatively long narrative poem" hardly exists at all in sub-Saharan Africa, but her definition seems to depend on a text being wholly

---

doma, caring above all for truthful transmission" (218). The "traditionalist-*doma*" is a "griot-king," part of the circle of initiates from which casted griots are generally excluded. Ba also points out that between the true versions of the traditionalist-*doma* and the suspect versions, there is common basis of facts, which are "rarely transformed." Casted griots are nonetheless the people Ba refers to as the principal archivists of African society; it is they who are the professional "guardians of the word." The case that Ba presents is a specific one of a casted griot becoming a traditionalist-*doma* and thereby renouncing his privilege to lie, becoming "constrained by the interdiction on lying" (ibid.). The French transcriptions of griots' texts do not, however, generally tell the reader whether the griot in question is an initiate in the realm of *doma*.

44. Diabaté, *Le Lieutenant de Kouta*, 95.

narrative and divorced of panegyric, and on a clear distinction between poetry and prose.[45] At least in the Mande context, these distinctions would appear to be inappropriate. Isidore Okpewho describes the epic in Africa as "a tale about the fantastic deeds of a man or men endowed with something more that human might and operating in something larger than the normal human context and . . . of significance in portraying some stage of the cultural or political development of a people."[46] *Sunjata* in all its written versions is just such a text. In matters of performance and form, Mande griots produce their epics in ways similar to the Serbo-Croation epics described by Albert Lord in his classic *The Singer of Tales.*[47]

However, one notable exception must be made: the Mande epics seem to adhere to no regular meter of stresses or syllables, at least none that has yet been described (see Bird, "Oral Art," 19). John William Johnson has written the most complete description of Mande epic form; he finds that it is poetic, with three different modes; without any strict syllable count; uninterruptable; and constructed of episodes, some of which are "core" and some "augmenting" (*The Epic of Son-Jara*, 31–39). Among the constants one would find in different versions of an epic are praise-names, songs, and etiological explanations of natural phenomena and human relationships. The language of Mande epic is close to that of everyday speech, with the exception of certain formulas that griots themselves either do not understand or are unwilling to betray.

The griot knows that his audience knows the basic story of Sunjata, but he is free and even duty-bound to make his own version of the epic more pleasing to the particular group in front of him. This may involve taking considerable liberties—those granted by Mande culture to casted griots—such as flattering an important official in the audience by making one of his ancestors a star of the epic, without any historical justification, like a Renaissance painter depicting his patron as present at the Nativity.[48] The Mande audience listens in silence, without any interjections, to the epic that is for them a source of great pride and a standard by which to judge their own lives. Listeners are expected to participate in one way: by coming forward with gifts of money for the griot, who will

45. Finnegan, *Oral Literature*, 108–10.

46. Isidore Okpewho, *The Epic in Africa: Towards a Poetics of the Oral Performance* (New York: Columbia University Press, 1975): 34. See also John William Johnson, "Yes, Virginia, There is an Epic in Africa," *Research in African Literatures* 11, no. 3 (Fall 1980): 308–326.

47. Albert Lord, *The Singer of Tales* (Cambridge: Harvard University Press, 1960).

48. Okpewho, commenting on one of the versions in Innes's *Sunjata*, highlights this phenomenon of "dragging an ancestor forward" in the epic; for Okpewho, this illustrates the inappropriatness of making a sharp distinction between "epic" and "panegyric" (*The Epic in Africa*, 70).

tailor his performance for the greatest possible flattery of those present and the greatest possible financial reward for himself. Meanwhile, the griot is accompanied on a guitar (*kora*) by his *naamunaamuna* ("yes-sayer"), who interjects encouragement and reinforcement (see Johnson, 69, n. 15).

Flattery of listeners for profit is just one factor that offsets and complements the respect for factual tradition or truth in the performance of *Sunjata*. I would like to examine the ways in which one griot represents his art and his caste, in effect how he flatters himself as well as his masters, in Djibril Tamsir Niane's *Soundjata ou l'épopée mandingue*. In doing this, one cannot ignore the mediating and interfering role of writing, the means by which these epics become accessible to Westerners. Niane's transcription/translation appeared in 1960; it is published in a popular, accessible form with few footnotes.[49] It is written in prose without archaisms and divided into chapters—all characteristics that would attentuate its so-called orality. The griot whose words are transposed is Djeli Mamadou Kouyaté, whose clan, the Kouyatés, have "since time immemorial" been in the service of the most prestigious noble clan in the Mande, the Kéitas, descendants of the Emperor Sunjata himself: this clan has held the dynasty of the traditional Mande kingdom continuously since the eighth century (Niane, *Recherches*, 9). The epic is to a certain extent the story of how the Kouyatés came to have a privileged relationship with the Kéitas: this, as many other aspects of Mande daily life and history, can be explained by telling the story of Sunjata, the greatest of the Kéitas and the greatest Mande emperor, founder of the Empire of Mali in the thirteenth century.

For purposes of comparison, I will also refer to other versions of *Sunjata* that are available in French and English transcriptions. The most interesting of these from a literary standpoint is *Le Maître de la parole*, the last book written by Camara Laye, author of *L'enfant noir* (*The Dark Child*, the subject of the next chapter of this study) and *Le Regard du roi* (*The Radiance of the King*). Camara says in his introduction that his text is the result of a recording session with a griot that took place between March 16th and April 16th, 1963. Camara's griot was Babou Condé, of the Condés of Kouroussa, Guinea, descended from the griot of Sunjata Kéita's *brother*.[50] Camara's griot and Niane's are thus "cousins" in a cer-

---

49. Niane's research on the history of the Mali Empire also resulted in a thesis for a diplôme d'études supérieures at the Faculté des Lettres de Bordeaux: *Recherches sur l'Empire du Mali au Moyen Age* (République de Guinée, Ministère de l'Information et du Tourisme: Mémoires de l'Institut National de Recherches et de Documentation, no. 2, 1962).

50. Camara Laye, *Le Maître de la parole: Kouma Lafôlô Kouma* (Paris: Plon, 1978): 31; trans. James Kirkup, *The Guardian of the Word* (New York: Vintage Books, 1984): 28–29.

tain sense, and their texts show a family resemblance, with differing degrees of emphasis within the same basic epic. Some other versions, produced by Western anthropologists, appear to be "closer" to the original oral texts, if only in the sense that they are translated verse by verse, placing Mandekan transcription and European translation on facing pages (e. g. Innes, *Sunjata*).[51] I have also seen a verse translation by the Mande scholar and novelist Massa Makan Diabaté, a novelized version by the same author, and three plays.[52] Niane's *Soundjata* and Camara's *Maître de la parole* are in effect *novelizations*, conveniently packaged, readable texts in which the long recitations, litanies, circumlocutions and repetitions of the oral epic are missing.[53]

The written text bearing D. T. Niane's name on the cover presents us with several layers of defense and justification. Opening the book, we come first to a foreword by Niane that quietly suggests the opening of an era in which orality will gain its due respect in the new world of literacy: "The word of the traditionalist griots deserves something other than contempt." Niane's presentation of the oral tradition is extremely reverent:

Puisse ce livre ouvrir les yeux à plus d'un Africain, l'inciter à venir s'asseoir humblement près des Anciens et écouter les paroles des griots qui enseignent la Sagesse et l'Histoire. (7)

May this book open the eyes of more than one African and induce him to come and sit humbly beside the ancients and hear the words of the griots who teach Wisdom and History. (viii)

---

51. John William Johnson's edition of *The Epic of Son-Jara*, with a text by the griot Fa-Digi Sisòkò, is the state-of-the-art scholarly edition in English at this point. Johnson adheres to verse form in his translation and includes a column of responses uttered by an apprentice ("indeed," "mmm").

52. Diabaté's *L'Aigle et l'épervier ou la geste de Sunjata* (Paris: Pierre Jean Oswald, 1975) is organized verse by verse: "Nous avons divisé ce texte par la syntaxe du rythme qui soutient le texte du début jusqu'à la fin. Aussi sommes-nous allés à la ligne quand Kele Manson [the griot] a marqué un temps d'arrêt" (10). This version is also heavily footnoted. Diabaté played a somewhat different role in producing his *Kala Jata* (Bamako: Editions Populaires, 1970), which begins with a dialogue between the griot Kele Monson and an inquiring visitor. Here there are no footnotes, and, with the exception of certain formulaic songs represented in verse, the book bears the form of a novel: broken into chapters, with narration and dialogue alternating. *Kala Jata* was republished in a new edition, with a new introduction, as *Le Lion à l'arc* (referred to above). One play version is Sory Konaké's *Le Grand Destin de Soundjata* (Paris: ORTF-DAEC, 1973); another is Koudou Gbagbo Laurent's *Soundjata le lion du Manding* (Abidjan: CEDA, 1979). The latter, in verse, uses the voice of Mamadou Kouyaté, who collaborated with Niane, but contains much less detail. The third play version is Ahmed-Tidjani Cissé's *Le Tana de Soumangourou* (Paris: Nubia, 1988).

53. Dorothy Blair refers to "Niane's novel *Soundjata*" (*African Literature in French* [Cambridge: Cambridge University Press, 1976]: 97).

The question of the contempt, fear and respect that Mande nobles feel toward casted griots is thus skirted by emphasizing only respect. The writer-transcriber humbles himself before the speaker-traditionalist to reverse the Western pattern in which "anything that is not written black on white [is] considered groundless" (orig. 6; trans. viii). The text thus prepares to transport the griot's words from orality to literacy, while at the same time taking the literate reader "back" to world of orality.

Turning the page, one sees the heading "La Parole du Griot Mamadou Kouyaté" ("the words of Griot Mamadou Kouyaté"), and one passes from the original French of Niane to the translation of Kouyaté's Mandekan. In his prologue, the griot seems concerned primarily with fending off the Mande attitude toward the spoken word, by asserting his authority and claim to truth:

> Je suis griot. C'est moi Djeli Mamadou Kouyaté, fils de Bintou Kouyaté et de Djeli Kedian Kouyaté, maître dans l'art de parler. Depuis des temps immémoriaux les Kouyaté sont au service des princes Kéita du Manding: nous sommes les sacs à paroles, nous sommes les sacs qui renferment des secrets plusieurs fois séculaires. . . . Sans nous les noms des rois tomberaient dans l'oubli . . .
>
> Ma parole est pure et dépouillée de tout mensonge; c'est la parole de mon père; c'est la parole du père de mon père. Je vous dirai la parole de mon père telle que je l'ai reçue; les griots de roi ignorent le mensonge. (9–10)
>
> I am a griot. It is I, Djeli Mamadou Kouyaté, son of Bintou Kouyaté and of Djeli Kedian Kouyaté, master in the art of eloquence. Since time immemorial, the Kouyatés have been in the service of the Kéita princes of the Mande: we are vessels of speech, we are the repositories which harbor secrets many generations old. . . . Without us, the names of the kings would vanish into oblivion . . .
>
> My word is pure and free of all untruth; it is the word of my father, it is the word of my father's father. I will give you my father's words just as I received them; the griots of kings do not know what lying is. (1, AT)[54]

Kouyaté clearly wants to disassociate himself from the common breed of griots. Griots in the courts of Mande kings and emperors could indeed be distinguished persons, used as ambassadors and wielding some influence in state affairs. They could also be buffoons (see S. Camara, *Gens*, 136, 206–10). Kouyaté's claim to truth must be understood in the context of a culture that needs to be convinced of such a claim when it comes from a griot. Like a European novel in the eighteenth century, a Mande oral text is obliged to make a bold claim to truth in the face of a reputation that says otherwise. Camara Laye, in his introduction to *Le Maître*

---

54. If the French phrase "griot de roi" refers to the Mande notion of a traditionalist-*doma* as described by A. H. Ba, then there is a clear grounding for the claim to exemption from the untrustworthiness of the word. Niane's edition does not, however, provide this information.

de la parole, makes clear that even a true griot, a Belen-Tigui or "master of the word" who has studied for years, who is "sworn" and "imbued with the imperative of respecting the truth," is still an "artist who, like all artists, lets his heart talk" (Camara, *Maître*, 32). Historical truth as we expect it in the West may thus be "drowned," says Camara, in chant or legend. In both versions of the Sunjata epic, the griot has the title of Master of the Word; but according to Camara Laye, this is no guarantee of historical truth. Kouyaté's claim to an unaltered truth thus becomes more rather than less ambiguous as it is placed in its particular cultural context. All interpreters of the Mande oral tradition seem to reach this aporia concerning the status of truth: the griots are allowed and expected to distort it, but their claim to authority must also be respected.

Since the Kouyatés are traditionally griots to the Kéitas, Mamadou Kouyaté's text would normally be addressed to a gathering of Kéitas and be designed to please them. At the center of the epic (no matter who it is addressed to) are the exploits of Sunjata Kéita. Sunjata was born paralyzed from the waist down, but at the age of seven he declared that he would walk, and rose up, bending a huge metal bar into a bow; he was driven into exile by the first wife of his late father, who was angered by the predictions of grandeur that were made regarding Sunjata; against all odds, he fought his way back after eight years to reconquer the Mande kingdom and to found the Empire of Mali. All this is bound to please an audience of Kéitas. Sunjata embodies and personifies Mali: he creates and fulfills Mande ideals, and distinct "sociogonic" agendas and strategies can be discerned within the epic.[55]

But another significant function of the epic is to remind the Kéitas how indebted they are to the Kouyaté griots because of the actions of Sunjata's personal griot and "guardian angel," Balla Fasséké Kouyaté. In Mamadou Kouyaté's version, his ancestor Balla Fasséké is a pivotal figure. On the eve of his departure into exile, Sunjata finds that, through the political machinations of his half-brother the king, his trusty griot has been taken from him and made an ambassador. His reaction is outrage:

"Frère Dankaran Touman, tu nous as enlevé notre part d'héritage. Chaque prince a eu son griot. Tu as enlevé Balla Fasséké, il n'était pas à toi; mais où qu'il soit, Balla sera toujours le griot de Djata. Et puisque tu ne veux plus nous sentir auprès de toi, nous quitterons le Manding et nous irons loin d'ici." (56)

55. For a detailed interpretation of political and "sociogonic" elements in *Sunjata*, with particularly valuable attention to issues of gender and interaction with other oral genres, see Stephen Bulman, "The Buffalo-Woman Tale: Political Imperatives and Narrative Constraints in the Sunjata Epic," in Barber and Moraes Farias, eds., *Discourse and its Disguises*, 171–88.

"Brother Dankaran Touman, you have taken away our part of the inheritance. Every prince has had his griot, and you have taken Balla Fasséké. He was not yours, but wherever he may be, Balla will always be Djata's griot. And since you do not want to have us around you, we shall leave the Mande and go far away from here." (27, AT)

Mamadou Kouyaté's version also states clearly that the war that would end in Sunjata reclaiming the Mande was at least provoked, if not actually caused by a question of griot ownership. The sorcerer-king Soumaoro is so seduced by Balla Fasséké's verbal talents that he claims the griot as his own, "ravishing [Sunjata] of his precious griot" for a second time. The epic states that at this point, "war thus became inevitable between Sunjata and Soumaoro" (77; 40). In other words, having left his kingdom in the first place because Balla Fasséké was sent away, Sunjata fought his war not to regain his kingdom but to regain his griot. In the Camara Laye version, there is an oral declaration of war in which Sunjata affirms his ancestral right over the Mande; the Niane/Kouyaté version has the hero say he is going to reclaim his kingdom (87; 46) but implies that his motivation comes from his feeling for his griot.[56] Such plot devices have been attacked by one Western critic as self-glorifying fabrications on the part of the Kouyaté griots, as "non-historical elements," "boasts," and "embellishments," leading him to ask "Which lineage is being glorified by these accounts—the line of the Kéita kings of Mali, or the line of Kouyaté griots?"[57] Clearly, we are dealing with kind of literature here that makes such questions impertinent: it is the inherited duty of Kouyaté griots to cast this tale in a certain light; it is their right to earn their living through exaggeration and misrepresentation; the claims of Western positivist history can be seen as quite irrelevant.

It is not only by exaggerating the importance and helpful deeds of their

56. Balla Fasséké Kouyaté plays an entirely different role in Diabaté's *L'Aigle et l'épervier*: here it is implied that Balla Fasséké was the first *male* griot on earth: "Il n'y avait pas de griots au Mande, / Il n'y avait qu'une seule griote au Mande, / Du nom de Tumu Manyian" (49). To this Diabaté adds a footnote: "L'art oratoire a peut-être commencé par les femmes, et les hommes y sont venus par intérêt." Cf. Camara Laye, *Maître*: "La parole était un art femelle" (56). In *L'aigle et l'épervier*, Sunjata's elder brother (his rival for the throne) sends the Kouyaté ancestor, who is named Jukuma Doka, to give his daughter to the sorceror king Sumanguru so that he, Sumanguru, will kill Sunjata. Sumanguru responds: "C'est bien," and, giving his balafon to Kouyaté, renames him Balla Fasséké. According to this version, therefore, the clan of griots faithful to the Kéita dynasty originally got their powers from Sunjata's evil enemy. In *Maître*, there is nothing like the closeness between Balla Fasséké and Sunjata that is described in the Niane/Kouyaté version. At the moment of the declaration of war, there is no mention of an alienated griot being a cause (71).

57. Austin J. Shelton, "The Problem of Griot Interpretation and the Actual Causes of War in Sondjata," *Présence Africaine* 66, no. 2 (1968): 152.

ancestors that griots remind nobles of their never-ending debt to the faculty they distrust, the faculty of speech. In the middle of the epic, at the point where Sunjata's exile is about to end, Mamadou Kouyaté reminds his listeners again of the importance of griots and of the primacy of the spoken word:

Les griots connaissent l'histoire des rois et des royaumes, c'est pourquoi ils sont les meilleurs conseillers des rois. Tout grand roi veut avoir un chantre pour perpétuer sa mémoire, car c'est le griot qui sauve la mémoire des rois, les hommes ont la mémoire courte. . . .

D'autres peuples se servent de l'écriture pour fixer le passé; mais cette invention a tué la mémoire chez eux; ils ne sentent plus le passé car l'écriture n'a pas la chaleur de la voix humaine. Chez eux tout le monde croit savoir alors que *le savoir doit être un secret*; les prophètes n'ont pas écrit et leur parole n'en a été que plus vivante. Quelle piètre connaissance que la connaissance qui est figée dans les livres muets. (78–79)

Griots know the history of kings and of kingdoms, and that is why they are the best counsellors of kings. Every great king wants to have a singer to perpetuate his memory, for it is the griot who rescues the memories of kings from oblivion, as men have short memories. . . .

Other peoples use writing to record the past, but this invention has killed the faculty of memory among them. They do not feel the past any more, for writing lacks the warmth of the human voice. With them everyone thinks he knows; but *knowledge must be a secret*. The prophets did not write and their words have been all the more vivid as a result. What paltry knowledge is that which is frozen inside dumb books. (40–41)

The defense against writing is relevant to two incursions on Mande culture: that of Islam, the first conqueror, a process that was already underway at the time of Sunjata,[58] and that of European colonialism. Writing is inferior for two reasons: it kills memory, and it lacks warmth. On the subject of memory, Mamadou Kouyaté now repeats his claim to exact transmission without alteration or lies: "I am the result [l'aboutissement] of a long tradition. . . . The word was passed on to me without alteration, and I will deliver it without alteration, for I received it free from all untruth" (79; 41). But the unwritten word is also *alive* ; the written word is frozen, dead. The plenitude of the voice in performance—which we know involves *variation*—coexists with the claim to have altered nothing over the centuries. This seems like a contradiction to the Western reader: on the one hand, books are condemned for their stagnancy, and on the other, the oral tradition is advertised as itself immutable. At the same

58. The beginning of written information about the Mali Empire coincides with the first conversion of a Mande king to Islam: "Nous n'avons de renseignements écrits sur Mali qu'à partir de 1050, date de la conversion à l'Islam d'un Roi Manding." Niane, *Recherches*, 8.

time that Mamadou Kouyaté reminds the listener-reader that griots are the depositaries of Mande history and wisdom, he closes the hermeneutic circle by stating that "knowledge must be a secret."

The bard's invocation of secrecy is not specifically aimed at frustrating the transcriber-historian, although that is the effect. Silence and secrecy have an ontological status here that is far superior to speech and knowledge. Speech must be controlled and contained if silence is to exercise its powers of truth, authenticity, seriousness, and healing. Proverbs say: "Silence is the antidote to everything, speech opens doors to all [evil]"; and "All things serious are done in silence, all things futile in tumult" (Zahan, *Dialectique*, 154). The relation of griots to silence is obviously a problematic one. The griot, by speaking at all, has already compromised secrecy. As a "depositary of the knowledge [*science*] of the past," Mamadou Kouyaté throws the status of his knowledge into question with this statement that "knowledge must be a secret." The knowledge contained in his recitation is obviously no longer secret; he has opened it to the world, as is his job. He indicates, however, that he knows more than he says, and that some of his knowledge will remain in silence and secrecy. One transcriber identifies the etymology of the griot Balla Fasséké's name as meaning "There is a secret between you and me."[59] Now it would appear that the function of speech in relation to silence in the Mande tradition—a function of revelation but also of betrayal—is repeated by the role of the historian-transcriber who pries secrets out of the oral tradition in order to publish them. *Writing is to speech as speech is to silence*: in both cases there is movement *from authenticity to alterity, from truth to tropes*. In Mande terms these transformations are all associated with the release of *nyama*, the necessary but dangerous force of action in the world. But in spite of the similarity between the role of the bard and that of the transcriber, the stakes change when one focusses on the role of the historian Niane in relation to his oral source.

At the point where Mamadou Kouyaté says "knowledge must be a secret," Niane inserts a footnote that highlights the difference between Kouyaté's philosophy of speaking and Niane's philosophy of writing in French:

Voici une des formules qui revient souvent dans la bouche des griots traditionalistes. Ceci explique la parcimonie avec laquelle ces détenteurs des traditions historiques dispensent leur savoir. Selon eux les Blancs ont rendu la science vulgaire;

---

59. M. M. Diabaté gives the etymology of the griot's name as follows: "Bala Faseke Kuyate: étymologiquement, *Bala* (balafon) *Fasere* (témoin) *Kuyate: kuyante* (il y a un secret de toi à moi). Toi qui as vu mon balafon et l'as joué, il y a un secret entre toi et moi" (Diabaté, *L'Aigle et l'épervier*, 60n.).

quand un Blanc sait quelque chose tout le monde le sait. *Il faudrait que nous arrivions à faire changer cet état d'esprit si nous voulons un jour savoir tout ce que les griots ne veulent pas livrer.* (78–79n, emphasis mine)

Here is one of the dicta that often recurs in the mouths of the traditional griots. This explains the parsimony with which these vessels of historical traditions give their knowledge away. According to them, the Whites have vulgarized knowledge. When a White knows something everybody knows it. *We will have to be able to change this state of mind if we ever want to know all that the griots decline to give away.* (92, n. 51, AT, emphasis mine)

Elsewhere Niane wrote, "Our knowledge . . . will remain incomplete so long as we have not *extracted* from the traditionalists . . . the secrets they hold." [60] Niane is a modern historian (as well as an author of fiction) and as such subscribes to distinctions between history and legend, exaggeration and truth. Writing elsewhere about the Sunjata epics, Niane complains: "It seems that the traditionalists are pleased to surround the great conqueror with mystery, and willfully maintain legendary narratives which, while interesting for those who enjoy epics, leave the historian unsatisfied." [61] At the same time, Niane is concerned with promoting the reputation of the oral tradition in the West, finding "a concern for truth that is entirely to the credit of the griot caste." One notes a slight condescension in his tone, again the need to state that casted griots are capable of truth after all. Niane is caught in the middle, as an African "insider" for Westerners but a professional stranger within the Mande, practicing a form of "permanent transgression." [62] When he speaks of changing the traditionalists' "state of mind," one hears the voice of progress—the hopeful feeling shared by many Africans at the time of Independence, the conviction that Africa could take from its traditional past only what would be useful for advancement, and leave the rest behind. In that same portentous year of 1960, the year of the Independences, Niane also wrote, "We will only get to the truth about the Mande royal family by *entering into the confidence* of the traditionalists, which is certainly not easy, for

60. Niane, *Recherches*, 7, emphasis mine. In a footnote to this remark, Niane allows that it was necessary to seek information outside the area in question, due to the "closed" attitude of certain griots.

61. Niane, "Le Problème de Soundjata," *Notes Africaines* 88 (October 1960): 123.

62. The phrase comes from Mamadou Diawara's fascinating testimony on the ambiguities of being an anthropologist of one's own culture: "Les recherches en histoire orales menées par un autochtone, ou l'inconvénient d'être du cru," *Cahiers d'études africaines* 97, no. 1 (1985): 14. Diawara writes: "Mes informateurs me dévoilent plus volontiers les secrets d'autrui"; "Je suis donc socialement marqué: je suis partout un étranger, même si les traitements en tant que tels varient selon les conditions sociales. Pourtant, je continue à aller à l'encontre de l'ordre des choses, mon métier se confond avec une transgression permanente" (13–14).

quite often they are sworn to secrecy." ("Le Problème," 123, emphasis mine). But Mamadou Kouyaté's message here is categorical: you cannot transcribe and translate me without destroying me. Any attempt to verify the oral tradition using written sources, archeology, or any other means, would sacrilegiously destroy the life of orality and reduce it to the state of writing: dead and mediocre.

Western readers are of course peeping Toms in this affair. By virtue of being able to read Mamadou Kouyaté's words, we know that his fortifications and defenses of the oral world have failed and that he himself is complicit in the reduction of his living words to dead letters. This conflict between tradition and progress comes to a head in the final chapter of Niane's book, titled "The Eternal Mande." Concluding by stating that kings may come and go but that the Mande is eternal, Kouyaté addresses the question of Sunjata's death and of the actual location of the legendary cities of ancient Mali. Mamadou Kouyaté again invokes his privilege of secrecy and actually refuses to go on narrating:

Le Manding garde jalousement ses secrets; il est des choses que le profane ignorera toujours car les griots, leurs dépositaires, ne les livreront jamais. (150)

The Mande keeps its secrets jealously. There are things which the uninitiated will never know, for the griots, their depositaries, will never betray them. (85, AT)

At this point Niane inserts another footnote:

Ici Djeli Mamadou Kouyaté *n'a pas voulu aller plus loin* . . . (150n)

Here Djeli Mamadou Kouyaté *declined to go any further* . . . (95, n. 78)

Niane goes on to explain various theories that can be pieced together, citing a Western historian (Delafosse) and various other traditionalists. Niane's project—of tying together the discourses of traditional orality and modern chronological history—thus makes him frankly disobey the warning Mamadou Kouyaté issues as his last words:

Malheureux, n'essaye point de percer le mystère que le Manding te cache; ne va point déranger les esprits dans leur repos éternel; ne va point dans les villes mortes interroger le passé, car les esprits ne pardonnent jamais: *ne cherche point à connaître ce qui n'est point à connaître.* (152, emphasis mine)

Never try, wretch, to pierce the mystery that the Mande hides from you. Do not go and disturb the spirits in their eternal rest. Do not ever go into the dead cities to question the past, for the spirits never forgive. *Do not seek to know that which is not to be known.* (84, emphasis mine)

The last words of the Niane/Kouyaté collaboration thus mark an impasse between writer and speaker, new and old, history and secrecy. (In spite of Mamadou Kouyaté's warning, Niane led excavations which exposed the site of Sunjata's capital, Niani.)[63]

The Politics and Religion of *Sunjata*

Versions of *Sunjata* are produced dialectically, in a conscious, symbolic relation to changing political and cultural circumstances. This is to say that *Sunjata* is always allegorical, always implying, inciting, insinuating, and teaching. "Only the desire for praise incites men to great actions," says the traditionalist, and this means that the lessons of the past are to be constantly translated into the terms of the present. "Actualization" is therefore basic to the production and the interpretation of *Sunjata*. Two Malian scholars, Sékou Oumar Diarra and Massa Makan Diabaté (a homonymous cousin of the novelist Massa Makan Diabaté), shed this light on Niane's work:

> If Djibril Tamsir Niane shows a great deal of interest in demonstrating the splendor of Sunjata, it is in order to provide a model for the politicians of the young independent states of black Africa, or more specifically for the people of Guinea and their president [Sékou Touré]. . . . *Soundjata* appears as a psychological support, in the face of the enemy's [France's] subversive manoeuvers.[64]

According to Diarra and Diabaté, the versions of *Sunjata* published by Niane and Camara Laye are inevitably addressed to and concerned with Sékou Touré, whose long shadow keeps crossing the chapters of this study. In Niane's *Soundiata*, there is support and praise for a leader against an onslaught of enemies. Again, reading the *future* in Guinean writings of the year 1960, we see the portents of a different enemy: Sékou Touré the tyrant who will imprison Niane from 1961 to 1964 in a one-by-two meter cell and drive him into exile in 1971.[65] In Camara's *Le Maître de la parole*, Diarra and Diabaté see Camara Laye attacking

63. Lilyan Kesteloot, "De Baro à Boiro: Djibril Tamsir Niane," *Notre Librairie* 88/89 (July-September 1987): "Il entreprend des fouilles qui mettent à jour la grande mosquée de Niani et des cases à fondations de pierre dans le quartier royal" (99).

64. Sékou Oumar Diarra and Massa Makan Diabaté, *Etude comparée de trois versions de l'épopée mandingue*, Mémoire de fin d'études, Ecole Normale Supérieure, Bamako, 1982–83, p. 23. They also comment on the same process in Diabaté's *Kala Jata*: "D'abord Kélé Monson Diabaté [the griot who "speaks" in this book] veut altérer l'histoire pour se remettre en valeur et cela partant des liens de fraternité qui unissent les Diabaté et les Traoré. . . . D'autre part *Kala Jata* a été publié en 1970, or nous savons que deux ans avant cette date, un Traoré [Moussa Traoré] a pris le pouvoir au Mali; on serait tenté de croire dans le réhaussement de Tiramaghan [a griot ancestor] par Kélé Monson, à une manière de valoriser le nouvel homme fort" (23).

65. See Kesteloot, "De Baro à Boiro," 97–99.

Touré, who had sent him into exile. It is quite clear who is being referred to in this passage from the end of Camara's introduction:

> Nos hommes politiques d'aujourd'hui, à l'exception de quelques-uns, sont-ils de grands hommes? C'est douteux: ils font de la politique une entreprise sanglante. Ils affament nos peuples, exilent nos cadres, sèment la mort! . . . Ils ne servent pas l'Afrique; ils se servent de l'Afrique; ils ne sont pas précisément des bâtisseurs, des organisateurs, des administrateurs de cités, mais des geôliers qui se comportent avec les femmes, les hommes, les enfants de nos peuples, comme avec du bétail. (34)

> Today, are our political leaders really great? Apart from one or two, it is really doubtful whether they are; they turn politics into a bloody massacre. They starve our peoples, exile our executives, sow death and destruction! . . . They do not serve Africa, they make Africa serve them. They are far from being builders, organizers, city administrators, but are rather jailers who deal with the men, women and children of our peoples as if they were cattle. (32, AT)

Massa Makan Diabaté (the novelist) described *Sunjata* as a "living epic" syncretically adapted by griots to enhance the leader of the moment. Thus when someone named Modibo Kéita was president of Mali in the 1960s, the epic was pressed into service as "a material force and a weapon of mobilization" for him as a descendant of Sunjata; when a Traoré became president, the focus shifted to the glories Sunjata's companion at arms, Tira Magan Traoré. Thus temporal power is able to enhance itself with spiritual power.[66]

One of the most significant dynamics that *Sunjata* participates in is the rise and spread of Islam in the Mande area. The emperor Sunjata can be depicted as either "the first true Muslim sovereign of Mali" (according to Niane) or "a great magician king faithful to the [non-Muslim] heritage of his ancestors" (according to a tradition reported by Vincent Monteil).[67] The griot Wâ Kamissoko declares, "Sunjata was never Muslim!" (in Monteil, *L'Islâm*, 90). But Sunjata *can be* Muslim or animist according to the present designs of the griot.

Muslim or not, the historical Sunjata appears to have acted as a mediator between Muslim and non-Muslim sectors of his expanding empire, laying early groundwork for the syncretic success of Islam in West Africa. The Arab traveller Ibn Battuta found Sunjata's capital to be "a completely Muslim metropolis" in 1352; two hundred years later, Leo Afri-

66. Massa Makan Diabaté, *Le Lion à l'arc*, 22–23.
67. Niane cited in René Luc Moreau, *Africains musulmans: Des communautés en mouvement* (Paris: Présence Africaine, 1982): 92; Monteil, *L'Islâm noir: Une Religion à la conquête de l'Afrique* (Paris: Seuil, 1980): 89–90.

canus found Islam to be flourishing in the Mande.[68] But the masses of the population remained non-Muslim and devoted to their ancestors' forms of worship. So even three hundred years after Leo's visit, the great Mande warrior Samory Touré was still wrestling with the limited efficacy of Islam as a social force: Islam remained for all that time the religion of only a small, privileged elite. The upheavals and migrations of the turbulent nineteenth century—culminating in French conquest—resulted in a great expansion of Muslim conversions, both forced and voluntary.[69] Islam presents West Africans with an alternative: a wholly non-Western system of culture and belief. Yet pre-Islamic traditions show a remarkable ability to survive and flourish both within and alongside Islam. Non-Islamic, non-Western, *indigenous* black African culture interweaves with each successive importation, thereby perpetuating itself. Griots are said to practice a form of cultural dualism or detour, giving lip service to Islam while maintaining Mande autonomy on a deeper level. Legends of the origins of griots cast their ancestors as both the faithful companion and the adversary of the prophet Mohammed.[70]

One of the theatrical versions of the Sunjata story is heavily Islamic in its ideological stance. Ahmed-Tidjani Cissé's *Le Tana de Soumangourou* casts the griot Wâ Kamissoko (whom I have been quoting) as a narrator who opens the play with the following exercise in discursive syncretism:

Gloire à Dieu notre créateur; unique détenteur du destin des astres et des hommes. Gloire au Tout-Puissant qui nous recommande, à nous autres griots, de ne pas fabriquer l'histoire des rois à partir des histoires d'alcôve. (13)

Glory to God our creator, He who alone controls the destiny of the heavens and of men. Glory to the All-Powerful, who advises us griots not to make the history of kings out of idle gossip.

The god of Islam is thus invoked as a super-ego overseeing the Mande oral tradition and the griot's propensity for gossip (this is reminiscent of the role attributed to Islam in the passage I quoted from Kane's *L'Aventure ambiguë* in the introductory chapter). Cissé depicts Soumangourou as a rabid anti-Muslim who promises to "cut off the head of anyone caught prostrating themselves like the Muslims" (27); he combats both

---

68. *Encyclopedia of Islam* (London: Luzac & Co., 1936), s.v. "Mali."

69. See Yves Person, "Samori and Islam," in John Ralph Willis, ed., *Studies in West African Islamic History*, vol. 1, *The Cultivators of Islam* (London: Frank Cass, 1979): 259–77; on the spread of Islam, see also Monteil's *L'Islâm noir*, and for a study of Islam's syncretic impact on West African culture, see René A. Bravmann, *Islam and Tribal Art in West Africa* (Cambridge: Cambridge University Press, 1974).

70. Laura Makarius, "Observations sur la légende des griots malinké," *Cahiers d'études africaines* 36, vol. 9, no. 4 (1969): 630. See also Hugo Zemp, "La légende des griots malinké," *Cahiers d'études africaines* 24, no. 6 (1966): 611–42.

Islam and slave trading. Sunjata is the champion of militant but syncretic Islam, declaring, "Islam lives happily [fait bon ménage] with our traditions" (67). The epic within which this statement occurs—*Sunjata* as a corpus of oral texts—is itself a part of this *bon ménage*, adapting itself as the Mande changes over time.

Orality in Theory

Le raisonnement, la déduction, appartiennent au livre.
—Baudelaire, "L'art philosophique"

Does the syncretic flexibility of the Mande oral tradition exempt it from outside manipulation? Or is this tradition, which is so capable of appropriating and incorporating new realities, itself susceptible to appropriation by non-Mande forces that may compromise its integrity? I will begin addressing this question by invoking a symbol.

There is a street in the Ivory Coast capital city of Abidjan called *Impasse des Griots*, the "Griots' Dead End." Many of the dead-end streets in Abidjan have names referring to traditional African culture and nature (Impasse des Tam-Tams; des Masques; des Manguiers), whereas the avenues and boulevards tend to take their names from Europe and colonial history, as seen in figure 2 (names include Boulevard de France; Avenue

Fig. 2. Street signs in Abidjan, Côte d'Ivoire.

Général-de-Gaulle; Avenue Faidherbe; Avenue Delafosse [Touré, *Civilisation*, 261–65]).[71] The simplest political model we can offer toward interpreting the transition from orality to literacy would take this bit of everyday civilization as its symbol: in contemporary Africa, precolonial culture is a dead-end in the mind of the ruling elite, those who name streets and read books. The world of orality has nothing to contribute to material progress, with which it is incompatible.[72] It is a dead end in and of itself, but it must be *saved*, encompassed, and coopted (*aufgehoben*) so that it may lend its mystique of authenticity to the new order. Progress will come through westernization; prestige will come from westernization but also, as it always has, from association with orality. Political power, like that of Sékou Touré, will carefully appeal to both the old and the new for self-justification. Orality will be elevated and cancelled out, like the masks and religious objects often called "fetishes," removed from

71. The gleaming, modern city of Abidjan is approached from its airport by the Boulevard Valéry Giscard d'Estaing; crossing the Pont du Général de Gaulle, which symbolically parallels the Pont Houphouët-Boigny, one reaches the Boulevard du Général de Gaulle (there is also the Avenue du Général de Gaulle). From there one has a choice of colonial conquistadors: Boulevard Angoulvent or Avenue Marchand, both named for French military men who subjugated the territory. What is the response of those who live among these ghosts of conquests past? As in many African cities, the visitor is struck by the uselessness of street names. People do not know and do not use the names of streets but refer instead to landmarks. In Abidjan, local parlance has produced nicknames that subvert the colonial references: names such as "Dallas" and "Soweto" are used to slip out from under the irrelevance of official culture. In those two nicknames one sees the kind of choices that present themselves: either solidarity with a South African township or the use of American popular culture as a wedge against French high culture. Among the intellectuals of the Ivory Coast, the symbolism of these names has not escaped critique. Léonard Kodjo of the University of Abidjan has analyzed the system of nomenclature in detail, starting from the premise that "to name is to construct, to build, to link, to make over." Names of public spaces "reflect the idea that a people holds regarding its own history, its culture." The avenues of Abidjan "describe a gash, traced in red steel, which obliterates the identity of the city. The central axis, the royal road leading from the south to the north of the city appears as the master's brand, indicating who owns the thing that has been thus marked" ("Noms de rues, noms de maîtres," paper given at the colloquium, "Noms et Appellations en Afrique," University of Abidjan, January 1987). I am grateful to Mr. Kodjo for providing me with a copy of his paper. Symbolically, when I looked for Impasse des Griots in March 1987, the street was unmarked.

72. This attitude is taken in certain UNESCO reports: "The illiterate man's thought . . . remains concrete. He thinks in images and not in concepts. His thought is, in fact, a series of images, juxtaposed or in sequence, and hence it rarely proceeds by induction or deduction. The result is that knowledge acquired in a given situation is hardly ever transferred to a different situation to which it could be applied." "UNESCO Regional Report on Literacy" of 1972, quoted in Sylvia Scribner and Michael Cole, *The Psychology of Literacy* (Cambridge: Harvard University Press, 1981): 14; see also Street, *Literacy*, especially chapter 7: "Unesco and Radical Literacy Campaigns."

Fig. 3. A bookstore in Abidjan, advertising "Inexpensive books—affordable for everyone."

the cultural context in which they were useful, placed in museums as dead artifacts.

From this point of view, the incursion of the book into black Africa is an imperialistic process of conquest and pure loss. Echoing Mamadou Kouyaté, a radical African critic calls the *book* an "appropriation of memory," irrelevant to African reality:

What the book has to say, what use is it for Africa so long as written language is fed by the form of a civilization whose solitude the writer is exposing? . . . [The book] is endowed in Africa with an autonomous power that is almost magical and without any grasp on the everyday reality of Africans.[73]

Another critic points out that the book is "not an innocent commercial 'product' in Africa"; it is still caught in "the dizzying spiral of political mythologies," including elitism, censorship, and irrelevance to peoples' daily lives.[74] In a rapidly-modernized state like the Ivory Coast, the capitalist system nonetheless promises literary democracy, with "inexpensive books, affordable for everyone" (see figure 3).

73. Stanislas Adotevi, *Négritude et négrologues* (Paris: Union Générale d'Editions: 1972): 275.
74. Pius Ngandu Nkashama, "L'Edition et le livre en Afrique," *La Quinzaine littéraire* 435 (March 16–31, 1985): 8–9.

Seen from this radically critical angle, Niane's role as a transcriber-historian is insidious, part of a process of handing African culture over to Western modernity so that it may be packaged and sold as folklore or as history in a Western sense of the term. Orality is betrayed, in this case by a "confidence man" ("entering into the confidence of the traditionalists") and his griot collaborator. The impasse reached at the end of Niane's *Soundjata* would thus manifest the resistance of orality to the superior technical power of literacy and the book. Mamadou Kouyaté's refusal to narrate certain secrets indeed represents a revolt against the process of reification and sublation: he draws a circle within which Mande African culture would remain unscathed, sacred, authentic, and secret.

Such an argument depends, however, on the assumption that orality *on its own terms* is innocent of reification, free of the manipulative binary structures of unequal exchange that we recognize immediately in colonialism and postcolonial Africa. This is a nostalgic view that uses precolonial Africa as the Other of a European mode, be it primitive as opposed to modern, concrete as opposed to abstract, symbolic exchange as opposed to the code of capitalism.[75] Even attempts to describe the so-called intrinsic effects of orality have tended to overemphasize the directness of a totalized, collective, "mechanical solidarity," an immediacy that the Mande tradition—for one—seems to call into question.

Jack Goody, one of the most influential theoreticians of orality, outlines a strategy for circumventing past ethnocentric approaches by stating: "The idea of two distinct approaches to the physical universe [the "Great Divide"] seems scarcely justified"; "In looking at the changes that have taken place in human thought, then, we must abandon the ethnocentric dichotomies that have characterized social thought in the period of European expansion."[76] This is entirely laudable: Goody advocates that the study of nonmodern cultures shift its emphasis away from hypothetical "mentalities"—such as Lévi-Strauss's *bricolage*—toward the study of something more concrete: the difference between orality and literacy. It is not ethnocentric to point out that there are cultures that write and cultures that do not. But one wonders how well Goody suc-

---

75. On symbolic exchange, see Jean Baudrillard, *L'Echange symbolique et la mort* (Paris: Gallimard, 1976). For a relevant critique of Baudrillard, see Joseph Valente, "Hall of Mirrors: Baudrillard on Marx," *Diacritics* 15, no. 2 (Summer 1985): "[Baudrillard's] call to deconstruct and transgress the general code is self-evidently quixotic. . . . He ultimately envisages a spontaneous, impassioned, almost mystical overthow of the general code. . . . In order to make a clean break with the rational finality of the code, Baudrillard is driven to a position unmistakably akin to the noble savage mythos so prevalent during the early stages of capitalism" (62–64).

76. Jack Goody. *The Domestication of the Savage Mind* (Cambridge: Cambridge University Press, 1977): 8–9.

ceeded in escaping ethnocentrism when one reads in his seminal article "The Consequences of Literacy" (written in collaboration with Ian Watt):

> The intrinsic nature of oral communication has a considerable effect upon both the content and the transmission of the cultural repertoire. In the first place, it makes for a *directness* of relationship between symbol and referent. There can be no reference to 'dictionary definitions,' nor can words accumulate the successive layers of historically validated meanings which they acquire in a literate culture. Instead, the meaning of each word is ratified in a succession of *concrete* situations, accompanied by vocal inflections and physical gestures. . . . This process of *direct semantic ratification*, of course, operates cumulatively; and as a result the *totality of symbol-referent relationships is more immediately experienced* by the individual in an exclusively oral culture, and is thus more deeply socialized.[77]

The term "concrete" has strong Lévi-Straussian overtones, as does the assertion that a more "direct" relationship with the referent obtains in oral cultures. Immediacy and directness, a diminished capacity to distinguish signifier and signified (Goody's "symbol" and "referent") have long been touchstones of Western myths of the "primitive." In *The Domestication of the Savage Mind*, Goody develops the idea that there are *intrinsic* differences between oral and written cultures, that "writing makes speech 'objective' " and that " 'traditional' societies are marked not so much by the absence of reflective thinking as by the absence of the proper tools for constructive rumination" (44). While Goody has distanced himself slightly from the ethnocentric vocabulary of the past, he still uses it, between quotation marks, sanitized.[78] Claiming a break with the value-laden and ethnocentric models of the past, Goody has only reconfirmed in a subtler way the superiority of the West as "proper" and "constructive," the proprietor of "thinking."

Goody and Watt further state: "Literate society, merely by having no system of elimination, no 'structual amnesia,' prevents the individual from participating fully in the total cultural tradition to anything like the extent possible in nonliterate society." Again, this presupposes "traditional society" to be homogenous and collective. Literate society, for Goody and Watt, because it does not adapt or omit knowledge, presents

77. Jack Goody and Ian Watt, "The Consequences of Literacy, in Jack Goody, ed., *Literacy in Traditional Societies* (Cambridge: Cambridge University Press, 1968, 29, emphasis mine). Although this article predates *The Domestication*, Goody states in the later text, "I want to pursue an argument that has been outlined elsewhere," presumably in "The Consequences of Literacy."

78. Walter Ong advocates a similar change of vocabulary: "We can avoid the earlier invidious terms [of "primitivism"] by translating the difference between the two poles as that between literate and oral peoples." "Orality-Literacy Studies and the Unity of the Human Race," *Oral Tradition* 2, no. 1 (January 1987): 374.

"the vista of endless choices and discoveries," which can foster "alien-ation" (57). The hapless literate has so much knowledge available to "him" that "the odds are strongly against his experiencing the cultural tradition as any sort of patterned whole" (58). They then resolve the tension by downgrading the power of literacy, asserting that even within literate cultures, oral communication remains "the primary mode of cul-tural orientation" (ibid.). But their vision of orality is primarily nostalgic, in that differentiation is associated only with literacy, wholeness only with orality. They offer no way to conceptualize difference within oral culture.

What does an examination of one specific oral culture do to Goody's model? The supposed "totality" and unity of the Mande tradition, for one, depends entirely on the *mediation* of a caste of bards, who are re-sponsible for preventing the immediacy of the spoken word, which rep-resents a threat. An apprenticeship such as that of a Mande "master of the word," lasting for decades, is surely a sign of differentiation. The endogamous caste of bards as a whole may serve the "collective" needs of Mande society, but it is also a sign of the social differentiation that is supposed to be "intrinsically" absent from an oral culture. Goody and Watt are right to insist on the fundamental importance of literacy as a tool of social change; but by attributing "intrinsic" qualities to writing, they short-circuited their attempt to get away from the "diffuse relativism and sentimental egalitarianism" of Rousseau and the "indivisible whole-ness" of Lévy-Bruhl (68).

The most common gesture made by the West has been to perceive in Africans a people so different that they do not know difference itself. The West has a millennial history of making such theoretical headway by using Africa as a figure of what the West is not. Any and all descriptions of difference between primitive and modern, even between oral and literate, run the risk of forcing upon the Other terms projected out from the Self—the risk of ethnocentrism—and of indulging in value judgments.

There is another argument that therefore needs to be made, an argument that begins by asking, Whose oral tradition is this anyway? In Africa, "word, power and domination are quite often inseparable" (Touré, *Civ-ilisation*, 44); the sacred words of Bamana initiation societies and the words of the griot in Sunjata epics both serve particular elites. An anthro-pological approach tends to rely on texts that may be faulted for "insti-tuting the thought of some as the thought of everyone" in an African culture (Touré, 44): anthropologists have produced images of harmoni-ous African societies by listening only to their male elites. Hence the ho-mogenized "*La*" *Pensée dogon*, "*La*" *Philosophie bantoue*. The political tensions within a precolonial autonomy may thus be ignored in favor of the dominant group: the males, the notables, the nobles, and freemen. We have seen a symbiotic relationship between Mande nobles and the griots that serve them. We can reconstruct rivalries between groups of nobles by listening to other oral texts serving other self-interests. Each will reflect a different "control of the past by the powerful," in Mamadou Diawara's phrase ("Les recherches," 13). But of marginalized groups within the Mande—the women (who are excluded from the most powerful use of orality, the recitation of *Sunjata*), the captives, the slaves, the artisans—we know much less. Theirs is a story that remains secret in another, more literal sense.[79]

The griots' own ambiguous status, along with their function of speaking for others, makes it difficult to see any clear distinction between marginalization and elitism; griots are thought of as both underprivileged and overprivileged.[80] They are allowed within the most powerful circles, but only because they are people of words, not action. Their *difference* allows them to shore up the unity of Mande culture and to justify the subjugation of others whose status is unambiguously inferior.

Niane's role as a Western-trained historian seeking factual illumination is indeed subversive. He risks exposing the self-justification of a power structure built on the subjection of certain tribes or castes.[81] His

79. This inequality in the representation of noble males versus other groups is particularly true in regard to the Mande oral traditions that have found their way into published form, because both *francophonie* and academic anthropology have favored the most prestigious genres; within the whole of Mande orality—including hunters songs, proverbs, and initiation chants, the configuration would be different and in some cases more egalitarian. Gerald Cashion states: "Whereas in Malinke society in general, ethnicity, age, noble birth, freeman status, ... are all hereditary determinants of status or political power, *none of these distinctions apply* within the hunter's society" ("Hunters of the Mande: A Behavioral Code and Worldview Derived from the Study of their Folklore," [Ph.D. diss., Indiana University, 1984, 102, emphasis mine]). For a broader approach to Mande narrative within the Kuranko group of Sierra Leone, see Michael Jackson, *Allegories of the Wilderness: Ethics and Ambiguity in Kuranko Narratives* (Bloomington: Indiana University Press, 1982).

80. Cf. Nicholas S. Hopkins: "The government [of Mali] periodically became concerned with the situation of the members of castes ... , especially the *dieli* [griots], alternatively considering the castes to be underprivileged groups whose status should be raised and overprivileged groups whose privileges needed to be reduced." *Popular Government in an African Town: Kita, Mali* (Chicago: University of Chicago Press, 1972): 20. See this work for interesting information on the role of griots, and the prejudice against them, in the postcolonial politics of Mali (139–40, 128–29).

81. In "Mythes, légendes, et sources orales dans l'oeuvre de Mahmoud Kati" (*Recherches africaines* 1–4 [1964]: 36–42), Niane exposes just such an agenda in a text with oral roots, the *Tarikh el Fettach*: "le mythe ... apparaît nettement comme une justification des structures sociales existantes, une explication de l'existence des castes serviles. ... Ces tribus successivement esclaves des Mansa du Mali et des Rois du Gao, tireraient leur origine

resistance to the secrecy of orality could lead him to a demystifying critique of precolonial society. That demystification is, however, a function of the Western discourse of history that Niane has assimilated. Western readers, knowing about orality only what is written in books, are twice removed from the truth of Mande orality: first through the process of transcription and translation, which suggests loss and betrayal; second through the traditional Mande attitude toward knowledge and power, which favors secrecy. The appropriation of orality for our literate purposes may be represented as a betrayal, but it is interesting that that betrayal echoes and repeats *ironically* the transformation of silence into speech by Mande griots. Literacy may be in the process of appropriating orality, but orality has been appropriating silence "since time immemorial."

I am aware that chips have fallen here in such a way as to create ghostly echoes with the Western philosophical tradition. It has been pointed out that the Mande mistrust of the spoken word is downright "Platonic."[82] Sory Camara's paraphrase of his culture's attitude sometimes sounds like Rousseau talking: "Although the organ of speech is natural to man, speech itself is not natural to him."[83] Faced with this predominant view, which is hostile to the difference that speech engenders, the griots are an oppositional group who thrive on difference. Their work might be interpreted as an example of what Derrida calls *archi-écriture*, his trademark for a generalized notion of difference, inscribed in all language whether spoken or written, implying violence, division, and the impossibility of total presence.

My argument against Jack Goody has in fact run parallel to what Derrida wrote about Lévi-Strauss's anthropology in *De la grammatologie*. Goody's insistence on "directness," taken in Derrida's terms, is a logocentric—and therefore invalid—form of anti-ethnocentrism, which works by projection, nostalgia, and the ignorance of its own condition.

de femmes esclaves de Noé. . . . En sorte que les Empereurs du Mali et les Rois du Gao n'étaient que les héritiers d'un ordre social établi depuis Noé! Personne n'aura à se reprocher un état de fait dont l'origine remonte dans la nuit des temps." Niane is nonetheless careful to plead for understanding of this maneuver: "Aujourd'hui nous comprenons aisément le sentiment qui poussait un Virgile à faire descendre Auguste de la déesse Vénus et du prince troyen Enée; ayons la même disposition devant Mahmoûd Kâti ou Babou Condé [the latter being the griot recorded and transcribed by Camara Laye in *Le Maître de la parole*] quand ceux-ci rattachent les rois, leurs bienfaiteurs à quelques héros de légende du monde arabe" (39–42).

82. Jacques Cochin, review of Sory Camara's *Gens de la parole, Notre Librairie* 88/89 (July-September 1987): 183.

83. Jean-Jacques Rousseau, "Discours sur l'origine de l'inégalité," in *The Political Writings of Jean-Jacques Rousseau* (New York: John Wiley & Sons, 1962): 209.

For Derrida, there is no society without "writing" (in his sense) and without violence; only a deluded anthropology leads one to believe that there is. The value of Derrida's work must be recognized here, along with its relevance to a Western reading of Mande tradition: given the opposition set up by Derrida (against Lévi-Strauss and Rousseau), between total difference (endlessly self-regenerating *différance, écriture*) and total presence (the vision of an ethical utopia-of-the-voice), one must admit that he has a point.[84] Recognition of hierarchization, internal opposition, and deferral within the cultural system of the Mande has been fundamental to what we have seen here. Reading Sory Camara, Abdoulaye-Bara Diop, Abdou Touré, and others has made it necessary to recognize difference.

But the entanglement of our reading with Western philosophemes is a treacherous, and ultimately frustrating, exercise. To assimilate Mande griots to a certain Western school would be folly and would do them no great honor. There are indeed echoes; of course we find configurations that seem to replicate Western debates. But this is a case where the Western debate is not at all inscribed in the African corpus we have been studying—it is instead an alien projection. Its real relevance here is as part of my own intellectual background. The essential point is that here, as elsewhere, the Western debate imposes a false opposition on the interpretation of African culture: total difference or total identity. Too many

---

84. See Jacques Derrida, "La violence de la lettre: de Lévi-Strauss à Rousseau," in *De la grammatologie* (Paris: Minuit, 1967):149–202. The problem with what Derrida does in this chapter is that he so powerfully invalidates Lévi-Strauss's work that he seems to throw out the baby with the bathwater, that is, all of anthropology *and ethics* with "logocentric" anti-ethnocentrism. Finding the "*éthique* de la parole vive" to be "un leurre" (201), Derrida disallows (for himself and his followers) the value of "social authenticity." The latter collapses into a form of totalitarianism that permits no difference and is therefore a travesty of ethics, because (to take up the point I arrived at in chapter 2) "Il n'y a pas d'éthique sans présence *de l'autre*" (202). But in continuing the same sentence, Derrida imposes the conditions under which he will allow the ethics of difference to be thought: " . . . mais aussi et par conséquent sans absence, dissimulation, détour, différance, écriture." Here we reach the "ouverture non-éthique de l'éthique," the point at which ethics is deconstructed, and any request for "an ethics" (or an authenticity or an anthropology) becomes naïve (see chapter 2, note 75). The attempt at an ethical description of the other has only one example in the chapter, that of Lévi-Strauss; his embarassing failure seems to have fatally compromised anthropology as a whole. This text of Derrida's is thus at the root of deconstruction's mistrust of systems and cultural descriptions (see, for example, my description of my student's attitude toward the "veil" between cultures, in the introduction, p. 10). It is here that the door slams shut, and the critique of totalitarian systems engenders a form of tunnel vision, a refusal to see anything but patented *différance*. The question left unanswered is one of ethical *distinctions* (in the face of *différance*) and of the non-totalizing description of *systems* of culture. For an extended analysis of Derrida's reading of Lévi-Strauss, leading to a different conclusion, see Tobin Siebers, *The Ethics of Criticism* (Ithaca, N.Y.: Cornell University Press, 1988): chapter 4, "Ethics in the Age of Rousseau: From Lévi-Strauss to Derrida," 69–97.

discussions of African literature turn around this same manichean choice, forgetting what seems to me the only interesting task: the analysis of particular configurations of culture, which are most likely to involve compromises *between* identity *and* difference. Of course there is a "quest for identity" in the Mande verbal arts; of course it takes place within a structure of difference. If the echoes of certain Western traditions help to analyze these configurations, so much the better; when they cease to be helpful, they should be left behind.[85]

Appendix: Caste in the Novel

The question of caste distinctions is a political and social hot potato in countries of the Sahel such as Sénégal and Mali. It is only in recent years that intellectuals have begun to discuss the problem in print. In the colonial period, when opposition to a common oppressor made unity among Africans imperative, it would obviously have been imprudent to dwell on the cleavages and prejudices that exist within traditional African societies. Europeans were too eager to conclude that "tribalism" and "feudalism"—vestiges of a past that Europe claimed to share with Africa—continued in Africa. But as African intellectuals begin to address each other more than the West, as the preoccupation with the Western "image of Africa" recedes ever so slightly, these social and cultural questions are finding their way into literature. Two novels by Ousmane Sembène serve to illustrate the two moments: first the confrontation with the colonizer, then the airing of internal differences.

In Sembène's classic novel of the colonial period *Les Bouts de bois de Dieu*, the ideological emphasis is on the solidarity of all those associated with a strike against the Dakar-Niger railroad. Distinctions of caste (and, in A.-B. Diop's terms, of "order") are mentioned, but the most important distinction, that between slaves and freemen, is complicated by the issue of being "enslaved" to the French railroad company. In the colonial context, slavery is redefined as a state of mind: "The real slaves aren't those who are taken by force, chained and sold as slaves, but those who accept

85. Karin Barber experimented with the application of deconstructive criticism to one form of African oral poetry in "Yoruba *Oríkì* and Deconstructive Criticism," *Research in African Literatures* 19, no. 4 (1984): 497–518. She found, first, that deconstruction was "so appropriate that it could have been modelled" on the Yoruba *oríkì* in question and many other oral texts (512); but, after further consideration of the issues, Barber finds that the appropriateness is only "superficial" and that deconstruction "rules out all the significant questions—ultimately questions about power and ideology—that are raised so insistently by *oríkì*" and reduces the "thinking critic/author . . . to impotent self-reflection" (513–14). She seems to conclude, as I do, that deconstruction is a useful but not sufficient component within the process of reading African literatures.

slavery morally and physically."[86] This idea comes from a character named Bakayoko, who is criticized for being too "theoretical;" the criticism comes from characters who are still concerned with the old sense of slavery and caste: "Besides, this has really got nothing to do with me, *I'm* not lower-caste," says one character, to which his friend replies, "You think that I am? I am a smith by birth and by trade, and if my parents were forced to accept a low condition because of circumstances, I still won't be anybody's slave" (45–46).

Between Bakayoko's use of the word "slave" and the use to which it is put by these two other characters, there is a world of difference: the difference between a modern world of shifting, ideological meanings and a traditional realm in which heredity and activity are supposed (by these characters) to determine meanings independent of interpretation. *Les Bouts de bois de Dieu* describes a world in which, in Marx's words, "all that is solid melts into air, all that is holy is profaned, and men at last are forced to face . . . the real conditions of their lives and their relations with their fellow men."[87] A character named Keïta sums it up:

Il y a bien longtemps . . . bien avant votre naissance, les choses se passaient dans un ordre qui était le nôtre, et cet ordre avait une grande importance pour la vie de chacun. Aujourd'hui, tout est mélangé. Il n'y a plus de castes, plus de griots, plus de forgerons, plus de cordonniers, plus de tisserands. Je pense que c'est l'oeuvre de la machine qui brasse tout ainsi.

A long time ago . . . well before your birth, things happened within an order that was ours, and this order had a great importance for everyone's life. Today, everything is mixed up. There are no more castes, no more griots, no more smiths, no more shoemakers, no more weavers. I think that it's the working of machines that blends everything together like this. (153–54)

It is not by chance that Sembène's novel follows the pattern described by Marx. The real conditions of life are determined by the machine—the locomotive—, and in *Les Bouts de bois*, this is not seen as a negative thing. The machine destroys tradition, but tradition was corrupt and inequitable; the machine equalizes, "mashing" everything together. The theorist Bakayoko says it: "The man that we were is dead, and we can only save ourselves for a new life through the machine, which has no language, no race" (127). Without language or race, the machine liquidates distinctions and renews the world. The political action of *Les Bouts de bois* points to a renewed world without caste, class, or gender, but

---

86. Ousmane Sembène, *Les Bouts de bois de Dieu* (Paris: Presses Pocket, 1960): 45.

87. Quoted in Marshall Berman, *All That Is Solid Melts into Air* (New York: Simon and Schuster, 1982): 21.

stops short of utopia. Bakayoko's vision of a new life remains as only a vision, a model.

Twenty years later, Sembène published *Le Dernier de l'Empire*, a two-volume novel describing a political crisis that is brought on by the prospect of a person of caste assuming the presidency of a country like Sénégal. After two decades of independence, the machine of modernization has failed to eradicate the caste system. Regarding the succession, capability is only one factor:

—*Joom Gallé*, ne sais-tu pas qu'en ton absence, Daouda ne peut pas remplacer le Vénérable . . . ni être président.
—Pourquoi? Daouda est plus capable que beaucoup de gens de ton groupe.
—Il ne s'agit pas de cela. Daouda est un casté. Et cela le peuple ne l'avalera pas.[88]

"*Joom Gallé*, don't you know that in your absence, Daouda can't replace the Venerable One, nor be president?"
"Why? Daouda is more capable than many people in your group."
"It doesn't matter. Daouda is a person of caste, and the people won't swallow that."

Daouda is the son of a griot (1: 101). A nobleman gives up his government post rather than work under him (1: 222). The very word caste has "the effect of a cold shower" (1: 135). According to the constitution, Daouda as Prime Minister will succeed to the presidency, but he is opposed by the finance minister Mam Lat Soukabé, a nobleman with "a prestigious name that local history, from generation to generation, had enriched and readapted, a name with which he identified" (1: 100). And it happens that the prime minister's father was the griot, and therefore the subservient, of the finance minister's father: there has been an "unnatural" reversal of the hierarchy. There are those *Modernes* in the novel who believe that all questions of caste must be swept aside, but the effect of the novel is to make *public*—i. e., readable, accessible throughout the world—a problem within the African political family.

In *Le Miroir de la vie*, Aminata Maïga Ka, one of Senegal's women novelists, describes a similar conflict, but within the realm of the family rather than in politics. The noble Madame Cissé's daughter wants to marry the son of Madame's *griotte* Astou Mbaaye, in a forbidden marriage:

Non, ce n'était pas possible que sa fille Ndèye, si douce, si gentille, noble par son père et par sa mère, s'abaissât à commettre une telle mésalliance, en épousant un homme de caste! . . . "Je préférerais mourir plutôt que de me souiller en envisa-

---

88. Ousmane Sembène, *Le Dernier de l'Empire* (Paris: L'Harmattan, 1981): I: 128.

geant une mésalliance avec un homme qui ne peut oser m'approcher que pour recevoir mes dons! . . . As-tu seulement pensé aux enfants que vous aurez?"[89]

No, it wasn't possible that her daughter Ndèye, so sweet, so nice, noble by both her father and her mother, would lower herself to committing such a misalliance, by marrying a man of caste! . . . "I would sooner die than soil myself by envisioning a misalliance with a man who can dare approach me only to receive gifts from me! . . . Have you given any thought to the children you will have?"

The similarity between this prejudicial discourse and the thought patterns of racism as we know them in the United States makes it less surprising that Abdoulaye-Bara Diop, in his ethnography of the Wolof, concludes that the caste system amounts to a form of racism.[90]

89. Aminata Maïga Ka, *La Voie du salut suivi de Le Miroir de la vie* (Paris: Présence Africaine, 1985): 160–64.

90. *La Société wolof: Tradition et changement* (Paris: Karthala, 1981): Diop describes racism as "always mythological," always trying to pass the cultural (i. e. social stratifications) off as *biological* (see 38–45).

4

L'Enfant noir, Totemism, and Suspended Animism

Camara Laye, Laye Camara

The texts that we have examined so far have been closely tied to tradition. Yet in the process of reading transcribed oral texts, we found that the tensions of colonial and postcolonial politics, overt or latent, were already present. Now if we wish to talk about the *novel* in Africa, and if we want to be precise in our use of terms, what distinguishes transcribed oral texts from novels? I mentioned earlier that Niane's *Soundjata* is often referred to and interpreted as a novel; its title page bears the single name of Djibril Tamsir Niane, making no mention of the oral author Mamadou Kouyaté. The name of a single author, legally responsible for the text that follows, belongs to the domain of written literature; the fragmented authorship and deferred authority of an oral text, inherited and modified, belongs to a different notion of originality and creation. Transcriber-historians, under pressure from their griots, are now sharing, "decolonizing," their title pages.[1]

Individual versus collective authorship is thus one of the watersheds between Western and African notions of literature, between traditional and modern African literatures, between orality and literacy. It has been used to explain the recurrent accusations of plagiarism or imitativeness that have troubled the African literary scene.[2] This opposition is both a

1. E. g., *The Epic of Son-Jara: A West African Tradition*, analytical study and translation by John William Johnson; text by Fa-Digi Sisòkò (Bloomington: Indiana University Press, 1986). The title page also names five individuals who helped transcribe and translate the text.

2. Cf. Jabbi Bu-Buakei, "Influence and Originality in African Writing," *African Literature Today* 10 (1979): 106–23; Donatus I. Nwoga, "Plagiarism and Authentic Creativity in West Africa," *Research in African Literature* 6, no. 1 (1975): 32–39; Christopher L. Miller, "Dis-figuring Narrative: Plagiarism and Dismemberment in Yambo Ouologuem's *Le Devoir de violence*," in *Blank Darkness: Africanist Discourse in French* (Chicago: University of Chicago Press, 1985): 216–45; Wole Soyinka, "From a Common Back Cloth: A

truth and a truism: it is grounded in real evidence, but too much is often made of it, and, as in Goody's interpretation of orality, it becomes a Trojan horse for the self-congratulation or guilt of the West.

In approaching francophone novels of the Mande, we should bear this opposition in mind as a question rather than a foregone conclusion. We take it for granted in the West (or we used to) that the novel, particularly the autobiographical novel, both illustrates and performs "individuation," the coming into individual selfhood. (If we contradict this, it is a consciously subversive move.) Without even considering the theme of individualism in the African novel, thinking only of the sociology of novel production, we must pose a number of questions. Africans who have written novels are people who have detached themselves from traditional society or who were detached from it, who went to French school and learned to write as individuals. Writing, as it was imported to Africa by colonialism, would indeed appear to be less collective than speaking. From the individual compositions written in school to the published works of a professional writer, each written text bears a single name.

An author's name must bear a considerable legal and philosophical burden. It must be different from all other names in some way; the author must be an individual. If name alone does not eliminate confusion, then in the libraries of the West we attach birth dates and other identifying marks. The legal status of copyright depends on a legal notion of individual identity, backed up by the techniques of literate culture: birth certificates, identity cards, signatures. Although there are certainly such things as collective works, these are built on a notion of multiple individuality; and it is important to note that novels and poems are almost never collective works in the modern Western literary tradition.[3] Since it is only through written documentation that the literate societies of the West—the colonizing powers—recognize and confer legal identity, the oral societies of Africa, when colonized, were bound to be radically altered in their mechanisms for giving identity, perhaps in their very notion of identity. When the French system of direct rule—seeking total control and standardization—imposed itself on the ancient societies of West Africa, how much of the old system was destroyed by the new one? And how can the postcolonial reader see through various layers of conflicting systems?

Reassessment of the African Literary Image," *The American Scholar* 32, no. 3 (Summer 1963): 387–96. The last article concerns what Soyinka calls "imitativeness" in the relation between Camara's *Le Regard du roi* and Kafka's *Castle*.

3. If they are collective in any way, we explain it as intertextuality, allusion, influence, imitation, or plagiarism.

Personal names are a reflection of cultural politics, bearing the mark of Christianity, Islam, and local cultures. The order and usage of names varies widely from culture to culture in Africa, even in those places where Islam and Christianity have imposed standardized "first" names by the millions. The order of the names does not necessarily give the outsider a clue as to proper usage. In the Mande, we have already seen the importance of the family name or *jamu*; to address people by their *jamu* is to invoke the identity that their genealogy defines; *jamu* is synomymous with honor. But because there are so many individuals with the same *jamu*, the given names or *tògò* must be used for differentiation. It is common therefore to use the first two names alone to refer to a person whose *jamu* has been established in the context: thus "Massa Makan" instead of "Diabaté." Within the confines of the Mande, *jamu, tògò*, and Islamic given names are recognizable as such, so that word order in names need not be confusing. Camara is one of the Mande *jamuw*; Laye is an Islamic given name, a shortened form of Abdoulaye.[4] But outside the Mande, the distinction is lost and confusion reigns, a confusion that is symptomatic of the clash between the West and Africa.

All of the leading works on African literature refer to Camara Laye as "Laye," although none of them would call Gordimer "Nadine" or Soyinka "Wole."[5] Almost alone among critics, Eric Sellin states: "His real

4. The correct usage is illustrated in *L'Enfant noir* by this passage, in which the boy-narrator explains his jovial exchange of greetings with one of his aunts: [The aunt says,] "'Voici que tu as encore fait attendre Mme. Camara nº 3!' Madame Camara nº 3, c'était le nom qu'elle donnait à Marie . . . 'Bonjour madame Camara nº 3, disais-je.' 'Bonjour, *Laye*, répondait-elle.'" *L'Enfant noir* (Paris: Plon, 1953): 181–82; emphasis mine; trans. James Kirkup and Ernest Jones, *The Dark Child* (New York: Farrar, Strauss and Giroux, 1954): 160. Further references to the novel and this translation, respectively, will be included in the text. Altered translations will be marked "AT."

5. However, Adele King points out that "Camara is the family name," ("Camara Laye," in B. King and K. Ogungbesan, eds., *A Celebration of Black and African Writing* [London: Oxford University Press, 1975]: 123n); and Eloise Bière refers to "the Camara family," in "*L'Enfant noir* by Camara Laye: Strategies in Teaching an African Text," *The French Review* 55, no. 6 (May 1982): 808; Mohamadou Kane indexes him under C, in *Roman africain et tradition* (Dakar: Nouvelles Editions Africaines, 1982): 502. Sonia Lee writes, in *Camara Laye* (Boston: Twayne, 1984): "The author's real name is actually Laye Camara, sometimes spelled Kamara. However, all his work is published under Camara Laye, which is the name he was given by the colonial school system." Maurice Delafosse, in an article concerning a time and place still mainly beyond the reach of French schools, confirms that the original order is 1) individual name, 2) *jamu*: "En fait, il est d'usage chez certaines populations ouest-africaines, telles que les Ouolofs, les Toucouleurs, les Mandingues [Mande], les Sarakollé, de faire suivre le nom d'un individu, quand on parle de lui, de son *snta* ou *yettôdé* ou *diamou* [jamu] . . . , absolument comme, chez nous, on fait suivre le prénom du nom de famille" ("Des soi-disant clans totémiques de l'Afrique Occidentale," *Revue d'ethnographie et des traditions populaires* 1 [1920]: 105).

name is Laye CAMARA."[6] How did this happen? There are several plausible explanations. One is that the reversal of names is the result of French regimentation, which uses the order *nom-prénom* for official documentation: "Lacombe Lucien."[7] Another explanation refers to the fact that Arabic script reads from right to left; "the confusion arises from the incompatibilities between the European and Arabic scripts which procede in opposite directions" (Sellin, "Alienation," 471). Whatever the explanation may be, the reversal of correct usage in Camara Laye's names is now institutionalized, inscribed on all his publications, indexed in all the bibliographies, with the exception of certain research libraries that catalogue him under C. Although it may be somewhat perverse to do so at this late date, I will swim against the current here and refer to the author by his *jamu*, Camara, as I attempt to show that the relation to the father's *jamu* is a paramount issue in *L'Enfant noir*.

Since his initial literary triumph in the early 1950s, Camara has thus been called by a name other than his family name. This is not so much a "mistake" as a gesture with certain symbolic significance in the context. Critics have ignored the name that evokes the author's identity in the Mande tradition, the name that ties him to the world he describes in *L'Enfant noir*. The family name, identifying the person by ethnic group, clan, and caste, is usurped by the given name, which individuates within the group but is meaningless as a key to identity within the collective as a whole. This is not the result of any conspiracy to rob Camara Laye of his identity; in the context of colonialism and colonial publishing, no conspiracy was necessary. It is a consequence of literacy, of writing and reading an author's name. There is nothing wrong in the word order "Camara Laye," no need for the author to correct it on the page proofs; it is in the usage of the names as *French* names that things have been altered. It is hard not to think that something has been lost, namely the symbolic power of the name Camara. Our question thus becomes: can we read "Camara" through, with the help of and also in spite of everything that has been written about "Laye"—can we see the Mande through and in the French words of this novel?

We must start from the premise that the "identity" of a Mande writer of Camara's generation is firmly connected to the devices and processes of the oral tradition that we examined here earlier. At the same time, the problem with Camara's name should alert us to the first hurdle of infor-

6. Eric Sellin, "Alienation in the Novels of Camara Laye," *Pan-African Journal* 4, no. 4 (Fall 1971): 471. Sellin follows convention, however, in refering to the author as "Laye" throughout his article.

7. The young French Nazi collaborator in Louis Malle's film *Lacombe Lucien* carries the practice over into the oral realm by introducing himself in this fashion.

mation and misinformation that we must jump, the possible distortions imposed by the transition to literate expression. If the author's very name has been more or less mistaken for decades, we have to wonder how far the distortion carries. Could it be that not only the author's name and identity but also his thoughts and words may have been adulterated? Within a system that claims and desires total control, the system of colonialism, what degree of hegemony can actually be imposed? Is any published source from the colonial period to be considered suspect, tainted by French sponsorship and interference? To what extent could an African writer, particularly at the apogee of colonial power in the early 1950s, manipulate European forms; to what extent was he restricted to generic, grammatical, rhetorical, even ideological norms?

These questions would be best answered by delving into the files of Paris publishing houses. The story of publication and rejection of African manuscripts in the colonial period is one that has not yet been told. In the case of Camara Laye, we have one bit of information to work with: we know that Camara's original title, *Enfant de Guinée*, was changed to *L'Enfant noir* by the publishers. They must have felt that racial generality was more appealing than national particularism. It is interesting to note that the most precise title, *Enfant du Mande*, was not even considered.[8] Ironically, French publishers were seeking universality in the 1950s, whereas in the 1980s they have decided that the specificity of national literatures is the order of the day. It is one thing for African authors to identify their works as *national*, as "Senegalese" or "Congolese" novels; it is quite another for editors in Paris to "encourage" or impose literary nationalism. The latter is precisely what was done to novels published in the 1980s by Jean-Pierre Makouta M'Boukou and Ismaila Samba Traoré.[9] This is in keeping with a pattern in the literary history of francophone African, a movement away from allegorical idealizations (such as

8. The question of national literatures is a topic of current debate, divided between critics such as Mohamadou Kane of Senegal, who advocates broad cultural and traditional categories he calls "aires culturelles" (cf. John William Johnson's use of the word "nation" in reference to the Mande; see above, p. 75) and critics like Adrien Huannou, for whom national literatures are already a fact. See Kane, *Roman africain et tradition* (Dakar: Nouvelles Editions Africaines, 1982); Huannou, *La Littérature béninoise de langue française* (Paris: Karthala and ACCT, 1984); and *Notre Librairie*'s series of special issues on national literatures in Africa: 83 (April-June 1986); 84 (July-September 1986); and 85 (October-December 1986).

9. *Les Exilés de la forêt vierge* by Makouta M'Boukou was subtitled "roman congolais" by its publishers, L'Harmattan, without the author's approval; *Les Ruchers de la capitale* by Traoré was subtitled "roman malien" by the same publishers, also without consulting the author. These books are thus made to participate in a nationalization process with which their authors may or may not wish to associate themselves. My thanks to Makouta M'Boukou and Traoré for this information.

Negritude), toward analytical specifics, nations, and ethnic allegiances. But the underlying problem is Parisian control of African literary life.

I do not mean to suggest that *L'Enfant noir* was rewritten by its editors, although rumors to that effect have circulated among critics. But between rewriting and simple "stylistic" editing, there is much room for ambiguity and adjustment. It would not be surprising if the prose of a young African factory worker had been retouched and "improved" by benevolent editors mindful of their duty to protect the French language against *barbarismes,* hoping to ensure the success of the novel.[10] It is not until 1968, with the publication of *Les Soleils des indépendances,* in Montréal and not in Paris, that the standard is broken and difference is allowed outside the bounds of quotations marks. We can only speculate as to the manuscripts that were rejected or altered in the early years of francophone African literature.

But if it is suggested that adherence to a French standard (or to standard French) was imposed by editors, it must also be acknowledged that the imposition can come from within the author, through his or her internalization of the standard. French schools taught not only French grammar but the "grammar" of colonial ideology, along with its "genealogy," which taught colonized children the world over to respect "their [sic] ancestors the Gauls." Camara himself described this influence or inculcation as the imprint of "the Classics" on his style. "There is no fruit without a tree," he remarked in an interview, "We are obliged to follow the advice we got in school."[11] The tree is the system of French colonial schools; the fruit is the francophone novel.

10. Blair asserts that the manuscript "underwent a certain amount of stylistic editing," *African Literature in French* (Cambridge: Cambridge University Press, 1976): 198.
    11. "Chacun a son maître, et je puis dire que Flaubert est le mien. . . . Evidemment, c'est ce que je disais: 'il n'y a pas de fruit sans arbre!' Depuis l'école primaire, on a lu *Le Grand Meaulnes*; on a lu tous les Classiques, *c'est ce que l'on faisait en Afrique. . . .* Comme [la tradition orale] n'est pas encore étudié[e] à fond, nous sommes obligés de suivre les conseils que nous avons reçus à l'école. Donc, *nous sommes obligés d'écrire comme eux, les Classiques*" (Jacqueline Leiner, "Interview avec Camara Laye," *Présence francophone* 10 [Spring 1975]: 155–56, emphasis mine). The basic facts of Camara Laye's biography are the following: born in Kouroussa, Guinea, in 1928, Laye was one of ten children; his educational trajectory took him from Koranic school to French (colonial) primary school, to a technical institute in Conakry, then to two different technical academies in France—his education was not "literary." Employed as a worker at a Simca factory, Camara wrote *L'Enfant noir* in his spare time; it won the Charles Veillon Prize. His brilliantly humorous and mystical second novel, *Le Regard du roi,* appeared only a year later, in 1954. In 1956 he returned to Guinea and began to work in various positions of public service. *Dramouss,* an autobiographical sequel to *L'Enfant noir* that tells of his return and subsequent disillusionment, was not well received by critics, nor was it appreciated by the regime of Sékou Touré, whom it criticized. Camara fled Guinea rather than submit to changing the manu-

I raise these problems here in order to further the sense of uncertainty and tentativeness that should characterize our approach to the seemingly straightforward and simple text of *L'Enfant noir*. For the "identity" of the author is often called into question in Western literature—literature itself seems to problematize the relation of a subject to identity through language—but it is rarer that the identity of the text need be called into question. It would be strange indeed for there to be a heated debate over whether a certain novel is "really French" or "really American" (although such debates were of course fought in the past). But in any number of veiled or overt forms, the question of identity is constantly thrown at the African text: commentators and critics, both African and Western, working from any number of ideological definitions of "Africa," "Africanity," or "the African personality," expect their notion to be revealed and honored in literary texts. Quarrels result when texts do not adhere and models clash; often the disagreements have a specifically political character. It is important, therefore, to study the peculiar reputation of *L'Enfant noir*, the strange ambivalence that surrounds it.

The Fallen Idyll

When *L'Enfant noir* first appeared in 1953, it was received with adulation in France and won the Charles Veillon prize. The Western critics who have written on *L'Enfant noir* have focussed on themes of alienation, individualism and collectivity, autobiography, "timeless values," social context: in general the Western approach has been to accept the novel's apparent political quiescence at face value, to concentrate on the text itself as a social and psychological document.[12] But that documentary approach has not led most critics beyond a superficial reading of the text; they have not delved into other documents that enrich one's understanding of the Mande context (many of which, to be fair, were simply not available).[13] The dominant interpretation sees *L'Enfant noir* as a text

---

script, and lived in Dakar, Senegal, from 1965 until his death from kidney disease in 1980. During his exile, he published his last work, *Le Maître de la parole*.

12. See Paul R. Bernard, "Individuality and Collectivity: A Duality in Camara Laye's *L'Enfant noir, The French Review* 52, no. 2 (December 1978): 313–24; Blair, *African Literature*, 194–96; Lilyan Kesteloot, *Black Writers in French: A Literary History of Negritude* (Philadelphia: Temple University Press, 1974): 324; Jacques Chevrier, *Littérature nègre* (Paris: Armand Colin, 1984): 108.

13. There is one notable exception, an anthropological reading of *L'Enfant noir* within Mande blacksmith culture: Jacques Bourgeacq's *"L'Enfant noir" de Camara Laye: Sous le signe de l'éternel retour* (Sherbrooke, Québec: Naaman, 1984), henceforth referred to as *Eternel retour*. Bourgeacq puts anthropological information to creative use and sheds a

of "happy moderation" (Kesteloot, *Black Writers*, 324). Arguments then arise as to the legitimacy and value of the happiness that the novel is supposed to depict, with African critics, at least in the 1950s, differing sharply from Western ones.

The purpose of the text, according to general agreement, is the description and preservation of "African" values, even if the analysis of those values as systems of local knowledge has been lacking. Although *L'Enfant noir* ostensibly describes a traditional African culture, it has been read more as an assault on specificity than as a support for it: "At the end of this book," writes a French journalist, "filled with tenderness and filial love, giving the image of a collective peasant mentality that is no longer strange or primitive, one has the impression that the African and his tribe are a man and a society like any other."[14] Such a characterization does not seem to be aberrent to Camara Laye's view of the world as he articulated it in an interview: "Man is the same everywhere, on all continents."[15]

But the novelist's personal view of things may not act as a real limitation on his work. I will argue here that the apparent happiness, universal sameness, and simplicity of this novel are figures within a more complex scheme that remains to be understood, and that the meaning of the novel is not evident or simple at all. This can be guessed from reading the same critics who think *L'Enfant noir* is happy. Dorothy Blair writes: "Laye has rejected all but the happy memories of a childhood in which the basic elements were love and mystery, and *his only dilemma* was whether to continue his studies in a Western institution and a technological discipline, and so *to associate himself irrevocably with an alien civilization*, or to join his father in the goldsmith's workshop and become an initiate

---

good deal of light on the text; his stated motivations are much the same as mine, to contextualize the novel and resist its assimilation to Western norms (8). I have one reservation about this work: that the author too hastily assimilates different discourses to each other. Camara Laye's novel, Germaine Dieterlen's ethnography of the Mande, and Mircea Eliade's "universal" theories about forging are rapidly stitched together. Eliade commands the interpretive level, as the "theorist" so often does; this is a problem I will discuss in this chapter with reference to Lévi-Strauss and the appeal of a "general level." In addition, Bourgeacq was not able to benefit from the work of Patrick McNaughton, whose *The Mande Blacksmiths: Knowledge, Power, and Art in West Africa* (Bloomington: Indiana University Press, 1988) was not yet published. I will refer to McNaughton's book as *MS*. Also see Robert Philipson, "Literature and Ethnography: Two Views of Manding Initiation Rites," in Kofi Anyidoho, ed., *Interdisciplinary Dimensions of African Literature*, Annual Selected Papers of the African Literature Association, no. 8 (1982): 171–181.

14. Claude Wauthier, *L'Afrique des Africains: inventaire de la négritude* (Paris: Seuil, 1964), 73–74.

15. Leiner, "Interview," 156.

into the sacred mysteries of his craft" (*African Literature*, 195, emphasis mine). This "only dilemma" is hardly a trivial matter in the novel; the dilemma and its consequences color all aspects of the narrative, produce considerable anguish, and form its very condition of possibility. Blair again reveals the crucial problem by glossing it over when she writes: "Because he succeeds in his evocation of a mythic, universal super-reality that gives meaning to existence, *even when it is only half comprehended*, *L'Enfant noir* deserves to be included in the outstanding works of fiction of the twentieth century" (196, emphasis mine).[16] If that which gives meaning is only half comprehended, how reliable can the preservation of values be in *L'Enfant noir*? Does this not undercut the text's whole raison d'être?

Meanwhile, some African critics have also seen in *L'Enfant noir* a "simple" work, one in which the author "doesn't deal with 'problems.'"[17] But most Africans have resoundingly disagreed with Western critics as to whether simplicity and quiescence are legitimate. What appeared to many Europeans as a fine aesthetic style struck many Africans as "mawkish personal lyricism."[18] In a scathing article in *Présence Africaine* entitled "Afrique noire, littérature rose" (Black Africa, Rosy Literature), the novelist Mongo Beti started with the assertion that there is an "absence of works of quality inspired by Africa and written in

16. Eustace Palmer (in *An Introduction to the African Novel* [New York: Africana Publishing Corp., 1972]) has similar difficulties with *L'Enfant noir*, but he is far more judgmental: questioning the novel's "sincerity," labelling it a "nostalgic picture of peasant soul-harmony and noble savagery" (92), Palmer seems to perceive in it an attack on Western civilization. He writes: "There is nothing inherently wrong in nostalgia about a way of life which one valued, but it is quite another matter to ascribe its passing to the impact of Westernization, growing technology, or progress. These factors may well be responsible for the disappearance of traditional civilization, but the fact must be demonstrated; it is not enough just to say so" (91). One problem with this is that *L'Enfant noir* simply does *not* "say so"; another problem is Palmer's apparent defensiveness against what he sees as creeping Rousseauism in Camara. He quotes another pair of critics (K. Ramchand and P. Edwards), who write: "Laye wishes to insinuate the same criticism of European civilization that Rousseau and his followers made" (91). Palmer's confused and shallow critique concludes with a litany of the novel's "flaws": "over-idealization, confused [i. e., complex] point of view, the propensity for assertion, rather than demonstration [the latter being an unusual thing to look for in a novel], . . . and the addiction to clichés, stock phrases and stereotypes, all of them associated with Camara Laye's attempt to impose a philosophy which he has not substantiated" (95). His opinions, while extreme, are nonetheless an apt caricature of the broad pattern of criticism interpreting *L'Enfant noir* as sweetly deceptive.

17. Peter Igbonekwu Okeh, "Two Ways of Explaining Africa: An Insight into Camara Laye's *L'Enfant noir* and Ferdinand Oyono's *Le Vieux Nègre et la médaille*, in Rowland Smith, ed., *Exile and Tradition* (New York: Africana Publishing Co., 1976), 80.

18. M. A. E. Okilie, "Nostalgia and Creative Secret: The Case of Camara Laye," *Okike* 23 (February 1983): 8.

French," whether by Africans or Europeans.[19] Because of the colonial situation, the very act of writing on Africa in the 1950s implies "taking a position for or against colonization—there is no getting out of it" (138). *L'Enfant noir* cannot be called *authentic* because it ignores the reality of colonialism and seems to hide its head in the sand: Beti writes, "*L'Enfant noir* wanted to make us believe in an idyllic Africa, but this was implausible because the White man was absent from the scene" (144). In another article, Beti attacked *L'Enfant noir* for projecting "a stereotyped—and therefore false—image of Africa:"

univers idyllique, optimisme de grands enfants, fêtes stupidement interminables, initiations de Carnaval, circoncisions, excisions, superstitions, oncles Mamadou dont l'inconscience n'a d'égale que leur irréalité. . . . Lorsqu'il parle de totem, sort, génie, il fait tout simplement pitié.

an idyllic universe, a child's optimism, stupidly interminable celebrations, carnival initiation ceremonies, circumcisions, excisions, superstitions, Uncle Mamadous whose lack of awareness is matched only by their unreality. . . . When he talks of totem, fate, and spirits, he is simply pathetic.[20]

In a sustained Marxist critique of *L'Enfant noir*, Nicole Medjigbodo accuses Camara of irresponsibility, of having created a book in which "none of the world's peoples will recognize themselves."[21] Reviewing the political situation of Guinea during the period of Camara's childhood, she sees in *L'Enfant noir* "a deliberate will to mask the sad and negative aspects in the village, to give the reader an image of order and beauty" (63), and an attempt to create an "illusion of immobility . . . a myth of static and happy societies" (71). But worse than the apolitical character of the novel is the atypicality of all its characters and situations: *L'Enfant noir* thus fails the litmus test of socialist realism. What we have here is a clear case of ethnicity versus ethics, with a certain notion of ethical struggle against colonialism making everything else seem quietistic and irrelevant.

At the moment when nationalistic sentiments were on the rise in Africa, when independence was beginning to be discussed openly, Camara's novel made it seem as if Africa *had always been* independent. No French colonial administrators interfere in the Mande world of *L'Enfant noir*; the tension comes not from overt resistance to colonialism but from a

19. A. B. [Alexandre Biyidi, who writes under the name Mongo Beti], "Afrique noire, littérature rose," *Présence Africaine*, n.s., nos. 1–2 (April-July, 1955): 133.

20. A. B., "*L'Enfant noir*," in *Trois écrivains noirs: Présence Africaine* 16 (1954): 420.

21. Nicole Medjigbodo, "Quelques réflexions sur la responsabilité de l'écrivain en Afrique colonisée et néo-colonisée: le cas de Camara Laye," *Présence francophone* 19 (Fall 1979): 86.

feeling of *falling away* from traditional culture. There is a clear model, that of traditional Mande society, but it is a model that is shown to be losing its grip; and that toward which the world is falling—French modernity—is never openly discussed.

Wole Soyinka evidently shared much the same opinion when he wrote in 1963:

> The cultivated naïveté of *The Dark Child* charmed even the African reader. Even if it often grew precious, it carried an air of magic, of nostalgia, which worked through the transforming act of language. If the author was selective to the point of wish fulfillment, it was unimportant. That a reader could be so gracefully *seduced* into a *village idyll* is a tribute to the author.[22]

It is as if there were something slightly dishonest and suspect about the whole project of *L'Enfant noir*. An idyll in 1953 was illegitimate, politically incorrect, even reprehensible. If an *idyll* is a form of expression that is dependent on stability, we will see that *L'Enfant noir* is a strange mutation, fallen away from the stability it reaches out to describe. One goal of this chapter will be to analyze the changing criteria by which an African novel like *L'Enfant noir* has been appraised; for, in a certain sense, the whole notion of what is "political" has changed in the postcolonial era: political vision and symbolic representation are no longer held to be mutually exclusive. African readers are now less likely to demand explicit political content and are more attuned to the symbolic politics of *L'Enfant noir*; there is a greater willingness to see *L'Enfant noir* as a work of subtly *sublimated*, rather than *repressed* politics.[23]

Looking at the broad pattern of criticism from a certain distance, an uncanny echo emerges: if *L'Enfant noir* is sweetly seductive, idyllic, and mythically idealized; if it betrays a nostalgic obsession with a lost past; and if its apolitical character is deceptive and misleading, then it sounds a lot like the Mande oral tradition. Sweetness and seductivity, we should recall, are qualities of griots' speech in the traditional Mande: "Smooth talkers are always mistrusted" because they deform the truth of silence when they transform it into noise; true knowledge should remain secret.[24] Critics, especially African critics, have unwittingly echoed the

---

22. Wole Soyinka, "From a Common Back Cloth: A Reassessment of the African Literary Image," *The American Scholar* 32, no. 3 (Summer 1963): 387, emphasis mine.

23. A. L. Brench took such a position in his interpretation of *L'Enfant noir*, in *The Novelists' Inheritance in French Africa* (Oxford: Oxford University Press, 1967): 46; and Jingiri J. Achiriga saw in *L'Enfant noir* a form of "discreet revolt" (*La Révolte des romanciers noirs de langue française* (Ottowa: Naaman, 1973): 34. The latter interpretation may reflect, however, a certain projection of militantism onto Camara's novel, the myth of "revolt" against which Guy Ossito Midiohouan argues (see above, chapter one).

24. Sory Camara, *Gens de la parole* (Paris: Mouton, 1976): 239.

Mande nobles' mistrust of smooth talk, of verbal art in general, as they have attacked *L'Enfant noir*. The criticism of *L'Enfant noir* may therefore point to a cultural authenticity within the novel while stating the exact opposite: the sweet deceptiveness of the novel may be a direct outgrowth of Mande tastes and modes of artistic production, specifically those of the *nyamakala*. To state it simply, *L'Enfant noir* may be closer to traditional Mande art than has been suspected; there may be a concrete sense in which Camara was a *literate griot*. The fact that Camara was born into *nyamakala* status, as the son of a smith, forces us to confront the question of transformation and retention of traditional aesthetics within new media such as the francophone novel.

If Camara's first novel succeeded in France because it seemed to be an exotic African idyll, and failed in Africa for the same reason, *L'Enfant noir* has nonetheless gone on to become the best-known francophone African novel, the most widely read, in many ways the "first" in its genre. Not the first chronologically of course: there was a distinguished, if short, list of precursors. But *L'Enfant noir* was the first to gain canonical status, and we must briefly consider what this means. There can be no canon without a number—preferably a large number—of non-canonical works among which masterpieces can be selected. In the early years of francophone African literature, the production was so small that it would be difficult to speak of an African francophone canon; rather the works of this literature were assimilated within the margins of a French, or worldwide, canon. But institutional support in France—the consacration of texts on programs of study such as the French *agrégation*—was lacking until very recently.[25] (The theory of what is canonical is a subject I will address in the last chapter of this book.) *L'Enfant noir* has probably been taught, read, and analyzed more than any other francophone African novel and has circulated widely in translation. Its canonical status is supported by the volume of criticism it has produced and by its inscription in African and non-African programs of study. For many years, it could almost have been considered a canon of one.

The identity of *L'Enfant noir* as a text is therefore singular. It attracts unparalleled attention, yet passes for a simplistic "idyll." Underneath decades of reading and interpretation, its meaning is somehow enigmatic, and its position between Mande tradition and francophone modernity remains largely unexplored. The riddles are in fact inscribed within the text. The ostensible subject of the novel is the development of a young

25. The first African text to be part of the *agrégation* was Senghor's *Poèmes*, on the 1987 program, 3 years after he was inducted to the French Academy.

African's identity, from his traditional upbringing to his break with Africa and departure for France. Yet the narrator seems unsure whether he ever gained the identity that the story is supposed to reveal, unsure whether he is in command of his culture and his narrative subject. When analyzed carefully, as I propose to do here, the complacency or idyllic simplicity that appear on the surface of *L'Enfant noir* are figures in a larger, more complex hermeneutic that emerges from Mande systems of thought, to involve itself with Western discourse.

If the changed political situation in postcolonial Africa has made it possible for Africans to see *L'Enfant noir* anew, Western readers are now in a much better position to understand the text as well; increasingly sophisticated ethnographies have appeared, making it possible to approach Mande systems on a higher level. I propose to reappraise this "idyll" in a consciously disruptive fashion, veering between close reading of the text and far-reaching intertextual speculation. I also propose to do this *slowly*, giving *L'Enfant noir* the attention it deserves.

Childhood and Readership

The surface simplicity of *L'Enfant noir* is such that its narrative seems to boil down to these three quotations:

> —J'étais enfant . . . (11)
> —Je grandissais. (103)
> —Je quittais mes parents . . . (153)

> —I was a child . . . (17, AT)
> —I was growing up. (93)
> —I was leaving my parents . . . (153)

Since these three moments accurately summarize the *events* that take place in *L'Enfant noir*, one is tempted to see in them a complete, if skeletal, representation of the novel as a whole. What else is there, need there be to an autobiography? No "plot" is required in the story of a life, particularly that of a child. The structure is that of a straightforward progression from childhood to adulthood, an unproblematic progression in which the distance between the narrator and the character of his childhood self diminishes steadily, if incompletely. The mature narrator, writing from the assurance of adulthood, describes his past as a path out of ignorance and into knowledge. The virtues and the happiness he evokes may be lost to him in the moment of writing—a moment that is referred to in *L'Enfant noir*—but that loss comes from a rupture at the story's end. The last of the three sentences above need not trouble the authority of the first two.

It is on assumptions like these that interpretations of *L'Enfant noir* have rested. Critics who praise *L'Enfant noir* as an idyll share with those who condemn it as an idyll an unquestioning acceptance of the text's constant assertions of happiness. It goes without saying that the happiness has been lost; such is the condition of writing about it. But I believe that what *L'Enfant noir* has to say about happiness—and it has a lot to say—is conditioned and overdetermined by the cultural, political, and rhetorical situation of the novel. I do not intend somehow to disprove or refute the notion that *L'Enfant noir* is a "happy" text or to prove that it is unhappy (which is not the same thing) but to analyze a limited number of the ways in which this novel challenges understanding. These considerations will be ordered according to the three stages outlined above, although I hope they will eventually show the inadequacy of such a linear reduction.

The first sentence of *L'Enfant noir* ("J'étais enfant . . .") could not be more predictable or appropriate for the beginning of an autobiography. The narrator as the presiding subjectivity establishes himself in the first word in relation to his past self as a child; the relation between the two is mediated through language, specifically the suspended temporality of the verb "to be" in the imperfect tense. But in addition to this narratological scheme, there is another, self-reflexive consideration that parallels and, in a certain sense, disrupts our analysis: the question of the Western reader and his/her status as a "child." It is not a negligible fact that the first word in the title of this "first" francophone African novel describes the condition of the average Western reader: innocent of knowledge about Africa, uninitiated to African culture, uneducated about the world that he/she is about to enter. The first sentence, and *L'Enfant noir* as a whole, therefore makes no assumptions, but starts from zero, from an opening: I was a child. When considered in its address to the Westerners that Camara Laye knew would be the vast majority of his readership, the sentence seems to say, "I used to be a child, but you still are, and it is only through this fictitious version of my own childhood that I can hope to teach you anything."

Seen in this perspective, the process of growing up, learning, and being initiated as a Mandeka serves not only the obvious purpose of recording and illustrating an African culture; it also attempts to educate and initiate outsiders. *L'Enfant noir* may appear to be a rather unexceptional Bildungsroman, but when we take a step back from textual and generic interpretation, its peculiar situation as an African novel leads to the recognition of other functions: as a novel of education, *L'Enfant noir* does not remain in the realm of the descriptive (constative) function of language; it performs education as well.

The idea of childhood, both in the descriptive and in the performative domain, is therefore connected to the idea of ignorance (by which I mean simply the absence of information, the opening for knowledge). But the figure of childhood in *L'Enfant noir* cannot be separated from the political control of knowledge in the colonial context. Childhood in connection to Africa is anything but an innocent idea. The identification of the Western reader as a child would probably have been considered risible in 1953, for the idea of Africa as a repository of systems of knowledge was not widely recognized. The Western stereotype, racist in nature and centuries old, was of Africa as a continent of childhood and of Africans as children, and this extra-African point of view further complicates our present task. In African critiques of *L'Enfant noir*, there was the fear that Camara Laye's book would perpetuate the myth of African culture as primitive, stuck in a timeless condition prior to the intervention of the colonizers. His insistent use of the imperfect tense seems to support such an interpretation, by creating a feeling of "suspension." Yet when analyzed as a strategy for the manipulation of the Western reader, childhood becomes a shrewd metaphor, a tactic used to gain influence, and ultimately an ironic comment on the politics of knowledge. How can we situate the condition of childhood between these competing claims?

The Opening Passage: Between Mother and Father

Camara Laye said in an interview that, in the construction of a book, "everything is in principle in the first chapter." [26] To let the text speak for itself, I will quote extensively from the opening passage of chapter one, in which the problems of ignorance and education, childhood and identity are opened for consideration. The first three pages follow a movement of dilation and contraction, of investigation and reflection, confidence and insecurity, that is repeated many times throughout the novel.

J'étais enfant et je jouais près de la case de mon père. Quel âge avais-je en ce temps-là? Je ne me rappelle pas exactement. Je devais être très jeune encore: cinq ans, six ans peut-être. Ma mère était dans l'atelier, près de mon père, et leurs voix me parvenaient, rassurantes, tranquilles, mêlées à celles des clients de la forge et au bruit de l'enclume.

Brusquement j'avais interrompu de jouer, l'attention, toute mon attention, captée par un serpent qui rampait autour de la case, qui vraiment paraissait se promener autour de la case; et je m'étais bientôt approché. J'avais ramassé un roseau qui traînait dans la cours—il en traînait toujours, qui se détachait de la palissade de roseaux tressés qui enclôt notre concession—et, à présent, j'enfonçais

26. Leiner, "Interview," 160.

ce roseau dans la gueule de la bête. Le serpent ne se dérobait pas: il prenait goût au jeu; il avalait lentement le roseau, il l'avalait comme une proie, avec la même volupté, me semblait-il, les yeux brillants de bonheur, et sa tête, petit à petit, se rapprochait de ma main. Il vint un moment où le roseau se trouva à peu près englouti, et où la gueule du serpent se trouva terriblement proche de mes doigts.

Je riais, je n'avais pas peur du tout, et je crois bien que le serpent n'eût plus beaucoup tardé à m'enfoncer ses crochets dans les doigts si, à l'instant, Damany, l'un des apprentis, ne fût sorti de l'atelier. L'apprenti fit signe à mon père, et presque aussitôt je me sentis soulevé de terre: j'étais dans les bras de mon père!

Autour de moi, on menait grand bruit; ma mère surtout criait fort et elle me donna quelques claques. Je me mis à pleurer, plus ému par le tumulte qui s'était si inopinément élevé, que par les claques que j'avais reçues. Un peu plus tard, quand je me fus un peu calmé et qu'autour de moi les cris eurent cessé, j'entendis ma mère m'avertir sévèrement de ne plus jamais recommencer un tel jeu; je le lui promis, bien que le danger de mon jeu ne m'apparût pas clairement.

Mon père avait sa case à proximité de l'atelier, et souvent je jouais là, sous la véranda qui l'entourait. C'était la case personelle de mon père. Elle était faite de briques en terre battue et pétrie avec de l'eau; et comme toutes nos cases, ronde et fièrement coiffée de chaume. On y pénétrait par une porte rectangulaire. A l'intérieur, un jour avare tombait d'une petite fenêtre. . . . A la tête du lit, surplombant l'oreiller, et veillant sur le sommeil de mon père, il y avait une série de marmites contenant des extraits de plantes et d'écorces. Ces marmites avaient toutes des couvercles de tôle et elles étaient richement et curieusement cerclées de chapelets de cauris; on avait tôt fait de comprendre qu'elles étaient ce qu'il y avait de plus important dans la case; de fait, elles contenaient les gris-gris, ces liquides mystérieux qui éloignaient les mauvais esprits et qui, pour peu qu'on s'en enduise le corps, le rendent invulnérable aux maléfices, à tous les maléfices. Mon père, avant de se coucher, ne manquait jamais de s'enduire le corps, puisant ici, puisant là, car chaque liquide, chaque gri-gri a sa propriété particulière; mais quelle vertu précise? *je l'ignore: j'ai quitté mon père trop tôt.* (11–13; emphasis mine)

I was a child playing around my father's hut. How old would I have been at that time? I cannot remember exactly. I must still have been very young: five, maybe six years old. My mother was still in the workshop with my father, and I could just hear their familiar voices above the noise of the anvil and the conversation of the customers.

Suddenly I stopped playing, my whole attention fixed on a snake that was creeping around the hut. After a moment I went over to him. I had taken in my hand a reed that was lying in the yard—there were always some lying around; they used to get broken off the fence of plaited reeds that marked the boundary of our concession—and I thrust it into his mouth. The snake did not try to get away: he was beginning to enjoy our little game; he was slowly swallowing the reed; he was devouring it, I thought as if it were some delicious prey, his eyes glittering with voluptuous bliss; and inch by inch his head was drawing nearer to my hand. At last the reed was almost entirely swallowed, and the snake's jaws were terribly close to my fingers.

I was laughing. I had not the slightest fear, and I feel sure that the snake would not have hestitated much longer before burying his fangs in my fingers if, at that moment, Damany, one of the apprentices, had not come out of the workshop. He called my father, and almost at once I felt myself lifted off my feet: I was safe in the arms of one of my father's friends.

Around me there was a great commotion. My mother was shouting hardest of all, and she gave me a few sharp slaps. I wept, more upset by the sudden uproar than by the blows. A little later, when I was somewhat calmer and the shouting had ceased, my mother solemnly warned me never to play that game again. I promised, although the game still didn't seem dangerous to me.

My father's hut was near the workshop, and I often played beneath the veranda that ran around the outside. It was his private hut, and like all our huts built of mud bricks that had been pounded and moulded with water; it was round, and proudly crowned with thatch. It was entered by a rectangular doorway. Inside, a tiny window let in a thin shaft of daylight. . . . At the head of the bed, hanging over the pillow and watching over my father's slumber, stood a row of pots that contained extracts from plants and the bark of trees. These pots all had metal lids and were profusely and curiously garlanded with chaplets of cowry shells; it did not take me long to discover that they were the most important things in the hut; they contained magic charms—those mysterious liquids that keep the evil spirits at bay, and, if smeared on the body, make it invulnerable to every kind of evil sorcery. My father, before going to bed, never failed to smear his body with a little of each liquid, first one, then another, for each charm had its own particular property: but exactly *what* property? *I do not know: I left my father's house too soon.* (17–19, AT, emphasis mine)

What did the narrator know and when did he know it? That is, what state of consciousness or knowledge is attributed to *l'enfant noir*, and how is the narrative authority established? From the second sentence of the novel, there is a problem of knowledge and recollection that disrupts the narrative process and seems to call the narrator's authority and command into question, even before it is established. At first the action is described, albeit it the suspended animation of the imperfect tense; immediately a limit is imposed by the narrator's failure of memory. Forgetfulness returns regularly in *L'Enfant noir*: for every "I see it all again" (such as 199; 173) there seems to be an "I don't remember" (such as 124; 112, AT). The narrator's project of relating his education and upbringing is full of holes, lapses of memory, and excuses for never having known. We will see how this works when we analyze the end of the opening passage.

Whatever may be the significance of childhood in a Western reading, its signficance within Mande culture must be considered. Unfortunately no studies have been written on childhood as such in the Mande; but ethnographers and critics have described Mande concepts of childhood that are relevant here. Opposing modes of childhood (which are also adult attitudes) are derived from relations with the mother and the father.

Fadenya or "father-childness" is the condition of being a father's son or daughter; it refers to the complex of feelings and relations that obtain between offspring of a single father, who in a polygamous society are often half-siblings. Rivalry is expected between such siblings and even with one's father.[27] *Fadenya* instills competition and vying for inheritance and glory; this is done with a view to posterity, in relation to the ancestors who must be equalled: "In the Mande world, a *name* must be won not only in the arena provided by one's peers, but also in that abstract arena created by one's ancestors."[28] *Fadenya* is described as "centrifugal," tending to spin the actor out toward social disharmony, jealousy, competition, etc. *Badenya* or "mother-childness" is translated as "affection" (Johnson, 9) and is associated with "submission to authority, stability, cooperation, those qualities which pull the individual back into the social mass" (Bird and Kendall, 15).

The disposition of the opening passage of *L'Enfant noir* seems to work from an assumption underlying the concepts of *fadenya* and *badenya*: that any notion of childhood must be derived from a relation to the parents, who are the vessels and enforcers of their culture. The first paragraph is evenly divided between the father ("près de la case de mon père") and the mother ("ma mère était dans l'atelier"), following one of the principal axes of the novel. But that evenhandedness is not to last: it is the image and name of the father that is to dominate *L'Enfant noir*; as the child tries to fall asleep at the end of chapter 1, he says, "the image of my father under the lantern wouldn't leave me . . . and I wept silently" (23–24). Later in the book, Camara makes an argument for the *powers* (plural, magical powers) of the mother, but the way in which he does this only further affirms the *power* (the singular authority) of the father.

Although it seems to me that the symbolics of gender association in *L'Enfant noir* tilt heavily in the direction of the father, it should be noted that the book is dedicated with a poem "To my mother." Filled with longing for childhood, the poem credits the mother as being "the first one to open my eyes to the marvels of the earth." This poem is remarkably similar in tone and theme to Léopold Sédar Senghor's famous "Femme noire" (which I will discuss later in this study); it echoes Negritude in its address to an allegorical, idealized "femme africaine."[29] The

27. See John William Johnson, *The Epic of Son-Jara*, 9.

28. Charles S. Bird and Martha Kendall, "The Mande Hero: Text and Context," in *Explorations in African Systems of Thought*, Ivan Karp and Charles S. Bird, eds. (Bloomington: Indiana University Press, 1980): 14, emphasis mine.

29. On the role of the mother, see Fritz H. Pointer, "Laye, Lamming, and Wright: Mother and Son," *African Literature Today* 14 (1984): 19–33; and Alphamoye Sonfo, "La Mère dans la littérature romanesque de la Guinée, du Mali et du Sénégal," *Revue ouest-africaine des langues vivantes* 2 (1976): 95–107.

mother is the spiritual equal of the father: coming from a great family of smiths herself, she is endowed with occult powers. However, in spite of the parity between father and mother as they are depicted in the novel, the child-narrator fixates on the father and undergoes a complex process of attempted identification with him. It is through the father's *name* that the child-narrator seeks, and fails to find, total identity in the Mande. By focussing on this process, I wish to imply nothing about the real anthropology of identity in the Mande as a function of either *badenya* or *fadenya*—a subject that goes beyond the question of Camara Laye's narrative strategy in *L'Enfant noir*. Returning to the opening passage, we can see how Camara Laye depicts the child's attention being drawn to the father's presence.

The child is playing, close to the father's house, within the father's compound or "concession," outside the father's forge. Although the mother is mentioned halfway through the paragraph, it is the father who dominates the geography of "case," "atelier," and "forge." The arrangement of the compound is such that "anyone who came or went had to go through the workshop"; but the child's domain was "not yet there; it was not until very much later that I got into the habit of crouching in the workshop to watch the forge glow" (14; 20, AT). The fire of the forge is thus the symbol and the real source of the father's authority and power, deriving from the privilege and the dangerous responsibility of transforming materials, unleashing *nyama*.[30]

The second paragraph seems to follow the classical narrative pattern of breaking a continuity established at the beginning of the novel. In French this is usually effected by a switch from the imperfect to the *passé composé* (*Madame Bovary*: "Nous étions à l'étude quand le proviseur entra . . ."); in a novel that is thought to be fixated on continuity itself, overlooking the violence of colonialism, what sudden event breaks the murmuring tranquility of the first paragraph? The arrival of a snake.

The prominence given to this snake has puzzled critics. Its position as a signifier seems to portend great importance, calling for the intervention of all the critical hooks and ladders that can be mustered. Crying "symbol!" critics have taken recourse to universalizing theories of totemism. Sonia Lee writes:

In Laye's story the symbol is clearly spelled out, but *the actual choice of symbol is not explained, although it would seem to have a totemic significance* due to the close relationship between the father and the animal; as J. E. Cirlot points out in his *Dictionary of Symbols*, "In the world of symbols, totemistic interpretation

---

30. See Bourgeacq, *Eternel retour*, 13–15, for an interpretation that applies Dieterlen's ethnography of smithing to this chapter.

does no more than demonstrate relationship, *without elucidating meaning*: it forges connecting links between beings endowed with 'common rhythm,' but it does not indicate the meaning of these beings." *Laye never explains* why the spirit of the father is symbolized by a little black snake rather than some other animal form. (*Camara Laye*, 21–22, my emphasis)

Lee seems to misread Cirlot's commentary, which suggests that totemism is about the *limitations* of meaning as free "choice." Still, Lee wants to know *why* one "symbol" was selected by Camara instead of another, and this is not an unreasonable desire. If no choice were involved, one could question whether the signifier were actually a symbol. How can an element be invested with meaning if it is free of *intent*, the intention to use this element instead of another? What kind of meaning is free of intent?

If we consider *L'Enfant noir* to be a product of Mande culture, if we seek interpretive models within that culture and not only in supposedly universal (usually Western) sources, then the significance of the snake will have to be found in the text of the novel and in other Mande sources. Yet the Western analytic literature on totemism is enormous and impossible to ignore; I will attempt to deal with it presently. The snakes that fill the opening passage of *L'Enfant noir* are a central enigma. We are told that they are "totemic," but we don't know what it means to be a totem. Can we elucidate their meaning beyond the level that seems immanent to the Western reader?

The tension of the second paragraph comes from the child's captivation with the snake. Not perceiving any danger, he sees the snake as a being which "seemed to be taking a walk," which "was beginning to enjoy our little game . . . , his eyes glittering with voluptuous bliss." Through the child's eyes, in free indirect discourse, the snake is anthropomorphized. This is a moment of suspended action: there had been an interruption at the moment when the snake caught the child's attention ("j'avais interrompu"), but now time stands still in a hypnotic present ("à présent, j'enfonçais ce roseau dans la gueule de la bête"). The moment of narrative action, the first moment at which an action actually takes place, is represented by the verbs "faire signe" and "se sentir" in the *passé simple*: "L'apprenti *fit* signe à mon père et presque aussitôt je me *sentis* soulevé de terre: j'étais dans les bras d'un ami de mon père!" The harmony of the first paragraph is reestablished, again under the sign of the father. It is the mother who administers the punishment, but the subject quickly returns to the father and his domain.

The relation between the incident with the snake and the narrative concentration on the father is not explained, not yet. But that relation is essential to understanding these pages of *L'Enfant noir*. The last paragraph above describes the mysterious interior of the father's house, filled with "gris-gris," materials that aid in controlling dangerous forces—those released in smith's work in the forge or in everyday life. The narrative has taken us from a small household drama that everyone can understand to the world of magic, by definition located on the margins of understanding.

Thus far, in a few paragraphs, the non-Mande reader has already been thrust into a very specific world, and allowed a degree of understanding of a certain family structure, architecture, and spiritual belief system. The *on* who enters the father's house through the rectangular door obviously represents the family member who would "really" be there (referentially), but *on* is also the reader being led by the child/adult-narrator. The second occurrence of the *on* in this paragraph demonstrates the educational function of the narrative: "on avait tôt fait de comprendre . . . " introduces a lesson in Mande culture. This *on* does not refer to the Western reader, who would not yet have understood what is in those containers, but it leads such a reader into complicity. Of all the methods for educating the outsider to African cultures, this is the most graceful and diplomatic; the pedagogical dimension is finessed, sublimated, veiled. But that dimension is there: when the narrator refers to "*our* huts," there is an implied reference to a "you" that *L'Enfant noir* is too discreet to name. We are a long way from the boisterous playfulness of the narrator of *Les Soleils des indépendances*, who will openly point his finger at the Western reader and proclaim, "You don't know this because you're not Malinke."

But if the narrator of *L'Enfant noir* is discreet, he is also less than authoritative. In the last sentence of the passage, we run hard into the limits of the narrator's competence, limits that he calls to our attention. The movement of penetration and education, from the establishment of an atmosphere at the beginning to the moment of entering the father's house, is violently interrupted by the phrase "Je l'ignore: j'ai quitté mon père trop tôt." Why does the narrator let us down so soon? He states a very simple, very significant reason: he left his father too soon. The father is knowledge; in the pages that follow he will begin to reveal some of his secret knowledge to his son. But for every movement of advance in education, there is a moment of shortfall, a realization of the deficit between desire and the real. Thus, when the riddle of the snake is unravelled, there is a similar movement from revelation to emptiness.

The boy's continuing relationship with snakes returns quickly, seemingly by a metonymical path, when he brings up the subject of the railroad that borders the family compound.

Nous habitions en bordure du chemin de fer. Les trains longeaient la barrière de roseaux tressés qui limitait la concession, et la longeaient à vrai dire de si près, que des flammèches, échappées de la locomotive, mettaient parfois le feu à la clôture. (15)

> We lived beside the railroad. The trains skirted the reed fence of the concession so closely that sparks thrown off from the locomotive set fire to it every now and then. (21, AT)

It would be pointless to resist interpreting the train as a sign and symbol of colonial penetration; the relation is synecdochal in that the railroad was the principal tool of colonial occupation and exploitation in the interior of West Africa—it is part and parcel of the political phenomenon that it represents here. When the walls of the traditional family enclosure are set on fire by the passing train, a small allegory of "things falling apart" is more than evident. Critics and readers interested in rehabilitating the politics of *L'Enfant noir* often point to this.

Then the narrator brings in the snakes, for the second time:

> Les rails luisaient cruellement dans une lumière que rien, à cet endroit, ne venait tamiser. Chauffé dès l'aube, le ballast de pierres rouges était brûlant; il l'était au point que l'huile, tombée des locomotives, était aussitôt bue et qu'il n'en demeurait seulement pas trace. Est-ce cette chaleur de four ou est-ce l'huile, l'odeur d'huile qui malgré tout subsistait, qui attirait les serpents? Je ne sais pas. Le fait est que souvent je surprenais des serpents à ramper sur ce ballast cuit et recuit par le soleil; et il arrivait fatalement que les serpents pénétrassent dans la concession. (16)

> The iron rails glistened cruelly in a light which nothing in that place could relieve. Baking since dawn, the roadbed was so hot that oil which dropped from the locomotives evaporated immediately, leaving no trace. Was it the oven-like heat or the smell of oil—for the smell remained in spite of everything—which attracted the snakes? I do not know. But often I came upon them crawling in that hot roadbed. And inevitably the snakes got into the concession.[31] (21, AT)

The metonymic link between railroad and snake draws the subject toward its ultimate destination in this chapter, the unveiling of the totemic relation between the Camara patrilineage and one species of snake. The snakes that come off the railroad and into the compound may be a threat, like the fires, but their identity must be established. If it is just any snake ("un serpent comme tous les serpents—en fait, ils différaient fort!"), the mother will beat it to a pulp. We are to assume that the first snake, the one encountered on the first page, was one of these undesirables. Yet the narrator's continuing fascination with snakes is preparing the first cultural lesson that will be offered by the father, the first unveiling of his knowledge.

31. The last sentence is mistranslated in *The Dark Child* as, "It would have been fatal if they had gotten into the concession."

The lesson begins when the mother points out to the child a snake that is different from the others.

—Celui-ci, mon enfant, il ne faut pas le tuer: ce serpent n'est pas comme les autres, il ne te fera aucun mal; néanmoins ne contrarie jamais sa course.

Personne, dans notre concession, n'ignorait que ce serpent-là, on ne devait pas le tuer, sauf moi, sauf mes petits compagnons de jeu, je présume, qui étions encore des enfants naïfs.

—Ce serpent, ajouta ma mère, est le génie de ton père. (17)

"My son, this one must not be killed: he is not like the other snakes, and he will not harm you; you must never interfere with him."

Everyone in our concession knew that this snake must not be killed—everyone except myself, and I suppose, my little playmates, who were still ignorant children.

"This snake," my mother added, "is your father's guiding spirit." (22)

The children are the only members of the community who might be ignorant of this vital information; they must be initiated. The process of learning their own culture begins with a perception of *difference*—"en fait, ils différaient fort"—that appears to be zoological but is revealed to be symbolic and cultural. Again, the child's reaction is that of the ignorant outsider, asking a thousand questions, like a Westerner uninitiated to Mande culture:

Bien que le merveilleux me fût familier, je demeurai muet tant mon étonnement était grand. Qu'est-ce qu'un serpent avait à faire avec mon père? Et pourquoi ce serpent-là précisément? On ne le tuait pas, parce qu'il était le génie de mon père! Du moins était-ce la raison que ma mère donnait. Mais au juste qu'était-ce qu'un génie? Qu'étaient ces génies que je rencontrais un peu partout, qui défendaient telle chose, commandaient telle autre? Je ne me l'expliquais pas clairement, encore que je n'eusse cessé de croître dans leur intimité. Il y avait de bons génies, et il y en avait de mauvais; et plus de mauvais que de bons, il me semble. Et d'abord qu'est-ce qui me prouvait que ce serpent était inoffensif? C'était *un serpent comme les autres*; un serpent noir, sans doute, et assurément un serpent d'un éclat extraordinaire; *un serpent tout de même*! J'étais dans une absolue perplexité, pourtant je ne demandai rien à ma mère: je pensais qu'il me fallait interroger directement mon père; oui, comme si ce mystère eût été *une affaire à débattre entre hommes uniquement, une affaire et un mystère qui ne regardent pas les femmes*; et je décidai d'attendre la nuit. (17–18, emphasis mine)

Although the supernatural was familiar to me, this sight filled me with such astonishment that I was struck dumb. What business would a snake have with my father? And why this particular snake? No one was to kill him because he was my father's guiding spirit! At any rate, that was the explanation my mother had given me. But what exactly *was* a "guiding spirit?" What were the guiding spirits that I encountered almost everywhere, forbidding one thing, commanding another to be done? I could not understand it at all, though their presences surrounded me as I grew up. There were good spirits, and there were evil ones; and more evil than good ones, it seems to me. And how was I to know that this snake was harmless? He was *a snake like the others*: black, to be sure, with extraordinary markings—*but for all that a snake*. I was completely perplexed, but I did not question my mother: I had decided that I must ask my father about it, as if this were *a matter to be discussed only between men, a matter and a mystery in which women had no part*. I decided to wait until evening to speak to him. (22–23, emphasis mine, AT)

The gendered nature of Mande knowledge is thus openly stated, if only as a child's intuition. The mother has pointed the son in the direction of occult knowledge, but he senses that the full content of knowledge will come only from his father. With this, the novel takes one step further the shift of attention from mother to father.[32]

Having been taught the difference between this kind of snake and all others, the child grapples with the basic problem of identity and symbolism. After all, a snake is a snake ("C'était un serpent comme les autres"); although he dwells in an environment where *génies* are everywhere, he has difficulty accepting the whole notion of an animal invested with power. The problem is not just one of identification; there is a decision whether to kill such a snake or not. Snakes that are not totemic *génies* are to be killed; but to kill one's *génie* would be a monstrous crime of betrayal, of symbolic patricide. The *enfant noir* does not yet know this. The condition of childhood here is thus not one of simple unity with one's culture; it is a relation of resistance, doubt, and possible violence. The upcoming conversation with the father will end the movement toward explication of the snake motif that has dominated the opening pages of *L'Enfant noir*. How much will be learned, either by the child or by the reader?

The father, faced with a barrage of questions from his son, somewhat reluctantly explains the history of his relation to the snake.

—Ce serpent, dit-il, est le génie de notre race. Comprends-tu?
—Oui, dis-je, bien que je ne comprisse pas très bien.
—Ce serpent, poursuivit-il, est toujours présent; toujours il apparaît à l'un de nous. Dans notre génération, c'est à moi qu'il s'est présenté.
—Oui, dis-je.
Et je l'avais dit avec force, car il me paraissait évident que le serpent n'avait pu se présenter qu'à mon père. N'était-ce pas mon père qui était le chef de la concession? N'était-ce pas lui qui commandait tous les forgerons de la région? N'était-il pas le plus habile? Enfin n'était-il pas mon père? (19)

32. On the final outcome of this process, see note 68, below.

"That snake," he said, "is the guiding spirit of our race. Can you understand that?"

"Yes," I answered, although I did not understand very well.

"That snake," he went on, "has always been present among us; he has always make himself known to one of us. In our time, it is to me that he has made himself known."

"Yes," I said.

And I said it with all my heart, for it seemed obvious to me that the snake could have made himself known to no one but my father. Was not my father the head man in our concession? Was it not my father who had authority over all the blacksmiths in our district? Was he not the most skilled? Was he not, after all, my father? (24, AT)

The father then recounts the story of the snake's visitations, first in dreams, then in reality. Like the son, the father as a child mistook the snake for "a snake like the other, and I had to hold myself back from killing it." The snake then speaks to him in a dream:

"Je suis venu comme je t'en avais averti, dit-il, et toi, tu ne m'as fait nul accueil: je lisais dans tes yeux. Pourquoi me repousses-tu? Je suis le génie de ta race, et c'est en tant que génie de ta race que je me présente à toi comme au plus digne. Cesse donc de me craindre et prends garde de me repousser, car je t'apporte le succès." (20)

"I came as I foretold," he said, "but you did not receive me kindly; I perceived it in your eyes. Why do you reject me? I am the guiding spirit of your race, and it is as the guiding spirit of your race that I make myself know to you as to the most worthy. Therefore look on me without fear and do not reject me, for I bring you success." (25, AT)

From his unique relation with the snake, the father derives numerous special powers, to which he attributes his success as an artisan. Through his dreams he is able to predict events and respond accordingly. Among the blacksmiths of the region, the Camara father alone rules like a monarch: "I am better known than the others, and *my name* is on everyone's tongue, and it is I who have authority over all the blacksmiths in the five cantons of this zone" (21; 25, emphasis mine, AT).

The fact that all of this success and reputation is attributable to the snake is the fact at the heart of this text, and the word "Camara" in its totemistic sense, although never written in this chapter, is the text's secret knowledge, now revealed. Revelation of the totem produces a plateau of higher knowledge and understanding for the child and for the reader. The narrator emphasizes the positive nature of the moment:

Il se tut, et *je sus alors* pourquoi, quand mon père revenait de promenade et entrait dans l'atelier, il pouvait dire aux apprentis: "En mon absence, un tel ou un tel est venu, il était vêtu de telle façon, il venait de tel endroit et il apportait tel travail." Et tous s'émerveillaient fort de *cet étrange savoir. A présent, je comprenais* d'où mon père tirait sa connaissance des événements. (21–22; emphasis mine)

He was silent; and *then I understood* why, when my father came back from a walk he would enter the workshop and say to the apprentices: "During my absence, this or that person has been here, he was dressed in such and such a way, he came from such and such a place and he brought with him such and such a piece of work to be done." And all marveled at *this curious knowledge. At that moment, I understood* where my father got his knowledge of events. (26, AT—the last sentence is absent from the published translation)

Having reached this plateau in the text, where the novel seems closest to a positive fusion of ethnographic and autobiographical authority, I would like to conduct an experiment in the relation between African literature and anthropology.

Totem and *Jamu*

Il me faut le cacher au plus intime de mes veines
L'Ancêtre à la peau d'orage sillonnée d'éclairs et de foudre
Mon animal gardien, il me faut le cacher
Que je ne rompe le barrage des scandales.
Il est mon sang fidèle qui requiert fidelité
Protégeant mon orgueil nu contre
Moi-même et la superbe des races heureuses . . .

—Léopold Sédar Senghor, "Le totem" [33]

This study—like others before it—is based on a desire to escape the nets of Western discourse and see Africa on its own terms; but we have seen that this desire must be tempered by the knowledge that, through colonialism, Europe wrote itself into the tradition of European-language literatures in Africa. Anthropology plays a dual role here, as a window and a mirror: as the means of gaining "local knowledge" and as a reflection of European preoccupations projected onto Africa. The further back in the history of anthropology that one ventures, the more obvious is its function as mirror (and one contribution of the new critical anthropology is to recognize that function in *all* ethnographies). In colonial times, when *L'Enfant noir* was written, anthropology was a European field—there were few Sory Camaras—and access to the African world of that period demands reliance on these alien sources.

Camara's use of the word "totem" dramatically highlights the irony of our position. How are we to read this word? As a self-evident cultural reference that the text fully accounts for or as a bridge to the body of

33. From the collection "Chants d'ombre" in *Poèmes* (Paris: Seuil, 1984): 24.

Western anthropological writings on totemism? In the pages that follow, I will conduct an experiment in the relation between *L'Enfant noir* and anthropology. Beginning with a survey of recent information on smiths in the Mande, I will try to show the importance of the father's name and status within the narrative, as a model of authority to which the son-narrator aspires. This reveals itself to be a question of "totemism," and my efforts to understand this concept within the novel will entail a radical detour through the cobwebbed halls of ethnography. "Totemism" is no longer referred to except in histories of anthropology, and this indicates that we can only approach it as an artifact within literature, leaving its anthropological validity within brackets. The pages that follow will amount to a comparison of ethnographic authority and narrative authority, as both work around the topos of totemism.

Much has been written on the role of the smith in West African societies. In many parts of Africa, and not just in the casted societies of the Mande, smiths are the object of special, often ambivalent, feelings. The first point to bear in mind is that Mande smiths are *nyamakala* along with the griots; they too produce and manipulate *nyama* and are subject to similar restrictions and privileges. There has been much speculation as to how this came about.[34] Patrick McNaughton, in his recent and incisive ethnography of Mande smiths, describes how the *nyamakala* birthright predisposes smiths to knowledge and power (*MS*, 150). In comparison to griots, smiths are more likely to possess arcane knowledge of the spirit world and an ability to deal with it; they act as healers, circumcisors, and excisors. In a way that does not happen in regard to griots, the word "power" keeps returning in discussions of smiths; although McNaughton claims that there is no hierarchy, Bokar N'Diaye states that the smiths "occupy the summit of the *nyamakala* hierarchy," while remaining inferior to nobles.[35] Smiths are highly respected, yet nobles may rationalize their fear by damning them (*MS*, 160); ambivalence reigns.[36] Smiths "intervene and negociate"; they possess trade secrets, and "hardly anyone outside their clans can acquire" this knowledge, for "endogamy is too

34. It seems that in the less hierarchical cultures of Central Africa, the smith is more esteemed than feared and may even be of royal lineage. But in societies where agriculture and livestock are the economic domain of a class of nobles, "depressed castes of iron-workers are [more accurately, may be] the remains of indigenous people who have been enslaved and kept at their work by more powerful but less ingenious conquerors" (Walter Buchanan Cline, *Mining and Metallurgy in Negro Africa* [1937], quoted in Pierre Clément, "Le Forgeron en Afrique Noire: quelques attitudes du groupe à son égard," *Revue de géographie humaine et d'ethnologie* [April-June, 1948]: 38).

35. Bokar N'Diaye, *Les Castes au Mali* (Bamako: Editions Populaires, 1970): 72.

36. McNaughton points out that Sumanguru Kante, the sorceror-blacksmith king in the Sunjata epic, reflects "the darker side of the blacksmiths' gift"; his "image is the essence

deeply ingrained" (*MS*, 40–41). Birth is therefore key, and paternity determines much of what one will know.

Before considering Camara Laye's use of the term "totem"—which is related to the acquisition of knowledge and power—we should first consider what the name Camara evokes in the collective memory of the Mande, the prestige it bears. The Camara clan is the second largest in the Upper Niger valley, and among smiths, the *jamu* Camara is one of the most distinguished.[37] In Kita (Mali), a clan of Camaras "is reputed for magic . . . as intermediaries between humans and protector spirits; the Camaras are true authorities in law, morals and religion . . . , the uncontested guarantors of the whole social order."[38] The identity of the clan comes from the common ancestor Fran Camara, whose story is told in the epic of Sunjata: Fran was a blacksmith,[39] king of Tabon, and faithful ally of Sunjata in the time of his exile. Fran was a friend of Sunjata's from childhood; in the campaign to conquer the empire, the help of his army of blacksmiths was instrumental. In *Le Maître de la parole*, Camara Laye's version of the Sunjata epic, there is a curious qualification of Fran Camara's status:

L'armée de Fran, roi du pays après la mort de son père Sadi So-oro, était composée de forgerons et de Djallonkès; *mais qu'importe! ce n'était pas l'origine des archers qui importait à présent*, c'était leur disponibilité et leur extraordinaire élan de vouloir accompagner leur roi et son ami Diata dans la grande aventure.

The army of Fran, king of the country since the death of this father Sadi So-oro, was composed of blacksmiths and Djallonkés, *but never mind! What mattered at the moment was not the origin of the archers*, but their availability and their

---

of fearsome, death-dealing, unstoppable power" (*MS*, 161). Yet he is not a villain in an ordinary Western sense. Johnson writes: "The contrast between Son-Jara and Sumamuru [Sumanguru] is not considered one of good versus evil, of admired hero verus scorned antihero" (*The Epic of Son-Jara*, 42).

37. Adele King, *The Writings of Camara Laye* (London: Heinemann, 1980): 1.

38. Diango Cissé, *Structures des Malinké de Kita: Contribution à une anthropologie sociale et politique du Mali* (Bamako: Editions Populaires, 1970): 211, 249. One cannot be certain that this clan of Camaras, located at a good distance from Camara Laye's birthplace, is actually related to his. Such are the complications of genealogy in this area that the two groups could bear the same name but issue from different branches of the clan, or according to Germaine Dieterlen, even be unrelated (*Essai sur la religion bambara* [Paris: Presses Universitaires de France, 1951]: 74). The name on its own is however sufficient to suggest a genealogy.

39. The "dalikïmbon" Camaras ("princes forgerons") are apparently to be distinguished from noble Camaras—see the reference to the name Camara in Sunjata's family in *Le Maître de la parole* (Paris: Plon, 1978); Sunjata's half brother Nan Boukari is son of a Camara woman (133).

extraordinary fervour and willingness to accompany their king and his friend Diata on a grand adventure.[40]

Their origins—their caste—can be overlooked and forgiven because of the noble deeds they perform; at the end of Le Maître de la parole, Fran Camara swears fealty to the emperor and is given full title to his kingdom by Sunjata. But the emperor then goes one step further in granting to the Camara clan equal status with the Kéita: "Henceforth we will be united. . . . The Camara princes of Tabon will grow up in Niani with the Kéita princes, and they will be treated as equals" (232). This is the explanation of the exalted status of Camaras in the Mande. As the father works in the forge in L'Enfant noir, and as he refers to his reputation as the standard-bearer of his generation, this is the heritage he bears.[41] But we have only begun to explore the meaning of identity and identification with the father in this context.

The identity of the father figure, le nom du père, is the condition to which the narrator aspires and to which he cannot seem to gain access. In the passages of Le Maître de la parole pertaining to Fran Camara, Camara Laye was working on the same problem of origin, identity, and status. To be a "father-child" (faden) is to have or to seek a certain relation with the father's totem. So when we read about the ancestor's relation to a snake in Le Maître de la parole, explaining genealogically the totemic relation, we will be in a better position to continue reading L'Enfant noir.

On the eve of the great battle, Fran Camara is visited by a snake:

> Le serpent noir, totem-ancêtre de Tabon Wana Fran Camara, pénétra sous la tente et vint se lover sous la couche de son possesseur. Bref, tous les chefs de guerre, avant que l'aube ne blanchît l'espace, avaient reçu ou perçu leur génie.
>
> Mais n'était-il pas extraordinaire, n'était-il pas miraculeux qu'en la circonstance, tous ces totems-ancêtres se manifestassent l'un après l'autre? Ils ne se montraient pas toujours. Mais aux heures décisives, leur apparition était une caution, la caution effective qu'ils donneraient à l'entreprise de leur possesseur. (217)

> The black serpent, the ancestral totem of Tabon Wana Fran Camara, entered the tent and came creeping under his couch, where it coiled up. In short, all the warrior chiefs, before dawn whitened the vastness of space, had received or heard their guardian spirits.
>
> But was it not extraordinary, was it not miraculous that in those circumstances all those ancestral totems should have manifested themselves one after the other?

<hr>

40. Camara Laye, Le Maître de la parole : 202, emphasis mine; trans. James Kirkup, The Guardian of the Word (New York: Aventura, 1984): 188, emphasis mine. Further references to the text and the translation, respectively, will be in parentheses.

41. Of course we should bear in mind that Le Maître de la parole reflects a performance paid for by a Camara, Camara Laye, and that this exaltation is designed to please that clan.

They did not often show themselves. But at critical times, their apparition was a warning, an effective warning they gave for their possessors' enterprises. (202)

In *L'Enfant noir*, the father's story of being visited by the totemic snake is directly, *genealogically* linked to the the Sunjata text, which precedes the novel by centuries of oral tradition but also follows it by 25 years, in the form of *Le Maître de la parole*, published in 1978.

Viewing the whole series of snake figures in the opening pages of *L'Enfant noir* in light of this information, we can put forth an anthropological hypothesis, with which I will experiment for a moment. There are three points at which snakes are discussed—the one the boy plays with, the snakes on the railroad tracks, and the snake that is the father's *génie*—, and from an anthropological perspective all could be subsumed to the last type of relation. The first two moments serve only to prepare the revelation of the totem.

From this perspective, Sonia Lee's puzzlement over the "choice" of the snake as a symbol is the result of a mistaken premise: that the snakes are figures freely drawn, *individual* signs. The explanation is that there is no "choice" of the snake here, not in the usual sense of the word. By indirect means, from the first paragraph of the novel, Camara is preparing the ground for the revelation of his problematic relation to his father's totem. Seen genealogically, in the Mande cultural world of the Camara clan, the snake is not chosen, it chooses. Camara Laye's use of the snake from the first page of his first novel is his way of honoring his ancestors, and in that he participates in and reproduces the most authentically Mande function of the word in literature, be it written or oral. In the three-tiered development of the snake motif, Camara Laye is honoring his father and is not far removed from the paradigmatic syntax of Mande verbal art: "*I fa k'anyi!*" (Your father is good!).

Following this logic, "meaning" becomes a function of cultural coherence. A culture is a system that can be penetrated from the outside and explained. Careful use of anthroplogical sources will help the reader advance even beyond the knowledge that is acquired by the child narrator of *L'Enfant noir*. "Understanding" may be limited: we cannot say that we really understand how the father can predict events; we may simply not believe it. But we can accept the internal logic of the system, admit its coherence, acknowledge its difference.

The meaning of the snake is thus totemic. It is not a matter of "choice" but of inheritance and genealogy; it marks a relation to a plenitude. This is to say that—even though the snakes in the opening pages of *L'Enfant noir* were clearly objects of the author's choice and intent, even though in writing his novel he could clearly have used any figure he wished in that passage—once he uses the totem of his father as a figure in the novel, *the meaning of the figure is not determined solely by writing and is not wholly subject to the power of reading.* In other words, the text itself and the practice of purely textual reading are not sufficient for the interpretation of *L'Enfant noir*.

I realize that such a statement may be controversial in some salons of Western criticism. But the process of contextual reading forces us to admit that there is something outside the text. This is to say that for the moment we will allow some autonomy to the notion of totemism; but Camara's use of this loaded, dated anthropological term will require efforts on our part to examine its history and consequences. At this point, the experiment demands a radical bracketing of the problems associated with ethnographic authority, a surrender to the history of colonial anthropology, in order to see what results.

Old anthropological sources are full of information on totemism in the Mande, one of the most striking features of the local "religion" or belief system. The new sources nearly are silent (James Fernandez is the only exception I have found). In one of the first full ethnographies of the region, Charles Monteil, a colonial administrator, described the *tne* or totemic taboo among the Bambara in some detail:

> Among the laws that the Bambara imposes on himself or on his fellows, the most widespread and, *in any case, the most striking to the European observer*, are the interdictions (*tne*): the Bambara forbids himself, his family and his fellow Bambara to perform certain acts, to pronounce certain words . . . , and the area of these restrictions is, in principle, unlimited. A hasty—and therefore superficial and incomplete—study of what can be called the honorific name (*jamu*) advanced ethnographers' knowledge of these *jamu* alone; it is especially in this restricted area that interdictions have been analyzed.
>
> In reality, the interdiction (*tne*) reaches every part of the native milieu, as its very law. Its object is to prevent any contact whatsoever with the invisible, with the thought that if this contact is made, it will automatically result in the punishment of the person who did it, unless the person has the time and the means to purify himself ritually. . . .
>
> In the family, the heart of the collectivity, the individual finds himself surrounded, during his entire lifetime, by these *tne*. The *tne* establish and maintain the authority of the elders (*koro-u*), and *particularly of the first among them, the* fa; the *tne* are active in the imposition and elaboration of ancestral traditions, laid down in successive layers since earliest times. The full set of these traditions form precisely the family custom.
>
> The patriarchy, the fraternities, the State, all Bambara collective units proceed in the same fashion, for all the collective units of society are modeled in some way on the natural family.
>
> Religion, the family, the society as a whole—in a word, Bambara civiliza-

tion—have been and continue to be to a large extent under the dependence of the *tne*.[42]

Leaving aside for the moment the commentary that a Clifford Geertz or a Jean Bazin might make on this passage (on the forced unification of a culture, reduced to a "typical" single "Bambara"; on the prominent place accorded the European observer, at the center of a tableau that unfolds around him, which in turn commands a total view of all "Bambara" civilization),[43] we can acknowledge a certain coherence between Monteil's ethnographic observations of 1924 and Camara's autobiographical novel of 1953. To the question that the child-narrator asks—"Qu'étaient ces génies que je rencontrais un peu partout, qui défendaient telle chose, commandaient telle autre?"—there is the answer provided by the father in *L'Enfant noir*; to this we can add the outsider's inside information that anthropology provides.

From the child's perspective we understand that the snake, his father's *tne*, is the foundation of the father's authority; Monteil takes the power of the totem from the level of the family, beginning with the *jamu*, to the level of the entire civilization. Between *L'Enfant noir* and Monteil's *Les Bambara* we go from the microscopic to the telescopic: Camara gives us the point of view of one child in the process of acculturation; Monteil describes the totality of a culture using the device of a unifying citizen-type, "le Bambara." In both texts, there is a crossing of voices, a sort of dialogue. The narrator of *L'Enfant noir* is not just the child, but also the adult looking back from an alienated perspective, as an insider turned outsider. Monteil admits his status as an outsider along with the superficiality of some of his research, but this does not prevent him from speaking in the place of "the Bambara"; he is an outsider in control of the insider's thought. Both "narrators" issue disclaimers, limiting their authority and competence (Camara: "Je l'ignore: j'ai quitté mon père trop tôt"; Monteil: "Une étude hâtive, et par suite superficielle et incomplète"), but it is the European outsider who seems *more* in command. The ethnographic text even seems to increase its power and further validate its enterprise by calling attention to certain faults, for by doing so, the ethnographer highlights his own honesty.

Another early authority on Mande totemism is Maurice Delafosse, whose study debunking the notion of "totemic clans" I used earlier, in discussing the role of the *jamu*. His work is essential because he rejects

---

42. Charles Monteil, *Les Bambara du Ségou et du Kaarta* (Paris: Emile Larose, 1924): 131–32, emphasis mine.

43. Not to mention Monteil's colonial condescension: "le Noir ne s'abstrait pas de la nature environnante, il n'est pas arrivé à ce stade" (156, see also 307n).

"totem" as a valid term for the context, in a gesture parallel to Mc-Naughton's rejection of "caste." Delafosse also insists on the *figural* nature of the relation to an animal in Mande culture. A more recent African ethnographer, Alpha Condé, confirms that there is "no identification" between the being (animal or vegetable) and the ancestor and that "the *tana* is certainly 'taboo' but not at all a totem." [44] This contradicts Arnold van Gennep's theory, which insists on the belief in a "parental," that is, *literal* link between person and animal. [45] The distinction is essential for understanding *L'Enfant noir* and its position on totemism, and I will return to Delafosse's argument presently.

It is evident that my experiment is getting more deeply drawn into increasingly European concerns. We are crossing an invisible border between direct ethnographic "information" about Mande beliefs and the Western anthropological, theoretical machine. Maintaining an awareness of the risks involved, I would like to see what Western theory has to offer here.

Totemism is one of the great topoi of classical anthropology; the literature on the subject is vast, and I do not intend to give an account of it here. [46] Rather I will touch on two twentieth-century theories of totemism—Freud's and Lévi-Strauss's—, and make a detour through a relevant ethnopsychoanalytical theory to see what help is provided, if any, by these Western theories with universal pretensions.

When he wrote the word "totem" in *L'Enfant noir*, Camara Laye was using a French word that was derived from the English version of a native American (Algonquin) word. When Freud defined a totem in 1913 as "an animal (whether edible and harmless or dangerous and feared) and more rarely a plant . . . , which stands in a peculiar relation to the whole clan . . . [as] the common ancestor of the clan . . . [and as] their guardian spirit and helper," [47] he was borrowing from the classics of late nineteenth-

44. Alpha Condé, "Les sociétés traditionnelles mandingues," typescript without place or date, but probably written around 1972.

45. See Delafosse, "Des soi-disant clans," 89. On Mande totemism, see also Henri Labouret, *Les Mandings et leur langue* (Paris: Larose, 1934): 130–32. See also Arnold van Gennep, *Tabou et totémisme à Madagascar: Etude descriptive et théorique* (Paris: E. Leroux, 1904).

46. See Edmund Leach, ed., *The Structural Study of Myth and Totemism* (London: Tavistock Publications, 1967); Marvin Harris, *The Rise of Anthropological Theory* (New York: Columbia University Press, 1968): 40, 193–94, 425–33; and Marcel Mauss, "Le Totémisme: problèmes et faux problèmes," in *Oeuvres 1: Les Fonctions sociales du sacré* (Paris: Minuit, 1968): 162–89.

47. Sigmund Freud, *Totem and Taboo*, trans. James Strachey (New York: W. W. Norton, 1950), 2. Further references, abbreviated *TT*, will be included in the text.

century anthropology. In works such as Sir James Frazer's *Totemism and Exogamy* (1910), a four-volume monument to the West's self-confident ability to compare and judge customs from around the world, Freud found the raw material for his theory of totem and taboo. (His title is actually a paraphrase of Frazer's, the *incest* taboo—which imposes the law of exogamy—being the key to totemism for Freud.) Freud's extremely heavy reliance on Frazer's "almost parodic reduction" of social evolutionary thought[48] left *Totem and Taboo* an easy target for attack.

The political underbelly of Freud's theory is revealed in his subtitle: "Some Points of Agreement Between the Mental Lives of Savages and Neurotics"; *Totem and Taboo* is a classic case of the West seeking answers to its own problem (neurotics) by pursuing an analogy to other, more distant, suppressed groups (savages, the colonized). I would like consciously to bracket the obvious problem that the subtitle raises, for a moment at least, because it is so obvious and because the validity of *Totem and Taboo* has, almost from its initial publication, been said to come not from its anthropological base but from its psychology.[49] In other words, while Freud may have relied on sources that were outdated even in 1913, while he can be faulted for having disguised a "timeless psychological explanation" as *history*,[50] and while his sources may now show themselves to be tainted by colonialism, he may have nonetheless hit upon a theory with universal significance.

The intellectual scheme of *Totem and Taboo* is not in fact limited to a face-off between what we would now call the first world (Freud's neurotics) and the third world (Freud's savages). The chapter that offers the main theoretical thesis of the book is called "The Return of Totemism in Childhood." The universal factor of childhood provides a bridge within Freud's theory, between on the one hand the present world of civilization and its discontents and on the other the primal world of present-day savages and prehistoric men. Central to Freud's theory is the idea that each child everywhere reenacts the evolution of the human race, emerging from a belief in the "omnipotence of thoughts" toward an ability to distinguish between psychical and factual reality (*TT*, 159). Totemism "constitutes a regular phase in all cultures" (109) and lies at the root of "all later religions" (145). Freud gives the example of a childhood phobia

48. George W. Stocking, Jr., *Functionalism Historicized: Essays on British Social Anthropology, The History of Anthropology, vol. 2* (Madison: University of Wisconsin Press, 1984): 137–38.

49. See Edwin R. Wallace IV, *Freud and Anthropology: A History and Reappraisal* (New York: International Universities Press, 1983), and Robin Fox, "*Totem and Taboo* Reconsidered," in Leach, *The Structural Study*, 161–78.

50. A. L. Kroeber quoted by Fox, in Leach, *The Structural Study*, 167.

in which "psycho-analysis has revealed that the totem animal is in reality a substitute for the father" (141). The totem is a way to kill the father but also to identify with him. The two taboos of totemism—not to kill the totem and not to marry a spouse with the same totem—correspond exactly to the two repressed wishes of the Oedipus complex (143). The identification is *total* within what Freud calls psychical reality, and his explanation of "the return of totemism in childhood" as an atavistic manifestation of the Oedipus complex might be applied to a reading of *L'Enfant noir*.

Such an application, while tempting, would require an attempt to tip-toe through the ideological minefield that surrounds *Totem and Taboo*; it would require the bracketing of the political problems I mentioned above (a bracketing that can only be momentary). The analysis that follows will therefore be my parody of an approach about which I remain skeptical. What we have seen of Mande totemism in *L'Enfant noir* presents certain aspects that are compatible with Freud's basic theory. That the snake is a substitute for the father is one of the obvious points of the narrative: unlike the childhood phobia that Freud analyzes, this case of totemism is open and diagnoses itself ("Toujours [le serpent] apparaît à l'un de nous. Dans notre génération, c'est à moi [le père] qu'il s'est présenté," 19). That the nature of the identification father/snake is total is also explicitly stated in the novel ("Il y a identité entre le totem et son possesseur; cette identité est absolue," 80 ["The totem is identified with its possessor; this identification is absolute," 74]). Seen through the analytical framework of the Oedipus theory, the *father's* relation to the totemic snake is an example of a happily resolved act of repression and sublimation: there is no neurosis here because Mande tradition and ritual have offered a system—the system of totemism—by which Oedipal energies can be channelled and bound. The unqualified happiness of the father, secure in his magical powers and in his position in the family, is the model of a resolved totemic-Oedipal relation; his story of encounters with his totem is an exotic allegory of the Oedipus complex; his unproblematic identity results from this relation to the totem. The *son's* very problematic relation to the totem (which we are about to explore), on the other hand, is a sign of an unresolved Oedipus complex. More generally, Camara Laye's inability to say—as we shall see—whether he had a totem of his own or not, is a sign of a deep, unresolved problem of identity, which is an Oedipal problem. *L'Enfant noir* is from this perspective a symptom of an unresolved Oedipus complex.

The fact that this exercise in applied theory has appeared to "work" should not be mistaken for a confirmation of its validity. The power of a theory to assimilate phenomena to itself should neither be ignored nor mistaken for truth itself.

Marie-Cécile and Edmond Ortigues made a classic attempt to explore the consequences of such an application in their *Oedipe africain*, a record and analysis of their experience as clinical psychiatrists in Dakar from 1962 to 1966.[51] Complex and subtle, *Oedipe africain* is a fine example of the triumphs and pitfalls of Western theories applied to Africa. The Ortigues' conclusion is that "the Oedipus complex exist[s] in the African populations," but that "the conditions of its repression did not present themselves in the same way as in Europe" (342):

> The father figure tended to be absorbed into a global figure of his age group; the fantasm of the father's death tended to be transferred to the ancestor, to a father who is already dead, who cannot be attacked and who represents the authority of Custom; rivalry tended to be displaced onto the "brothers" or those called "equals" (*nawle*), and at the same time aggressivity repressed by the law of solidarity would be turned into paranoid [*persécutives*] interpretations. (339–40, my translation)

In allowing that the Oedipus complex presents itself differently among Africans, the Ortigues are careful to distance themselves from earlier anthropologists such as Bronislaw Malinowski, who asserted that the Oedipus complex was "restricted to the Aryan, patriarchal society."[52] Among the Trobriand Islanders that are the object of his study, matrilineal family structure allegedly provides for "almost complete harmony with the biological course of development," with "nothing suppressed,

51. Marie-Cécile and Edmond Ortigues, *Oedipe africain* (Paris: Union Générale d'Editions, 1973). Melville J. and F. S. Herskovits analyzed a different "African rephrasing" of the Oedipus complex in their study of Dahomey (now Benin); see their "Sibling Rivalry, the Oedipus Complex and Myth," *Journal of American Folklore* 71, no. 279 (1958): 1–15. The other classic attempt at an application of Oedipal theory to Africa was made by Meyer Fortes in his essay *Oedipus and Job in West African Religion* (Cambridge: Cambridge University Press, 1983 [1959]). The Fortes piece is followed by a cogent critique, with considerable relevance to my experiment here, by Robin Horton, "Social Psychologies: African and Western." See also James W. Fernandez, "Filial Piety and Power: Psychosocial Dynamics in the Legends of Shaka and Sundiata," *Science and Psychoanalysis* 14 (1969): 47–60. In contrast to these works, which try to adapt Western paradigms to Africa, Awa Thiam flatly rejects any theory of an African Oedipus complex, because "la famille négro-africaine est polynucléaire. . . . A priori on peut présumer de l'inexistence du complexe d'Oedipe en Afrique dans les familles traditionnelles"; for her, the Ortigues' work consists "non pas à découvrir autrui tel qu'il est dans sa culture, mais à y mettre ce qu'on aimerait y trouver." *Continents noirs* (n.p.: Tierce, 1987): 79–81.

52. Bronislaw Malinowski, *Sex and Repression in Savage Society* (New York: Harcourt, Brace & Co., 1927): 173. See also Melford E. Spiro, *Oedipus in the Trobriands* (Chicago: University of Chicago Press, 1982).

nothing negative, no frustrated desire," because the father is "first a nurse and then a companion" rather than the brutal despot that he is in Europe (75–77).[53] The Ortigues find little of value in Malinowski's "long, uninterpretable pages" of "happy naturalism" (*Oedipe africain*, 348).

The Ortigues see no evidence in Africa of such an escape from sexual repression: "the incest taboo presents itself as a difference which tends asymptotically toward zero, but can never disappear entirely, *unless culture and language are to collapse into the void*" (381, emphasis mine). In other words, only a blind romanticism can make such an escape appear possible. The argument here is parallel to Derrida's critique of Lévi-Strauss, asserting the universal inescapability of difference. Referring to the "chicken or the egg" problem that recurs in Oedipal theory—which came first, culture and its taboos or nature and its family ties—, the authors comment:

> Let us not disdain this difficulty: no vocabulary will triumph over it; it comes from language itself. It is as if we wanted to transport ourselves back to the origins of language and name the unnameable. . . . Thus, in order to conceive logically what the incest taboo means psychologically, in order to avoid the vicious circle of the chicken and the egg, what else are we to do but acknowledge from the start a *pure differential* [*une pure différentielle*], a gap (as small as you like) relative to some "zero point" which is given *fictively*. (380–81, emphasis mine)

By asserting a purely differential, structural theory, considering relations between terms rather than the terms themselves, and based on an *aporia*, a fiction of origin, *Oedipe africain* rises to a level of generality that ap-

---

53. Malinowski does not wish to reject Freudian psychology altogether but rather to challenge its applicability: "By my analysis I have established that Freud's theories not only roughly correspond to human psychology, but that they follow closely the modification in human nature brought about by various constitutions of society. . . . It appears necessary [however] . . . not to assume the universal existence of the Oedipus complex, but in studying every type of civilization, to establish the special complex which pertains to it" (81–82). He then advances his theory on the Oedipus complex within matrilineal societies, based on his research among the Trobriand Islanders: he describes the "avunculate complex," by which the maternal uncle is given the role of primal father and scapegoat for the hatred of the son, whereas the real father is allowed to be kind and lenient; sexual desire is displaced from the mother to the sister (see 74–84; 138–39). There are two striking problems with Malinowski's writings: first, the agenda that requires non-European societies to respond to and provide escape from European problems (namely, escape from sexual repression); and second, his brand of common-sensical, intuitive psychology, which reduces complexes to "attitudes" of the most domestic and familiar sort and depends on the author's personal feelings and observations ("Why should the young males remain hanging around the parental horde, why should they hate the father and desire his death?" [164]; in Central and Eastern Europe, "when a father returns home from work, or drunk from the inn, he naturally vents his ill-temper on the family, and bullies mother and children" [29]).

proches irrefutability. The purer the differential nature of the theory, the less it should be susceptible to the content-loaded, ethnocentric datedness of Malinowski. *Oedipe africain* thus presents the possibility of a value-neutral Western theory of Africa.

But it is precisely for its supposed neutrality and universality, compromised by an underlying belief in origins and progress, that the theory of *Oedipe africain* may be criticized. Although the Ortigues are a long way from Freud's value-laden subtitle, we may inquire if their highly sophisticated rendition of ethnopsychoanalysis—or any other theoretical model based on a notion of origins and progress for that matter—is so purely universal that all questions of ethnocentrism may be dismissed. Can a theory reach beyond contingency and specific reference, to a universal point of origin, valid for all cultures? Within its own coherent terms it certainly can, but only at a certain cost. The Ortigues frankly admit this when they reveal the "fictive" basis of their theory.

Agreeing that all theories are based on fictions, and congratulating the Ortigues for recognizing this within their own theory, we might leave it at that. However, it is equally important to discuss the consequences of this fictivity, one of which is the imprint of a certain discourse on the Ortigues' work. I cannot help but notice that the Ortigues couch their work in a romantic vision of evolution and primitivism that is descended from Rousseau, through the long history of Orientalism, to Freud and the subtitle of *Totem and Taboo*. Their Africa is a place where Europeans travel backward in time:

> Thus, if only in order to better understand Freud's hypothesis, why not try to do his own procedure over again? Why not expatriate ourselves in time and space, toward lands where the sky is clearer, where in the evening, when the shade of the trees thickens, they say, the voice of dead fathers—spirits of the lineage—still murmur in the branches? (10)

These sentiments, which conclude their introduction, are harmless enough, but they arrange for certain stakes to be played out in the book that follows. The Ortigues feel that Freud's armchair anthropology will be better understood if it is reappraised under the clear skies of Africa. Their image of Africa is firmly grounded in primitivism, in the premise that what Europe has lost—the voices of the ancestors—Africa still has. The Ortigues set off in search of the fictive crossroads between nature and culture (the "zero point"), with the assumption that Africa is closer to it than Europe is.[54] But if this is so, their African Oedipal theory is

54. This notion of proximity to nature seems almost unshakable; it is found even in James Fernandez's remarks on totemism in *Persuasions and Performances* (Bloomington: Indiana University Press, 1986): "Totemism is one of a variety of tropic structures—apt in

more like the unfolding of a timeless, immutable *essence* than a purely differential, neutral construct; more than they think it is. If Africa is closer to the crossroads, then cultural neutrality is compromised by the superior advancement of the West, the greater distance of the West from that crossroads. The evolutionary model, with its inexorable (if reversible) judgments of superiority and inferiority, is at odds with the desire for a value-free differential field. We are left in an aporia between conflicting discourses with conflicting claims, somewhere between the chicken and the egg.[55]

If Freud and various Oedipal theories leave us in doubt as to the neutral "applicability" of a universal Western theory, in turning to the theory that Lévi-Strauss expounded in a book-length essay called *Le Totémisme aujourd'hui*, we find a more appropriate model, one which attempts to take into account both totemism itself and the problem of Western perceptions of totemism. Writing as a critic or a meta-anthropologist, Lévi-Strauss analyzes totemism as an *illusion* fabricated by the West to suit its own needs. Totemism, like hysteria, was made to appear "more different" than it is, by scholars working "under the guise of scientific objectivity" to "mark off certain human phenomena—as though they constituted a natural entity—which scholars preferred to regard as alien to their own moral universe, thus protecting the attachment which they felt toward the latter."[56] The word totemism itself is a "distortion of [the] semantic field" (18). This perspective allows us better to deal with political problems of anthropological discourse; Lévi-Strauss's study calls much of the literature on totemism into question by showing its ideological willfulness. Totemism is thereby shown to be akin to Orientalism.

Yet Lévi-Strauss does not, as has been claimed, "abolish totemism" rather than "understand" it (although abolition might not have been such a bad thing); in fact, he only reforms it.[57] He launches the study by discussing totemism posthumously, as an already "demolished," "liqui-

---

the archaic world *because of the proximity of that world to nature*—arising out of the earliest experience of inchoate subjects attempting through various concrete predications upon themselves to escape the anxiety of inchoateness" (36, emphasis mine).

55. But so is *L'Enfant noir*, we should not fail to notice; the theoretical validity of *Oedipe africain* may be separated from its relevance to our reading. An evolutionary model is implied in the novel by the metaphor (and fact) of childhood that Camara uses; the necessary link between totemism and linguistic difference is seen in the process of the child learning to differentiate between snakes ("Celui-ci, mon enfant, il ne faut pas le tuer: ce serpent n'est pas un serpent comme les autres [17]).

56. *Totemism*, trans. Rodney Needham (Boston: Beacon Press, 1963): 1.

57. Peter Worsley, "Groote Eylandt Totemism and *Le Totémisme aujourd'hui*, in Leach, ed., *Structural Study*, 142: "For Lévi-Strauss, indeed, the problem is not to understand totemism, but to abolish it."

dated" (5) term. But, as a professional anthropologist, he clings to what he sees as the vital mission of his discipline: to seek among the disparate fragments of evidence a "level so general that all observed cases may figure in it as particular modes."[58] "Atomization," the refusal to make broad comparions between cultures, then, is a threat to the anthropological endeavor. Systems can and must be described.[59]

Totemism as a system is, in one of Lévi-Strauss's formulations here, "what remains of a diminished totality" (26). I will place more weight on this phrase than Lévi-Strauss does; it is actually his paraphrase of other anthropologists. On the one hand, this formulation does seem to represent Lévi-Stauss's own view of totemism, and on the other, it fits the theory that *L'Enfant noir* implies. In his conclusion, Lévi-Strauss describes totemism as an *intellectual* phenomenon (a point that did not go without saying at the time), as the primal trace of figural language, trope, metaphor, emotion, and poetry (102). This is where Lévi-Strauss wishes to bring an ideological correction to bear: Western anthropology had exaggerated the "difference" of totemism by interpreting it as a kind of fetishism. The latter term, a notorious invention of Western discourse on non-Western beliefs, refers to the collapse of representation, the primitive inability to tell sign from being.[60] Lévi-Strauss discovers the mediating, metaphorical nature of totemism in "native theory itself" (20). By insisting on its *representational* nature, by showing its close relation to Rousseau and to Bergson, Lévi-Strauss redeems totemism as a viable mode of intellection. The Ortigues' version of the incest taboo is clearly linked to Lévi-Strauss and the differential notion of the origin of language.

58. Criticizing Raymond Firth's and Meyer Fortes's work on totemism, Lévi-Strauss writes: "Now we shall never get to the bottom of the alleged problem of totemism—and on this point we are in agreement with Radcliffe-Brown—by thinking up a solution having only a limited field of application and then manipulating recalcitrant cases until the facts give way, but by reaching a level so general that all observed cases may figure in it as particular modes" (77).

59. Lévi-Strauss takes Adolphus P. Elkin to task for placing theory over the facts:

Elkin dissociates the facts so that theory shall be saved . . . in order to preserve the reality of totemism at any price . . . But, faced with a situation of this type, there are two ways of proceeding: either to throw out the baby with the bathwater, i. e., to give up all hope of reaching a systematic interpretation rather than start all over again, or to be inspired by sufficient confidence in the outlines of order already discerned to broaden one's perspective, seeking a more general point of view which will permit the integration of forms whose regularity has already been established but whose resistance to systematization may perhaps be explained, not by intrinsic characteristics, but by the fact that they have been ill defined, incompletely analyzed, or viewed in too narrow a fashion (46).

His distinction between "placing theory over facts" (which he is against) and "seeking a more general point of view" (which he is for) is highly problematic.

60. On fetishism, see my *Blank Darkness: Africanist Discourse in French*: 39–49.

Switching to the Mande context and to Delafosse's argument, we find a similar insistence on the figural:

Many natives of the Western Soudan declare, "Our family and the panther are the same thing," or "the panther is my brother." But they mean by this nothing different from what we mean ourselves when we speak of the brotherly ties between the French and the Belgians. As we do in this case, they speak *figuratively* and do not at all mean that they are descended from a panther or that their family and the panther came from a common ancestor. ("Des soi-disant clans," 90, emphasis mine)

Leaving aside what appears to be a "Belgian joke" here, Delafosse provides a bridge between Lévi-Strauss (who is completely extracontextual) and *L'Enfant noir* within the Mande. Both Delafosse and Lévi-Strauss are reformers of the old-fashioned totemism of Frazer and company; although Delafosse rejects the word itself as "vain," he "listens to what the natives say" and argues that their concept of *tana* is a figural one.

Lévi-Strauss's theory and Delafosse's testimonial ethnography should—if everything is working correctly—allow us to translate the figure of the totem in *L'Enfant noir* from the Mande world that is remembered by the narrator to the francophone dimension of his writing and our reading. Within the Mande, the totem would indeed appear to be "that which remains of a diminished totality," the totality being the orderly systems of relations, customs, and beliefs that hark back to the glory days of the empire. The Sunjata epic is the principal reminder of the lost plenitude; the griots' verbal art seeks to revive the totality but is suspected of diminishing it. Totemism is another reminder. The snake is to the father in *L'Enfant noir* a sign of his kinship, his powers as a smith, and his prestige in the community.

But there appears to be a disjunction between Lévi-Strauss and Delafosse on the one hand and Camara Laye on the other. *L'Enfant noir* does not show the Mande totem to be a metaphor *consciously recognized as such* within the culture: rather it is magic; it performs; it acts. The father insists on the reality of the snake's appearances to him ("Je le vis *réellement*," 20). Later in the novel, Camara states that there is "total identification" between the totem and its possessor (80; 75); that is, that a totemic relation is unmediated, a relation of self to itself. It is a re-presentation rather than a representation. By his very use of the word "totem," Camara puts himself at odds with Delafosse.

Within the obviously figural frame of the novel genre, Camara seems to deny the figurality of totemism, and I would like to examine the implications of this in relation to Western anthropology. Does he actually contradict Lévi-Strauss's theory and Delafosse's ethnography?

At the least, there is a gap between interpretation from the outside (through anthropology) and experience on the inside. The latter, which we know only through the father's words as reported in this novel, is of course "always already" representational; the reader's experience will never be direct. But the outside—anthropological analysis—must not be imposed on the inside as a truth that the insiders do not realize about their own culture. To do so would be to adopt the paternalistic position of Tempels or Frobenius that I criticized at the beginning of this study. It is preferable to leave the gap as it is, with the truth of Mande "totemism" still somewhat of a secret (as we are told it ought to be).

The real object of my analysis is, in fact, not the totem itself, but its remains within the francophone novel. Through the prism of the colonizer's written language, the totality of totemism is remembered and diminished, as is the glory of Sunjata's empire in the oral epic. The crux of James Fernandez's remarks on totemism are relevant here. Leaving aside his (I think) misguided statements about the greater proximity of "archaic" societies to nature, I find the following formulation helpful: "The power in totemism is that it at once preserves a sense of . . . primordial identification processes and achieves a sense of separation both from nature and from other social subjects" (*Persuasions*, 36). In other words, totemism is a question of both identity and difference.

It is in the context of this understanding, caught between two worlds, that Lévi-Strauss is more relevant. The last chapter of *Totemism* is called "Totemism From Within," but it is based on a reading of Rousseau and Bergson, European philosophers as removed as one could imagine from the anthroplogical totemism that is the ostensible object of the study. The estrangement is purposeful on Lévi-Strauss's part: it elevates his discourse to a plane of generality, "a level so general that all observed cases may figure in it." But in redeeming totemism as an intellectual mode, we must wonder, has Lévi-Strauss assimilated it to Western discourse, casting totem-believers as precursors or unwitting followers of Rousseau and Bergson? In seeking to correct the exaggeration of difference, does Lévi-Strauss exaggerate sameness? Is it necessary that the "general level" be commanded by European thought? Since Lévi-Strauss's move toward theoretical synthesis in some sense parallels the move that is described in *L'Enfant noir*—from local to general, from Kouroussa to Paris, from *nyamakala* art forms to the francophone novel—we should spend a few more moments on this question before seeing how the theory of totemism is played out in *L'Enfant noir*.

What do we gain from comparing *L'Enfant noir* with Monteil, Lévi-Strauss, the Ortigues, and other anthropological sources? In spite of the tensions and historical frictions that come between *L'Enfant noir* and these anthropological texts, there is a theoretical basis for comparing them. If criticism of African literature is going to interact with anthropology, it will inevitably borrow some of the assumptions that underpin that discipline. We have uncovered one of those assumptions here in reading Monteil: the tendency—perhaps inevitable—for the ethnographer to use collective entities and personalities as his/her object. "The Bambara," "the Bantu," "the Mande nobleman," are all condensations made in the ethnographer's thought and prose, producing a coherent unity out of the many interviews and contacts that took place in the field. If one were to imagine that this process of condensation suddenly became illegal or inadmissible, the cost would obviously be a loss of the ability to write understandable, synthetic studies of cultures. More up-to-date ethnographers may leaven their work with fragmentation and self-reflexivity, but the basic project remains the same: the description of other cultures as systems, not of individuals taken in and of themselves or of random observations. There would be nothing wrong with the latter project; it just does not seem to be what most anthropology does.[61]

Lévi-Strauss's argument in favor of the "general level" is elucidated in his masterful essay "Introduction à l'oeuvre de Marcel Mauss." Here Lévi-Strauss makes clear the reasoning behind the anthropological penchant for collective wholes, including Mauss's "total social phenomenon" (*fait social total*). Discussing at length the tension between psychic activity, which is seen as individual, and collective social systems, Lévi-Strauss describes the relation between the two as complementary: the psychic is a simple "élément de signification" within a greater system, but (and this is the crucial complication) it is also *the sole means of verification* for the system as a whole. "The only guarantee we can have that a total fact corresponds to reality, instead of being an arbitrary accumulation of more or less truthful details, is if that fact is demonstrable in concrete experience [saisissable dans une expérience concrète]." But individual experience in and of itself, according to Lévi-Strauss, has no *symbolic meaning*. "Normal individual behaviors *are never symbolic by themselves*: they are the elements with which a symbolic system, *which can only be collective* [emphasis mine] is built."[62] This notion of collec-

---

61. There is of course a subgenre, the ethnographic biography or individual case study, which ostensibly focusses on individuals, but most often it is only in service of a wider, more collective notion. Vincent Crapanzano's *Tuhami: Portrait of a Moroccan* (Chicago: University of Chicago Press, 1980), is an excellent example: the first word refers to an individual, but the rest of the title introduces a collective construct, "the Moroccan."

62. Claude Lévi-Strauss, "Introduction à l'oeuvre de Marcel Mauss," in Marcel Mauss, *Sociologie et anthropologie* (Paris: Presses Universitaires de France, 1950): xxvi–xxvii; xvi. For a commentary on Lévi-Strauss's insistence on modes of thought that are shared by all humans (as opposed to exclusive, particular, *ethnic* beliefs and structures), see Dan Sperber's chapter "Claude Lévi-Strauss aujourd'hui," in *Le Savoir des anthropologues* (Paris: Hermann, 1982): 89–128.

tivity is of course only a prerequisite for the level of real analysis: the level of "elementary structure," "the unconscious," and "universal laws."

An anthropological approach to *L'Enfant noir* and to the specific problem of the snake motif will therefore naturally and logically be drawn to an interpretation that inserts the motif within a collective system. This is what I have tried to do by showing the relation between the snake as totem and the identity of the Camara clan through the name of the father. The nuances that Freud, Lévi-Strauss, and others have introduced here are merely expansions on the basic idea that there is a collective system at work here: this idea makes up the epistemological frame of "totemism."

When V. Y. Mudimbe addressed the question of ethnopsychoanalysis and the universality of the Oedipus complex, it led him into a meditation on the inevitability of subjectivity in discourse. Intellectual undertakings are "prisoners of [their] epistemological frames"; they "only unfold the consequences of [their] own postulates."[63] In other words, there is no alternative to "finding" the bone you've buried yourself. The topos of totemism within its anthropological frame dictates certain "findings," with a bias toward collective coherence and a penchant for primitivism.

Falling Short

The neat coherence of this interpretation accounts for only one side of the pendulum swing that recurs constantly in *L'Enfant noir;* further evidence must be considered. The movement outward toward the expansion of the child's knowledge and the narrator's power is quickly undercut by the complementary movement of retreat and limitation. While the expansiveness of the novel—its moments of ethnographic authority—allowed us to go far afield in search of relevant information, its complementary moments of slippage invite a reappraisal of anthropology's penchant for the collective.

The father's lesson ends with the following passage:

Quand je relevai les yeux, je vis que mon père m'observait.

—Je t'ai dit tout cela, petit, parce que tu es mon fils, l'aîné de mes fils, et que je n'ai rien à te cacher. Il y a une manière de conduite à tenir et certaines façons d'agir, pour qu'un jour le génie de notre race se dirige vers toi aussi. J'étais, moi, dans cette ligne de conduite qui détermine notre génie à nous visiter; oh! inconsciemment peut-être, mais toujours est-il que si tu veux que le génie de notre race te visite un jour, si tu veux en hériter à ton tour, il faudra que tu adoptes ce même comportement; il faudra que tu me fréquentes davantage.

---

63. V. Y. Mudimbe, *L'Autre face du royaume: une introduction à la critique des langages en folie* (n.p.: L'Age d'homme, 1973): 93.

Il me regardait avec passion et, brusquement, il soupira.

—J'ai peur, j'ai bien peur, petit, que tu ne me fréquentes jamais assez. Tu vas à l'école et, un jour, tu quitteras cette école pour une plus grande. Tu me quitteras, petit. . . .

Et de nouveau il soupira. . . . Il me parut soudain comme vieilli. (22)

When I raised my eyes, I saw that my father was watching me.

"I have told you all these things, little one, because you are my son, the eldest of my sons, and because I have nothing to hide from you. There is a certain form of behavior to observe, and certain ways of acting in order that the guiding spirit of our race may approach you also. I, your father, was observing that form of behavior which persuades our guiding spirit to visit us. Oh, perhaps not consciously: but nevertheless it is true that if you desire the guiding spirit of our race to visit you one day, if you desire to inherit it in your turn, you will have to conduct yourself in the same manner; from now on, it will be necessary for you to be more and more in my company.

He gazed at me with burning eyes, then suddenly he heaved a sigh.

"I fear, I very much fear, little one, that you are not often enough in my company. You are all day at school, and one day you will depart from that school for a bigger one. You will leave me, little one. . . ."

And again he heaved a sigh. . . . He suddenly seemed to me an old man. (26–27, AT)

Camara *père* is not merely part of a biological progression; his bloodlines have been complemented by a "line of conduct" that made him worthy of the blessings of the snake. His singularity within his caste and clan is however, not a case of modern individualism. He is more like a condensed representation of the collectivity, and thereby invested with special powers, than an exception or aberration. He displays spectacular qualities of *fadenya*, which distinguishes him and differentiates him within the group. In this, the figure of the father in his very singularity is analogous to the anthropologist's condensation of group characteristics into a single type. The father in *L'Enfant noir* is "the father," "the Mande blacksmith"; and importantly, *he is the son's native informant*. In the (diegetic) space of the narrative, the power relations are the opposite of what they are in the process of the novel's narration: within the story, the father commands; but in retrospect, the son reorders and reshapes the father's knowledge to a new form and purpose, the agendas of the francophone novel.

There is therefore a hinge of difference between the father's relation to the culture and the son's; that hinge is in the passage cited above. The father followed a strict line of conduct and was rewarded by a privileged relation to his totemic snake. He admonishes the son to do likewise if he wants to enjoy the same privileges, but he expresses his fear that the son will fall away. Between his two phrases "Il faudra désormais que tu me

fréquentes davantage" and "Tu me quitteras, petit" there are two projected futures. One envisions the child becoming worthy of his honorable
jamu and of his casted profession as a blacksmith; the other conjures up
the future that we already know will come true, a future outside of the
coherence of local culture. We were already told by the narrator, "J'ai
quitté mon père trop tôt." This conversation, which should have been the
first of many initiation sessions, was the first and the last, the narrator
now tells us ("After that we never mentioned the little black snake again:
my father had spoken to me about him for the first and last time" [24;
28]), meaning that this is all that he and we will learn on the subject. The
relation to the totemic snake, so closely linked to the notion of identity
here, will now follow a path of divergence and alienation, leading back
cyclically to nostalgia, recollection, and narration. This cycle is perfectly
represented by the last two paragraphs of the chapter:

> Oui, c'était comme une conversation. Est-ce que moi aussi, un jour, je conver-
> serais de cette sorte? *Mais non: je continuais d'aller à l'école!* Pourtant j'aurais
> voulu, j'aurais tant voulu poser à mon tour ma main sur le serpent, *comprendre*,
> écouter à mon tour ce frémissement, *mais j'ignorais* comment le serpent eût ac-
> ceuilli ma main et *je ne pensais pas qu'il eût maintenant rien à me confier*, je
> craignais bien qu'il n'eût rien à me confier jamais. . . .
> Quand mon père jugeait qu'il avait assez caressé le petit animal, il le laissait;
> le serpent alors se lovait sous un des bords de la peau de mouton sur laquelle
> mon père était assis, face à son enclume. (24–25, emphasis mine)

> Yes. It was like a conversation. Would I too converse that way some day? *No.
> I continued to attend school.* Yet I should have liked so much to place my hand,
> my own hand, on that snake, and *to understand* and listen to that tremor too;
> *but I did not know* if the snake would have accepted my hand, and *I felt now
> that he would have nothing to tell me.* I was afraid that he would never have
> anything to tell me.
> When my father felt that he had stroked the snake enough he left him alone.
> Then the snake coiled himself under the edge of one of the sheepskins on which
> my father, facing his anvil, was seated. (28–29, emphasis mine)

As the father "leaves" the snake and lets it go, it is symbolic of a trans-
position in the next generation, for the son will "leave" behind the culture that the snake represents. The closure of this ending is complete
between the totemic snake, the blacksmith, and his forge, all connected
by tradition and ritual.[64]

It is a closure that leaves the son, turned narrator, on the outside,
observing, wishing he understood. But he already doubts that there is

---

64. Deep inside *Le Maître de la parole*, we find a reference to the same snake doing the
same thing ("le serpent . . . pénétra sous la tente et vint se lover sous la couche de son
possesseur"; see above, p. 142).

anything more to be revealed, and from the adult perspective tells us that in any case this is all he ever learned. In turning from "I didn't know" if the snake would welcome me to "I felt now that he had nothing to tell me," the narrator places himself in the precarious position, suspended between inside and outside, of the prodigal who questions the totality he has left behind, which in turn appears to be "diminished" by his look back upon it.

Here, then, is the hinge between "Camara" and "Laye." The *jamu* includes the father, the son, and the snake in a binding identification that the son must adhere to or risk losing. The *tògò*, Laye, refers to the son alone and the path he will follow by himself, through the French schools that will reform him, give him an identity card, and make of him a novelist named Laye. He will not be a smith of whose *jamu*, Camara, the griots will sing. The unity between father and totem, excluding the son, at the end of the first chapter, is symbolic of the individuation and differentiation without which the writing of a novel seems impossible. This is the brave new world of the colonial francophone novel.

I would like to attempt an analysis of this new situation—the alienation of the narrator—using one of the tools employed above to analyze the collective symbolics of the totem. Lévi-Strauss's theory stated that a symbolic system can only be collective, that individual behavior in and of itself is not symbolic. Within the anthropological frame of reference, this makes perfect sense: the informant who thinks differently from everyone else in the group is an unreliable source. But in the context of written literatures, this theory itself seems aberrant: individuality and originality are the ideological cornerstones of modern (Western) literature. How should we turn this corner; how can we adapt our methodology to follow and understand the change that we have just observed in *L'Enfant noir*? Lévi-Strauss offers us a means of bridging the gap between collectivity and individual, between Camara and Laye.

Having stated that individual acts are only symbolic as elements in a collective system, Lévi-Strauss returns to clarify the interpretation of individual difference.

> Any society is therefore comparable to a universe in which discrete bodies alone would be highly structured. In all societies therefore, it would be inevitable that a percentage (and a variable percentage at that) of individuals are placed, so to speak, outside of the system or between two or several irreducible systems. . . . Their peripheral position in relation to a local system does not prevent them from being an integral part of the total system, just as the local system is. ("Introduction," xx)

Lévi-Strauss describes ways in which aberrancies are merely translations of various "constants" within a society; the individual difference is still dependent on the collectivity for its meaning and interpretability; the exception proves the rule. But our problem is in deciding, *What is the system?* The traditional Mande world can clearly be considered a total system in Lévi-Strauss's sense. However, the only perspectives we have on this total system are given by representations which are *aberrant to the system itself*: oral traditions that are transcribed and translated, ethnographies written by Europeans or European-trained Africans, a novel that foregrounds its own unreliability. *L'Enfant noir* wants to describe the coherence of the traditional Mande world but keeps tripping over the condition of its own creation: the break with the total system that motivates the nostalgic return.

Rereading Lévi-Strauss's phrases, we could consider the "total system" to be colonialism rather than the traditional Mande. If the Mande is a "local" system within a greater whole—French West Africa, twentieth-century imperialism, colonialism—then Camara Laye's position as peripheral to the world of his birth is attributable to his participation in the larger system.

The larger system, for all it may try, however, does not succeed in "totalizing," in establishing hegemony over all means of production of meaning; *L'Enfant noir*, published at the height of the colonial era yet ignoring its impact, appears as a defiant proof of this resistance. Any signifier within the larger system must be looked at differentially, in function of the dualism that conditioned its creation. Anthropology, as defined by Lévi-Strauss as a total system capable of explaining "all behaviors,"[65] can and must be referred to in order to interpret certain signs, such as the totemic snake, which are imbued with the kind of symbolism that anthropology has described: inherited, collective, magic. But what about the other snakes in chapter one? They are not totemic; what kind of meaning are we to attribute to them?

The "brusque" appearance of a snake on the first page of the novel, seen retrospectively and in light of the totemic significance of the last snake, cannot be seen as arbitrary. The first snake appears to the uninitiated reader as an arbitrary symbol, a slightly exotic figure serving to introduce the child's innocence. Any other animal would have served to reinforce the ostensible theme of security threatened and restored, but Camara's use of a nontotemic snake in this strategic position is indicative of his relation to the totem. The product we are looking at when we open *L'Enfant noir* comes from a larger system than the one that is described within it. New possibilities of meaning are refracted between the world

65. "Une *anthropologie*, c'est-à-dire un système d'interprétation rendant simultanément compte des aspects physique, psychologique, psychique et sociologique de *toutes les conduites* [emphasis mine]" ("Introduction," xxv).

of the referent (the Mande) and the world of the signifier (France). The first snake is a creation of the world of writing that serves to lead toward the totem. The function of the first snake, and of the those that appear on the railroad tracks, is also to mark the distance that separates the novel from the totem. There are three careful steps, therefore, leading into the recollected Mande of *L'Enfant noir*: the first snake, with which the child plays, appears to be a seductive plot device; the second passage, with the snakes on the railroad tracks, has the resonance of a political allegory; and the final encounter leads to the (partial) revelation of the totem.

Do these steps represent "stages" in some evolution? The metaphor of childhood invites such speculations, which may be misleading. There are steps toward a limited revelation, moving seemingly from an arbitrary, modern kind of symbolism to an allegorical one, then to totemism, in which meaning is predetermined and partially concealed. In the first step, meaning would appear to be tied to the metaphor of childhood, kept simple and unassuming. In the second step, the signifier seems to have acquired a dual valency, banal and anecdotal on one level, charged with political commentary on the other. The third step represents arrival to a collective notion of symbolism, explicable in anthropological terms. Yet we have seen that that arrival is qualified, hesitant, and ultimately unreliable. The revelation is never fully accomplished but rather hinted at. Totemic meaning itself remains a mystery; the magic of its re-presentation can only be represented, diminished.

L'Enfant noir and *Nyamakala* Art

Reading the modest opening of this "simple" novel has proved to be a complicated project in interpretation. The principal thematic concerns of the novel are identity, happiness, and loss (with the last two coming together in the form of nostalgia). The development of these themes is enriched by the condition of the text as a product suspended between opposite systems of meaning. The product is a francophone novel, supposedly subject to universal (Western) explication and understanding; but the purpose of the product is to expose and explain a very different system of meaning and identity, that of the Mande. We have found the gap between the two systems difficult to close. The functioning of the thematic system—the desired closure of identity and happiness—to some extent depends on the success of the novel in participating in, being part of, the culture it depicts. Does *L'Enfant noir* go beyond the pedagogical function we have described here, to *perform* the artistic transformations that Camara Laye was called to by his birth in the *nyamakala*? Did he conceive of his own production as a writer as in any way connected to the traditional arts of the Mande? I have described *L'Enfant noir* as *suspended* between two systems, but we must still wonder whether suspension means "both . . . and" or "neither . . . nor"; whether the francophone novel is part of any "total system" or part of none. I will address these questions by looking at the ways in which the thematic and theoretical problems I have raised are played out both in the rest of *L'Enfant noir* and elsewhere.

The pattern of dilation and deflation established in the opening passage recurs throughout *L'Enfant noir*. The second chapter describes the father's work as a goldsmith: a woman arrives with some gold to be made into jewelry; she is accompanied by her griot, who sings the praises of the smith and his ancestors, inciting him to finer work. In this passage, the close relation between different *nyamakala* modes of production is described. In order to praise his father's work, Camara invokes the oral tradition of the griots that supports the work of the smiths:

A mesure que les couplets se dévidaient, c'était comme un grand arbre généalogique qui se dressait, qui poussait ses branches ici et là, qui s'étalait avec ses cent rameaux et ramilles devant mon esprit. La harpe soutenait cette vaste nomenclature, la truffait et la coupait de notes tantôt sourdes, tantôt aigrelettes. (27)

As the couplets were reeled off it was like watching the growth of a great genealogical tree that spread its branches far and wide and flourished its boughs and twigs before my mind's eye. The harp played an accompaniment to this vast utterance of names, expanding it with notes that were now soft, now shrill. (32)

The musicality of this passage, with its playful alliteration ("ses cent rameaux et ramilles"), shows a *participation* of Camara's writing in the oral tradition it describes. We are a long way here from the faithful prose transcription of *Le Maître de la parole*; here the practice of orality is evoked rather than reproduced and translated. Griots are referred to several times in *L'Enfant noir* (including those who sing the praises of the departing *enfant noir* as he is leaving home by train), but they are never quoted. The novelist's verbal art has displaced the griots' and appropriated their role.

In this passage (27; 32), Camara's first written commentary on Mande verbal art, he immediately raises the question of truthfulness and flattery:

Où le griot puisait-il ce savoir? Dans une mémoire particulièrement exercée assurément, particulièrement nourrie aussi par ses prédécesseurs, et qui est le fondement de notre tradition orale. Y ajoutait-il? C'est possible: c'est métier de griot que de flatter! Il ne devait pourtant pas beaucoup malmener la tradition, car c'est métier de griot aussi de la maintenir intacte. Mais il m'importait peu en ce temps, et je levais haut la tête, grisé par tant de louanges, dont il semblait rejaillir quelque chose sur ma petite personne. (27–28)

Where did the griot get his knowledge? In a particularly well-practiced memory, certainly, particularly nourished as well by all his predecessors; such memories are the foundation of our oral tradition. Did he add to it? It is possible: the griot's profession is to flatter! He was not supposed to stray too far from tradition, however, because the griot's profession is to maintain tradition intact as well. But that was of little importance to me then, and I raised my head high, giddy from all the praises, some of which seemed to rain down on my little self. (my translation—this passage is left out of the published translation, p. 32)

The smith reacts as would a nobleman: with pride that is hidden behind ostensible embarrassment. The griot is to the smith here as the smith is to the client: the *nyamakala* craftsman is hired to augment the prestige of a client, either with praisesongs or with jewels. Both productions involve risky transformations, of silence into speech and of raw gold into a finished jewel. The commentary here raises the question of transformations and of legitimacy: the opposition between flattery and tradition is posed as a question, then answered by asserting that the opposition is false. Transformations are suspect but give joy to the patron.

The direct and concrete relation between the art of the griot and that of the smith is developed as the ritual of smelting gold reaches its solumn climax, a moment of "transubstantiation:" [66]

Il arrivait aussi que, gêné dans ses mouvements, mon père fît reculer les apprentis. Il le faisait d'un simple geste de la main: jamais il ne disait mot à ce moment, et personne ne disait mot, personne ne devait dire mot, le griot même cessait d'élever la voix; le silence n'était interrompu que par le halètement des soufflets et le léger sifflement de l'or. Mais si mon père ne prononçait pas de paroles, je sais bien qu'intérieurement il en formait; je l'apercevais à ses lèvres qui remuaient . . .

Quelles paroles mon père pouvait-il bien former? *Je ne sais pas; je ne sais pas exactement: rien ne m'a été communiqué de ces paroles.* Mais qu'eussent-elles été, sinon des incantations? N'était-ce pas les génies du feu et de l'or, du feu et du vent, du vent soufflé par les tuyères, du feu né du vent, de l'or marié avec le feu, qu'il invoquait alors; n'était-ce pas leur aide et leur amitié, et leurs épousailles qu'il appelait? Oui, ces génies-là presque certainement, qui sont parmi les fondamentaux et qui étaient également nécessaires à la fusion. (30–31, emphasis mine)

If he felt he had inadequate working space, my father had the apprentices stand well away from him. He merely raised his hand in a simple gesture: at that particular moment he never uttered a word, and no one else would: no one was allowed to utter a word. Even the griot's voice was no longer raised in song. The silence was broken only by the panting of the bellows and the faint hissing of the

66. Bourgeacq compares this ritual to the sacrament of the Eucharist, *Eternel retour*, 17.

gold. But if my father never actually spoke, I know that he was forming words in his mind. I could tell from his lips, which kept moving . . .

What words did my father utter? *I do not know. At least I am not certain what they were. No one ever told me.* But could they have been anything but incantations? On these occasions was he not invoking the genies of fire and gold, of fire and wind, of wind blown by the blast-pipes of the forge, of fire born of wind, of gold married to fire? Was it not their assistance, their friendship, their espousal that he besought? Yes. Almost certainly he was invoking these genies, all of whom are equally indispensable for smelting gold. (34–35, AT; emphasis mine)

"Génie" in this context seems to refer to *nyama*, the dangerous forces, sacred and unclean, that are released in the performance or violation of ritual: the stock in trade of the *nyamakala*. Looking at this text as anthropological and in light of anthropological information, we see that Camara is reaching for command of the most sacred (and secret) rites of his father's caste. But the description is forged in the same hermeneutic of secrecy that we have encountered previously, the catch-22 that was stated by Mamadou Kouyaté in *Soundjata*: anything worth knowing is worth keeping hidden; "knowledge must be secret."

The moment of transformation in which the spirits are invoked is the moment of silence, of secret knowledge. The smith alone murmurs, but his words are unknown to the narrator and to the reader. We again reach the "navel" of *L'Enfant noir*, the information and credibility gap that the narrator keeps calling to our attention: "I don't know; I don't know exactly; nothing was told to me"; I know "almost certainly," but not certainly; I *would* know now, except that "I left my father too soon;" "at that time I had neither the maturity nor the curiosity to ask the old men, and when at last I was old enough, I was no longer in Africa" (57).[67] The silence in the forge at this moment, the silence in the text, is therefore both a central component of *nyamakala* artisanship and a condition of the production of this francophone novel.

Silence in the Mande, as we saw in the previous chapter, is the condition of equilibrium that speech violates. The incantations that the father *speaks silently*, with only his lips moving as he smelts the gold, must be surrounded by silence so that the danger may be kept to a minimum. There is an "absolute silence" and an "anxious wait" as the "magic operation" takes place. Again, the father is the repository of knowledge, the son can tell us what is happening, but only through *visual* evidence: the

---

67. Bourgeacq discusses these moments of uncertainty and questioning in the novel as a form of *dialogue*, rooted in African traditions of oral discourse, "où l'assistance participe à la parole du conteur" (*Eternel retour*, 67).

operation "took place *before my eyes*"; hearing and the possibility of verbal understanding are excluded:

Ces paroles que nous n'entendions pas, ces paroles secrètes, ces incantations qu'il adressait à ce que nous ne devions, à ce que nous ne pouvions ni voir ni entendre, c'était là l'essentiel. L'adjuration des génies du feu, du vent, de l'or, et la conjuration des mauvais esprits, cette science, mon père l'avait seul, et c'est pourquoi, seul aussi, il conduisait tout. (32–33)

Those inaudible, secret words, those incantations that he addressed to something we shouldn't and couldn't either see or hear, that was the essential thing. Calling on the spirits of fire, of wind, of gold, and exorcising the evil spirits—this was a knowledge he alone possessed, and that was why he alone conducted everything. (36, AT)

In the pages that follow, Camara provides a good deal of information about the rituals of goldsmithing in the Mande. The child has discovered that the father's totemic snake plays a role in the process; the father caresses the snake, which appears "miraculously," coiled under the sheepskin rug each time before work is to be done. The participation of the griot is described as "curious" but "direct" and "actual"; "he too was intoxicated by the joy of creating" (36), and when the father has finished the work, the griot performs a song of unique power and significance, the Douga:

Et quand mon père, après avoir soudé le gros grain qui achevait la pyramide, faisait admirer son oeuvre, le griot n'aurait pu se retenir plus longtemps d'énoncer la "douga," ce grand chant qui n'est chanté que pour les hommes de renom, qui n'est dansé que par ces hommes. (36)

And when my father, after having soldered the large grain of gold that crowned the summit, held out his work to be admired, the griot would no longer be able to contain himself. He would begin to intone the *douga*, the great chant which is sung only for celebrated men and which is danced by them alone. (39, AT)

The Douga, as we saw in the context of Kéita Fodéba's poem "Aube africaine," is the honorary sign of the vulture, corresponding to a high order of achievement. Camara goes on to explain the danger associated with the song of the Douga:

Mais c'est un chant redoutable que la "douga," un chant qui provoque, un chant que le griot ne se hasarderait pas à chanter, que l'homme pour qui on le chante ne se hasarderait pas non plus à danser sans précautions. Mon père, averti en rêve, avait pu prendre ces précautions dès l'aube; le griot, lui, les avait obligatoirement prises dans le moment où il avait conclu marché avec la femme. Comme mon père, il s'était alors enduit le corps de gris-gris, et s'était rendu invulnérable aux mauvais génies que la "douga" ne pouvait manquer de déchaî-

ner, invulnérable encore à ses confrères mêmes qui, jaloux peut-être, n'atten-
daient que ce chant, l'exaltation, la perte de contrôle qu'entraîne ce chant, pour
lancer leurs sorts. (36–37)

But the *douga* is a formidable chant, a provocative chant, a chant which the
praise-singer dared not sing, and which the man for whom it is sung dared not
dance before certain precautions had been taken. My father had taken them as
soon as he woke, since he had been warned in a dream. The griot had taken them
when he concluded his arrangements with the woman. Like my father he had
smeared his body with magic substances and had made himself invulnerable to
the evil spirits whom the *douga* inevitably set free; these potions made him invulnerable also to rival griots, perhaps jealous of him, who awaited only this song
and the exaltation and loss of control which attended it, in order to begin casting
their spells. (39, AT)

One of the problems with the reputation of *L'Enfant noir* is that its
reporting of magic practices comes through the eyes of a child, whose
information was taken by some critics as unreliable and childish ("piti-
ful" according to Mongo Beti), as if he were talking about Santa Claus.
But this is only the case as long as readers fail to take into account the
Mande context as the referential network. When we read about "mauvais génies" in the passage above, the referent is *nyama*, and the vocabulary with which the narrator describes these forces echoes that of
anthropologists describing *nyama*: "redoutable," "perte de contrôle,"
"précautions." The signs and symbols that are described here are not the
wild fantasies of a child or the vague ruminations of a deracinated intellectual: they are specific to the Mande and can only be understood within
its system of references.

In spite of a provisional investment of faith in the coherence of "systems,"
we have thus far been unable to pinpoint the place that *L'Enfant noir*
occupies between and within the systems to which it is subject: the totemic system of the Mande and the alienating system of colonialism.
There is of course no single position that the novel takes: it is itself a
system, interacting with other systems. Final answers to the questions we
have raised here—identity, totemism, alienation—will be all but impossible. However, there is one more part to the puzzle that will help us
toward a conclusion.

A few years before his death, Camara Laye was interviewed by the
astute critic Jacqueline Leiner. In the published version of their conversation, from which I have already quoted, Camara discusses the relationship he sees between the traditional arts of the Mande practiced by his
father and his own art as a writer; this topic is at the crux of our analysis

here. Turning from comments on the loss of "spiritualism" in European art, Camara describes the process of "deformation" that was at the root of his father's art, a deformation that captures reality by distorting it:

J'ai vu mon père, par exemple, dessiner pour un administrateur des colonies, quatre femmes. . . . Mais, on a failli avoir des ennuis! Ça plaisait à tous, sauf au monsieur, et mon père m'a dit: "C'est à cause des seins! Trop vieux!" Ce monsieur qui avait un casque colonial qui cachait sa tête blanche, il n'acceptait pas ça: la réalité; n'est-ce pas c'était faux pour lui. . . . Mon père, lui, laissait parler son coeur. . . .

D'où grosseur première, déformation première, qui n'est pas voulue. Mais alors, si cette femme-là, qui est sculptée, a un gros ventre, il faudra de gros mollets, pour soutenir ce gros ventre, il faudra de grands pieds. Avec la première déformation qui est sentie par l'auteur, il y a d'autres déformations résultantes, conséquences de ça, n'est-ce pas? Ce qui fait un certain nombre de vues qu'on sent. (159)

I saw my father, for example, draw four women for a colonial administrator. . . . But we almost got into trouble! Everyone liked it except the gentleman, and my father said to me: "It's because of the breasts! Too old!" This gentleman had a colonial pith helmet which hid his white face; he didn't accept that: reality, you see, was false for him. . . . As for my father, he let his heart speak. . . .

From which [you get] a primary bigness, a primary deformation, which is not wanted. But then if that woman who is sculpted has a big stomach, she'll have to have big legs to support it, and big feet. With the first deformation that is felt by the author, there are other, resultant deformations, consequences, you see? Which makes for a certain number of views that one feels.

Up to this point, Camara has been describing an aesthetic that derives from a verisimilitude of *feeling*, a realism that he says comes from the inside. There is an affinity between African art and modern European sculpture like Picasso's, Camara remarked earlier: "When I see a modern sculptor, I know what he wants to do; when I see a modern painting, I know exactly where the painter got it; I know it by the form . . . I know it from the inside" (Leiner "Interview," 159). The colonial administrator represents those who know reality only on the surface; the father's mode of creation proceeds through a chain of interlocking deformations toward the expression of a hidden reality. The ultimate achievement is to "let the heart speak," consistent with the Mande notion of truth as contained within the biological body. But the truth that is released is not unitary; it is comprised of "a certain number of views," like a cubist painting, like the art of Picasso, which Camara knows "from the inside."

Immediately following the passage quoted above, Camara goes on to make the connection between visual and verbal arts:

Par exemple, chez le griot, quand il fait son discours, il y a aussi déformation, il
y a répétition. Pour un professeur de français, c'est mauvais. . . . Par exemple,
moi, je pense que si vous donniez une de mes conférences à un professeur de
français, il dirait que c'est très mauvais . . . parce que je reprends, je répète, j'ai
un mot-clef, je reprends le mot-clef . . . comme pour une sculpture, il y a un mot-
clef. Ainsi, par exemple, au début de *L'Enfant noir* j'écrivais: *seul*. C'est pour
moi un mot-clef, *seul*. Je veux que cela rentre dans la tête du lecteur; j'écrivais
seul, seul. Automatiquement, après l'avoir entendu cent fois, vous comprenez. Je
reprendrai ensuite les mots conformément à un rythme, de sorte que même si
l'auditoire n'est pas attentif à la première phrase, à la fin du discours, il aura
compris. Finalement, avant que je termine mon idée, tout le monde aura compris
ce que je voulais dire. C'est ça, le discours!

. . . C'est avant tout, un rythme. Prenez le tam-tam, c'est pareil. Pour des oreilles non habituées, c'est monotone. Pour nous, il y a un certain rythme. Moi, je
reprends toujours la même chose. Si j'écris: "*seul*, dans la chambre, *seul* j'écrivais," j'ajoute tout de suite: "j'écrivais, j'écrivais . . ." Voyez, je reprends comme
dans une sculpture, et il y a une déformation. (159–60)

For example, when a griot speaks, there is also a deformation and repetition. For
a professor of French, that's bad. . . . For example, I think that if you gave one of
my lectures to a professor of French, he would say that it's very bad . . . because
I pick things back up, I repeat, I use catch-phrases. Thus, for example, at the
beginning of *L'Enfant noir*, I wrote: *Alone*. That for me is a key word, *alone*. I
want that to sink into the reader's mind; I wrote, *alone, alone*. Automatically,
having heard it a hundred times, you understand. I will pick words back up in
order to build a rhythm, so that even if the listeners aren't attentive to the first
sentence, at the end of the speech they will have understood. Finally, before
I finish my idea, everyone will have understood what I mean. That's what discourse is!

. . . It's first of all a rhythm. With drums, it's the same thing. For ears that
aren't used to it, it's monotonous. For us there is a certain rhythm. I personally
always repeat the same thing. If I write: "*Alone*, in the room, *alone*, I was writing," I immediately add: "I was writing, I was writing . . ." You see, I repeat as
in a sculpture, and there is a deformation.

The most striking aspect of these remarks is Camara's assumption that
sculpting, speaking, and writing are all the same. With the phrase "for
example," he passes from the father's sculpting to the griot's art, then to
his own oral lecturing style, and then again, to his writing in *L'Enfant
noir*. The three art forms repeat and exemplify each other. We know that
the sculptor-blacksmith and the griot come from the same caste and the
same tradition; anthropological sources have shown us how both manipulate the forces of *nyama* in certain ways. But when it comes to carrying the comparison over to Camara's production as a speaker and a
novelist, the jump is of an entirely different magnitude, and any attempt

on our part to analyze this assertion will meet certain difficulties. It is clear that Camara sees continuity between his father's work and his own, through the intermediary of the traditional bards. It is not difficult to accept this comparison; the francophone novel is certainly heir to the oral tradition in many ways that we have been exploring. But it is curious that the word "seul," part of what Camara describes as an insistent rhythm at the beginning of *L'Enfant noir*, is nowhere to be found in the text.

Camara Laye believed in the unity of all things. In the Leiner interview, he states, "There is no hatred. All men are the same." He has not asserted that all art forms are the same, but he has made clear his vested interest in maintaining the *identity* between traditional Mande forms and his own work. The logic and the necessity of such a claim are self-evident: faced with critics who use the word "alienation" as an accusation of inauthenticity, the African author is constantly called upon to demonstrate the rootedness of his or her art.

Jacqueline Leiner asks Camara: "If you had been a griot, for example, your family would surely have had for you the veneration they had for your father, the smith and sculptor, wouldn't they?" Camara is too diplomatic to point out the fallacy in the question, the idea that smith and griot are interchangable "métiers" rather than hereditary casted roles with different status. He replies:

> Je suis, si vous voulez, "un artiste" . . . Bon, d'accord! Mais, *d'une autre langue, inaccessible à eux*, quoi! C'est pour cela qu'ils ne comprennent pas très bien. . . . Ainsi quand j'allais à l'école, à sept ans, à huit ans, je rapportais à la maison des tableaux d'honneur ou des bonbons. Pour mon père, c'est quoi tout ça? *Ce n'est pas son contexte*. (163, emphasis mine)

> I am, if you will, "an artist" . . . So, all right! But *of another language, which is inaccessible to them*! That's why they don't understand very well. . . . Thus when I went off to school at the age of seven, eight, I brought home awards or candy. For my father, what is all that? *It's not his context*.

It is therefore the language barrier that accounts for the lack of understanding, according to him. The practice of writing in French can still adhere to tradition, even if those closest to tradition can not understand it.

Camara seems to imply that francophone writing can be "authentic" in two ways: either as a description of traditional forms or as an actual performance of a traditional aesthetic in a new form. On the most basic level, *L'Enfant noir* is simply concerned with representing the traditional arts, describing the totemic relations that the boy's father and mother enjoyed with certain animals. Although we have seen that the novel works just as constantly to undercut its own authority on these subjects, to confine its competence to the level of knowledge of an uninitiated young boy, this strategy allows the outsider to enter and be educated within certain limits. The descriptive function clearly ties *L'Enfant noir* to its traditional background and makes it a precious document.

The performative function is more problematic, and holds more at stake on the theoretical level. If francophone novel-writing performs the same functions and manipulates the same forces as the father Camara's work at the forge, are we to interpret it as a real *nyamakala* mode of expression? It would therefore be subject to the same laws, totems, and taboos, and it would command the same prestige. The descriptive function of the novel would in turn reflect the performative function; the passages on the father's work at the forge would serve as allegories on Laye's act of writing. In the Leiner interview, Camara Laye draws this comparison between his father's performance and his own. Even if he is mistaken in his reference to *L'Enfant noir*, much of the reading we have done here would tend to support the general comparison, if not a total identification, between traditional *nyamakala* arts and Camara's activity as a novelist. But we must also recognize that, according to what the novel says, there is one thing only at the heart of *nyamakala* performance, and that is the totem.

The father's totem is the condition of his creative powers; the mother's is the condition of her magic. While we have thus far been unable to *define* totemic meaning in a theoretical way, we have been able to describe it as a relation of total identification, derived from a certain narrative of origin, perhaps impossible to recover. The question of the totem in Camara Laye's own work remains, and is addressed both in *L'Enfant noir* and in the Leiner interview. With one more look at each text, our puzzle will be complete.

In the novel, the mother's presence and influence have been felt and eventually come to play a central role in defining totemism. In the passage about gold smelting discussed above, the mother's attitude toward the father's work with gold provides a moral counterweight to his reckless heroics. The language in which the mother expresses her disapproval seems to be practically oriented; she seems to be thinking only of questions of safety; but her mistrust has deeper resonances.

—Où étais-tu? disait-elle, bien qu'elle le sût parfaitement.
—Dans l'atelier.
—Oui, ton père travaillait l'or. L'or! Toujours l'or!"
Et elle donnait de furieux coups de pilon sur le mil ou le riz qui n'en pouvait mais.
—Ton père se ruine la santé! Voilà ce que ton père fait!
—Il a dansé la "douga," disais-je.

—La "douga"! Ce n'est pas la "douga" qui l'empêchera de s'abîmer les yeux!
Et toi, tu ferais mieux de jouer dans la cour plutôt que d'aller respirer la poussière
et la fumée dans l'atelier! (38–39)

"Where have you been?" [she asked], although she knew perfectly well where
I had been.
"In the workshop."
"Of course. Your father was smelting gold. Gold! Always gold!"
And she would beat the millet or rice furiously with her pestle.
"Your father is ruining his health!"
"He danced the *douga*."
"The *douga*! The *douga* won't keep him from ruining his eyes. As for you,
you would be better off playing in the courtyard instead of breathing dust and
smoke in the workshop." (40)

When the mother talks about the father damaging his health, the son
responds that the father had danced the Douga, indicating that "health"
here does not mean only physical welfare. The mother's insistence on
the physical side is in opposition to the father's mystical performance,
in which the physical is subordinated to the spiritual. The mother's concern for physical health reflects a concern for the binding, safer forces of
badenya; while the father's daring feats of *nyama*-manipulating reflect
fadenya.

In the fifth chapter of *L'Enfant noir*, an important addition is made to
Camara's literary ethnography of totemism. While the son's access to his
totem can only come through the father, it was the mother who taught
him the difference between the snakes, giving him information necessary
for apprenticeship with the father. So it is ironic and significant that the
most definitive statement about totemism in the novel comes in relation
to the *mother's* totem, which the son cannot "have." Descended from a
line of smiths and "sayers of hidden things," the mother has inherited the
crocodile as totem. She is therefore able to draw water even in crocodile-
infested waters, for they will not attack one of their own kind:

Mais les crocodiles ne pouvaient pas faire de mal à ma mère, et le privilège se
conçoit: il y a *identité entre le totem et son possesseur; cette identité est absolue,*
est telle que le possesseur a le pouvoir de prendre la forme même de son totem;
dès lors il saute aux yeux que le totem ne peut se dévorer lui-même. (80, emphasis mine)

But the crocodiles could do no harm to my mother; and this privilege is quite
understandable: the totem is *identified with its possessor: this identification is
absolute,* and of such a nature that its possessor has the power to take on the
form of the totem itself; it follows quite obviously that the totem cannot devour
itself. (75, emphasis mine)

The son stands in a marginal relation to "absolute identity." His mother has this kind of identity, but her totem cannot be his ("Naturally I watched her from a distance, for my totem is not my mother's"); and later in the novel, the coming of manhood will increase the distance between them.[68] The father has it, but school—the call of the West—removes the child from the father's sphere. "Laye" is closed off on both sides. The novel nonetheless insists on the reality it has left behind: the actuality of totemism. The passage quoted above is the closest we get to a statement of definition and belief.

Once this is done, however, the novel reverts to the pattern established from its beginning, as the witness first underscores the veracity of his testimony, then undercuts it. The paragraph that immediately follows the last quotation above poignantly accentuates the suspension of the novel between belief and loss:

> Je ne veux rien dire de plus et je n'ai relaté que ce que mes yeux ont vu. Ces prodiges—en vérité, c'étaient des prodiges!—j'y songe aujourd'hui comme aux événements fabuleux d'un lointain passé. Ce passé pourtant est tout proche: il date d'hier. Mais le monde bouge, le monde change, et le mien plus rapidement peut-être que tout autre, et si bien qu'il semble que nous cessons d'être ce que nous étions, qu'au vrai nous ne sommes plus ce que nous étions, et que déjà nous n'étions plus exactement nous-mêmes dans le moment où ces prodiges s'accomplissaient sous nos yeux. Oui, le monde bouge, le monde change; il bouge et il change à telle enseigne que *mon propre totem—j'ai mon totem aussi—m'est inconnu.* (80–81, emphasis mine)

> I do not wish to say any more, and I have told you only what I saw with my own eyes. These miracles—they were miracles indeed—I think about now as if they were the fabulous events of a far-off past. That past is, however, still quite near: it was only yesterday. But the world rolls on, the world changes, my own world perhaps more rapidly than anyone else's; so that it appears as if we are ceasing to be what we were, and that we were not exactly ourselves even at the time when these miracles took place before our eyes. Yes, the world rolls on, the world changes; it rolls on and changes, and the proof of it is that *my own totem—I too have my totem—is unknown to me.* (75, AT, emphasis mine)

The last two phrases perfectly reflect the state of *suspended belief*, "suspended animism," so to speak, which is the condition of *L'Enfant noir.*

68. In the eighth chapter, Camara describes the ritual and experience of circumcision, including the period of isolation from women and girls afterwards. He is allowed a two-minute visit from his mother, which is a turning point in their relationship: "Quand j'avais quitté ma mère, j'étais toujours un enfant. A présent . . . Mais étais-je vraiment un homme, à présent? Etais-je déjà un homme? . . . J'étais un homme! Oui, j'étais un homme! A présent, il y avait *cette distance entre ma mère et moi: l'homme!*" (147;131, emphasis mine).

"I have my own totem, but it is unknown to me" makes no sense from a totally literal point of view. Possession combined with ignorance would appear to be paradoxical, especially in regard to an identification that must by the author's definition be absolute. But in the swirling temporality of this passage, paradox marks the author's relation to his past, to his people, to himself, and to his art. If totemism—regardless of any "universal" significance that anthropologists might want to attach to it—is within this novel a *figure* of the notion of identity, then this paragraph is the perfect articulation between the figure and the notion. Totemism is possessed but unknown; identity is never renounced but changes so constantly that it almost disappears. At any given moment, and particularly at moments of self-revelation ("où ces prodiges s'accomplissaient sous nos yeux"), what we are has already given way to what we will be.

In the Leiner interview, Camara makes some fascinating and highly ambiguous remarks about totemism. Asked by Leiner if he believes in the totemic power of the crocodile as described in *L'Enfant noir*, Camara responds:

Ouais! Il faut voir ça, avec les yeux d'un enfant. Moi, j'ai quitté ma famille quand j'avais quatorze ans. On m'a envoyé au collège, à Conakry, donc jusqu'à quatorze ans, j'ai cru à cela, et comme le livre s'appelle *L'Enfant noir*, c'est l'enfant noir qui parle et non l'homme. (162–63)

Yeah! You have to see it with the eyes of a child. I left my family when I was fourteen. I was sent to secondary school in Conakry, so until I was fourteen I believed in that; and, since the book is called *The Black Child*, it is the black child who speaks and not the man.

The answer clearly implies that he ceased to believe in totems at the age of fourteen.

Later in the interview, Camara appears nearly to lose his composure when he is asked for a second time about totemism. The question and answer directly echo the last passage from *L'Enfant noir* quoted above.

C. L. Nous, les Africains, nous sommes très à l'aise avec eux [les surréalistes]. Dans notre monde moyenâgeux, moi, par exemple, *j'ai mon totem*, ma mère a son totem, mon père a son totem.

J. L. Comment? . . . *Vous n'avez pas votre totem*, puisque vous m'avez dit, tout à l'heure, que vous ne le connaissiez pas?

C. L. *Vous êtes en train de me coincer* . . . Voyez-vous ici on est davantage surréaliste, quoi! C'est ça surtout que je veux dire . . . Quand on affirme, par exemple, que je copie Kafka . . . Non! Au contraire c'est peut-être Kafka qui nous copie? Kafka copie l'Afrique sans le savoir . . . (165, emphasis mine)

C. L. We Africans are very comfortable with them [the surrealists]. In our medieval type of world, I, for example, *have my totem,* my mother has her totem, my father has his totem.

J. L. What? . . . *You don't have a totem,* do you, since you just told me that you didn't know it?

C. L. You're backing me into a corner! . . . We're more surrealist here, don't you see? That's what I really mean . . . When they say, for example, that I'm copying Kafka . . . No, on the contrary, maybe it's Kafka who's copying us? Kafka is copying Africa without knowing it . . .

Toward "Francophonie"

This inquiry into totemism and identity in one francophone novel has repeatedly been confronted by moments of *suspension*: breaches of knowledge on the narrator's part, perhaps a reluctance to tell what he knows; gaps between theories of totemism and testimony about it from the narrator and his father; and above all, a theory (Lévi-Strauss's) that defines totemism itself as a state of suspension between totality and loss. Earlier, I asked whether suspension should mean "either/or" or "neither/ nor"; by way of conclusion, I will apply this question to two topics: first, the hermeneutics of Mande secrecy in *L'Enfant noir,* and second, the status of language and of the French language in particular.

Recalling Mamadou Kouyaté's dictum that "knowledge should remain secret," that anything worth knowing is worth keeping quiet, it is not surprising to learn that *L'Enfant noir* was seen as an act of cultural betrayal in some circles, for to reveal is to betray. These comments are most relevant to the seventh chapter of the novel, in which Camara describes and in effect demystifies the initiation rite of the Kondén Diara or "children's lion." Narrating from the child's point of view, he writes,

Ce n'est qu'après avoir participé plusieurs fois à la cérémonie des lions, que nous commençons à vaguement entrevoir quelque chose, mais *nous respectons le secret*: nous ne faisons part de ce que nous avons deviné qu'à ceux de nos compagnons qui ont une même expérience; et l'essentiel nous échappe jusqu'au jour de notre initiation à la vie d'homme.

Non, ce n'étaient pas de vrais lions qui rugissaient dans la clairière, c'étaient nos aînés, tout bonnement nos aînés. . . .

Mais les hommes? Mais tous ceux qui savent?

Eh bien, ils ne disent pas une parole, ils tiennent leur science strictement secrète. Non seulement ils laissent femmes et enfants dans l'incertitude ou dans la crainte, mais encore ils y ajoutent en les avertissant de tenir rigoureusement closes les portes des cases. . . .

Il va de soi que si le secret était éventé, la cérémonie perdrait beaucoup de son prestige. . . .

... Mais, au vrai, qu'en subsiste-il à l'heure où j'écris? Le secret ... Avons-nous encore des secrets! (119–22, emphasis mine)

We begin to have a vague understanding of the ceremony of the lions only after we have taken part in it many times. But even then, *we respect the secret*; we are careful to share our knowledge only with those companions who have had the same experience. And the real secret lies hidden until the day when we are initiated into our life as men.

No, they were not real lions that roared in the clearing, for it was the older boys, simply the older boys. . . .

But what about the men? What about those who *do* know?

They won't breathe a single word about it. They keep their knowledge a close secret. Not only do they keep women and children in a state of uncertainty and terror, they also warn them to keep the doors of their huts firmly barred. . . .

It is obvious that if the secret were to be given away, the ceremony would lose much of its power. . . . But, at the moment of writing this, does any part of the rite still survive? The secret . . . Do we still have secrets! (106–9, AT, emphasis mine. The translation of the last phrase is problematic, and I will comment on it below.)

Respect for the secrecy of the ceremony is no sooner declared than violated by the narration itself. The powerfully demystifying phrase, "No, they weren't real lions," is exactly the thing that is supposed to be kept secret and sacred. *L'Enfant noir* seems to praise the idea of secrecy while betraying particular secrets. Speaking in the Leiner interview about the negative reaction that this passage provoked among his fellow Africans, Camara defended his "betrayal" as a quest for truth: "If I'm truly writing, then I have to tell the truth."[69] This kind of truth sounds like the kind that the historian Niane wants to practice in relation to oral traditionalists: corrosive, compromising, treacherous to local secrets. Truth subordinates specificity to a universal value. In the last two sentences quoted, that ambivalence is plain: first questioning whether anything remains behind him, whether there is anything left to be nostalgic about, then "Le secret . . ." and the exclamation ("Avons-nous encore des secrets!") that seems to point to an inexhaustible secret Mande culture, far beyond the corrosive power of this one novel. But the latter phrase is difficult: the published translation renders it as a question, "Do we still have secrets?" but in the original text, the question is more implied than

---

69. Leiner, "Interview," 162: "*J.L.*—Il y a un passage qui m'a tout particulièrement intéressée: c'est la démystification de l'initiation. Qu'en ont pensé vos compatriotes?

C.L.—Ah! Ils n'ont pas bien réagi . . . ils n'ont pas bien réagi! Mais on est obligé, la sincérité est obligée de . . . En tout cas, moi, en ce qui me concerne, si vraiment j'écris, alors, je suis obligé de dire la vérité, je ne peux pas tricher. Quand je triche, en bien je ne peux pas m'empêcher de corriger ensuite. Le manuscrit est porté, je le reprends six mois après; il faut que je dise la vérité."

stated. The phrase is in fact suspended between interrogative and affirmative modes.

A reservoir of secrets is precisely marked by the *points de suspension* that precede this phrase, a sign of the suspension of narrative discourse, and by the suspension of the last phrase between knowing and asking. The *Petit Robert* dictionary, defining *points de suspension*, quotes Bachelard: "Les points de suspension 'tiennent en suspens ce qui ne doit pas être dit explicitement'" (Suspension points "hold in suspense that which is not to be said explicitly"). The seventh chapter of *L'Enfant noir* gave away enough secrets of Mande culture to be controversial; but in those suspension points and in the sentence that follows, the power of the francophone narrator is suspended, and Camara, like Mamadou Kouyaté, gives silence and secrecy their due. Another passage from *L'Enfant noir* illuminates the role of silence; here the narrator describes the silence of his uncle after a day's work in the fields:

car les pensées ne se laissent jamais tout à fait pénétrer; ce mutisme des choses, des raisons profondes des choses, conduit au silence; mais il suffit que ces choses aient été évoquées et leur impénétrabilité reconnue, il en demeure un reflet dans les yeux. . . . (54)

thoughts don't let themselves be completely penetrated; this reticence of things, of the deep reasons of things, conduces to silence. But it is sufficient for these things to be evoked and their impenetrability recognized, for a reflection to remain visible in the eyes. . . . (52, AT)

Profundity and silence go together; complete penetration is betrayal, and "things" resist it. The suspension points in the phrase, "Le secret . . ." may be seen as precisely a *reflection of silence*, a recognition of the unpronounceable. (It is interesting to note also that the Senghor poem on the totem, which I used above as an epigraph, p. 139, ends with suspension points as well.) [70]

Returning to Camara's remark about telling the truth in writing, I would like to close this chapter with some thoughts on the function of language and specifically of the French language in *L'Enfant noir*. "If I'm truly writing, then I have to tell the truth"—this quick remark is important because it shows a certain relation between writing and the betrayal of truth. I most definitely do not think that the relation is an intrinsic one, as Goody would have it; literacy *per se* has no patent on a specific brand of truth. The kind of demystifying truth that *L'Enfant noir* gave away is not the sole property of writing. As we saw in the chapter on orality and

70. For a structuralist-semiological analysis of this poem, with reference to totemism and Lévi-Strauss, see Sunday O. Anozie, *Structural Models and African Poetics* (London: Routledge & Kegan Paul, 1981): 174–87.

literacy, the Mande tradition conceives of orality as already holding that potential in the treacherous noise of speech.

How, then, should we account for that kind of truth, and how can we characterize the role of language in *L'Enfant noir*? If an important goal of *L'Enfant noir* is to reveal and honor a totem through the name of the father, then language—specifically, French—is the means by which the writer scratches his way back toward a diminished totality; yet it is also, one suspects, the means by which that totality is diminished. Written French reveals truths, describes identity, praises ancestors, teaches non-Mande readers about Mande culture, and perhaps even (if we go along with the Ortigues) attempts to crawl back to the fictive point of collapse between nature and culture. In this, the written French of *L'Enfant noir* adheres to a (speculative) etymology of the word *griot*: "climbing back up the course of time through speech,"[71] if we change "speech" to "writing." In many respects, the two appear to be interchangable; the comparisons between *L'Enfant noir* and Mande oral traditions reveal a deep continuity between the griot's art and that of the "gratte-papier" (174), the novelist. But we have seen that that is not the whole story.

If the French of *L'Enfant noir* does all the things I have just named, it also interferes with the functions it is supposed to be performing. Thus as the narrator tries to work his way toward secret truths and knowledge, he keeps tripping over the condition of possibility of the narrative itself: French and the education in colonial schools without which it would not be before the reader's eyes. Time after time he tells us that he would be able to tell us what we want to know, if only he hadn't "left his father too soon." But if he hadn't left his father, the novel would not exist; Camara Laye's artistic birthright would perhaps have been played out in the forge. French, simply put, is the medium of alienation, the perfect synecdoche for Camara's exile, his imperfect knowledge of his own culture, and his inability to tell the reader what is what. French is what makes Camara "Laye."

If our final question is the relation between the francophone novel and its traditional precursors, then the above remarks leave us with a problem

71. "La racine dya implique, comme le remarque Delafosse, l'idée de 'longueur, hauteur, éloignement dans le temps' et le mot *dyeli* ou *dyali* concernerait tout d'abord l'action de remonter le cours du temps par la parole." Dominique Zahan, *La Dialectique du verbe chez les Bambaras* (Paris: Mouton, 1963): 125. This appealing hypothesis—sounding like Proust above all—is rejected by Hugo Zemp, who sees in *jeli* a link with the word for blood (see "La Légende des griots malinké," *Cahiers d'études africaines* 24, no. 6 [1966]: 630–32); Zemp's idea is in turn rejected by Sory Camara, who sees in *jàlí* (the older form of *jeli*) the "action of lodging, of offering hospitality" (*Gens*, 101). All three scholars find corroboration in the social practices of the Mande.

outstanding. The "positive" (pedagogical, mythical, praising) function of French in *L'Enfant noir* is clearly in harmony with the oral tradition. But the "negative" side—that which seems to diminish the totality it tries to describe—gives just as strong an echo; griots are distrusted because of their peculiar manipulations of truth and flattery. If the "authenticity" of a francophone novel depends not just on its depiction of themes, characters, and ethnic reality but on its adherence to a certain philosophy of language, then the suspension of *L'Enfant noir* between competent knowledge of secrets and ignorance of them is in fact a sign of its participation in the system it seems to have left behind. It is in the nature of *nyamakala* artisanship to betray and reveal at once, to claim mastery and then hide the truth. *L'Enfant noir* seems to be a *nyamakala* work of art. To interpret *L'Enfant noir* in this way is to find authenticity on a deeper level than that of image and politics.

But to leave it at that—with *L'Enfant noir* safely and unproblematically rooted in an aesthetic tradition that we have recuperated through recourse to anthropology—would be to ignore the ways in which the stakes change as that aesthetic is translated from orality to literacy. We would be kidding ourselves to think that nothing is lost, that there is a simple harmony between the two contexts, Mande and francophone. The watershed is to be found, again, in the political antinomy between ethnicity and ethics. *L'Enfant noir* is, as Mongo Béti wrote in the 1950s, a work of "littérature rose," in which the conditions of colonialism are nuanced and muffled. Its carry-over of *nyamakala* aesthetics and its translation of ritual secrets into French make it appear that the contexts are equal, that it is the same to betray secrets within the culture and beyond its confines. *L'Enfant noir* blurs the boundaries between systems by creating a hybrid between them. To do this, to ignore the manichean, black-versus-white realities of colonialism, had to be controversial at the time. The warm welcome given to the Western reader confirms a Western desire to be included in African culture and to have a good conscience. Camara Laye was therefore ignoring Mamadou Kouyaté's warning: when a white man knows something, everyone will know it, and knowledge itself will disappear.

Times have changed somewhat. In the postcolonial period and context, particularly to outsiders, the "betrayal" seems less important than the revelation and preservation. What appeared to be a repression of politics in the 1950s now looks like a subtle subversion of colonial domination from within. Camara's handling of outsiders—with diplomacy and tact—can no longer be dismissed as a form of either naïveté or simple "alienation." The discourse of *L'Enfant noir* is suspended between older worlds, between, on the one hand, the traditional Mande and, on the other, a secure French colonialism that will not survive the 1950s. Camara Laye is part of these two worlds, but by his act of writing he places himself in a new space as well, one which both overlaps and goes beyond what came before. The new position, the new space that Camara Laye occupies with both unease and grace, is the space of *francophonie*. When Camara wrote *L'Enfant noir*, this term was not yet in use; its ramifications and problems—which are the subject of the next chapter—were not yet clear. It will be a more than a decade later before the body of French-language literature by Africans will gain institutional recognition (by which I mean inclusion in school and university curricula, both in the West and in Africa) and before its problems come into sharper focus.

Thus while Camara's "suspension" may initially appear as a purely negative state, when viewed historically it becomes understandable as a position of its own. As an heir to the tradition of *nyamakala* art, Camara is particularly well qualified to handle dangerously ambiguous materials (like the French language). What he *forges*, along with his contemporaries Mongo Beti, Ferdinand Oyono, and others, is the new francophone novel. Camara has lost none of the power implicit in his family name; he has merely transposed it into a new idiom.

5

Les Soleils des indépendances and Francophone Dialogue

Francophonie and Dialectics

La langue française est entourée d'une grande dévotion. Objet d'une sorte de fétichisme stérile qui a hypothéqué jusqu'à ces derniers temps les travaux d'écrivains non français mais possédant en elle leur unique moyen d'expression. . . . Oui, c'est le mot: un fétichisme, une sorte d'amour outrancier que les Français ont voué à leur langue.

The French language is surrounded by great devotion. It is the object of a sort of fetishism which has until recently held hostage the works of non-French writers who possessed it as their only means of expression. . . . Yes, fetishism is the word: a sort of unbridled love that the French have given to their language.[1]

—Ahmadou Kourouma

Francophonie rime d'ailleurs avec hégémonie. (Besides, francophonie rhymes with hegemony.)[2]

—*Peuples noirs, peuples africains*

In the early 1960s, when statutory independence had come to all of francophone Africa, everything about the continent seemed open to question. Decolonization was a political fact; sixteen states, including Senegal, Mali and the Ivory Coast, became independent in the year 1960 alone. But beyond the level of governmental status, how far did decolonization reach? How effective has the process been after thirty years? These questions continue to motivate and vex inquiries in many areas of African studies, most pertinently in the case of literature. One goal of this chapter

1. Interview by Moncef S. Badday, "Ahmadou Kourouma, écrivain africain," *Afrique littéraire et artistique* 10 (1970): 6–7.
2. Editorial, *Peuples noirs, peuples africains* 11, nos. 59–62 (September 1987-April 1988): 6.

will be to map the ideological and literary space of decolonization in the francophone Africa of the 1960s as it appears in Ahmadou Kourouma's *Les Soleils des indépendances*. Kourouma's novel constitutes a kind of declaration of independence for the francophone African signifier. Its status as a canonical classic inside and outside Africa is well beyond dispute; the author was pleased to note in the mid-1970s that his novel was known throughout his country, the Ivory Coast.[3] But before examining the implications of *Les Soleils des indépendances* for this continuing inquiry into literature and anthropology (an area in which this novel could not be ignored), it will be useful to pose a question that underpins the whole corpus that we are exploring: the question of *francophonie*, of the material and ideological value of the French language. For if *Les Soleils des indépendances* modifies the shape of francophonie, steering out of the space inhabited by Camara in *L'Enfant noir*, this reorientation takes place in a context that cannot be ignored.

The word *francophonie*, in spite of appearances, does not simply refer to the fact of speaking French. More ambitious, idealized connotations have gathered around it, with a marked increase in density and importance since the late 1960s. Francophonie cannot be interpreted without looking at the ideology and the institutions that support it; this is the context in which *Les Soleils des indépendances* appeared, a context that this novel significantly altered. As a cultural construct, francophonie represents an appeal to reciprocity and dialogism, ethical imperatives that I have already discussed in relation to the new styles of ethnography. A contextualized reading of *Les Soleils des indépendances* will therefore provide a useful locus for more specific consideration of ethical representation in politics, anthropology, and literature.

With the coming of political independence, it was assumed by many that cultural decolonization would be necessary and inevitable, and that language was the key to decolonizing the mind. So long as Africans continue to use European languages in politics, literature, law, and everyday life, the argument goes, they will be chained to the colonial system and compelled to follow its patterns. In 1963, the East African journal *Transition* published an article calling African literatures written in European languages a "dead end": "The whole uncritical acceptance of English and French as the inevitable medium for educated African writing, is misdirected, and has no chance of advancing African literature and culture. . . . Until these writers and their Western midwives accept the fact that any

---

3. Gérard Dago Lezou, *La Création romanesque devant les transformations actuelles en Côte d'Ivoire* (Abidjan: Nouvelles Editions Africaines, 1977): 224.

true African literature must be written in African languages, they would be merely pursuing a dead end, which can only lead to sterility, uncreativity, and frustration."[4] Why this prediction has proved to be wrong—or at least premature—is a question that I will not be able to answer fully here. But one basic distinction is clear: beginning with the article in *Transition* and continuing through Ngũgĩ wa Thiong'o's recent "departure from Afro-Saxon literature" (in other words, African literature tied by language and genre to the British colonial tradition),[5] the abandonment of European languages has been more *thinkable* in anglophone than in francophone Africa. The reasons for this go deep into colonial history, and lie principally, I believe, in the opposition between the British policy of indirect rule and the French notion of assimilation. Indirect rule encouraged and justified greater attention to the development of local-language literacy; francophone Africa is still far behind on this score.[6] Although in practice the two systems behaved more similarly than their theories should have allowed, the opposed ideas have left a distinct imprint. I will return to the comparison of French and English presently.

A volume of the "Que Sais-Je?" series of easy-reference books, exuding a semi-official aura, makes a convenient starting point for a survey of francophonie. Authored by Xavier Deniau, "Président du Comité de la Francophonie," *La Francophonie* deals authoritatively with its subject. The word *francophonie* is shown to have a full spectrum of "linguistic, geographical, spiritual or mystical, and institutional" meanings. Most revealing is the introduction, in which Deniau quotes from a speech he himself made in the National Assembly in 1976:

... [La Francophonie,] c'est une prise de conscience de cette solidarité naturelle: née d'une approche analogue des affaires du monde à l'aide d'un même instrument, née d'une expression semblable des idées. ... La langue, la culture et la civilisation française appartiennent à toutes les familles spirituelles et politiques de notre pays et des autres pays qui se réfèrent à notre langue. *La langue française est médiatrice et non pas impératrice.*

... [Francophonie] means becoming aware of this natural solidarity: born from an analogous approach to world affairs, using the same tool, born from a similar expression of ideas. ... French language, culture and civilization belong

4. Obiajunwa Wali, "The Dead End of African Literature?" *Transition* 3, no. 10 (September 1963): 14.

5. Ngũgĩ, *Writers in Politics* (London: Heinemann, 1981): i.

6. On indirect rule, see Frederick, Lord Lugard, *The Dual Mandate in British Tropical Africa* (London: Frank Cass, 1965); Hubert Deschamps, "Et Maintenant, Lord Lugard?" *Africa* 33, no. 4 (October 1963): 293–306; and Michael Crowder, "Indirect Rule—French and British Style," *Africa* 34, no. 3 (July 1964): 197–205.

to all the spiritual and political families of our country and of the other countries that rely on our language. *The French language is a mediator, not a dictator.*[7]

Throughout the book, Deniau protests (too much) that francophonie is "not political" and must not be "confused with any ideology" (6): "francophonie is situated beyond the causes of combat because it seeks no power," and even Marxists have been forced to admit the purely cultural, apolitical nature of the movement (he does not say which Marxists have done this) (96). Francophonie is built on the myth of universalism: Charles de Gaulle identified the French language as the root of France's mission in the world, a mission to "make available to the world a language perfectly adapted to the universal nature of thought" (quoted in Deniau, 21).

No one in Africa speaks for the significance of francophonie better than Léopold Sédar Senghor. He has been one of the movement's staunchest supporters and leaders. According to the literary historian Albert Gérard, Senghor's leadership of francophone writers brought Africa out of "isolation." Gérard writes: "It was a French troop, guided by Senghor, that brought Africa up to the podium of universal literature."[8] What is francophonie for Senghor?

La francophonie est un mode de pensée et d'action, une certaine manière de poser les problèmes et d'en chercher les solutions. Encore une fois, c'est une communauté spirituelle, une noosphère autour de la terre. Bref, la francophonie, c'est, par delà la langue, la civilisation française; plus précisément, l'esprit de la civilisation, c'est-à-dire la culture française. Que j'appellerai la *Francité*.

Francophonie is a mode of thought and action, a certain way of posing problems and seeking their solutions. Again, it is a spiritual community, a noosphere around the earth. In short, beyond language, francophonie is French civilization; more precisely, the spirit of civilization, that is, French culture. Which I will call *Francité*.[9]

These remarks are taken from an address given in 1966 at Laval University in Québec, an address in which Senghor admits that "the only incontestable principle on which [francophonie] rests is the usage of the French language." How one derives a "noosphere" (from the Greek *noos*, "spirit") from the simple use of a language is the mystery at the heart of francophonie. As the Holy Trinity manages to be three and one at the

---

7. Xavier Deniau, *La Francophonie* (Paris: Presses Universitaires de France, 1983): 5, emphasis mine.

8. Albert Gérard, *Etudes de littérature africaine francophone* (Dakar: Nouvelles Editions Africaines, 1977): 59.

9. Léopold Sédar Senghor, "La francophonie comme culture," in *Liberté 3: Négritude et civilisation de l'universel* (Paris: Seuil, 1977): 80.

same time, francophonie purports to embody simultaneously the central power of France and the multitude of regional interests from around the globe.

What allows Senghor's idea of francophonie to operate is his accurate perception that languages are not neutral. Languages implicitly or explicitly convey attitudes and ideologies. But it seems unlikely that they do this in the way Senghor thinks. Instead of focussing on the historical and political conditions that have made the French language what it is, Senghor speaks to the "virtues of the French language" itself, its supposedly intrinsic qualities rather than its contingent situation: "French offers us at once clarity and richness, precision and nuance" (81). His defense and praise of French seem to become a justification of his own political and poetic practice:

> Les mots français sont clairs et précis. C'est qu'ils ont tendance à l'*abstraction*, qui en fait un merveilleux outil du raisonnement. Et il n'est pas vrai que l'abstraction ignore le réel; elle le réduit à son squelette, à son réseau de relations, qui est son essence. (81)

> French words are clear and precise. This is because they tend toward *abstraction*, which makes them a marvellous tool of reasoning. And it is not true that abstraction ignores the real; it reduces the real to its skeleton, to its network of relations which is its essence.[10]

Senghor's consideration of the French language therefore begins with grammar, but leads into questions of stylistics, "the relation between thought and its translation," in other words, ideological linguistics. French ultimately offers its user nothing less than *logic*: it is "the efficient instrument of reasoning" (82). *La Francité*, mentioned above, is defined as "a rational way of posing problems and looking for their solutions..." (85). It is not at all clear how Senghor conceives of the importance of France itself in *Francité*; this is the central riddle of francophonie, around which Senghor's discourse turns in elaborate intellectual acrobatics. France is at the center, yet France is "universal" and "creolized." On a larger scale, "Western civilization" has maintained hegemony because it achieved "a kind of universality" in which Africa is always already

10. An abstraction that succeeds in not "ignoring the real" sounds curiously like a wishful description of Senghor's presidency of Senegal in the 1970s, increasingly cut off from the populace, preoccupied with global ideals such as francophonie, "technicity," and the "new humanism." Irving Leonard Markovitz writes: Senghor "has developed a systematically interrelated set of ideas which both justifies close French-African ties and legitimizes an elite rather than mass-based politics" (*Léopold Sédar Senghor and the Politics of Negritude* [New York: Atheneum, 1969]: 233). See also Jacques Louis Hymans, *Léopold Sédar Senghor: An Intellectual Biography* (Edinburgh: Edinburgh University Press, 1971): chapter 41, "Obstacles on the 'African Road,'" 206–10.

included; since Western culture is heavily indebted to African culture, the distinction between them can be ignored.[11]

The enigma of *francité* is important if only because the prize that *Les Soleils des indépendances* won in Canada, at the time of its initial publication, was the "Prix littéraire de la francité." The word *francité* is defined in the journal that controlled the prize as "francophonie *minus* France."[12] Subtracting France from francophonie makes it much easier to advertise francophonie as apolitical and reciprocal, and it obviously provides new opportunities to marginalized but now powerful communities like French Canada (which is, after all, rich by comparison to most of Africa). The idea of reciprocity fits well into Senghor's conception of the francophone community, but the means of putting reciprocity into effect—breaking ties with France—go against the most basic tenets of Senghor's political worldview. Senghor's version of francophonie appears to be a clear allegory of continuing dependence on the real France.[13]

The political fact of the imposition of French throughout an empire is translated by Senghor—and by the ideology of francophonie in general—into something quite different from a fact. Francophonie is represented as a neutral technology of reason, like literacy itself. Much of the mystique surrounding the French language, much of the mysticism within Senghor's praise of its use, is merely a translation of the myths of literacy that we examined earlier in this study. To say that francophonie is rooted in myth, however, is not to say that is is useless or devoid of positive value, particularly in opposition to the very real and increasing domination of world culture by American products.

The ideology of francophonie appears to be explicitly subservient to French national interests in the world, yet the French government was a reluctant participant in the early efforts to launch a global francophone organization. It was less clear to President de Gaulle in the 1960s (in spite of his sentiments about French itself) than it has been to President Mitterand more recently that cultural ties to former colonies must be preserved in order to protect markets and French national prestige. The first

11. See Senghor, *Ce que je crois: Négritude, francité et civilisation de l'universel* (Paris: Bernard Grasset, 1988): 208. The fourth chapter of this book, "Francité et francophonie," is Senghor's most comprehensive statement on francophonie, including his personal version of the sequence of events.

12. G.-André Vachon, "La francité," *Etudes françaises* 4, no. 2 (May 1968): 117, emphasis mine.

13. In his preface to the first *Lexique du français du Sénégal* (Dakar: Nouvelles Editions Africaines, 1979)—whose publication was an important step in the development of francophone pluralism—Senghor laid down the limitations he believes in: "Nous sommes pour une langue française, mais avec des variantes, plus exactement, des enrichissements régionaux" (3).

initiatives of francophone organization were understood "as insurance for continued French aid," insurance that France was then hesitant to offer. According to a number of observers, the French government had to be persuaded to recognize their own self-interest in the continuation of African allegiance to French culture.[14] Deniau wrote elsewhere in 1974: "It is remarkable that the francophone aspiration was born outside of the hexagon."[15] Although aid must be seen to perpetuate dependence on one level, the following quote from Senghor's speech at Laval shows that his conception of francophonie involves a certain realignment of power, a new era of reciprocity. There is also an implied warning to France:

> La Francophonie ne sera plus enfermée dans les limites de l'Hexagone. Nous ne sommes plus des "colonies": des filles mineures qui réclament une part de l'Heritage. Nous sommes devenus des Etats indépendants, des personnes majeures, qui exigent leur part de responsabilités: pour fortifier la communauté en l'agrandissant. . . .
>
> . . . L'essentiel est que *la France accepte de décoloniser culturellement* [emphasis mine] et qu'ensemble nous travaillions à la *Défense et Expansion de la langue française* comme nous avons travaillé à son illustration. Et elle accepte si elle n'en a pas pris l'initiative. (89)

> Francophonie will no longer be contained by the borders of France. We are not "colonies" any longer: underaged daughters who beg for a part of the Inheritance. We have become independent States, grown-ups, and we demand our share of the responsibilities, in order to strengthen the community by expanding it. . . .
>
> . . . The essential thing is that *France accept cultural decolonization* [emphasis mine] and that we work together for the *Defense and Expansion of the French language* as we have worked for its illustration. And France accepts this even if she did not take the initiative.

Senghor's version of francophonie may now appear hopelessly tied to the thought patterns of colonialism, but the kind of decolonization he speaks of here, the "initiative"that France would not take without prodding, was not negligible. His francophonie is not without oppositional force. What he is demanding is *dialogism*, the principal of supposedly equal exchange without which francophonie makes no sense. The essen-

---

14. Philip M. Allen, "Francophonie Considered," *Africa Report* 13, no. 6 (June 1968): 9; Robert Cornevin confirms that "le gouvernement français restait extrêmement réservé sur ces divers projets." *Littératures d'Afrique noire de langue française* (Paris: Presses Universitaires de France, 1976): 33. For the most comprehensive general treatment of francophonie, see Michel Tétu, *La Francophonie: Histoire, problématique et perspectives*, with a preface by Léopold Sédar Senghor (Montreal: Guérin Littérature, 1987); on De Gaulle's attitude, see p. 50.

15. Xavier Deniau, "La Dimension francophone dans la politique française," *France-Eurafrique* 247 (May-June 1974): 4.

tial thesis underlying postcolonial use of colonial languages is that linguistic, discursive, and political power are linked; that the imposition of greater "universality" through global languages like French and English is an *irreversible* process; that decolonization will only come through *appropriation* of the former master's tongue and—in most cases— through continued *dialogue* with the colonizing power. Reciprocity is the key, and it is evident from Senghor's speech that a small revolution had to take place before France would agree to participate. That revolution was the seizure of the French language by colonized subjects who, like Shakespeare's Caliban, turned the weapon against the former master, if only to get his attention. The French language is a "miraculous weapon," in Césaire's words.[16] Tchicaya U'Tamsi, the late Congolese poet, said, "If the French language colonizes me, I'll colonize it right back."[17] Hence the master's hesitation in regard to a formalized, multilateral francophonie.[18] The quotations from Senghor here reveal the moment of that seizure. At the moment of incipient decolonization, it represented nothing less than the seizure of "the means of expression," to borrow a Sartrean notion.[19]

If francophonie can be said to promote cultural independence, therefore, it is only within a peculiar dialectic of power in which metropolitan France alternately promotes and impedes advancement. This is in fact very much the reality of francophone African literature: France promotes by impeding and impedes by promoting. Francophonie serves as a principal motor of decolonization, but it forces those who would decolonize, at the least, to continue dialogue (exchange, trade, commerce) with the

16. Aimé Césaire's first volume of collected poetry was called *Les Armes miraculeuses* (Paris: Gallimard, 1946). The most complete elaboration of the philosophical theory behind this is to be found in Jean-Paul Sartre's "Orphée noir," published as a preface to Léopold Sédar Senghor's edited volume of Negritude poetry, *Anthologie de la nouvelle poésie nègre et malgache de langue française* (Paris: Presses Universitaires de France, 1948): ix-xliv.

17. "La langue française me colonise, je la colonise à mon tour." Quoted in Jacques Chevrier, "L'écrivain africain devant la langue française," *Notre Librairie* 53 (May-June 1980): 45.

18. "To France, the adoption of multilateral forms of decision-making in economic, educational, and foreign policy affairs would seem to impair freedom of initiative in areas where France believed it was already doing its utmost. From this point of view, only France would become more seriously bound by the formalization of Francophonie" (Allen, 10).

19. The literary history of francophonie, incidentally, runs counter to Sartre's claim (as elucidated by Denis Hollier), that "there is but one politics, the politics of prose" (Denis Hollier, *The Politics of Prose* [Minneapolis: University of Minnesota Press, 1986], 9). For it was negritude *poetry*, published in Senghor's *Anthologie de la nouvelle poésie nègre*, with a preface by Sartre himself ("Orphée noir"), that provided one of the strongest initiatives in an emergent black francophonie. Of course, according to critiques we have seen in this study, negritude was in any case apolitical.

métropole. France therefore has it both ways: as a former colonial power, France maintains colonial structures of aid and exploitation, yet at the same time offering a "nonaligned" alternative to American and Soviet hegemony in the world.[20] Again, Senghor sums it up: "The French language is the language of nonalignment and of the third world . . . when used in international reports, the French language corresponds to the affirmation of a policy of nonalignment."[21] The space of francophonie is therefore claimed to be a politically honorable one, overlapping with but not contained by any "world," first, second, or third. It is a transcendental political space whose ideological strength comes from its flexibility.

The most surprising element in all this, after more than two decades of organized francophonie and three decades of African independence, is the staying power of the ideology of francophonie. The movement continues to gather strength, as political action complements poetic intentions. In 1986, Jacques Chirac named a Guadeloupean woman, Lucette Michaux-Chevry, to a new cabinet-level post as Secretary of State for Francophonie. In 1989, a new magazine called *Francophonie* was launched; its "comité de soutien" is headed by François Mitterand, followed by Senegalese President Abdou Diouf, Jacques Chirac, Canadian Prime Minister Brian Mulroney, and others. The magazine expresses full confidence in "new solidarities" that will emerge within this movement whose "originality is in being the only international community based on a language."[22]

Writers from across the political spectrum, from Senghor on the right to the Haitian poet René Depestre on the left, speak in a harmonious chorus on the value of French (while dissenting voices are heard in the wings). A useful review of contemporary attitudes toward the French language was published in 1985 by the journal *La Quinzaine littéraire*, in the form of short articles responding to a questionnaire. Writers from around the francophone world were asked why they wrote in French,

20. For Pierre Biarnès, correspondent of *Le Monde* in West Africa, political independence is largely an illusion: "Bref, on [i. e. France] continuerait à exercer sur ces contrées une influence prépondérante et on garderait pour l'essentiel, en tout cas pour une large part, leur marché, mais à un bien moindre coût qu'autrefois, politique et financier." *L'Afrique aux Africains: Vingt ans d'indépendance en Afrique noire francophone* (Paris: Armand Colin, 1980): 61.

21. Quoted in Jean-Claude Luc, "Les chances de l'agence de coopération culturelle et technique des pays francophones" (*Revue française d'études politiques africaines* 57 [September 1970]: 78). Cf. Boutros Ghali, Egyptian Foreign Minister: "Le français est une langue non alignée, désintéressée" (quoted by Guy Ossito Midiohouan, "Le Sottisier francophone," *Peuples noirs, peuples africains* 11, nos. 59–62 [September 1987-April 1988]: 184).

22. Jean-Félix Mouloungui, editorial, *Francophonie Magazine* 2 (June 1989): 3.

whether it was by choice or constraint, how French fit into their social and intellectual background, and whether they saw French as an advantage for the future. The editor of the *Quinzaine* frames the discussion with a properly pluralistic introduction, even to the point of substituting the rubric "Ecrire les langues françaises" (Writing the French Languages) for "francophonie": "The term 'francophonie' has bad resonances for many; they hear echoes of a colonial history that has happily been left behind." The liberal position is thus that "the language belongs to those who use it."[23] What is most interesting in the responses from African and Afro-Caribbean writers is the strong current of idealization that runs through their attitudes toward French (this current is not the only one, and I will return to the dissenting view presently). Thus, for Mukala Kadima-Nzuji from Zaïre, French represents the "place of rootedness, of man's self-reconciliation, of the affirmation of all cultures," if only the francophone writer can succeed in making French "the place in which he takes on his own identity" (*QL*, 31). The degree of optimism present in Mukala's article is characteristic of many francophone writers: if they did not share at least some part of Mukala's belief, there would be no point to writing in French.

For perspective, it would be wise to bear in mind that in the late 1980s the use of French is widely considered to be a moot question. First-world readers, particularly Americans in my experience, tend to assume that local-language use and cultural liberation are one and the same thing, that writing in Swahili or Creole is a sufficient condition for the creation of national culture in Fanon's sense. Speaking as part of a panel in New York in 1986, the Congolese poet Tchicaya U'Tam'si was asked a question from the audience that was based on this assumption. Having apparently explained "why I write in French" ten thousand times over a period of thirty years, Tchicaya nearly exploded with frustration. He simply refused to answer what was, for him, a pointless question. The fact is that now, unlike in the 1960s, it matters less *why* than *how* francophone writers write in French. The institutionalized inevitability of French in "francophone" Africa must be kept in mind as the base condition underlying the history and the attitudes we are examining. Nonetheless, the impertinent question from the audience in New York unleashed a discussion that showed anything but total agreement among the African and Afro-Caribbean writers who were present.

23. Maurice Nadeau, "La langue appartient à ceux qui l'utilisent," *La Quinzaine littéraire* 436 (March 16–31, 1985): 3; further references to this number of the journal, abbreviated *QL*, will be included in the text. I am grateful to Cynthia Mesh for bringing this series of articles to my attention.

If Mukala's response represents a broad current in the francophone world, René Depestre's contribution to the *Quinzaine* survey is part of a narrower, more problematic tendancy. A Haitian poet, essayist, and critic exiled in Cuba for many years, Depestre is a strong presence on the ideological left. His contribution is a poem called "Bref éloge de la langue française" ("A Short Encomium to the French Language"). The poem is built on a metaphor of the French language as a human body, specifically a woman's, which the poet "leads to the river" in order to "rub her body with perfumed herbs;" he enriches the body of the language with creole vigor, "words of joy and of sowing" (*QL*, 33). The metaphor reaches its logical conclusion at the end of the poem:

> oui je chante la langue française
> qui défait joyeusement sa jupe
> ses cheveux et son aventure
> sous mes mains amoureuses de potier.
> (*QL*, 33)

> yes I sing the French language
> who gayly undoes her dress
> her hair and her chance
> under my loving potter's hands.[24]

This little poem bears a strong resemblance to one of Senghor's most famous works, "Femme noire," in which woman also plays the role of compliant inspiration for the male poetic consciousness.[25] In both cases, a discourse of liberation from a prior condition of oppression—racial in Senghor's text, cultural in Depestre's—is expressed through the exploitation (the word is not too strong) of woman as an allegorical commodity. Depestre represents his appropriation of French through the willing submission of a woman to a man's desires. It is as if equality of gender had to be sacrificed in order for "general" (i.e., male) liberation to take place (this is a central assumption, to which I will return in the next chapter). This current of idealization and metaphoricity in the characterization of francophonie makes strange bedfellows of Senghor and Depestre, who otherwise seem to have little in common.[26]

24. In translating the poem into English, one is forced to exaggerate the gender relations by choosing between "him" and "her" in the phrase "lui frotter le corps" ("rubbing *her* body").

25. Senghor, "Femme noire," in *Poèmes* (Paris: Seuil, 1984), 16–17. I will analyze this poem in the next chapter.

26. In his *Bonjour et adieu à la négritude* (Paris: Robert Laffont, 1980), Depestre issues a strong critique of negritude ideology, particularly as practiced by Senghor: "Léopold Sédar Senghor, dans une perspective plutôt romantique, vitaliste, voire mystique, considérait

The tendency to idealize the French language has, however, been sub-ject to criticism from the beginning. Ahmadou Kourouma himself, in an interview published in 1970, took a very clear position regarding the uses and abuses of French (see the epigraph at the beginning of this chapter). Educated in a French colonial system in which "little blacks were made to 'respect' a language that in no way corresponded to their vision of the world" (Baddey, 7), Kourouma found French to be anything but a neu-tral tool of reasoning and creativity. French is "born out of Latin genius" and has "grafted itself poorly to the African soul." Kourouma set out to do nothing less than "break" and "distort a classical language that was too rigid for my thoughts. . . ." French is "an iron collar" (*carcan*) with which the African writer must come to terms. The author of *Les Soleils des indépendances* takes a subversive attitude toward French; we will see how this translates into a specific style and lexical practice later in this chapter. Kourouma's remarks, taken in the context of an emergent fran-cophone movement, appear to be revolutionary. However, if franco-phonie is reciprocal and pluralistic, any revolt that takes place in French only strengthens the movement.

As the francophone movement began to institutionalize itself, scepti-cism followed. Conflicting attitudes toward language are a classical topos in the rivalry between Britain and France, which naturally was exported to anglophone and francophone Africa. In the same interview, Kourouma comments that fetishization of the colonial language was not a problem in the British colonies: "The English didn't brood over their own lan-guage as the French did, and that's a good thing" (Baddey, 7). Anglo-phone critics voiced derisive scepticism, referring to francophonie as "a secular state of grace with all the articulations and paradoxes of a latter-day City of God" (Allen, 6). There were those who asserted that "fran-cophonie has lost people and gained only governments," that French "is losing its vitality and withering into a kind of bureaucratic Latin" (7). Philip M. Allen attacks the most basic premise of francophonie when he

---

l'une des formes historiques de l'aliénation des hommes (l'aliénation raciale) comme un état qui serait intrinsèque à 'l'homme négro-africain'. . . . Cette position nous paraît plus proche du romantisme allemand, de Barrès, Drieu La Rochelle, Ernst Jünger, que des expériences réellement vécues par nos peuples à l'époque de la colonisation" (158). The rhetoric of liberation in *Bonjour et adieu* must nonetheless be juxtaposed to a real problem of gender objectification and romantic idealization in other works by Depestre, namely *Alléluia pour une femme-jardin* (Ottowa: Leméac, 1973). In a survey of writers' attitudes toward fran-cophonie, Jacques Chevrier identifies three groups: 1) "les inconditionnels," such as Sen-ghor, for whom French is nearly sacred; 2) "les réticents," who see French as inevitable but colonialist; and 3) "les réalistes," including Tchicaya, those who deal with French prag-matically (Chevrier, "L'écrivain africain").

states that francophone African writers, such as Marcien Towa, "cannot forge a French that is their own French, in the way that English has become the national possession of Welshman, Americans, Australians, and Nigerians—after a *dialectical* interaction of metropolitan and national influences. In Africa at least, *this dialectical process does not seem to apply to French*" (8, emphasis mine). Allen's statement, on the most elementary level, refers to the relative immutability of French, which in Africa appears to have been creolized—that is to say, *appropriated*—much less than English.[27] This is true to the extent that French remains a more institutionally protected commodity in the francophone nations, passed on only in schools that remain tied to the French system if only by the presence of French *coopérants* and the necessity of maintaining *équivalence* with French universities. Somehow—and again, literary history and the mere experience of conversation in Africa support this—French resists mutation more than English; there are real creoles (spoken as first languages) based on English in Africa, while French-based languages seem to remain pidgins, "used [only] by native speakers of other languages."[28]

French colonialism, built around a doctrine of assimilation, did little to encourage local language literacy. The British, as least partially subscribing to Lord Lugard's theory of indirect rule, worked to establish African language literacy and to encourage the development of literatures in local languages.[29] After Independence, British publishing houses established branches in Ibadan and Nairobi, while Présence Africaine struggled to survive in Paris. No French publisher has opened a branch in Africa (although Nouvelles Editions Africaines is partly French owned). The style and freedom of the respective literatures seemed to follow suit: anglophone writing seemed more open and "creole"; francophone literature remained wedded to the academism of Paris. Albert Gérard comments: "No such prodigious linguistic and literary burgeoning [as in anglophone Africa] produced itself in francophone Africa" (*Etudes*, 67).

All of these factors help to preserve the "quality" (that is, the uniformity) of the French language. Due to the viability of African lingua francas, there is little need for French as a means of everyday communication

27. Tchicaya U'Tam'si, in his contribution to the *QL* survey, mentions the nonreciprocity between French and African languages in the Congo: "On y parle les parlers nationaux en les truffant de mots français, mais pas le contraire" (*QL*, 30).

28. Adrian Akmajian, Richard A. Demers, Robert M. Harnish, *Linguistics: An Introduction to Language and Communication* (Cambridge: MIT Press, 1984): 319.

29. For example, without the missionary press in Morija (Lesotho), Thomas Mofolo's Sesotho-language novel *Chaka* would surely not have been published in 1925. See Daniel P. Kunene's introduction to Mofolo's *Chaka* (London: Heinemann, 1981): xi–xiv. Ironically, the missionary society that ran the press was French.

between ordinary people, further insulating it from dialectical change.[30] The astute francophone critic Jean-Pierre Makouta-M'Boukou sees the impenetrability of French as a paradox at the heart of francophone literature: "The advent of black literature changes nothing in the French language. . . . There is no cultural cross-breeding linguistically speaking," and Senghor's highly-advertised *métissage* is in reality "alienation."[31] African languages are shot through with Gallicisms, Makouta-M'Boukou points out, but standard French remains aloof, "pure."

The question of dialects and dialectics goes to the heart of the matter of francophonie. True believers of the movement, such as Senghor and Deniau, define francophonie as reciprocity, as a multilateral cultural formation in which *dialogue* may take place. This word *francophonie*, which on the most obvious level means only speaking French, is said to permit an unraveling of French hegemony: to continue to speak French is to work for decolonization. This makes sense from the perspective of the 1960s, when in the view of many African leaders the greatest danger of decolonization was to be totally cut off from the *métropole* (Sékou Touré of course saw things differently); francophonie was a device for continuing relations on a new basis. But how new are the new terms of the relationship? How does postcolonial francophonie really differ from colonial domination? The movement has clear answers to these questions, beginning with Senghor's remarks quoted above: the difference is that relations will now be between equals, "adults." The space of francophonie is a space of *dialogue*, in which power would be exercised by dialectical interaction with no predetermination of outcome; it is a space of "mediation" and dialogue, not imperialism or dictation. In the words of one French Africanist, francophonie should come to be "a common cultural homeland [*patrie*], in which French would no longer be the language of exile. . . . Instead of uprooting, it would irrigate all the different roots."[32]

But if, as Allen and Makouta-M'Boukou assert, the dialectical process does not apply to French in Africa, then the consequences are grave. To examine them, we will have to distinguish between the linguistic and the broader political and philosophical implications of the question, that is, between dialect and dialectic. Both terms come from the Greek *dia-* (be-

---

30. A notable exception is the Ivory Coast, where the lack of a viable lingua franca has pressed French into service; French has inevitably spawned a dialect form often called "le français de Moussa." See "Le français de Moussa," *Autrement* 9 (October 1984): 148–54.

31. *Introduction à l'étude du roman négro-africain de langue française* (Abidjan: Nouvelles Editions Africaines, 1980): 79, 73. See also Makouta-M'Boukou's *Le Français en Afrique noire* (Paris: Bordas, 1973).

32. Vincent Monteil, "Le problème linguistique en Afrique noire," *Esprit* 311 (November 1962): 809.

tween) and *legein* (to talk); both are closely related to the idea of *dialogue*. A dialect is a particular, local or individual manner of speaking; it is speech with a difference, often "considered as deviating from a real or imaginary standard speech" (Webster); it is a "subordinate form" (*Oxford English Dictionary*). As a technical term in linguistics, the word dialect "carries no negative value judgment and simply refers to a distinct form of a language."[33] A dialectic, in its simplest description, is a "logical argumentation or disputation" (*OED*); it could be construed as the process of give and take by which a dialect differentiates itself from the standard, if we can take "logic" as the cultural and political processes effecting linguistic change. This mutability is what Allen denies in the case of African French. To address the question of dialect and dialectic thus takes us back to the question posed at the beginning of this study: "What's the difference?" What is a "different" use of French, and by what process of "disputation" might it come about? It also poses once again the question of dialogism and its discontents and suggests a political question as well: What difference has Independence made?

If what Allen wrote were literally and totally true, if French could in no way be adapted to local needs, appropriated and turned to new purposes, then the founding premise of francophone African literature, and its current consensus, would be invalidated. Some take precisely this position: that European languages in general can never be Africanized. This is the pragmatic view taken by Ngũgĩ: decolonization begins with the tongue. Makouta-M'Boukou takes the position that any single language is wholly valid for only one culture. French, for example, can never coincide with "black concepts" (*Introduction*, 77); French "does not have enough virtue to fully express the black soul" (74). By implication, any literature written in one's native language would eliminate the gap between meaning and expression.[34] For Makouta-M'Boukou, the relation between French and African languages is nonreciprocal because of the historical situation: "If there is a meeting between black African languages and French, there is certainly no marriage in the sense of harmony, but rather domination of the black languages by French." Ahmadou Kourouma took a similar view in describing the conflict between two opposed cultural essences, Latin genius and the African soul (at the end of this chapter we will see his version of the marriage metaphor).

Maryse Condé, a novelist and literary critic originally from Guadeloupe but intimately connected with Africa, translates this view of the

33. Akmajian, et al., *Linguistics*, 287.
34. Makouta-M'Boukou is arguing against Sartre's notion that there is a "décalage leger et constant qui sépare ce qu'il [l'écrivain noir] dit de ce qu'il voudrait dire, dès qu'il parle de lui" ("Orphée noir," xix).

apparently greater flexibility of English into a nostalgia for anglophone freedom and pragmatism, for indirect rule rather than assimilation:

> Certain specialists of African literature vie with each other in emphasizing the "more precocious awakening" of francophone Africa to poetic and novelistic production. . . . In fact, these specialists, in their perhaps unconscious desire to prove the superiority of French colonization, turn their back on History. From the end of the nineteenth century, all of anglophone West Africa was the site of an intense intellectual activity which simply did not choose literature as its field. . . .
>
> If neither the content of the works nor the role and status of the writers are radically different, what makes the specificity of anglophone as opposed to francophone literature?
>
> One could answer schematically that the anglophone writers speak of a place that still exists. The francophones dream of a place that is already gone [*qui n'existe déjà plus*].[35]

Condé echoes a long tradition of characterizations—born in trans-Channel rivalry and carried over into colonial Africa—when she describes the francophones as wedded to an abstract classicism and the anglophones as free to be themselves:

> The work of the anglophone writer is immersed in a cultural ocean. The themes that are treated are not the only things that count, it is more *the direct grasp of the real* [*prise directe sur le réel*], the fact that the work does not raise the problem of "blackness" [*Négrité*] in an artificial or abstract manner, but in the most deeply intimate fashion. . . . From the start, then, anglophone literature is situated between two requirements which could appear to be contradictory: on the one hand, intimacy with the traditional culture and universe, and on the other, audacity and a feeling for innovation. (30; emphasis mine)

The "pragmatic" approach, producing a supposedly unmediated and intimate reflection of one's culture, is typical of the anglophone African literary world; it is as if Indirect Rule created conditions favorable to "direct" expression (for example, greater African-language literacy), while the French ideal of assimilation produced highly mediated abstractions such as Negritude.[36] The anglophone rejection of Negritude (such as Wole Soyinka's famous *bon mot*: "The tiger doesn't talk about his

---

35. Maryse Condé, "Anglophones et francophones: les frontières littéraires existent-elles?" *Notre Librairie* 65 (July-September 1982): 27.

36. Michel Tétu gives credence to this popular notion: "La littérature africaine d'expression anglaise . . . des années 1950 à 1970 . . . est précise, énumérative: la langue est un véhicule. Les romanciers tendent à coller à la vie, en nommant simplement les réalités qu'ils feront sentir plus profondément par le rappel de dictons, d'éléments ancestraux ou de bruits familiers. L'écrivain francophone, marqué par son éducation humaniste, ou simplement par la tradition littéraire française, analyse, dissèque, s'essaye à quelques synthèses et va parfois jusqu'à célébrer son pays . . . " (*La Francophonie*, 143).

tigritude") has often been phrased as an attack on obscurantistic abstraction (hence Senghor's rejoinder, an abstraction that does not "ignore the real").

The problem with anglophone pragmatism is that it often merely substitutes one allegory for another, "Africanity" or "the African personality" for Negritude. Condé may appear to have traded one idealization for another, but at least on the question of language, she seems to deny any intrinsic quality in language and focusses on its political situation. She sees colonial languages as the products of chance. Her response to the *Quinzaine* survey is called "Au-delà des langues et des couleurs" (beyond languages and colors); her conviction is that the ideology of both race and francophonie are null (*caduc*), that only "fraternity" has validity as an ideal (*QL*, 36).

Mongo Beti, the Camerounian novelist, as editor of the journal *Peuples noirs, peuples africains*, has produced one of the most comprehesive and stinging rejections of francophonie. In his own contribution to a special issue on the subject, Beti writes: "What is this act of allegiance or love for the French language that is expected of us? Why should I have to celebrate French? Because I write in French? Living in the suburbs, I use my car to get into the center of the city every morning; who would dare ask me to make a declaration of love to my car?"[37]

A more philosophical critique of francophonie comes from Edouard Glissant. Beginning with the paragraph I used as an epigraph to this book, Glissant labels the role of French as "maintaining [a false] transparency, perpetrating a kind of humanism that will henceforth be lukewarm, comforting and colorless."[38] The most spectacular and dubious claim made for the French language, in Glissant's analysis, is that it preexists differences, that it transcends divisions. This means that French can serve as the bearer of universal values like humanism and the dignity of man: "The French language would therefore have a function of humanization which would be inseparable from its nature and which would guard against the hastiness of what would be called an abusive collectivization of identity." Once these premises have been established—and our

37. Mongo Beti, "Seigneur, délivre-nous de la francophonie," *Peuples noirs, peuples africains* 11, nos. 59–62 (September 1987-April 1988): 105. It is interesting to note that Beti's rejection of francophonie, like Condé's, is accompanied by a grass-is-always-greener attitude toward the anglophone world; Beti writes: "La langue anglaise est aujourd'hui, mieux que la langue française, la langue de la liberté, autant dire de la créativité. Ce n'est certainement pas un hasard si le premier Prix Nobel Africain de littérature est anglophone" (106). For a critique of francophonie as neocolonialism, see in the same issue the editorial, "Le Degré zéro de la décolonisation," 1–7, and Guy Ossito Midiohouan, "Tiens, revoilà les tirailleurs," 53–58.

38. *La Quinzaine littéraire* 437 (April 1–15, 1985): 7. This issue of *La Quinzaine* contains several additional responses to the questionnaire on francophonie.

rapid review of francophonie here has shown how widespread they are—once French is identified with a certain set of values, a hierarchy of conformity must follow; some writers will express better than others the "transcendental values" of francophonie. Glissant sums up his attack:

Francophonie as a theory and as a practice therefore derives from the covetousness of the French spirit, from a pretension that is generous but destructive to other peoples, a pretension to nourish and convey universal values. This pretension is now a deadly one, for the language itself first of all.

To such questions [as the specific roles that French plays in varying contexts], francophonie as a theory cannot respond, because its nature, as we have seen, is to pre-exist anything that is done, suffered, or expressed. (7)

The value of Glissant's contribution lies in his unveiling of the monolithic substructure of an ideology that claims to be pluralistic. When analyzed as a discourse, as the sum of all utterances on the subject, francophonie would appear to be inseparable from an idea of France as a liberating influence throughout the world. French colonialism was, after all, a *liberal* undertaking, often promoted as the exportation of the values of 1789.[39] Francophonie as we have seen it described by Deniau and Senghor and critiqued by Glissant can be an ideological wolf in sheep's clothing, inviting dialectical exchange but subtly domesticating and assimilating to an unchanging standard.

The problem with this interpretation is that it rests on the assumption that francophonie succeeds in imposing immutable norms. Here we must distinguish between the hidden agenda of universal values exposed by Glissant—an agenda that may or may not succeed—and the ability of francophone writers to cope with francophonie, this "iron collar" (Condé, *QL*, 36), to bend and twist it to their own ends. That French is totally resistant to counterappropriation, to decolonization in any form, is obviously a thesis that will not withstand much scrutiny. Allen ridicules the Moroccan poet Abdel-atif Laabi, "who urges a 'decolonization of culture' without being able to express his own ideas in anything but the language of colonialism," who "cannot forge a French that is [his] own French" (8). Such a critique is facile, at least in regard to sub-Saharan Africa; it ignores the real politics of discourse, beginning with the conditions of literacy. How, then, do we assess the dialectization of French against a current telling us it isn't there?

39. For example, Hubert Deschamps describes the French policy of assimilation (as opposed to the disdainful "hands-off" policy of the British, indirect rule) as "la Révolution de 1789 débarquant en Afrique sur la pointe des pieds et avec un certain retard" ("Et Maintenant, Lord Lugard?" 300). See also Christopher L. Miller, "Unfinished Business: Colonialism in Sub-Saharan Africa and the Ideals of the French Revolution" (forthcoming article).

By listening and by reading. Any amount of time spent in francophone Africa will destroy one's idea that French does not change in local circumstances. Although many Africans speak "perfect," classical French, most make at least occasional use of phrases directly translated from their local languages. It is common usage in the Tshiluba-speaking parts of Zaïre to say "Comment?" instead of "Comment ça va?" and "Quelle heure fait-il?" instead of "Quelle heure est-il?" and to agree with a negative assertion by saying yes instead of no, reproducing Tshiluba usage. These forms of Africanisms are called *calques*, direct copies of African originals in French, and *Les Soleils des indépendances* is shot through with them. It is not my object here to prove the importance of Africanisms in African spoken French; linguistic studies of this question are available.[40] What concerns us now is the dialectization of written, literary French.

What are the modes of Africanization in French? Three types come to mind. First, Camara Laye, who was very much a part of the "classicism" referred to by Condé and who used French words in materially unmodified ways, nonetheless created a degree of conditional "intimacy." The conformity of this style to French norms did not preclude a close and subtle depiction of his African childhood, including a detailed appropriation of a word such as "totem." Second, starting in the 1950s Sembène Ousmane was already practicing a limited form of linguistic experimentation. Alioune Tine, a professor of African literature at Dakar, has analyzed the surprising degree to which Sembène practiced both a "Frenchization of Wolof" and a "Wolofization of French" in even his early novels.[41] And lastly, Senghor says that his participation as one of the "immortals" of the French Academy will allow him to "work on . . . the crossbreeding of the French language. . . . I hope to introduce into the French Academy's dictionary words like 'negritude.' "[42]

Within a space that clearly is full of complexity and nuance, one general observation can be made: the literary productions of francophone Africa were not able to take full account of the dialectization of spoken French. Written French remained classical and largely isolated from the mutations to which spoken French was subject in Africa. Until a certain

40. See especially Makouta-M'Boukou, *Le Français en Afrique noire*.

41. For example, the title *Les Bouts de bois de Dieu* is a direct translation of the Wolof expression "banty mam yall," which is in fact the subtitle of the book. See Alioune Tine, *Etude pragmatique et sémiotique des effets du bilinguisme dans les oeuvres romanesques de Ousmane Sembène*, dissertation (thèse de 3e cycle), University of Lyon II, 1981. Tine analyzes Sembène's linguistic practice as an effort to "fill in a void," that void being the absence of Wolof as a written language (5). See also Tine, "Wolof ou français, le choix de Sembène," *Notre Librairie* 81 (1985): 43–50.

42. Interview with Senghor by Stephen H. Grant, *African Report* 28, no. 6 (November-December 1983): 62.

point, therefore, this gap between the way Africans wrote and the way they spoke French seemed to support the notion of an impenetrable French language, forever removed from the life of the people. By general agreement, the watershed in the history of literary francophonie in Africa was the publication, in 1968, of *Les Soleils des indépendances*.[43]

The basic discourse of francophonie as value-bearer was already well established by 1968; against a background of rhetoric that sometimes bordered on anti-"Anglo-Saxon" paranoia,[44] the institutions that now support that ideology were just being formed. As I have indicated, Kourouma's novel was first published with a specific and explicit intention on the part of its Canadian publishers, as a showpiece of francophonie. In light of the author's stated attitude toward the French language, there is a considerable irony here. The condition of possibility for this minirevolution in African francophonie was the mediation provided by French Canada. It was a French-Canadian initiative that in 1961 led to the founding of AUPELF, the Association des Universités partiellement ou entièrement de langue française, the first organization dedicated to francophonie. And it is significant that AUPELF was founded at the University of Montreal, for it was the University of Montreal Press that first published *Les Soleils des indépendances*.

If francophonie appears from the outside sometimes to hide universalism in the clothing of pluralism, the Prix de la francité, as a Canadian initiative, comes out of a culture of difference. The journal *Etudes françaises* created its literary prize specifically for those who "feel, in a particularly bitter manner, the gap that separates their original culture from the cultural norm represented by Paris." The "meeting" and even the "conflict" between these non-French writers and French literature can produce a "creative shock" and lead to "the renewal of the language." Kourouma's novel is thus attributed a prize and published within the bounds of an *analogy* between French-Canadian culture and francophone African culture: "The Prize of the journal *Etudes françaises* was thus created with writers in mind who, in order to create their work, must overcome a problem of culture *analogous* to that which the French Canadians have been living for two centuries."[45]

In Quebec, the movement toward cultural liberation in the 1960s gath-

<hr>

43. Condé, in her article on anglophonie and francophonie, refers to *Les Soleils des indépendances* as the belated coming of cultural authenticity to francophone literature: "Il aura fallu attendre 1968 pour qu'un francophone, Ahmadou Kourouma, ose écrire: 'Il y avait une semaine qu'avait fini dans la capitale Koné Ibrahima . . . ' " ("Anglophones et francophones," 30).

44. See Gérard Tougas, *La Francophonie en péril* (Montreal: Le Cercle du Livre de France, 1967), reviewed in *Etudes françaises* 4, no. 1 (February 1968): 101–2.

45. G.-André Vachon, "La francité," 118, emphasis mine.

ered force around the issue of the French language, and in this context the ideology of pluralistic francophonie makes perfect sense. French in Quebec corresponds logically to the one language/ one culture theory espoused by Makouta-M'Boukou. There obviously would be no economic or cultural liberation for the Québecois unless it began with seizure of the "means of expression" on the signboards. The analogy between cultural oppression in Quebec and racial oppression elsewhere was made explicit by Pierre Vallière's *Nègres blancs d'Amérique*.[46] The cultural condition of Quebec would also appear to have served as the condition of possibility for a significant departure in the history of African literature.

Whether francophonie can be labelled as a form of either true or false cultural consciousness is a question that makes no sense outside of specific contexts. As French-speaking political leaders continue their efforts to organize common interests and goals, the cultural mysticism of Senghor may be left behind; on the other hand, it may only be replaced by a new form of francophonie as tourism in intellectual disguise.[47]

The preceding pages should illustrate how much significance is attached to the fact of writing in French, and how *Les Soleils des indépendances* was initially published as part of a concerted effort to demonstrate the dialectical viability of francophonie. In the close analysis of the novel that follows, I will try not so much to test that viability as to see how the dialectization of French fits in with anthropological concerns.

Kourouma's *Détour*

From its opening paragraph, *Les Soleils des indépendances* is written in a French that breaks classical norms and calls attention to a distinctive new way of writing:

> Il y avait une semaine qu'avait fini dans la capitale Koné Ibrahima, de race malinké, ou disons-le en malinké: il n'avait pas soutenu un petit rhume . . . [48]

46. *Nègres blancs d'Amérique: autobiographie précoce d'un "terroriste" québecois* (Paris: Maspero, 1969): "les travailleurs du Québec ont conscience de leur condition de nègres, d'exploités, de citoyens de seconde classe" (23).

47. In addition to the new *Francophonie Magazine* referred to above, there is a new tourist magazine called *Soleils et francophonie*. The first number (June 1989) featured dozens of luscious pictures of African tourist spots. The introductory editorial proclaims, falsely: "L'Afrique est un pays [*sic*] où le français prédomine" (3); in an interview, Jack Lang states with just a trace of uncertainty: "La France n'est plus suspectée, en tout cas je l'espère, de vouloir imposer ses façons de penser à travers sa langue" (5).

48. Ahmadou Kourouma, *Les Soleils des indépendances* (Paris: Seuil, 1970): 7. All further references to the novel, abbreviated *SI*, will be included in the text, followed by references to the published translation by Adrian Adams, *The Suns of Independence* (New York: Africana Publishing, 1981), abbreviated *Suns*. I will use the notation "AT" in the

One week had passed since Kone Ibrahima, of the Malinke race, had met his end in the capital city, or to put it in Malinke: he hadn't survived a little cold . . . (3)

Kourouma described his technique as an adaptation of French to African narrative rhythms: "Je l'ai pensé en malinké et écrit en français en prenant une liberté que j'estime naturelle avec la langue classique" ("I thought [the book] in Malinke and wrote it in French, taking liberties that seemed natural with the classical language" [Baddey, 7]). Examples of linguistic "deviance" are to be found on nearly every page.[49] By using African-language phrases translated word for word into French, and by using African words that he teaches to the reader, Kourouma goes further than previous African writers toward closing the gap between the way French is spoken by many Africans and the way it was written. His written French, having been "thought in Malinke," is always already a translated language, but the original *text* does not exist. We are faced with a sort of palimpsest, a poorly erased original, that affects the form and meaning of the French text. This compromise or *hybrid* between an African language and French has been hailed as the "coexistence of the French signifier and the Malinke signified, of the French word applied to a Malinke [Mande] reality."[50]

---

frequent cases where I have found it necessary to alter the translation. I have also preferred to stay with the French spellings of names (Doumbouya instead of Dumbuya).

49. Jean-Pierre Makouta-M'Boukou's linguistic analysis, in his *Introduction* (302–12), is the best. Makouta-M'Boukou distinguishes between three "levels" of style in *Les Soleils des indépendances*: first, "incorrect" or imprecise usage in French, such as "en pleine musulmane" instead of "en parfaite musulmane" (*SI*, 27), or "asseoir le deuil" instead of "porter le deuil" (*SI*, 132); second, *calques* that result in original, if not incorrect usage, such as "totem panthère" used as a family identification (*SI*, 9), or this description of a man as an accumulation of objects: "C'était un court et rond comme une souche, cou, bras, poings et épaules de lutteur, visage dur de pierre" (*SI*, 14); the third level is that of pure originality without derivation from Mandekan; Makouta-M'Boukou cites this sentence: "Les ténèbres de la nuit s'étaient réfugiées autour des recoins, dans les feuillages des arbres, sous les toits" (*SI*, 43). In the context of his *Introduction*, Makouta-M'Boukou demonstrates that Kourouma's stylistic practice flows out of a history in francophone African literature, that it is not without precedent: "Ahmadou Kourouma, comme beaucoup d'autres écrivains négro-africains, pense en sa langue, mais s'extériorise en français" (303; see also 267–302). For others, Kourouma has nonetheless staged a revolution in writing: "Nous n'avons pas encore vu cela chez les écrivains d'expression française. Ces derniers se voulaient un langage très académique, conforme en tout point à la norme de la grammaire française. . . . Kourouma fraie un nouveau chemin, qui a pour noms: fusion, décalque, violence, viol" (Joseph M'lanhoro, "Puisqu'il faut conclure . . . " in Joseph M'lanhoro, ed., *Essai sur "Les Soleils des indépendances"*, [Abidjan: Nouvelles Editions Africaines, 1977]: 96). I will henceforth refer to this volume as *Essai*. For further discussion of Africanisms in *Les Soleils des indépendances*, see J.-J. Séwanou Dabla, *Nouvelles écritures africaines: romanciers de la seconde génération* (Paris: L'Harmattan, 1986): 56–60.

50. M'lanhoro, *Essai*, 96.

I will concentrate less on analysis of Kourouma's language here, its sources and references, than on the ways in which he frames his own practice and redefines francophonie, consciously and actively. Critics have rightly focussed on the linguisitic details but have missed certain crucial points about the implications of Kourouma's practice. For example, the first paragraph of the novel, quoted above, does not do what it says it will do. The imperative statement "Let's say it in Malinke," when taken literally, calls quite simply for the end of francophonie, for the adoption of African languages as the means of literary expression. Had this call been followed on the other side of the colon, if a Malinke expression had been put there *in Malinke* (Mandekan), the history of African literature would have been quite different. Instead, what follows is a direct *translation* of a Malinke phrase: "il n'avait pas soutenu un petit rhume." The conditions of literacy being what we have seen them to be, this result is not surprising. The call "Let's say it in Malinke" must be seen as literary rather than literal: framed by the material conditions of literacy and publication, the "will-to-write-in-Malinke" (see A. Tine, *Etude*, n. 41 above) expressed here is *detoured*, resulting in a literary compromise, a stylistic innovation that operates between two languages.

To borrow terms used by Glissant in his *Discours antillais*, writing in Malinke represents the desire for Return (*retour*), for the repossession of a world of permanence and oneness. Return is however ruled out as a practical possibility by the material situation of the postcolonial world, and the only cultural praxis left open is one of *détour* or diversion: work by ruse, camouflage, and derision.[51] Significantly, the first example of *détour* that Glissant gives is the poetics of the Creole language of the "francophone" Caribbean, in which he sees "a permanent exercise of turning away" from a transcendental French source (32). Is Kourouma's creolization of French part of a similar exercise?

Francophonie, if defined as the mere use of French, thus does not disappear at the beginning of *Les Soleils des indépendances*. The suggestion of its actual disappearance should not, however, go unnoticed. In the wake of that suggestion, French is significantly modified; some would say it will never be the same. The ability of Kourouma to produce this compromised language, and to have it published and acclaimed, would appear to support the theory of francophonie as a participatory, reciprocal arrangement allowing numerous peoples to write their own cultures in a "universally" readable language: the pluralistic theory. As we will see in more detail presently, much of Kourouma's practice supports this theory, particularly his way of teaching Mande vocabulary to the non-Mande

51. Edouard Glissant, *Le Discours antillais* (Paris: Seuil, 1981): 28–36. These few pages contain a concise and brilliant appraisal of postcolonial culture.

reader. At this point such a conclusion would be hasty, however; we will have to look closely at the interaction between the French language and the Mande-Malinke world in this novel before we make any such ambitious claims.

The area that we need to explore and describe is therefore the space of Kourouma's detour between an intention to "speak Malinke" and the fact of writing in French. The broadest possible schematic rendering of *Les Soleils des indépendances* would be a triangle drawn between the Mande, Independence, and French. These three points are obviously not of uniform status; each represents a different combination of anthropological, political, and linguistic concerns, although the Mande would appear to be mainly an anthropological category, Independence political, and French linguistic. This discussion has revealed a process of a detour within the frame of the French language and francophonie, a detour that is evident from the first lines of the novel; now it is appropriate to ask where that detour leads, whether it produces a new and different way of describing the Mande and the politics of Independence. A continued reading of the first chapter will begin to provide an answer concerning Kourouma's treatment of the Mande; I will discuss the question of politics in a later section.

The Mande is simply the center of the world in *Les Soleils des indépendances*. Ethnicity is constantly referred to and explained, in a complex project of literary anthropology. The second paragraph opens with a phrase that is emblematic of the ethnic base: "Comme tout Malinké" (like all Mande people). As we have seen many times already in the course of this study, one of the most basic impulses of ethnography is to posit general and universal characteristics within a group of people. Kourouma's writing defines itself as anthropological in the most elementary sense from the moment it establishes and builds on an ethnic category. *Les Soleils des indépendances* may be one of the most anthropological novels in the francophone field, because it insists on ethnicity as the basis for knowledge and behavior. Thus the second paragraph explains the Mande way to die, telling what happens to the "shade" of Ibrahima Koné:

> Comme tout Malinké, quand la vie s'échappa de ses restes, son ombre se releva, graillonna, s'habilla et partit par le long chemin pour le lointain pays malinké natal pour y faire éclater la funeste nouvelle des obsèques. . . . Au village natal l'ombre a déplacé et arrangé ses biens. De derrière la case on a entendu les cantines du défunt claquer, ses calebasses se frotter; même ses bêtes s'agitaient et bêlaient bizarrement. Personne ne s'étaient mépris. "Ibrahima Koné a fini, c'est son ombre," s'était-on dit. L'ombre était retournée dans la capitale près des restes

pour suivre les obsèques: aller et retour, plus de deux mille kilomètres. Dans le temps de ciller l'oeil! (*SI*, 7)

As with every Malinke, once life had fled his remains, his shade rose, spat, dressed and set out on the long journey to its distant native land, there to impart the sad news. . . . In its native village, the shade rearranged its belongings, putting them in order. From behind the hut you could hear the deceased's tin trunk banging shut, his calabashes rattling about; even his sheep and goats were restless and uttered strange cries. No one was mistaken about what had happened. "Ibrahima Kone has finished," they said, "his shade has come." The shade then returned to the city, where lay its remains, to attend the funeral: a round trip of a thousand miles, in the time it takes to wink an eye! (*Suns*, 3, AT)

While the initial phrase articulates between an outside and an inside, the material that follows is offered as the factual telling of a tale, without analysis. If the frame is anthropological—showing the hinge between ethnic groups or between ethnic and "nonethnic"—, the body of the paragraph is simply ethnic, displaying a kind of knowledge that is shared only within a certain group. Thus "no one mistook" Ibrahima Koné's shade for anything else because the frame of human reference is limited to· those who can recognize such things for what they are, that is, the Mandekalu or Malinke (I will use the term Malinke, in accord with the translator of *The Suns of Independence*, except in cases where I want to broaden the reference to include the entire Mande).[52] To be Malinke here is to be a competent reader of signs.[53] With the notion of the shade, Kourouma begins his presentation of Malinke religious views to the reader; he will use other, untranslated terms such as *ni* and *dja* later in the novel (116, 120, 129). Now if all of the Malinke described in this paragraph are in a sense infallible (or at least competent) readers, what relation obtains between their acts of interpretation and ours? The first two paragraphs of the novel seem to launch a monological project of

52. "Malinke" is taken from the French designation *Malinké*, which has been used "to embrace all . . . Mandinka and Maninka peoples" (David Dalby, "Distribution and No-menclature of the Manding People and Their Language," in Carleton T. Hodge, ed., *Papers on the Manding*, [Bloomington: Indiana University, 1971]: 3). Charles Bird, whose usage I have been following in this study, says that the Malinke (or Maninka or Mandinka) are those who dwell in the western section of the Mande heartland ("Heroic Songs of the Mande Hunters," in Richard M. Dorson, ed., *African Folklore*, [Bloomington: Indiana University Press, 1972]: 275); but it should be kept in mind that Bird's restriction of the word "Malinke" is not consistently operative in French usage. In turn, Kourouma uses this ethnic designation within a fictive framework in which references are both realistic and playful.

53. On the psychology of cultural representation in *Les Soleils des indépendances*, see Guy Michaud, "Représentations culturelles dans *Les Soleils des indépendances* d'Ahmadou Kourouma," *Revue d'Ethnopsychologie* 2–3 (1980): 137–44.

Mande-to-Mande references: the shade walks and is recognized. The role of the reader would be to overhear these references and to decipher them, but the cultural authenticity of the novel will derive from its adherence to the inside frame of reference.

This is the case to a certain extent. More than the average African novel, more than *L'Enfant noir* certainly, *Les Soleils des indépendances* will insist on a community of reference, a unified field of vision. Small things in the novel illustrate the offhand, taken-for-granted character of a Mande community. The hero, Fama, meets a stranger while travelling; "obviously," Kourouma writes, the stranger knew Fama's village, his family, a certain cousin, etc. It is "obvious" because the two men belong to one community. Likewise Kourouma writes: "Avec les pas souples de son totem panthère . . . , Fama atteignit la cour des aïeux Doumbouya" ("With the supple stride of his panther totem, . . . Fama reached the dwelling-place of the Dumbuya ancestors" [*SI*, 106; *Suns*, 70]). There is no laborious explanation of what a totem is, nor is there a narration describing how one comes to have a totem, as there was in *L'Enfant noir*; *Les Soleils des indépendances* is more casual and self-assured in its references to cultural phenomena. Perhaps this is possible because of the work of preparation that had already been done in novels like *L'Enfant noir*.

The most fundamental armature of this novel is therefore Mande culture, its signs and symbols, its structure, its attitudes. The thematic structure derives, as I have indicated, from the interferences between the Mande world and the two other sides of the triangle, francophonie and the politics of independence. The degree of complexity that this interaction provides can be seen on the first page of the novel, to which I would like to return. If the first two paragraphs define a space of Mande authenticity, expressing a desire to speak or even write in Mandekan and plunging into a world of shadows that must be interpreted according to Mande customs, the third paragraph takes what was implicit in the failure to actually "speak" Mandekan and brings it to the foreground. We saw that the necessity to write in French overpowered the will to use an African language, producing a compromised, creolized French. The second paragraph, with its evocation of a world in which "no one made a mistake" because everyone was initiated to the same culture, expresses an analogous desire, a will to write only *about* the Mande, perhaps only for Mande readers. This is a desire for *monologue*, for a return to a world of oneness, the precolonial world of Mande autonomy.

In the third paragraph, this impulse meets the same fate as the desire to write in Mandekan: the apparent monologism of the second paragraph yields to a radical, *personified* dialogism between the narrator and the reader:

Vous paraissez sceptique! Eh bien, moi, je vous le jure, et j'ajoute: si le défunt était de caste forgeron, si l'on n'était pas dans l'ère des Indépendances (les soleils des Indépendances, disent les Malinkés), je vous le jure, on n'aurait jamais osé l'inhumer dans une terre lointaine et étrangère. (*SI*, 7–8)

You look sceptical! Well, I swear it's true, and what's more, I swear that if the deceased were of blacksmith caste, and if we weren't living in the era of Independence (the suns of Independence, the Malinke say), no one would have dared bury him far away in foreign soil. (*Suns*, 3, AT)

The fact that the reader is addressed directly by the narrator of course brings to mind the encounter between griot and listener in the oral tradition. By creating a fictive reader as a personified presence in the novel, Kourouma mimics the immediacy of oral exchange.[54] More importantly, he explodes the apparent monologism that preceded and throws Mande authenticity into the maelstrom of politics. Mande autonomy, the precolonial world, becomes an irreal condition: "*if* we were not living in the era of Independence . . ." The paragraph goes on to spell out what would happened in the lost world: "An elder of the caste would have travelled down from home . . . the shade would have re-entered the body, and the dead man would have risen. . . . The various exceedingly complicated funeral rites for a Malinke of blacksmith caste would have been performed in his native village" (*SI*, 8; *Suns*, 3–4).

The thematic outline of *Les Soleils des indépendances* derives from the impossibility of a return to the conditions of pure Mande autonomy and the necessity to deal with the politics of Independence and francophonie. Fama Doumbouya is the last prince of the Doumbouya dynasty, the infertile relic of a time when Mande nobles really ruled. The funeral of Ibrahima Kone demonstrates how the nobles have fallen on hard times: *like a griot*, Fama attends or "works" all the funerals he can find in order to receive handouts.

Comme toute cérémonie funéraire rapporte, on comprend que les griots malinké, les vieux Malinkés, ceux qui ne vendent plus parce que ruinés par les Indépendances (et Allah seul peut compter le nombre de vieux marchands ruinés par les Indépendances dans la capitale!) "travaillent" tous dans les obsèques et funérailles. De véritables professionels! Matins et soirs ils marchent de quartier en quartier pour assister à toutes les cérémonies. On les dénomme entre Malinkés, et très méchamment, "les vautours" ou "bande d'hyènes."

Fama Doumbouya! Vrai Doumbouya, père Doumbouya, mère Doumbouya, dernier et légitime descendant des princes Doumbouya du Horodougou, totem panthère, était un "vautour." Un prince Doumbouya! Totem panthère faisait bande avec les hyènes. Ah! les soleils des Indépendances! (*SI*, 9)

---

54. See Rosemary G. Schikora, "Narrative Voice in Kourouma's *Les Soleils des indépendances*," *The French Review* 55, no. 6 (May 1980): 811–17.

Since every funeral pays, one can readily understand why Malinke griots and elderly Malinke, those whose trading activities were ruined by Independence (and Allah alone knows how many old traders ruined by Independence there are in the capital city!) all "work" the burials and funeral rites. Real professionals! Morning, noon and night they keep on the move from one neighborhood to another, in order to attend all the ceremonies. The Malinke most unkindly refer to them as "the vultures" or "that pack of hyenas."

Fama Doumbouya! A true Doumbouya, of Doumbouya father and Doumbouya mother, the last legitimate descendant of the Doumbouya princes of the Horodougou, with the panther as his totem, was such a "vulture." A Doumbouya prince! A panther totem roaming in a hyena pack. Ah! the suns of Independence! (*Suns*, 4, AT)

Degradation, humiliation, and sterility are the trademarks of Fama's existence. Insulted by the griot conducting the funeral, Fama launches into an indignant monologue, only to be ignored by the assembled mourners, who have seen this spectacle too many times. The griot at the Kone funeral, having called attention to Fama's late arrival, remarks sarcastically: "That he is late, does not matter: the customary rights of the noble families have been respected; the Doumbouya have not been forgotten. The princes of the Horodougou have been put with the Kéita." This association of Fama's dynasty with that of the Kéita, descendants of Sunjata, is taken by Fama as an insult, "enough to make your eyeballs explode with rage;" the Doubouya do not need to borrow glory from anyone. For Fama, there are "no real griots left; the real ones died with the great masters of war, before the European conquest" (*SI*, 12; *Suns*, 6, AT). The fact that a nobleman should be so compromised by a griot is of course shocking but also part of an ancient tradition; caste and clan rivalry thus motivate the tension at the beginning of the novel. Everything evil, sterile, and offensive in the universe is described by Fama—through indirect discourse that monitors his thoughts—as attributable to the politics of Independence.

Kourouma's choice of name for his hero comes with glorious connotations that the hero cannot manage to live up to. "Fama" as a common noun is often translated as "lord"; derived from *fanga* (strength), "Fama" was one of the titles assumed by Samory Touré, the great Mande warrior of the nineteenth century.[55] In modern times, it also means simply "rich person." The following classic, rather clichéd ethnographic passage by Jacques Macquet reads like a description of the world as the character Fama would like it to be:

55. Yves Person, "Samori and Islam," in John Ralph Willis, ed., *Studies in West African Islamic History*, vol. 1, *The Cultivators of Islam* (London: Frank Cass, 1979): 267.

Political and ritual authority is exercised . . . by the *Fama*, the heir of the most powerful family. His power over men and goods is absolute. As a representative of the ancestors, he disposes of life. . . . He sets taxes, metes out justice, declares war, forges alliances, maintains the army of horsemen. But he makes no decision without consulting the notables and the delegates of each village.[56]

The agreement between old-fashioned ethnography and Fama's attitudes is significant. Both are representations of oneness, of a well-ordered world in which each sector of society "knows its place."

In order to facilitate the analysis that will follow, I will briefly summarize the development of the novel. *Les Soleils des indépendances* is the tragic and comic story of the end of a dynasty. Fama is unable to reproduce himself, and his sterility is symbolically linked to the commercial stagnancy of the independent Republic of the Ebony Coast (obviously a parody of the Ivory Coast) in which he lives: "the sun! the cursed sun of Independence filled half the sky, scorching the universe . . . " (*SI*, 9; *Suns*, 5). Legitimate heir to the throne of the Horodougou (a real territory of the Mande), Fama loses his succession first to a French administrator, a dirty "little boy," then to a distant cousin, Lacina, who had "cast spells, sacrificed beast after beast, intrigued, lied and crawled so low" (*SI*, 21–22; *Suns*, 13). The usurper cousin is however deprived of all power by the forces of Independence and the one-party state, which thus constitute forces of usurpation to a second degree. Fama, who had participated in the fight against French colonialism, finds himself unwanted and unemployable in the newly independent republic, specifically because of his illiteracy (*SI*, 23; *Suns*, 14).

This background information is made available to the reader through and is richly colored by the indirect discourse that blends Fama's consciousness with that of a first-person narrator who remains anonymous. By the end of the second chapter, a complex tableau has been drawn, showing Fama's cultural, political, and personal situation to be absolutely deplorable: "A life that was moribund, consuming itself in poverty, sterility, Independence and the one-party state" (*SI*, 29; *Suns*, 18, AT). Fama sees himself as part of a class that was "ruined by the Independances" (*SI*, 9; *Suns*, 5), one of the "Dyula" Malinke for whom trade was the "very *raison d'être*," and who at times "enjoyed a virtual monopoly

56. Jacques Macquet, "Les Bambara," in Veronica Görög, ed., *Contes bambara du Mali* (Paris: Institut National des Langues et Civilsations Orientales, 1979): 116. This is precisely the kind of writing that is called into question by works such as Jean Bazin's "A chacun son Bambara," in Jean-Loup Amselle and Elikia M'Bokolo, eds., *Au Coeur de l'ethnie: ethnie, tribalisme et état en Afrique* (Paris: La Découverte, 1985): 87–127.

of local trade," as part of a vast network of Mande-speaking traders extending throughout the western Sudan.[57]

At the beginning of the third chapter, a significant step is taken, as the baton of free indirect discourse is passed from male to female, from Fama to his wife Salimata: in a significant departure for a male-dominated literature, a woman's consciousness takes center stage, and the realities of women's lives begin to escape a long silence. The third and fourth chapters belong to Salimata and her preoccupations: the guilt associated with sterility and her efforts to overpower this curse through the use of "innumerable magic charms" (*SI*, 31; *Suns*, 19); her relationship with Fama, "a shameless husband"; but most importantly, the nightmarish memories of her excision and of her rape. Kourouma's rendition of Salimata's initiation ceremony stands in striking contrast to Camara Laye's recollections of circumcision in *L'Enfant noir*. Told by her mother that initiation was necessary in order to make "a break with the years of equivocal, impure girlhood" (*SI*, 33; *Suns*, 21), Salimata disgraced herself by fainting at the crucial moment. That night she was raped by the fetish-priest who was supposed to take care of her; the crime was later attributed to "a spirit." Delivered to her first husband, who "stank like a stale warmed-over version" of the rapist (*SI*, 39; *Suns*, 25), Salimata refused to let him touch her; the husband later died of a strangulated hernia. Her second marriage, to Fama, was initially happy but produced no child. A childless woman is stigmatized; she "lacks more than half of her femininity" (*SI*, 51; *Suns*, 33, AT). Although Fama has slept with other women, who all failed to get pregnant, he still considers Salimata to be the sterile one. At the moment that is represented as current in the novel, Salimata is in despair. She goes to a marabout, who performs elaborate divinatory rites and incantations. When he slits the throat of a chicken as a sacrifice, Salimata is seized with the recollection of her excision and rape; the chicken's blood makes a metonymical link with her experiences of violence. The association within Salimata's mind appears to be almost a sign of madness. But, once the marabout has pronounced his conclusion—that Fama is sterile, not Salimata—the link is made literal: the

57. Robert Launay, *Traders Without Trade: Responses to Change in Two Dyula Communities* (Cambridge: Cambridge University Press, 1982): 3. As a Mande-language speaker living in the "South," Fama would fall under the Dyula designation (although the word "Malinke" is used in the novel, not "Dyula"). The term "Dyula" varies according to context. The word *jula* simply means "trader"; but through the large presence of Mande traders in non-Mande areas of West Africa, it acquired ethnic meaning. Thus, in parts of Mali, Burkina Faso, and the Ivory Coast, "all native speakers of Manding call themselves Dyula. . . . Any individual calling himself a *dyula* might mean that he was a professional trader or simply that he was a native speaker of Manding" (ibid., 2). See Launay's book for further sociological information relevant to *Les Soleils des indépendances*.

marabout attempts to rape Salimata, who then escapes (*SI*, 66–80; *Suns*, 43–52).

The second part of *Les Soleils des indépendances* shifts the focus back to Fama and brings the news that his cousin has died, meaning that the last of the Doumbouya must return north to the Horodougou to recover his kingdom. His village, Togobala, is in the part of the Horodougou that is located across the border in the socialist republic of Nikinai (cf. Guinée); but "of the Togobala of his childhood, the Togobala he bore in his heart, there was nothing left, not even the whiff of a fart" (*SI*, 105; *Suns*, 70). The word "Togobala," referring to a "great name," is thus cruelly ironic. Fama nonetheless finds something of the traditional cultural structure: he is honored as a prince and treated with deference by his legitimate griot Diamourou; "just for a moment, the world as it should be soared anew" ("un monde légitime plana" [*SI*, 113; *Suns*, 76]). Fama "held power as if beggary, marriage to a barren woman, bastard Independence, all his past life and present worries had never existed" (ibid., AT). In short, a ghost of the traditional social structure remains in Togobala. The local fetish-priest is Balla, a former slave "who had remained with his masters," the Doumbouya, after emancipation (i. e., colonization) (*SI* 114; *Suns*, 76). He and Diamourou the griot are "owned" by Fama (*SI*, 117; *Suns*, 78, AT), yet Fama lives in Togobala on money given him by these two old men, as "his servants' parasite" (*SI*, 132; *Suns*, 88). The world is turned upside down even in this remote village.

If Mande tradition and the politics of Independence are to coincide, Fama will have to be made president of the Party's local committee: "Why not, when all the Horodougou belonged to him?" (*SI*, 136; *Suns*, 91). The current president of the committee, Babou, is the descendant of slaves. A great palaver is arranged; the conflict will be resolved by speaking. The griots preface the palaver, then Babou takes the floor and delivers "a stream of flattery," heavily seasoned with proverbs (*SI* 139; *Suns* 93). At the end, "Babou the slave's son had conquered the villagers by his eloquence." Fama, ever conscious of his own nobility and the pollution that speech invites, "did not condescend to utter so much as three words!" Why should he, when his griot is right there? Meanwhile, even before the palaver started, the secret council of village elders had assembled and decided the outcome, in order "to ward off the dangers of discord": "Fama would remain the traditional chief [*chef coutumier*], and Babou the official president" (*SI*, 141; *Suns*, 94, AT).

Ignoring the warnings of Balla, Fama sets out on a journey back to the capital city, with a new wife, Mariam, to put his affairs in order before settling in Togobala for good. Fractiousness ensues between Salimata and Mariam; Fama finds the perfect excuse to stay out of the house: palavers are taking place everywhere because the Ebony Coast "seemed on the brink of insurrection" (*SI*, 160; *Suns*, 107). Friends of Fama begin to disappear in the night. Soon enough, Fama himself is thrown in jail with no reason given (*SI*, 164; *Suns*, 110). The prisoners are taken to a camp that has no name, for "things that cannot be talked about do not deserve a name, and the truth about this camp could never be told." (Here one thinks about the fate of Kéita Fodéba, who apparently died in such a camp in Guinea). At his pretrial hearing, Fama learns of his crime: he had a dream concerning the minister of state Nakou, a Malinke acquaintance of Fama's. In the dream, Fama had foreseen the plot and Nakou's downfall. His crime was in not reporting the dream to the proper authorities so that "many subsequent misfortunes would have been avoided." A mass sentencing is held, with the judge speaking French: "You are all jackals. You can't speak French and you tried to kill the president" (*SI*, 173–74; *Suns*, 115–16). Fama is given twenty years of solitary confinement at hard labor. The Doumbouya dynasty will end in jail.

One day the prisoners are given new clothes and assembled. The entire government is present, surrounded by griots and dancers. The president of the republic himself delivers an address that is as sweet and treacherous as the village president's speech; he speaks "softly, quietly, in the low, persuasive tone of voice of which he alone held the secret." All the prisoners are to be liberated immediately. The president gives each one "a thick wad of banknotes" (*SI*, 180–82; *Suns*, 120–21). Parades, fireworks, and dances await them in the capital. Unimpressed, Fama returns to the city in silence. He is advised by an enterprising friend to take advantage of the opportunities of Independence, to forget about Togobala, and invest his money in the new economy: "let these new suns keep you warm!" (*SI*, 190; *Suns*, 126). Fama remains silent and leaves for Togobala, in order "to die there as soon as possible" (*SI*, 193; *Suns*, 128).

By the next morning, Fama is inside the unmarked boundaries of the Horodougou, where "everything belonged to him." But the new geography conflicts with the old: the border between the Ebony Coast and Nikinai, which cuts the Horodougou in two, is closed indefinitely. This is unacceptable to Fama, who needs no authorization from "all the bastard sons of dogs and slaves" to go to Togobala. Calmly, triumphantly, he crosses the bridge, shouting "look at me!" lest his departure be mistaken for flight: "Admire me, sons of dogs, sons of Independence!" Finding no hole in the barbed wire on the Nikinai side, Fama goes down to the riverbank, thinking the "sacred crocodiles of the Horodougou would never dare attack the last descendant of the Doumbouya" (as they would not attack the mother in *L'Enfant noir*). But things have fallen apart in the Mande universe: one does dare to attack Fama, and he is mortally wounded; a guard shoots the crocodile, and all of nature protests in a great howl of animals and wind: "all the Horodougou was inconsolable, because the Doumbouya dynasty was coming to an end" (*SI*, 198–200; *Suns*, 132–34). Retrieved by Nikinai soldiers, Fama is taken by ambulance toward Togobala. Hallucinating, with visions of white chargers, lightning, and cool sandy places, Fama dies only a few miles away from Togobala. The novel ends as it began, with the death of a Malinke.

Dialogue and Anthropology

We saw how Kourouma made use of a personified reader at the beginning of the novel ("You look sceptical!"), in a context where a monological desire (for Mande authenticity) and a dialogical imperative (francophonie) framed the space of narration. The necessity of writing in French detoured the desire to "put it in Malinke" and produced a dialogical compromise that attempted to satisfy the monological impulse. *Les Soleils des indépendances* is a magnificently dialogical text on several levels, even if its single-culture base cannot be forgotten. I would like to examine now the ways in which Kourouma uses dialogue and suggests dialogism within a literary-anthropological project of great complexity.

At several other points in the text, Kourouma creates a situation of personified dialogue between the narrator and either Fama or the reader. Beginning to explain Fama's attitude toward colonialism, the narrator breaks off (using suspension points) and begins again: "Let's talk about this for a moment" (*SI*, 21; *Suns*, 13, AT). During the funeral of Fama's cousin Lacina, the narrator says: "Let's skirt round the dancing: yagba, balafon, ngume. Let's sit down, however, and watch the hunter's ngoni" (*SI*, 149; *Suns*, 100). A few pages later, the narrator addresses a rhetorical question to the reader:

> Maintenant, dites-le moi! Le voyage de Fama dans la capitale (d'une lune, disait-il), son retour près de Salimata, près de ses amis et connaissances pour leur apprendre son désir de vivre définitivement à Togobala . . . , vraiment dites-le moi, cela était-il vraiment, vraiment nécessaire? Non et non! (*SI*, 151)

> Now tell me! Was Fama's journey to the capital city (for one moon, he said), back to Salimata and his friends and acquaintances, to inform them that he intended to settle permanently in Togobala . . . , now tell me truly, was that journey really necessary? Not at all! (*Suns*, 101, AT)

The immediacy, the illusion of presence and complicity created by these gestures should not be taken at face value. It is indisputable that they mimic the exchange of a spoken encounter; this narrator's speech

patterns are so characteristic of oral traditions that one critic has identified him as "a griot," although this is not literally the case.[58] Within the
fiction of the narrator's speech, there is an implied fiction of the reader's
role. This is strikingly clear at the moment of the funeral dances: the
personified reader is invited to sit down and observe the performance,
while the narrator issues a scathing critique. Who is this unnamed, un-
seen but constant presence in *Les Soleils des indépendances*, addressed
only as "vous?" He or she is not merely "the reader," any reader
belonging to any interpretive community. Kourouma makes things much
more explicit than that. Earlier in same funeral ceremony, four bulls
are slaughtered, leading to the following commentary on the blood of
sacrifice:

De grand couteaux flamboyants fouillèrent, dépecèrent et tranchèrent. Tout cela
dans le sang. Mais le sang, *vous ne le savez pas parce que vous n'êtes pas Malinké*, le sang est prodigieux, criard et enivrant. De loin, de très loin, les oiseaux
le voient flamboyer, les morts l'entendent, et il enivre les fauves. Le sang qui coule
est une vie, un double qui s'échappe et son soupir inaudible *pour nous* remplit
l'univers et réveille les morts. (*SI*, 147, emphasis mine)

Great glittering knives thrust, chopped and sliced. All amidst blood. But
blood—*you do not know this, because you are not Malinke*, blood is stupendous,
loud, gaudy, intoxicating. From far, very far away, birds see it blazing, the dead
hear it, and it makes wild beasts drunk. Blood that flows is a life, a double escaping, and its sigh, inaudible *for us* fills the universe and wakes the dead. (*Suns*, 98,
AT, emphasis mine)

With this wave of the pen, Kourouma provides a heavy anthropological
anchor for any dialogical interpretation of his novel: the reader is identified as non-Malinke, non-Mandeka, although not necessarily non-African.
Kourouma insists on ethnicity at every stage of the novel's progress. Between the *vous* and the *nous* in this paragraph is the space of dialogue;
the difference necessary for dialogue and dialectic is given a particular
character: it is a cultural, ethnic difference between the Mande and everything outside it.

At this point of clear divergence between writing culture and reading
culture, I would like to concentrate for a moment on one of the many

58. Bernard Magnier, "Les soleils des indépendances," in Ambroise Kom, ed., *Dictionnaire des oeuvres littéraires négro-africaines de langue française* (Sherbrooke, Quebec:
Naaman, 1983): 545. Frederic Michelman also refers to "the griot narrator," in "Indepen-
dence and Disillusion in *Les Soleils des indépendances*: A New Approach," in David Dorsey
et al., eds., *Design and Intent in African Literature* (Washington, D.C.: Three Continents
Press, 1982): 95. See also Claude Abastado's remarks on the "identity" of the narrator, in
"La Communication littéraire dans *Les Soleils des indépendances* d'Ahmadou Kourouma,"
Revue d'ethnopsychologie 2–3 (1980): 147, 149.

examples of Kourouma's aberrant (some would say bad) style, which produces not only an effect of the Mandekalu language in a creolized French but also ambiguities of literal meaning. The phrase *son soupir inaudible pour nous remplit l'univers* in the last sentence above was rendered in the published translation as "its sigh that we cannot hear fills the universe." Although this makes for a "better" English sentence, it abolishes an ambiguity in the original: *pour nous* could just as well apply to *remplit l'univers* as to *inaudible*, thus, "its unaudible sigh for us fills the universe." In either case the non-Malinke has been excluded from the collective "we," and the difference is only one of emphasis. But with the emphasis on inaudibility, on the failure to hear, the characterization of the Malinke *nous* is quite modest; the sigh would undoubtedly not be heard by any non-Malinke either, so the difference between inside and outside is not so great. "For us filling the universe and waking the dead" is a considerably more ambitious claim; it directly refers to a universe that is Malinke, that only Malinke can perceive. The reader, told that he or she is excluded from that universe, is nonetheless invited to learn about it. Thus the novel passes quickly from this moment of separation between *nous* and *vous* to another collective *nous* which includes the reader: "Asseyons-nous et restons autour du n'goni des chasseurs."

Kourouma's *mise en scène* of the reader raises the question of ethnography in an interesting way. The narrator leads the personified reader to the dance ceremony after reminding him/her of his/her status as an outsider. Chastened, the reader or interlocutor sits down to watch the hunters' performance. The result is a *parody* of participant observation, the keystone of anthropological authority. The reader watching this *n'goni* is not unlike the imago of the fieldworker as it emerged in the 1920s; James Clifford describes Bronislaw Malinowski, the leader of the "I know because I was there" school of ethnography as "squatting by the campfire; looking, listening, and questioning; recording and interpreting Trobriand life." [59] The persona of the fieldworker-theorist, gifted with special powers of observation and trained to separate essential from extraneous data, was the foundation of scientific participant-observation. According to Clifford, participant-observation "serves as shorthand for a continuous tacking between the 'inside' and the 'outside' of events," a prescription that may be taken seriously "if reformulated in hermeneutic terms as a dialectic of experience and interpretation" (34). Participant observation in classical anthropology produced an authoritative, monological discourse

59. James Clifford, "On Ethnographic Authority," chapter one of *The Predicament of Culture: Twentieth-Century Ethnography, Literature, and Art* (Cambridge: Harvard University Press, 1988): 28.

(in Bakhtin's sense of the word "authoritative") because a single subject, the anthropologist, appropriated both experience and interpretation.

Although Kourouma's personified reader may have been invited to "squat by the campfire," it is the narrator who controls the dialectic of "being there" and understanding. The narrator's role is not limited to that of the wily native informant. He controls the process through an elaborate dialogical movement, one of whose elements is the personification of the reader. But the positions of authority are reversed here: the outsider, who in classical anthropology was always in control of interpretation, is here stripped of all power, reduced to a mere physical presence. The subversion and parody of participant-observation is marvellous. The outsider is denied the illusion of "living one's way into an alien expressive universe" (Clifford, 36); he or she can only sit and listen to the narrator, who will control the relation between inside and outside. There is thus an implied critique of the Western penchant for understanding Africa better than Africans do. *Les Soleils des indépendances* defamiliarizes the outsider's relation to Africa (the making-strange of the French language is surely one of the principal means of doing this), while at the same time providing explicit lessons in Mande ethnography.

Les Soleils des indépendances does not pretend to have switched from an outside/inside relation to a purely inside/inside one; this was clear from the moment that the call "Let's say it in Malinke" was answered in French. Representation, division, and inequality all remain. This is to say that authority is not absent at all; it is largely vested in the narrator. But what form does his authority take? When he says, "You don't know this because you are not Malinke," the narrator does not sound terribly different from the participant-observer, who claims to knows because of experience. Has an existential claim—being Mande—replaced the scientific one? Only to a certain extent; the narrator of *Les Soleils des indépendances* is anything but an African Malinowski. Control and authority in this novel are dialogical, and must be seen in terms that go beyond the literal dialogue of a personified narrator and a personified reader.[60]

Through the massive use of indirect style, direct address, and informational devices (definitions given in parentheses, for example), Kourouma constructed a prismatic whole that belongs to no single subject. If novels and anthropologies can be compared at all, then, *Les Soleils des indépendances* resembles the dialogical model more than the classical participant-observer model. Using Clifford's definition, an anthropology

60. There are other cases of personified dialogism within the novel, notably the moments when the narrator addresses Fama as "tu" (*SI*, 152, 174).

that is "reciprocal" would be "a constructive negotiation involving at least two, and usually more, conscious, politically significant subjects" (41). In the literary realm, Kourouma's novel is a *fiction* of such a negotiation, involving male and female subjects, persons of caste, offspring of slaves, the non-Mande observer/reader, and many others. While we may still be far from the "utopia of plural authorship" that Clifford evokes (51), Kourouma offers us some simulacrum of it.

Before generalizing about Kourouma's literary anthropology and its implications, we need to establish exactly how this novel is anthropological, how it interprets a culture. We can begin with simple questions of vocabulary. One of Kourouma's most frequent devices for imparting anthropological information, and incidentally for reshaping francophonie, is the use of Mandekan vocabulary. In the funeral scene, the word *n'goni* is used without explanation at first, then given a synonym: "Une danse, un n'goni de chasseurs sans sang, disons-le, c'était décevant" ("A hunters' dance, a *n'goni* without blood is admittedly disappointing" *SI*, 149; *Suns*, 100). Meanwhile, the narrator's description of the *n'goni* explains the phenomenon by example and fills in the gap between the fiction of the reader's presence and the reality of his or her absence at the scene of performance:

> . . . Bâtardise! Vraiment les soleils des Indépendances sont impropres aux grandes choses; ils n'ont pas seulement dévirilisé mais aussi démystifié l'Afrique. Il n'y eut aucune diablerie ébahissante, mais de toutes petites, comme celle que Fama avait vues quatre-vingts fois parfaitement exécutées par un prestidigitateur toubab dans la capitale.
>
> Un chasseur s'enfonça une aiguille dans l'oeil gauche et la retira de l'anus. Un autre alluma quatre doigts de poudre bien tassée avec quatre plombs, dans une oreille droite et recueillit à l'oreille gauche une calebasse d'eau contenant les plombs. (*SI*, 149)

> . . . A bastard *ngoni*. Truly the suns of Independence are unsuited to great things; they have not only unmanned, but also unmagicked Africa. There was no startling wizardry to be seen, only a few little tricks that Fama had seen performed fifty times over by a white conjuror in the capital city.
>
> A hunter thrust a needle into his left eye and drew it out of his anus. Another fired four fingers of hard-packed powder, with four bullets, in his right ear, and produced at his left ear a calabash full of water, containing the bullets. (*Suns*, 100, AT)

There are many other cases where Kourouma teaches vocabulary through the use of parentheses, appositives, and explanations. Thus the word *kala* is defined as "un objet avec lequel on éteint la vie dans le corps . . . ; cet objet met fin à notre destin" ("a thing that will extinguish the life in his body . . . ; this thing cuts short our destiny" (*SI*, 130; *Suns*, 87). Kourouma, unlike his translator, does not often use italics or quotation marks to signal the first use of a word; the Mandekan words are incorporated seamlessly into the French once they have been defined. The first time the word *tara* is used, it is set off by quotation marks: "Fama et ses deux femmes occupaient la petite pièce avec un seul lit de bambou, un seul 'tara' " ("Fama and his two wives lived in the little room, with its one 'tara' or bamboo bed" [*SI*, 158; *Suns*, 105, AT]). In the next sentence, the word has become French, and French has become a little more African: "La femme (celle à qui appartenait la nuit) montait à côté du mari, l'autre se recroquevillait sur une natte au pied du tara" ("The wife whose night it was slept next to the husband, the other curled up on a mat at the foot of the tara").[61] The personified reader-interlocutor is then asked, "Have you ever slept on a tara?" ("Avez-vous déjà couché sur un tara?"); the direct address again emphasizes the cultural gap that Kourouma sees as separating the narrator and the reader. On the level of language, Kourouma's practice makes a dialect out of French, a new literary dialect composed of Mandekan words within French syntax ("au pied du tara," "c'est notre kala," and even "les soleils des indépendances").

Some very problematic anthropological concepts are introduced in this way, most notably in the case of the Mande notions of the soul and the double:

La colonisation, les maladies, les famines, même les Indépendances, ne tombent que ceux qui ont leur ni (l'âme), leur dja (le double) vidés et affaiblis par les ruptures d'interdit et de totem. (*SI*, 116)

Colonial rule, illness, famine, even Independence only strike those whose ni (soul) and ja (spirit double) are empty and weak because they have broken taboos and totems. (*Suns* 77, AT)

Kourouma repeats the lesson twice several pages later: "le double, le dja de Fama avait quitté le corps" ("Fama's ja, his double, had left his body"); "leurs djas, leurs doubles sont fougueux" ("Their ja, their doubles are vigorous" [*SI*, 123; *Suns*, 82]).[62] But then, as if to expand one's understanding of the idea, Kourouma uses a different synonym: "le dja de l'animal, le vital de l'animal" ("the animal's ja, its vital substance" [*SI*, 129; *Suns*, 86]). I will not pursue these terms into a full discussion as I did with Camara's use of totemism; I only want to emphasize here

61. The translator ignores Kourouma's practice of carefully introducing and then assimilating Mandekan words by rendering the end of this sentence: "at the foot of the bed."
62. It should be noted that, although Kourouma uses the Mandekan word, he spells it according to French orthographic standards and pluralizes it in French rather than in Mandekan, writing *djas* rather than *djaw*.

Kourouma's delicate handling of anthropological pedagogy.[63] He does not go as far as Camara in *explaining* local beliefs; rather he makes use of them. He gives the reader just enough information to keep abreast of the plot, but the movement of the text allows for no prolonged meditations on the nature of the *ni* or the *dja*.

Between the first *nous* that we looked at here—the exclusionary "we" that leaves all non-Mande out, not knowing because they are not Mande—and the second, inclusive one ("Let's sit down"), Kourouma has established the difference necessary for dialogue to take place. The anthropological device of teaching vocabulary depends on a structure of difference and dialogue, and reciprocally, when vocabulary is taught, such a structure is necessarily implied. Kourouma did not create the distance between the reader and the African text, but, more openly than writers before him, he made it an object of reflexion. The vocabulary lessons in *Les Soleils des indépendances* are a sign of dialogism, of the transcultural voicing, the ventriloquism of the text. It should also be noted that, according to Bakhtin, the distance necessary for dialogue is the distance that constitutes the novel: "Being *cuzoj* [alien] makes dialogue possible. The novel is that literary art form most indebted to *cuzdost'* [otherness]" (*The Dialogical Imagination*, 423).

Indirect style and free indirect discourse are important devices used by Kourouma to mediate between the inside and the outside of his characters' (including his narrator's) consciousness. Thus, at the funeral of Ibrahima Koné at the beginning of the novel, the narration switches from the direct speech of Fama, between quotation marks, to his reported but unspoken thoughts:

> Fama se récriait: "Bâtard de bâtardise! Gnamokodé!" Et tout manigançait à l'exaspérer. Le soleil! le soleil! le soleil des Indépendances maléfiques remplissait tout un côté du ciel . . . Et puis les badauds! (*SI*, 9)

> Fama grumbled: "Hell and damnation! *Nyamokode!*" And everything conspired to exasperate him. The sun! the sun! the cursed sun of Independence filled half the sky . . . And the gawkers in the street! (*Suns*, 5)

Although the quotation ends quickly, Fama's thoughts continue to be printed out, in free indirect discourse, which combines the grammar and

---

63. The classic anthropological analysis of *ni* (or *nyama*) and *dja* is to be found in Maurice Delafosse, "Souffle vital [i. e. *dja*] et esprit dynamique [i. e. *nyama*] chez les populations indigènes du Soudan Occidental," *Compte rendu de l'Institut français d'anthropologie* (1912): 89–94. Makhily Gassama has analyzed Kourouma's use of French and Mande vocabulary, as a necessary balance between terms which cannot share connotations, which he calls a form of "ethnologie" (*Kuma: Interrogation sur la littérature nègre de langue française* [Dakar: Nouvelles Editions Africaines, 1978]: 225–27).

tense of indirect speech with the expressivity of direct speech. Free indirect discourse has been characterized variously as a "dual voice," as a
coherent representation of one character's point of view, and, decon-
structively, as "the style of the undecidable."[64] For Bakhtin, of course,
reported speech is one of the main devices of dialogism, a "hybrid construction" constitutive of the novel as a genre; free indirect discourse is
one way in which the "borders" between speakers can be infiltrated and
polyphony heightened.[65] And Clifford, expanding on work by Dan Sperber, shows that indirect style is "the preferred mode of ethnographic interpretation": "ethnographies abound in unattributed sentences such as
'The spirits return to the village at night,' descriptions of beliefs in which
the writer assumes in effect the voice of culture" (47–48); according to
Sperber, the ethnographer's indirect style often makes any original ("native") utterance impossible to reconstitute.[66] How does Kourouma use
this style, to which such significance is attached and which has been one

64. See Roy Pascal, *The Dual Voice* (Manchester: Manchester University Press, 1977);
Ann Banfield, "The Formal Coherence of Represented Speech and Thought," *PTL* 3, no. 2
(April 1978): 289–314, and "Narrative Style and Direct and Indirect Speech," *Foundations of Language* 10 (1973): 1–39; and Claude Perruchot, "Le Style indirect libre et la
question du sujet," in Claudine Gothot-Mersch, ed., *La Production du sens chez Flaubert:
Colloque de Cerisy*, (Paris: Union Générale d'Editions, 1975): 253–74. The dispute over
the nature of free indirect discourse (FID), which is most visible in Perruchot's article, was
a perfect topos for 1970s issues of deconstruction of the subject. Banfield's single-minded
insistence on what she calls the "1E/1 Consciousness Principle" ("For every node E [ex-
pression], there is a unique referent, called the subject-of-consciousness, to whom all expressive elements are attributed" ["Narrative Style," 29]) reveals a true devotion to the idea
of personified subjectivity, even in very dubious cases of FID. For Perruchot, this was nothing but a "theology," "le despotisme du sujet 'unaire' " (260); FID for him "déchire l'identité elle-même et la dédoule à l'infini dans le miroir de l'altérité." In Perruchot's
description, FID becomes "l'Autre-de-la-parole . . . : la pensée, dira-t-on?—Non, l'écriture,
mais cachée par le trop grand glaïeul" (255). But outside of these philosophical issues, there
is agreement between Banfield and Perruchot on the fact that FID does not represent
thoughts as actually taking place in a character's head: "The free indirect style avoids sug-
gesting that the actual process of reflection and sensation occurs as internal speech, by
'distancing' the language which reproduces it from verbal communication in suppressing
first- and second-person pronouns" ("Narrative Style, " 29); Banfield, however, does not
invest as much philosophically in that "distance" as does Perruchot. For the purposes of the
analysis that follows, I will not hesitate to attribute instances of FID to specific characters;
not to do so would be to ignore the numerous indications Kourouma gives, "ses pensées,"
"ces réflexions," etc.

65. On Bakhtin's "hybrid construction," see Tsvetan Todorov, *Mikhail Bakhtin: The
Dialogical Principle* (Minneapolis: The University of Minnesota Press, 1984): 73. See also
Katerina Clark and Michael Holquist, *Mikhail Bakhtin* (Cambridge: Harvard University
Press): 233–36; and Brian McHale, "Free Indirect Discourse: A Survey of Recent Ac-
counts," *PTL* 3 (1978): 281.

66. Dan Sperber, "L'Interprétation en anthropologie," *L'Homme* 21, no. 1 (January-
March 1981): 76–77.

of the touchstones for the representation of *African* consciousness in particular?[67]

To begin with, Kourouma gives us no character outside of reported discourse, no neutral point of view. Even names are made expressive. The first time the hero's name is mentioned by the narrator, it is uttered as an exclamation: "Fama Doumbouya!" (*SI*, 9; *Suns*, 4). Rather than wondering what "center of consciousness" this emanates from, we might consider the rhetoric of the name in Mande culture and remember that the *jamu* is a mode of praise. The hand-wringing that follows ("Totem panthère faisait bande avec les hyènes. Ah! les soleils des Indépendances!") plays off against a usage that should invoke glory; to say "Fama Doumbouya!" is to speak volumes of (oral) history. If there is no utterance without a consciousness, if discourse is always the product of a controlling ego, we would be forced to see here a collective Mande consciousness, indistinguishable from the personified narrator of the novel and synonymous with narration itself. There is indeed validity to this interpretation, and the idea of a collective consciousness is an essential part of the anthropological dimension here. In statements like those that follow, the writer has assumed "the voice of [his] culture:"

—"Comme tout Malinké, quand la vie s'échappa de ses restes, son ombre se releva" ("As with every Malinke, once life had fled his remains, his shade rose" [*SI*, 7; *Suns*, 3]).

—"L'important pour le Malinké est la liberté du négoce" ("What matters most to a Malinke is freedom of trade" [*SI*, 21; *Suns*, 13]).

—"Les Malinké ont la duplicité parce qu'ils ont l'intérieur plus noir que leur peau et les dires plus blancs que leurs dents." ("Malinke are full of duplicity because deep down inside they are blacker than their skin, while the words they speak are whiter than their teeth" [*SI*, 108; *Suns*, 72]).

67. I am thinking of the first "African" novel, actually not written by an African, *Batouala* (Paris: Albin Michel, 1965 [first published 1921]), written by the Martinican black René Maran, who described himself in the preface as a French writer. Maran makes exceedingly heavy use of FID, to the point of attributing a "center of consciousness" to animals (most strikingly in another novel, *Djouma, chien de brousse* [Paris: Albin Michel, 1927]). FID is his means of shuttling between his own position, that of a colonial administrator, and the position of the native population: "allongé en ma chaise longue, une véranda, j'écoutais les conversations de ces pauvres gens" (*Batouala*, 10). On FID in *Batouala*, see Christophe Mfizi, "Qui a tué Batouala?" *Afrique littéraire et artistique* 46 (1977): 78–88. In an excessively anthropomorphic and judgmental interpretation, Mfizi sees FID as a form of false consciousness, as a refusal of the narrator's "responsibility" for discourse: "le narrateur refuse de se compromettre et met tout sur le compte d'un personnage qui n'est même pas *en situation*" (82). For Mfizi, the dualism of FID, its indeterminacy as a voice, represents a failure of *engagement*, an act of "colonization" of the text by Maran (87). Mfizi's article is, in spite of its faults, one of the few to recognize the political implications of FID in the colonial African novel.

These examples are not, however, marked by the expressivity of direct speech, one of the signs of free indirect discourse. Going back to the paragraph that begins "Fama Doumbouya!" we can see clearly that an *effect of orality* is present here; the free indirect utterance mimics the spoken tongue but is not reducible to it. A voice, be it "dual" or "unde-cidable," emerges from the text, and if we do not know its provenence, we at least know in what space it remains suspended: the space between Mande culture and francophonie. Fama as a name and as a character is a product of that space, and Fama's first appearance seems designed to blur distinctions between individual and collective consciousness.

Once Fama is named and his debased status deplored, the narrative moves toward the representation of his actual consciousness. The first step in this movement is the direct quotation "Bâtard de bâtardise!" Di-rect speech is modest in its implications; it tells only what is outwardly knowable, the spoken word; it makes no claims on inner consciousness. Direct speech is the material of literal dialogue. The second sentence ("Et tout manigançait . . .") shows narrative command of the character's con-sciousness, but in its formal aspect it remains on the outside; it is indirect but not free. In this sentence an implied dialogue takes place between Fama and the outside world, a dialogue that is smoothed into a single prose form, that of narration. When the narration switches to the free indirect mode ("le soleil! . . ."), the distinction between narration and consciousness falls away, and the text becomes dialogical on a different plane. Fama "becomes" the narrator in sentences like this one, which can even be transposed into the first person as Fama's "thoughts": "Lui, Fama, né dans l'or, le manger, l'honneur et les femmes!" ("He, Fama, born to gold, food in plenty, honor and women!" [*SI*, 10; *Suns*, 5]).

But Kourouma rarely, if ever, takes the process one step further, into the stream-of-consciousness style that aims to reproduce thought in a pure state, as in Molly Bloom's soliloquy at the end of Joyce's *Ulysses* or at various moments in Maran's *Batouala*.[68] Kourouma keeps his rendi-tions of characters' thoughts within the confines of the imperfect tense, free but still indirect. Many of these utterances have no verb; when they have one, it is in the imperfect:

Fama non plus! Celui-ci s'excitait, trépignait, maudissait: le fils de chien de Bamba montrait trop de virilité! (*SI*, 14)

68. Maran alternates between styles, switching rapidly from FID in the imperfect tense ("Aha! les hommes blancs de peau. Qu'étaient-ils donc venus chercher, si loin de chex eux, en pays noir?" [*Batouala*, 21]) and stream of consciousness in the present ("Vivre au jour le jour, sans se rappeler hier, sans se préoccuper du lendemain, ne pas prévoir, voilà qui est excellent, voilà qui est parfait" [21]).

And how could Fama? Worked up to a quivering rage, he was mouthing curses: that son of a dog Bamba thought he could play the man, did he! (*Suns*, 8)

From a technical standpoint, there is nothing particularly innovative in Kourouma's use of free indirect discourse. But the implications of his usage are subtle and relevant to our general concern. The introduction of Fama as a character comes after a context has already been established and a new practice of francophonie has been defined. As we saw earlier, that practice is one of detour between standard French and Mandekan. When Fama's words and then inner thoughts are first presented two pages later, the situation is similar: there is an implied call to "say it in Fama's thoughts." This call is so basic to the novelistic enterprise that it seems hardly worth examining; of course the novel will represent its characters' thoughts. But, as in the question of language, the answer can only be *indirect*. First Fama's words are reported between quotation marks, next a narrative version of his thoughts is given, then the compromise of free indirect style is reached. In each case, "thought" itself is not quite captured.

On the most general level, this is simply because no character's thoughts are made totally congruent with the language of the novel; seeking discourse, we always find only text.[69] But material considerations should not be ignored: the idea of writing Fama's thoughts is a subset of the project of writing a novel in Mandekan, for Fama's thoughts take place in that language only. What Bakhtin calls "the concrete social context of discourse"[70] is to be found in this case in the fact that the novel is francophone and Fama is not. This is the most fundamental incongruity between thought and writing in *Les Soleils des indépendances*. The impossiblity of a Mandekan novel in 1968 thus cannot be left out of our considerations of style. Indirect style and particularly free indirect discourse are the means of detouring the language barrier; the boundaries are infiltrated, and what was a roadblock becomes a permeable zone of communication. So just as Kourouma's language is suspended between French and Mandekan, his narration floats between voices.[71] Some of

69. On the distinction between discourse and text, see Clifford, 39.

70. Bakhtin, "Discourse in the Novel," *The Dialogic Imperative*, edited by Michael Holquist, translated by Caryl Emerson and Michael Holquist (Austin: University of Texas Press, 1981): 300.

71. A useful parallel is visible in Henry Louis Gates, Jr.'s interpretation of FID in Zora Neale Hurston's *Their Eyes Were Watching God*: Gates sees FID as "a third language, as a mediating term that aspires to resolve the tension between standard English and black vernacular." This corresponds to Kourouma's use of FID in the space between standard French and Mandekan (Gates, *The Signifying Monkey: A Theory of Afro-American Literary Criticism* [New York: Oxford University Press, 1988]: 215).

these voices can be identified, but in other utterances, difference more than identity seems to be the root condition.

The "ethnographic authority" of Kourouma and his narrator is thus a dialogical one, more like a "constructive negotiation" than an unreciprocal dictation. At the moments when the personified narrator emerges and reminds the reader of his superior knowledge, an authoritarian structure has been exposed and subjected to irony; irony because the authority of this narrator-character is limited by the dialogical exchange in which he participates with the reader. When Kourouma writes what appear to be sweeping ethnographic statements in indirect style (such as those I quoted above), their authority is only relative, because the voice pronouncing them is only one among several voices. When free indirect discourse is used, dialogism and polyphony are at their most obvious.

But to call narrative authority in Les Soleils des indépendances dialogical is too easy and leaves too many questions unanswered. As Clifford makes clear, there is no escape from authority itself, there are only different versions of it; and any authority claiming to be dialogical can be accused of merely representing dialogue to a monological end. The appearance of polyphony may only confirm "the final virtuoso orchestration by a single author of all the discourses in his or her text" (Clifford, 50). With the novel, this cannot help but be the case.[72]

Representing Salimata

These criteria only make sense when tested in specific cases, and one of the most interesting opportunities presented in Les Soleils des indépendances is the representation of a woman's point of view. A brief look at Kourouma's treatment of Fama's first wife Salimata is thus in order. Salimata first appears as an object of Fama's free indirect "thoughts":

72. For a general treatment of free indirect discourse in Kourouma's novel, see George Joseph, "Free Indirect Discourses in Les Soleils des indépendances" (The American Journal of Semiotics 6, no. 1 [1988–89]: 69–84). Joseph's article appeared after I had completed this chapter. While acknowledging the undecidability of voice in FID, Joseph remains somewhat literalistic in his interpretation of particular utterances (for example, assuming that the narrator is "not Malinke" because he refers to the Malinke as "they"); at the same time, I think he exaggerates the dialogical "free competition" of voices (using Bakhtin as a reference) when he claims that "all of the discourses of the text . . . remain equally limited and impotent to explain reality" (72); "the novel sets conflicting discourses on an equal footing with one another" (75). With such insufficient attention to the imbalances and unequal distribution of power through discourse in the novel, Joseph's interpretation winds up overstating the ambiguity of the text: "In the end we cannot be sure of the true significance of events related in the novel" (76).

Salimata! Il claqua la langue. Salimata, une femme sans limite dans la bonté du coeur, les douceurs des nuits et des caresses, une vraie tourterelle; fesses rondes et basses, dos, seins, hanches et bas-ventre lisses et infinis sous les doigts, et toujours une senteur de goyave verte. Allah pardonne Fama de s'être trop emporté par l'évocation des douceurs de Salimata . . . Allah! fais, fais donc que Salimata se féconde! (*SI*, 26)

Salimata! He clicked his tongue. Salimata, a woman abounding in goodness of heart, in sweet nights and caresses, a true turtle-dove; butttocks low-slung and rounded, back, breasts, hips and belly smooth and infinite to the touch, and always a scent of green guava. May Allah forgive Fama for evoking Salimata's charms too warmly . . . Allah! Let her, let Salimata conceive! (*Suns*, 16)

If what begins as a moral portrait and witness of tenderness becomes an earthy, objectifying evocation, excuses are begged for, as if anticipating the objection. The image of the fertile body that Fama relishes is deflated by his belief that she is sterile, as sterile as Independence; this belief will in turn be deflated by the realization, later in the novel, that it is Fama who is infertile. Salimata is thus initially a figment of Fama's delusions and wishes; she exists only within his fantasm. Within the frame of the novel as a whole, even as this woman comes into her own "thoughts," the male writer retains authority and lends it out through fictions of dialogical discourse.

As a matter of perspective, it is important to realize that *Les Soleils des indépendances* comes in the middle of a long silence, the "silence" of women's exclusion from black African literary francophonie. It is only in the mid-1970s that the first novels by women are published, making the first generation of women writers a greatly belated one. In the next chapter, I will explore some of the reasons for this state of affairs; for the moment I will concentrate on Kourouma's manipulation of female consciousness, which might justifiably be seen as a prefeminist work (the word feminism is to be used advisedly here, since many francophone African women writers themselves seem to keep it at arm's length.)[73] Much attention has been devoted to Sembène Ousmane and his "attempt to delve beyond the superficial portraits of the woman as mere exotic accompaniment to the male, in order to reveal her own psychic universe,"[74] but Kourouma's

73. See for example, Aminata Sow Fall, quoted in Kembe Milolo, *L'Image de la femme chez les romancières de l'Afrique noire* (Saint-Paul Fribourg: Editions Universitaires Fribourg Suisse: 1986): 293–94. "Je ne suis pas une féministe dans le sens où l'entendent les gens." See discussion in the next chapter.

74. Karen Smyley Wallace, "Women and Alienation: Analysis of the Works of Two Francophone African Novelists," in Carole Boyce Davies and Anne Adams Graves, eds., *Ngambika: Studies of Women in African Literature*, (Trenton, N.J.: Africa World Press,

Salimata represents an attempt that is at least equally important. In criticism of the representation of women by male African writers, Kourouma has been largely neglected. His role deserves attention within the history of the emergence of a literary discourse on womens' consciousness because of the step he takes beyond objectification. But in making this advancement, Kourouma's narrative has to claim greater command as well as greater sympathy, and this is why the case of Salimata becomes an interesting test for the "authority" of *Les Soleils des indépendances.*

The first view of Salimata, quoted above, could be seen as one of those "superficial portraits" that abounded in earlier years. Yet the thematic content of Fama's thoughts goes beyond this initial level and seems to lead toward the penetration (with all that that word implies) of Salimata's mind. Fama's initial ruminations about his wife take place in a mosque, where he has sought refuge from a violent thunderstorm; in counterpoint, Fama alternately concentrates on his prayers and mulls over the curse of Salimata's imputed sterility; the prayers are for an end to the curse. In free indirect style, Fama contemplates Salimata's pious nature, her adherence to the faith, her active search for a solution: "Et que n'a-t-elle pas éprouvé! . . . toutes ces pratiques exécutées chaque soir afin que le ventre se fécondât!" ("And hadn't she tried everything? . . . all these practices performed every evening, to make her belly fruitful!" [*SI*, 27–28; *Suns*, 16–17]).

Some of these rituals leave her "half unconscious," others produce a frenzy of passion to which Fama is barely able to respond, "limp and cold in the lower belly" as he is. But Fama must respond for fear of "Salimata's stormy and worrisome fits" ("les orageuses et inquiétantes fougues de Salimata" [*AT*]). At this point, still within the framework of Fama's free indirect thoughts, Salimata's discourse breaks through: "Elle s'enrageait, déchirait, griffait et hurlait: 'Le stérile, le cassé, l'impuissant, c'est toi!' et pleurait toute la nuit et même le matin" ("She would rave, tear, scratch and scream: 'You're the one who's sterile, worthless, impotent!' and she would weep all night and half the morning too" (*SI*, 29; *Suns*, 18). Thematically, the moment of Salimata's eruption is significant

1986): 65. Victor Aire calls Sembène "le premier écrivain féministe africain," in "Mariama Bâ, 'Une si longue lettre:' compte rendu," *Canadian Journal of African Studies* 16, no. 3 (1982): 636. See also Jarmila Ortova, "Les femmes dans l'oeuvre littéraire d'Ousmane Sembène," *Présence Africaine* 71, no. 3 (1969): 69–77, and Karen Smyley Wallace, "*Les Bouts de bois de Dieu* and *Xala*: A Comparative Analysis of Female Roles in Sembène's Novels," *Papers in Romance Studies* 5, no. 3 (Autumn 1983): 89–96. Arlette Chemain-Degrange recognizes Kourouma's importance but devotes only a few pages to Salimata in her important study *Emancipation féminine et roman africain* (Dakar: Nouvelles Editions Africaines, 1980): 282–84.

because she directly contradicts Fama's idea that she is sterile; she will be proven right later in the book.

On the level of discourse, this eruption of direct speech marks the watershed between the male and female characters; the process of transferring discourse from one character to another begins at this point. The first character acquires subjectivity, marked by free indirect discourse attributable to him; what he reports about the other character is what he sees and hears, that is, image and direct speech.[75] In the following paragraph, a crucial step is marked by the phrase "les pensées de Salimata":

> Blasphème! gros péché! Fama, ne te voyais-tu pas en train de pécher dans la demeure d'Allah? C'était tomber dans le grand sacrilège que de *remplir tes coeur et esprit des pensées de Salimata* alors que tu étais dans une peau de prière au sein d'une mosquée. (*SI*, 29, emphasis mine)

> Sin and blasphemy! Fama, did you not know you were sinning in Allah's dwelling-place? What desecration, *to fill your heart and mind with thoughts of Salimata / of Salimata's* while sitting on a prayer rug in the middle of a mosque! (*Suns*, 18, AT, emphasis mine)

This is a passage of very explicit dialogism, with the narrator addressing Fama directly while referring to Salimata. The first translation I have given of the phrase *des pensées de Salimata* ("thoughts of Salimata") is the literal one. But there is an ambiguity here between objective and subjective genitives, between Fama's (objective) thoughts about Salimata, and Salimata's own (subjective) thoughts that she thinks. The significant corner that is about to be turned—and which begins with her direct speech as it is "heard" by Fama—is the transition toward the printing out of her own thoughts. As the next chapter begins, Fama literally falls asleep, creating an empty space in the narrative, a space that is filled as the narrative enters the fiction of Salimata's consciousness.

Kourouma marks this transition from male to female not only by the start of a new chapter but also by stating explicitly that we are entering Salimata's thoughts: "Et alors pour elle partit une nuit longue et hérisée d'amertume. Elle entretint et activa des pensées amères et brûlantes . . . les oreilles tendues a ses pensées" ("Then began for Salimata a long night bristling with bitterness. She fanned burning bitter thoughts . . . her ears alert to the thoughts" [*SI*, 30; *Suns*, 19]).[76] Ourselves alerted to the fact

75. This is a classical pattern, most clearly visible in Flaubert's *Madame Bovary*. See Perruchot, "Le Style indirect libre."

76. Kourouma periodically reminds the reader that chapters 2 and 3 are made up of Salimata's thoughts, using phrases like "ses pensées" or "Salimata fut interrompue dans ses réflexions . . . " (*SI*, 33; *Suns*, 21; he uses this phrase again later, at the end of chapter 4, to close off her discourse: *SI*, 57; *Suns*, 36).

that these are Salimata's thoughts and no one else's, we read the first free indirect utterance attributable to her: "Malédiction! Malchance!" ("Curse and misfortune!" [AT]). Thus begins the recounting of a woman's desperate life, victimized by tradition, Islam, and Independence. Now that the roles are reversed, it is Fama who is reduced to a merely physical presence; he lies there snoring, "grunting like a boar . . . [lying] like a fallen tree-trunk, blocking off most of the bed with his arms and knees" (*SI*, 31; *Suns*, 20). The reversal of perspective might appear to be unremarkable (as pure technique it is not original), but in the context of francophone African literary history it is a significant development.

What kind of significance? That of revolt against tradition, that of putting the meaning of certain traditions into question, which is precisely what Salimata does. By asking herself in the quotation below, "Quelle grande signification?" ("What great meaning / significance?" [*SI*, 32; *Suns*, 21, AT]), Salimata dares to think of the sacred custom of initiation as an empty act of mutilation; in this she anticipates one of the great causes of African feminism. Again, the polyvocal composition of the text heightens the point: the voice of Salimata's mother is given within quotation marks, surrounded by a critique in Salimata's *free* (here the word takes on a double meaning) indirect discourse:

"Tu verras, disait-elle souvent alors que Salimata était une très petite fille; tu verras, tu seras un jour exisée. . . . C'est . . . une grande chose, un grand événement ayant une grande signification."
Mais quelle grande signification? . . .
. . . Et le jour fixé arriva. . . . "Ma fille, sois courageuse! . . . Mais j'ai peur, et mon coeur saute de ma peur, j'implore tous les génies que le champ soit favorable à mon unique fille!" Oui, les génies entendirent les prières de sa maman, mais comment! et après combien de douleurs! après combien de soucis! après combien de pleurs! (*SI*, 32–33)

"You'll see," she would often say when Salimata was a very little girl, "you'll see, one day you'll be initiated. . . . It's . . . something very important, an event with a deep meaning."
But what was the deep meaning?
And the day ordained duly arrived. . . . "Be brave, my daughter! . . . But I am afraid, my heart is leaping with fear, and I beg all the spirits that the field may be auspicious to my only daughter." Yes, the spirits heard her mother's prayers, but how? And after what sorrow! after what worries! after what tears! (*Suns*, 20–21, AT).

This is a dialogical arrangement of voices, but it is an unequal one. The mother's words, representing the authority of tradition and culture, are quoted directly but then undercut by Salimata's thoughts. Directly quoted speech is inflexible and authoritative; to borrow from the glossary of *The Dialogical Imagination*, it "permits no play within its framing context" (424). Proferred within free indirect discourse, these thoughts offer on the one hand the intimacy of consciousness itself and on the other the authority of narration, the voice of the Book. Temporal distance further complicates the dialogue with the mother: to the extent that these thoughts are Salimata's, they would be occuring years later. The overall effect is a subversion of direct speech by free indirect discourse and, consequently, a subversion of tradition by one woman's act of resistance. The passage that engages the mother in a dialogue shows how dialogism can be used as a principle of *unequal* exchange, of nonreciprocity between self and other.[77]

In one sense, this is a classical Bakhtinian example of how heteroglossia "dethrones" authoritative discourse, which then becomes "a dead thing, a relic," showing how "human coming-to-consciousness" involves the "freeing of one's own discourse from the authoritative word." But heteroglossia in Salimata's discourse is an embattled fortress, surrounded by hostile forces. The exchange between Salimata and her mother shows how free indirect discourse, itself a dialogical style, can be used to the end of empowerment, to subvert quoted authority and establish a new authority in its place. To whom does this new authority belong?

Within several frames, each of which must be considered, it belongs to Salimata and to African women in general. I have already summarized the contents of Salimata's indirect soliloquy, the story of her excision and rape. The effect of that story is to reveal how the question of gender cuts across images of traditional African culture and raises new questions. By the fact that Salimata is devoted and pious, loyal to her husband, and observant of Islam, the evils that happen to her cannot be construed as self-inflicted; they appear to come out of the system itself. Pius Ngandu Nkashama is simply wrong, as well as sexist, to imply that Salimata brings violence upon herself by "provoking" men and "preventing them from remaining within the strict limits of the social order."[78]

77. Joseph addresses the question of Salimata's discourse, but he does not focus on the contrast between the mother's direct address and Salimata's FID; he discusses a collective "voice of the community" that seems to be active within Salimata's thoughts (FID within FID). He asserts: "While [FID] in a dialect-free French implies the sympathy of the narrator for Salimata, it also creates between the poor woman and the collective voice a distance that undermines both" ("Free Indirect Discourses," 80). Again, this ignores the asymmetry with which FID operates, its unequal distribution of discursive power.

78. Pius Ngandu Nkashama, *Kourouma et le mythe* (Paris: Silex, 1985): 174. Ngandu Nkashama fails to point out that for all the reader knows, the marabout may behave this way with every female client. Ngandu Nkashama's reading of Salimata starts off badly, by evoking supposedly timeless and universal "myths" of woman as the "great earth mother" (155). In a gloss on Mircea Eliade (whose work was also used by Jacques Bourgeacq in his

Kourouma's critique of tradition is no more evident than at the moment when the sacrifice performed by the sorceror-marabout becomes a pretext for attempted rape (*SI*, 66–80; *Suns*, 43–52). The rituals to which Salimata is subjected involve the invoking of the dead, the calling up of spirits, and prayers to God. At the center of these rites, there is perfect silence: "Silence! Silence! Quelque chose parut introduire le silence dans la matière et les êtres de tout ce que la case contenait" ("Silence! Silence! It was as if something were instilling silence into the being and substance of everything within the hut" [*SI*, 69; *Suns*, 45]). This silence marks what should be a moment of real truth, arrived at by incantatory words, but itself beyond words, sacred. At the end of the process, the marabout, speaking with "an inside and a mouth that are clear," pronounces the truth: it is Fama who is sterile, but Salimata must suffer the consequences. Here, then, is totemism told from the other side. The marabout tells Salimata:

Allah a sacré le mariage, c'est un totem. Mais l'enfant pour une femme dépasse tout; le but de la vie est que naisse un rejeton. La vérité comme le piment mûr rougit les yeux mais ne les crève pas. . . . Ton mari, je te le dis d'un intérieur et d'une bouche clairs, ne fécondera pas les femmes. . . . Voilà la vérité, la seule. (*SI*, 77)

Allah has ordained marriage; it is a totem. But for a woman, a child is more than anything else; the aim of life is to bring forth offspring. Truth, like a ripe red pepper, reddens the eyes but does not blind them. . . . Your husband, I say this with a clear tongue and conscience, will never make a woman bear fruit. . . . That alone is the truth. (*Suns*, 50, AT)

To have this truth—invoked and divined under sacred circumstances and pronounced with a "clear mouth"—undercut by the attempted rape, to have Salimata's flashbacks to the scenes of her excision and rape made real, is a dramatic and subversive revelation. Islam and traditional Mande culture have both been wagered, and both are compromised by this episode. The authority of Salimata's two chapters derives only from the ability to recount misfortune and exploitation. That negative authority is, however, anything but negligible. Escaping the marabout's advance, Salimata stabs him with a curved knife and leaves him howling in pain;

---

study of *L'enfant noir*), Ngandu Nkashama describes the reproductive function of women as a realisation of "the desires of man for immortality" (156). Salimata's alleged sterility marks the end of human history (163); for him, Salimata is a victim ("suppliciée dans son corps, broyée, écrasée . . . ") who "installs disorder in the world" and defeats myth; she *acquiesces* to "cette force inactuelle et anti-mythologique," which is disorder (177–78). Ngandu Nkashama writes from within the very point of view that oppresses Salimata, from within the myths rather than their critique.

this narrative of one woman's experience has a similar value of defensive counterattack.

The frames around Salimata's story of course affect its overall value. Within the development of the novel, the takeover of discourse by Salimata ends abruptly with the beginning of part 2; *Les Soleils des indépendances* is once again Fama's story. While in prison, Fama reflects on his life and on eternity, foreseeing a place in heaven for Salimata because "she had done her duty, more than her duty" (*SI*, 177; *Suns*, 118). Fama leaves the capital for the last time hoping that Salimata will be happy with another man (*SI*, 193; *Suns*, 128). But Salimata's fate is obscure and marginal after she leaves center stage; hers is the kind of story that will only be told in detail ten years later, in novels by women such as Mariama Bâ. In *Les Soleils des indépendances*, the woman's story takes over for a significant period but remains partially extraneous to the rest of the novel.

The other frame is the gender of the writer. Unlike the personified narrator who "is Malinke" and therefore "knows," Kourouma is male, and representing Salimata places him in a more distanced relation to his subject. Does his manipulation of a female character amount to a mere display of male power, a "virtuoso" writer's performance, an act of false consciousness? From a 1980s perspective, such a view is conceivable, if ungenerous. But within the context of literary history as it happened, a context in which African women were written about ("spoken for") before they wrote about themselves, Kourouma's achievement is considerable. His artful manipulation of discourses, his dialogical ventriloquism, and his ethical, political courage, deserve greater attention than they have received.

Politics in Speech and Writing

If Kourouma is ahead of his time in regard to women's issues, and if his version of francophonie is somewhat revolutionary, *Les Soleils des indépendances* nonetheless has the overall reputation of being "ideologically weak."[79] Barthélémy Kotchy, a leading Ivoirian critic, says that the novel "simply points to a failure" and cannot serve any progressive or revolutionary purpose.[80] Harris Memel-Fotê sees within the novel and within Fama's mind "the nostalgic, reactionary and impotent position of an old social class, the aristocracy, that history has stripped of its economic,

---

79. Gérard-Dago Lezou, "Temps et espace," in *Essai*, 41; Lezou refers to this view of the novel but rejects it.

80. Barthélémy N'Guessan Kotchy, "Signification de l'oeuvre," in *Essai*, 93.

political and intellectual prerogatives."[81] *Les Soleils des indépendances* is indeed the swan song of the Mande aristocracy, as told with both irony and sadness by Kourouma. *Les Soleils des indépendances* is either a satire or a tragedy, depending on how you read its indirect style; this suggests that it is both. Any ideology within the novel must be interpreted as indirect, as partially belonging to fictive characters. What Fama has to say (or think) about the politics of Independence is thus a question that straddles anthropology and ideology, or, if you will, ethnicity and ethics. What emerges is a view of politics that has everything to do with the reputation of the spoken word.

For perspective, we should bear in mind that Fama sees colonialism and Independence as the same thing. When he shouts his last invective from the middle of the bridge, he addresses it to "tous ces enfants de la colonisation et des Indépendances" ("all these children of the colonial era and of Independence" (*SI*, 199; *Suns*, 132). Although he was active in the struggle against colonial rule, it was a return to tradition that he thought would be the result. The period of anticolonial agitation was known as "les soleils de la politique" ("the suns of politics") (*SI*, 22; *Suns*, 14), and politics was a question of "virility" and "vengeance" (*SI*, 56; *Suns*, 36, AT). But as for the economic situation, "Les Indépendances n'y pouvaient rien!" ("Independence couldn't do a thing about it!" [*SI* 18; *Suns* 11]). The word *politique* is used only in relation to the colonial period and Independence; it is associated with the illegitimacy and sterility of the present. Only the precolonial past is outside of *la bâtardise*.

The politics of colonialism and Independence exploit literacy in order to empower certain groups over others: "Avec les colonisateurs français, avaient débarqué des Dahoméens et les Sénégalais qui savaient lire et écrire et étaient des citoyens français ou des catholiques" ("The French colonizers had brought along people from Dahomey or Senegal, who knew how to read and write and were French citizens or else Catholics" [*SI*, 88; *Suns*, 59]). With Independence, Fama is passed over for various posts because he is illiterate:

. . . les Indépendances une fois acquises, Fama fut oublié et jeté aux mouches. Passaient encore les postes de ministres, de députés, d'ambassadeurs, pour lesquels lire et écrire n'est pas aussi futile que des bagues pour un lépreux. On avait pour ceux-là des prétextes de l'écarter, Fama demeurait analphabète comme la queue d'un âne. (*SI*, 22–23)

. . . once Independence had been won, Fama was thrown to the flies and forgotten. The appointments as minister, deputy, ambassador, all passed him by; for those, reading and writing are not quite as pointless as rings for a leper. There

---

81. Harris Memel-Fotê, "La bâtardise," in *Essai*, 54.

was an excuse for leaving Fama out of it, since he had remained as illiterate as a donkey's tail. (*Suns*, 14)

Literacy being almost exclusively a question of francophone literacy, it is clear that Fama's exclusion from the circle of francophonie has everything to do with his political disenfranchisement in the era of Independence.

The plotted tension of *Les Soleils des indépendances* comes from the impingement of the new politics on traditional means of decision-making, and from interference between the new politics and the traditional Mande attitude toward the spoken word. Kourouma rehearses that attitude in one of his most ethnographic passages:

Les Malinkés ont la duplicité parce qu'ils ont l'intérieur plus noir que leur peau et les dires plus blancs que leurs dents. Sont-ce des féticheurs? Sont-ce des musulmans? ... Rien en soi n'est bon, rien en soi n'est mauvais. C'est la parole qui transfigure un fait en bien ou le tourne en mal. (*SI*, 108–9)

The Malinke are full of duplicity because deep down inside they are blacker than their skin, while the words they speak are whiter than their teeth. Are they fetish-worshippers? Are they Muslims? ... Nothing is good or evil in itself. It is speech that transforms a thing into good or turns into evil. (*Suns*, 72, AT)

There is no need at this point to embellish on the ethnographic significance of this passage. Instead I would like to juxtapose it to the following characterization of politics, which comes just before the moment of Fama's arrest:

[Fama] aurait dû retirer ses mains et pieds de la politique pour s'occuper des palabres de ses femmes. La politique n'a ni yeux, ni oreilles, ni coeur; en politique le vrai et le mensonge portent le même pagne, le juste et l'injuste marchent de pair, le bien et le mal s'achètent ou se vendent au même prix. (*SI*, 164)

[Fama] should have pulled his hands and feet out of politics, and attended to his wives' palavers. Politics has no eyes, no ears, no heart; in politics, truth and lies wear the same cloth, just and unjust go hand in hand, good and evil are bought and sold at the same price. (*Suns*, 109)

What politics does have is a mouth. Speech and politics both defeat notions of intrinsic value; they make everything relative, suspect. And political speech is the most dangerous of all. Thus, if *illiteracy* is the cause of Fama's exclusion from the new regime, *orality* and its untrustworthiness are at the root of Fama's disdain for "politics."

Two political speech acts in *Les Soleils des indépendances* show the complexity of the relation between the old politics and the new. In the big palaver that is held in Togobala to decide on governance, the committee president Babou displays all the deceitful characteristics of a smooth talker:

Dès l'ouverture de la bouche tout le conciliateur, le rusé fils d'esclave se révéla. Le président du comité avançait dans le dire comme on marche dans un marais, en tâtant, en promenant des regards interrogatifs, recueillant quelques approbations avant de lâcher un autre mot. . . . Et un flot de flatteries coula. . . .

Oui, d'accord, Fama était sans pareil, sans limite. Oui! L'humanisme et la fraternité sont avant tout dans la vie des hommes. Mais après? Babou retournait ces deux thèmes et d'autres lieux communs toujours accueillis avec respect par des Malinkés musulmans: la miséricorde divine, le jugement dernier, la vérité qui est la canne dans le palabre. Mais tout cela s'amenait après des regards flamboyants, des intonations variées et des proverbes, s'accompagnait d'autres regards, de mouvements de la tête et des mains et d'autres proverbes, l'assistance exultait et buvait. Elle n'en demandait pas plus: le palabre pour le palabre! Babou, le fils d'esclave, avait conquis les villageois par la parole. (*SI*, 139–40)

As soon as he opened his mouth, he showed himself to be a wily, conciliatory son of a slave. The committee president delivered his speech like a man walking on marshy ground, one step at a time, looking about inquiringly and pausing for signs of approval before continuing. . . . There followed a stream of flattery. . . .

Yes, agreed; Fama was peerless and supreme. Yes! Humanism and fraternity are what counts in men's lives. But so what? Babou kept reiterating these two themes, and other commonplaces always respectfully received among Muslim Malinke: divine mercy, the Day of Judgement, truth the staff of righteousness in a palaver. But all of this was introduced with fiery looks, varied intonations, and proverbs, and delivered with more glances, gestures of the head and hands, and proverbs, and the audience joyfully drank it all in. They asked for nothing more: palaver for palaver's sake! Babou the slave's son had conquered the villagers with the spoken word. (*Suns*, 93, AT)

Although descended from slaves, Babou is a master of speech and of persuasion as much as any griot; his extravagant manners and manipulation of clichés delight the audience but constitute a threat to the power of nobility. Fama, refusing to lower himself, responds with noble silence. Politically, Babou appears to have won; Fama can only intervene through his legitimate griot Diamourou, and the "outcome" is a decision—previously made by the elders—for divided authority. The fact that the decision is made outside of the open arena, outside of the realm of "politics," by a secret council, makes the politics of the suns of Independence seem like an empty game. The sense of that council meeting is reported in free indirect discourse; it is said that politics as presently constituted will pass away and must only be humored for the moment. The palaver is allowed to continue as a diversion for the people, as an entertaining speech-fest. This clearly implies that the ancient political apparatus of this decrepit village is still capable of manipulating delegates of the party and the new politics as a whole. For the elders, the new politics is nothing but the latest use to which smooth talk has been put.

Such a view is certainly Fama's. The other political speech in the novel, a remarkable example of its genre, is made by the president of the republic of the Ebony Coast. His rhetoric is obviously the source of Babou's clichés about fraternity and humanism; in turn this president sounds much like the real president of the Ivory Coast, Félix Houphouët-Boigny, whose catchphrases include the very same terms, *fraternité* and *humanisme*.[82]

An underling conducts the crowd's response, orchestrating pandemonium and silence like an expert media advisor. A strangely indirect performative speech act forms the climax of the president's remarks:

> Il parla, parla de la fraternité qui lie tous les Noirs, de l'humanisme de l'Afrique, de la bonté du coeur de l'Africain. . . . Tout était bien dit, tout était ébahissant. Et c'était vrai, ce n'était pas un rêve; c'était réel. Le président demandait aux détenus d'oublier le passé, de le pardonner, de ne penser qu'à l'avenir, "cet avenir que nous voulons tous radieux." *Tous les prisonniers étaient libérés.* "Tous et tous. Immédiatement. Tous *allaient rentrer* dans leurs biens." (*SI*, 180–81, emphasis mine)

He talked and talked, about the brotherhood that binds all black men together, about the humanism of Africa and the good-heartedness of Africans. . . . Everything was well phrased, it was all astonishing. And it was true, it wasn't a dream; it was real. The president was asking all the detainees to forget the past, to forgive him, to think only about the future, "the glorious future we all hope

---

82. Houphouët has used the word "fraternité" consistently since at least the late 1950s, whenever he speaks on national unity and the need for a continuing French role in the Ivory Coast: see "Appel à la fraternité" (136–37) and other addresses in *Le Président Houphouët-Boigny et la nation ivoirienne* (Abidjan: Nouvelles Editions Africaines, 1975). The semiofficial and only daily newspaper in the Ivory Coast is called *Fraternité Matin*, published under the direction of the Ministry of Information; the weekly *Fraternité Hebdo* is produced by the political bureau of the party. On the culture page of *Fraternité Matin*, one can find echoes of official ideology translated into poetry. For example, a poem by Koula Lucien entitled "Fraternité" was published on March 3, 1987 (p. 11); another poem in that issue, by Simeon Aka N'Wozan, called "Sublime dialogue" (10), speaks of "la vraie Fraternité et la douce Paix." In an address given in 1971, Houphouët refers to his national policy as one of "liberal humanism": "Il est vrai que notre Côte d'Ivoire conduit, depuis son indépendance, avec beaucoup de conviction et de sincérité, une expérience d'*humanisme libéral* où les aspirations au mieux-être trouvent à s'exprimer dans la liberté la plus grande . . . " (*Le Président et la nation ivoirienne*, 172, emphasis mine). Houphouët seems to use the words "humain" and "humanisme" in order to appeal to an order that transcends politics and is therefore beyond question; in 1968, going against the Organization of African Unity, Houphouët supported secessionist Biafra and declared that the Biafra problem "est un problème humain plutôt que politique" (quoted in Marcel Amondji, *Félix Houphouët et la Côte d'Ivoire: l'envers d'une légende* [Paris: Karthala, 1984]: 242). Amondji contradicts everything in the offical discourse of fraternity and humanism.

for." *All the prisoners were to be set free.* "Every single one of them. At once. All their possessions *would be restored* to them." (*Suns* 120, AT, emphasis mine)

The purpose of the president's speech is to free his political prisoners. He uses a simple performative which consists of the words "I (hereby) liberate you." That performative is here but translated into indirect style: "Tous les prisonniers étaient libérés." In dialogical counterpoint with Fama's indirectly reported hearing of and reactions to the speech ("Et c'était vrai ... "), direct quotations cite the president's words. But the most directly functional utterance, the performative, reverts to the indirect style. Then, with the quotation marks reopened, an apparent mistake is made: the verb *rentrer* is used in a future-in-the-past tense that should belong to indirect rather than direct style. This "slip" breaks down the distinction between direct and indirect discourse, between the president and Fama, and seems to lead to a general takeover of narration by forces outside of Fama's control: namely, the politics of Independence.

The president is as duplicitous as Babou; his speech makes liberation itself suspect. Fama's reaction to this speech, as to Babou's, is silence, a silence that seems disdainful but also leaves the narrative open to be dominated by other voices. Fama will now fade away as a "center of consciousness." First the president's voice commands, then that of Fama's travelling companion Bakary. Fama considers his silence to be a victory, but it is a triumph that will only translate itself into the most noble of silences, that of death. When he becomes the "center of consciousness" again, it is to decide to die (*SI*, 193; *Suns*, 128). The slip in verb tenses is a small sign of the great forces that will kill Fama.[83]

Is it the politics of speech that kills Fama? Not literally, but rhetoric is a sign of the complex alienation of which Fama is a victim. It is difficult to sort out a single political viewpoint in *Les Soleils des indépendances*, partly as a result of the unrelenting polyvocality. Within the point of view of Fama and the narrator, the term "politics" is contingent, linked to specific moments and destined to vanish. Fama's adherence to the value of noble silence leaves him excluded from the new political discourse that Babou has learned to mimic from the president of the republic; his illiteracy guarantees his exclusion from the workings of the new state. According to Fama's ideology, all this will pass; he hopes only for a Mande utopia in which to die, and in his hallucinations, that is very much what he gets. He represents a dying class, a dying caste. Yet there is a clear

83. The same "mistake" is made elsewhere (142) in reporting what was said at the secret council meeting: "'Laissons le grand palabre se développer et se poursuivre, les villageois *l'aimaient* et le délégué *devait* être joué.'" Although written in direct speech, the verbs are in the appropriate tense for indirect style.

implication, in the last words of the novel, that the Mande is eternal and its values survive political change. The last paragraph repeats formulas from the first chapter and ends with a conjunction and suspension points that signal a cyclical continuation:

Un Malinké était mort. Suivront les jours jusqu'au septième jour et les funérailles du septième jour, puis se succèderont les semaines et arrivera le quarantième jour et frapperont les funérailles du quarantième jour et . . . (*SI*, 205)

A Malinké had died. Day would follow day until the seventh day and the seventh-day funeral rites, then after a few weeks would come the fortieth day and the fortieth-day funeral rites, and . . . (*Suns*, 136)

How can the impact of the novel as a whole be distinguished from Fama's point of view? Such a distinction is essential to any political interpretation, but the possibility of irony is all too often forgotten by critics discussing *Les Soleils des indépendances*. To begin with, there is irony in the tone of the personified narrator, evident in his use of words like "illiterate" and obvious at the points when he addresses Fama directly, needling him with questions like "Don't you see . . . ?" There is irony is Fama's very existence, his quixotic actions, and obsessive thoughts: this is not a "hero" for African postcolonial times but a funny and touching caricature of outdated values. The interpretive problem lies in trying to distinguish between the ironic and sincere aspects of the novel. Fama is an ironic hero, yet his point of view, his "ideology," his voice, so dominate the novel that they are taken to be synonymous with the voice and ideology of the novel itself and perhaps of its author (hence the judgments of "ideological weakness"). Fama is ironic, but the representatives of the new state are even more so, from the president with his phony slogans to Babou with his smooth verbiage. The polyvocality of discourse in *Les Soleils des indépendances* seems to guarantee that all points of view will be ironic in relation to each other.

Following this approach, a particular political interpretation would make sense: *Les Soleils des indépendances* is a carnivalesque arena in which competing voices perform; no single voice is able to dominate or silence the others; the political import of the book comes from its success in staging all of this rather than from any single message. Some would say that this is precisely an *apolitical* interpretation; if everything in the novel is "subordinated to the task of coordinating and exposing languages to each other," as Bakhtin puts it,[84] politics in the novel is only a question of language. On one level, the question of language cannot be dismissed, for "language" is not a simply matter of words but of the

84. *The Dialogical Imagination*, 365.

differential systems by which all meaning is produced. But two objections come to mind: first, that the labelling of the novel as an arena of coordinated and divergent languages begs too many concrete problems of interpretation of the novel as a whole. Second, to say that politics is "about" language is an assertion so abstract, elitist, and purely literary-theoretical in its construction (not to mention banal) as to be all but useless in an African studies context, where the borders between disciplines are the most significant places. I would like to explore those problems of interpretation and those borders, briefly, by way of concluding this chapter.

While acknowledging the "unofficial," antiauthoritarian and antiunitary power of Kourouma's novel, while recognizing for example the subversive impact of "Mandekanisms" within francophonie, we must not ignore other factors.[85] Some voices in Les Soleils des indépendances are less ironic than others, some have more authority, and some emerge with more political import than others. In the face-off between Fama and the representatives of the Party over governance of Togobala, the council of elders emerges as the most powerful force, capable of reconciling differences between all parties to the conflict. Their secret power, within the village, allows them to manipulate the villagers and the Party delegate from outside; in this, Fama and traditional ethnic values win: "La bâtardise n'avait pas gagné Togobala. Merci! Merci à tous!" ("The bastards had not won in Togobala. Thank you! Thank you all!" [SI, 142; Suns, 94]). The elders appear to have a superior, commanding perspective, and their appraisal takes on authority, especially in this statement: "les soleils des Indépendances et du parti unique passeront comme les soleils de Samory et des Toubabs, alors que les Babou, les Doumbouya resteront toujours à Togobala" ("The suns of Independence and the single party would pass away, as did the suns of Samory and of the Europeans, but there would always be the Babous and the Doumbouyas in Togobala").

This belief in an eternal ethnic and family structure, shown in the use of the jamu as that which will always remain, is profoundly ideological and forms the backbone of Fama's attitude. It is an attitude that directly contradicts the stated goal of most postcolonial African regimes, building a national identity by transcending, if not superseding ethnic affiliation: "by superposing a historically higher and ethically superior form of human solidarity."[86] In the Ivory Coast, President Houphouët-Boigny's insistence on the ideals of fraternity and humanism can only be understood

---

85. I am alluding to Bakhtin, The Dialogical Imagination, 20: "The novel . . . is associated with the eternally living element of unofficial language and unofficial thought (holiday forms, familiar speech, profanation)."

86. Crawford Young, "Patterns of Social Conflict: State, Class, and Ethnicity," Daedalus 111, no. 2 (Spring 1982): 84.

within this frame of reference. Can Fama's precisely *ethnocentric* belief, which runs counter to state ideology, be taken at face value, as the ideology "of" *Les Soleils des indépendances?*

The ending of the novel offers the other counterweight to the forces of dialogical entropy. An ending always appears to have greater authority, merely by virtue of its place, by having the last word. There are two things to consider in the ending of *Les Soleils des indépendances*: the fact that Fama dies and the vision that he has while dying. His death is clearly identified as the end of the Doumbouya dynasty, which is symbolic of a general cultural demise, perhaps even the fading away of the Mande itself. The secret knowledge of the village elders thus appears to be undercut; they too are reduced to an ironic condition of relativism. But the last word of the novel itself ("and . . . "), belonging to no personified "center of consciousness" but rather to a collective whole, seems to echo the elders' assertion by emphasizing the cyclical, endless patterns of Mande ritual. Ethnocentrism wins in the discourse of the novel, even if it has lost in the dramatic, political outcome. A Mande utopia has been lost on earth, but the implication is that it survives in the mind. Politics will belong to the new structures, but culture will remain unchanged.

Such a view is implicit in the end of *Les Soleils des indépendances*, and the weight that it is given cannot be ignored. There is no "ideological weakness" within this point of view, nor any great ambiguity: it is a clearly identifiable, class- and caste-based nostalgia for the precolonial period. Our question thus becomes one of weighing the monological power of this ideology against the dialogical forces that permeate the novel.

Flaubert, the supreme novelistic ironist, is said to have insisted that the character Félicité in his novella *Un coeur simple* was "not ironic," an assertion that I have always found hard to believe.[87] Félicité dies seeing an apotheosis of her deceased parrot Lulu, surrounded by blue vapor, "hovering over her head."[88] Kourouma's Fama sees himself on a white charger, surrounded by a retinue, which then disappears, leaving him alone in a "cool soft place under trees," until "everything softens and slips away . . . " (*SI*, 204–5; *Suns*, 135–36). Fama's utopia, like Félicité's, is an ironic one, the pipe dream of a debased and dispossessed character. In his dying vision, he sees the utopia of the past recaptured, but only in his dying vision. The final note of ethnocentric assurance in

87. "Flaubert himself, in sketching an outline of the story for Mme Roger des Genettes, insisted that it was in no way ironic, but rather 'serious' and extremely 'sad' " (Victor Brombert, *The Novels of Flaubert* [Princeton, N.J.: Princeton University Press, 1966]: 233).

88. Gustave Flaubert, "Un coeur simple," in *Trois contes* (Paris: Garnier-Flammarion, 1965): 83.

the novel is thus offset by the implication that the Mande utopia is to be found only in hallucination and death.

The conclusion of *Les Soleils des indépendances* is monological enough that we can situate this novel within an ideological trend, the literature of disillusionment that began to flood Africa in the wake of independence. By the late 1960s, satires and critiques of postcolonial regimes had become staple, if controversial, readings for the African elite and interested Westerners.[89] Kourouma's only novel remains the classic in this tradition on the francophone side. But unlike other critiques, *Les Soleils des indépendances* adopts a viewpoint that comes from outside the circle of the intellectual élite, most concretely distinguished from the masses by the factor of literacy. The most basic ventriloquism performed by Kourouma is therefore his representation of the illiterate, nonfrancophone Fama. Beyond that, it is pointless to speculate whether Fama serves as spokesman for Ahmadou Kourouma; what counts is the visible gap between literate and illiterate as a sign of class. *Les Soleils des indépendances* does not speak for the class it comes from but for another, in a language not known to those it speaks for: French. The ventriloquism is doubled in the treatment of Salimata, adding gender difference to class difference. This is the root of the dialogism in the text, and of the ambiguity of the novel as a political utterance.

A consideration of politics and dialogism in *Les Soleils des indépendances* would be incomplete if it neglected to mention the exploitation of "dialogue" by the President of the Ivory Coast, Félix Houphouët-Boigny. By referring to the political situation of the Ivory Coast, I do not mean to suggest that Kourouma's Côte des Ebènes is merely an encoded form of the real Ivory Coast; but beginning with the playful transformation of names, the relation is too clear to ignore. The connection has been somewhat neglected in criticism, a neglect that may be partially due to self-censorship among Ivory Coast literary critics.[90] The incipient insur-

89. For an overview, see Neil Lazarus, "Great Expectations and After: The Politics of Postcolonialism in African Fiction," *Social Text* 13/14 (Winter/Spring 1986): 49–63; and Guy Ossito Midiohouan, "La littérature négro-africaine depuis les indépendances," chapter 5 of *L'Idéologie dans la littérature négro-africaine d'expression française* (Paris: L'Harmattan, 1986): 147–212.

90. For example, Ch.-G. Wondji's contribution to the collective volume *Essai sur "Les Soleils des indépendances"* is called "Le Contexte historique" (17–26) but makes no mention of the attempted coup. In the same volume, Gérard Dago Lezou makes the connection to real places and events sound much more ambiguous than it is: "C'est un espace symbolique de l'Afrique de 1961, partagée entre de multiples tendances . . . La Côte d'Ivoire? Le Mali? La Guinée? Le texte permet de le soupçonner, mais peu importe. L'essentiel est que toute l'Afrique indépendante est confrontée aux mêmes problèmes" ("Temps et espace,"

rection in *Les Soleils des indépendances* roughly corresponds to events that took place in the Ivory Coast beginning in 1962: an alleged plot against the regime, the arrest of conspirators, followed by a magnanimous pardon and "political re-education" of the seditionaries, who included many notables.[91] In reaction to his opposition, Houphouët developed a specific theory and method of *dialogue: le dialogue fraternel permanent* (which stands in interesting contrast to Sékou Touré's *complot permanent*). Invoking the African tradition of *palabre*, in 1969 the President began a series of face-to-face meetings with groups representing all sectors of Ivorian society. According to his adoring biographer Paul-Henri Siriex, Houphouët listened patiently and tolerantly, "without the slightest sign of irritation," and responded methodically and at length to all the complaints that were aired (*Houphouët-Boigny*, 219). These encounters became regular events, and the political life of the Houphouët regime has come to be associated with the idea and perhaps the myth of *le grand dialogue*.

In his speeches, Houphouët defines dialogue as "first of all the respect of the other . . . , the desire to approach and to understand that which is not oneself or far from oneself."[92] That is the desire behind the practice of dialogues permitting "the sectors of the Nation, *through the voices of their most authorized representatives*," to express "*directly and freely*, in the most total frankness, their complaints and suggestions."[93] The contradiction between direct expression and indirect, authorized representation is to be noted. The President says that he is "comforted" to note that in this fraternal dialogue "no one questioned the regime of liberal

37). The *Essai* was published in the Ivory Coast by Nouvelles Editions Africaines, which is a state-supported and controlled enterprise. Lazou also, in his own book (*La Création romanesque*, 224), makes explicit reference to a "suppression" of allusions to the 1962 events in the text of *Les Soleils des indépendances*. He states that it is only this suppression by the editors (he does not say whether he means the University of Montreal or Seuil) that accounts for the predominance of Malinke themes in the novel, but he does not go into any detail. No other critic, nor Kourouma, has confirmed that any passage was suppressed. In any case, the allusion to the events of 1962 seems clear in the published text.

91. On the events of 1962–64 and their aftermath, see Aristide R. Zolberg, *One-Party Government in the Ivory Coast*, revised edition (Princeton, N.J.: Princeton University Press, 1969): 345–55; T. D. Roberts et al., *Area Handbook for Ivory Coast*, second edition (Washington, D.C.: U.S. Government Printing Office, 1973): xxxiv-xxxv; Paul-Henri Siriex, *Houphouët-Boigny ou la sagesse africaine* (Abidjan: Nouvelles Editions Africaines, 1986): 216, 221–22.

92. Félix Houphouët-Boigny, *Propos sur la culture: extraits de discours 1959–1980* (Abidjan: Ministère des Affaires Culturelles, 1980): 11–12.

93. "L'arme des forts: le dialogue," in *Le Président Houphouët-Boigny et la nation ivoirienne*, 167, emphasis mine.

economics" (168), in other words, the domination of the economy by foreign capital. If Houphouët's and Siriex's accounts of the 1969 dialogue—claiming that a totally free and reciprocal exchange took place—are hard to take at face value, another usage of the word "dialogue" invites further skepticism. In his international relations, Houphouët became notorious for his advocacy of dialogue with South Africa in the early 1970s: "I believe that dialogue with the Whites of South Africa is possible if we conceive it within a perspective of peace through neutrality and within political neutrality" (quoted in Siriex, 339). At a time when France was selling massive supplies of arms to South Africa, Houphouët's idea of dialogue was merely a reflection of Western interests as he saw fit to serve them.[94] For critics of the regime, the "permanent fraternal dialogue" within the nation and the dialogue with South Africa are both a sham. For Marcel Amondji, writing in the mid-1980s, the staged "confrontations" between the government and various sectors of the society are part of a plan "to maintain the balance essential to the good working of the system" (Félix Houphouët, 200). The supposed struggle within the dialogical process is an illusion because it opposes individuals or coteries that all share the same essential interest, the maintenance of the system. If that is the case, then Houphouët's "respect for the other" is in fact a defense of the self. Here then, is a clear political model in which dialogue seems to be a form of bad faith, a disguise over a monological intent.

For Houphouët's admirers, his ability to enfold numerous groups within the money-making enterprises of the state is the source of his success. Victor LeVine writes: "By judiciously distributing shares in the country's prosperity, he has co-opted the major ethnic groups and their leaders into a relatively stable (though occasionally internally contentious) system of reciprocal self-interest."[95] It would be difficult to say whether such a system corresponds to Houphouët's definition of dialogue as "respect for the other"; it is clear that reciprocity is subservient to the overarching need for order, control, and "authorized" expression. In Pierre Biarnès's view, Houphouët's system amounts to nothing more than "personal power tempered by palaver" (L'Afrique aux Africains, 194).

That monological intent—the needs and imperatives of the State—is well served by the myth of dialogism. But the forms of artistic expression and literary criticism that take place in a country like the Ivory Coast

94. See Yves Benot, "Le 'dialogue' avec l'Afrique du Sud, vu de Paris et vu de l'Afrique," La Pensée 160 (November-December 1971): 98–106; and Jacques Baulin, La Politique africaine d'Houphouët-Boigny (Paris: Eurafor-Press: 1980): 199–203.

95. Victor T. LeVine, "Cameroon, Togo, and the States of Formerly French West Africa," in Peter Duignan and Robert H. Jackson, eds., Politics and Government in African States 1960–1985, (Stanford, Calif.: Hoover Institution Press, 1986): 95.

demonstrate that artists and scholars see through the myth and tailor their expressions accordingly. *Les Soleils des indépendances* derives its discourse of playful disguise and polyvocality in part from political necessity, from an awareness of the monological climate of a one-party state. The novel must speak in veiled terms in order to survive and circulate, but it must also "speak" the language of national and international politics, French. The use of French guarantees state access and control by insulating the masses from whatever sedition the elite may want to indulge in. In many third world countries, there is far greater tolerance of dissent expressed in English or French; but once a local, popular language is used, censorship is more likely to be imposed.

Political self-censorship is not, however, a global explanation for the dialogism of *Les Soleils des indépendances*. It is only part of a constellation of factors, a crossing of needs and desires. In the 1970 interview, Kourouma commented on censorship, novelistic technique, and the difference between orality and literacy. These remarks provide a condensed summary of the questions raised in this chapter.

En ce qui me concerne, j'ai voulu simplement faire un livre. Je vous dirai d'ailleurs que la tradition écrite nuit à l'invention et que le classicisme tue la recherche. . . . Bien sûr, le dit est différent de l'écrit, mais qu'est-ce que cela prouve? Qu'il faut que l'écrivain africain devienne cinéaste ou metteur en scène de théâtre? Ecrire n'est pas filmer. Le roman a sa technique propre. Fama et Salimata, mes personnages, sont décrits selon ma propre technique romanesque indissociable de mon appartenance malinké, mais je prouve qu'on peut les faire vivre autrement que par l'image. Le roman a sa propre technique et existe par lui-même. . . . Mon héros, Fama, est un prince malinké victime des indépendances, qui sont "tombées" sur l'Afrique, mais, à travers lui, c'est une mise à nu de la déchéance; l'indépendance a profité à certains, pas à tous. Je crois fermement qu'on peut critiquer sans outrances et surtout en faisant oeuvre littéraire. *Peut-être que certains n'ont pas compris qu'on peut dire un tas de choses vraies sans s'attirer les foudres de la censure.* . . . Il y a bien sûr un *"mariage" contre nature* entre la langue française et la pensée africaine, mais l'intellectuel africain n'a que cet outil à sa disposition et il faut bien qu'il s'en serve. (Badday, 8, emphasis mine)

As far as I'm concerned, I just wanted to write a book. I can tell you that in any case the written tradition hinders invention and that classicism kills original thought. . . . Of course the spoken is different from the written, but what does that prove? That the African writer has to become a filmmaker or director of plays? Writing and filming are not the same. The novel has its own technique. Fama and Salimata, my characters, are described according to my own novelistic technique, which is inseparable from my belonging to the Malinké; but I prove that they can come to life other than in pictures. The novel has its own technique and exists by itself. . . . My hero, Fama, is a Malinke prince and a victim of the Independence that "fell" over Africa, but, through him, the book is a laying-bare of decadence; Independence is profitable for some, not for all. I firmly believe that it is possible to be critical without indulging in excesses, especially in works of literature. *Some people don't seem to have understood that one can say loads of true things without attracting the lightning bolts of censorship.* . . . Of course there is a *"marriage" against nature* between the French language and African thought, but the African intellectual has only this tool available to him, and he must indeed put it to use.

Kourouma conceives of literacy, and of francophone literacy in particular, as a necessary evil with which he has come to terms. Although he appeared earlier to subscribe to the one language / one culture theory of authenticity, he obviously sees the *gap* between the French language and "the African soul" as a space that the artist can and must inhabit. He has made his peace with francophonie while rejecting many of its ideological tenets (and of course francophonie as an ideological movement was only inchoate when he wrote *Les Soleils des indépendances*). He sees no contradiction between novelistic technique and Malinke/Mande ethnicity; they are "inseparable" because he has found a new way to combine them. Theater and cinema have an clear advantage in reaching the masses, but the novel, because of its "technique," is capable of unique critical descriptions. Although Kourouma does not say exactly what he means by "technique," we can be certain that the indirect style he uses so effectively, and his innovations in French, are his essential technical means. The novel allows for *indirection*, for ventriloquism and dialogism: it allows you to say "loads of things." The value of the written word—even of the written French words of an African novel that was published in Canada and in France—is not to be dismissed.

Kourouma's final image of the "marriage against nature"—a shotgun wedding, if you will—may seem to be an exceedingly unhappy metaphor for the francophone African novel. But when one takes account of colonial history, of the material conditions of literacy, and of the fundamental desire to express a culture in its own language, Kourouma's choice of words seems well justified. Earlier in this chapter, I wondered whether the publication of *Les Soleils des indépendances* should be interpreted as a support of francophonie ideology or as a revolt against it. The problem with liberal pluralism is that it can coopt whatever it wants, making any opposition into participation. Dialogism within a certain frame can ultimately serve a monological end; reciprocity may be a trap. Within the frame of Ivory Coast political life, Kourouma speaks for the "other," the illiterate, indirectly, and voices the concerns of a dying class; his discourse undermines official discourse but could be seen to support an official policy of dialogism, of criticism "without indulging in excesses." A critical novel such as *Les Soleils des indépendances* can be coopted, and it has been in the Ivory Coast, in the sense that the book now circulates freely and poses no threat to the regime.

A similar fate, a form of domestication, applies to the question of Kourouma's francophonie. His revolt against what he calls classical French helped launch the new, sophisticated, pluralistic, and reciprocal francophonie that has gained wider acceptance in recent years. The French of *Les Soleils des indépendances* is thus two things at once: a rejection of francophonie and an expansion that strengthens it. There is no contradiction in this; there is rather a recognition of material and historical conditions by one African author and an extremely inventive way of dealing with them.

6

Women have no mouth.

—Beti proverb, Cameroun[1]

Speech was a female art.

—Camara Laye[2]

Senegalese Women Writers, Silence, and Letters: Before the Canon's Roar

Voice and Silence

Il me semble que je vous parle quand je vous écris.

—Guilleragues, *Lettres portugaises*[3]

On the threshold of this last chapter, I am struck once again by an antinomy between a theoretical truth and a historical fact. The theoretical
truth is that gender is not merely a supplementary issue that can be
"added on" to a critical approach, like the caboose on a train; gender as
an issue and feminist criticism in particular invite a reappraisal of literature and culture from the ground up. I take this truth to be self-evident,
and in previous chapters I have tried to acknowledge the importance of
gender issues within the writings of male authors. But we must also consider a historical fact: francophone African women published no works
of literature before the mid-1970s, and their literature therefore came as

1. Mineke Schipper, "Women and Literature in Africa," in *Unheard Words: Women
and Literature in Africa, the Arab World, Asia, the Caribbean and Latin America*, edited
by Mineke Schipper and translated by Barbara Potter Fasting (New York: Allison & Busby,
1985): 20.
2. *Le Maître de la parole* (Paris: Plon, 1978): 56; trans. James Kirkup, *The Guardian
of the Word* (New York: Vintage, 1984). The words quoted here are attributable to the
griot Babou Condé.
3. *Lettres portugaises, lettres d'une Péruvienne et autres romans d'amour par lettres*,
edited by Bernard Bray and Isabelle Landy-Houillon (Paris: Flammarion, 1983), 87.

246

a belated "addition" to a preestablished male tradition before it could be seen as an *alteration of* the tradition. The glaring absence of women novelists before 1976—the deafening silence—commands any approach to this topic and demands explanation. In this chapter I will try to show how Senegalese women (the first to publish) have responded to this "supplementary" condition, and how one novelist in particular—Mariama Bâ—managed to begin the reappraisal of gender within the African novel while simultaneously confronting her own marginal status as a writer.

The belated emergence of women writers raises a large number of questions concerning the relation of literate culture to patriarchy, the control of literary production, and the process of canon formation outside the boundaries of first-world canons. One must consider not only how women were excluded from 1920 to 1976 but why they eventually bothered to write at all. Is it safe to assume that literacy and education are wholly beneficial and that the coming into "voice" through literature is part of a process of social improvement for women?

I would like to begin this inquiry with a question of rhetoric.

It is almost impossible to write about writing without using metaphors of speech. The dictionary "says"; the author "talks" about a subject; books are written to break "silence." When a text's meaning is revealed, we insist even more on metaphors of orality, as if communication itself were intrinsically oral and aural: a text that moves me "speaks to me." Archeologically speaking (sic), the inevitable recourse to figures of speech may be a vestige of orality within literacy; the metaphorical slip may be an atavistic trace of speech that writing cannot seem to avoid. We have been taught to be suspicious of these metaphors, to be embarrassed by these slips, which have been unveiled as an effect of Western logocentrism; the valorization of the oral and aural as immediate presence is stigmatized as naive. But in approaching what may be an inchoate canon of African women writers—one of the most significant recent developments in the literature of francophone Africa—I would advise caution once again before the reader applies the grid of any particular Western theory to the African context: everything must be reconsidered. If theoretical baggage cannot be left at home, we can at least offset our Derrida with a lesson from Walter Ong (while remaining unfaithful to both).

Ong pursues the opposite thesis: that the voice in the West has been suppressed, processed, silenced, and in effect colonized by writing. Derrida sees "writing" as the base condition of language, Ong sees "voice."[4]

4. See Jacques Derrida, *La Voix et le phénomène* (Paris: Presses Universitaires de France, 1967); *De la grammatologie* (Paris: Minuit, 1967), esp. "La Violence de la lettre:

Neither thesis can be ignored. The fact is that the privileging of the voice in the West that Derrida critiques has taken place within the medium of literacy. The West, through the "universalizing" of education at home and through colonialism abroad, has imposed literacy while endlessly dreaming of orality. Politically, the voice remains our central metaphor for political agency and power; "having a voice" means empowerment, even if power and literacy in fact remain inseparable in a context like the United States. The slippery old opposition between orality and literacy thus confronts us once again on the threshhold of a problem.

For the peoples and cultures of Africa, the Western ambivalence about writing and speaking is both irrelevant and of pressing concern. Precolonial African systems of signification—which for the most part eschewed writing as we know it—need not be held accountable for problematics that preoccupy the West; but with the imposition of colonialism, things changed. Western "technologies" (like literacy) and philosophical concerns (like the immediacy of the voice and the "differance" of writing) were *inscribed* onto the African intellectual landscape and became African concerns as well.

No consideration of an African literary corpus—not to mention a canon—can ignore two factors that we have seen many times in this study. First, the material conditions of literacy in Africa, the narrowness of its scope among populations that remain in the vast majority illiterate. African-language literacy and literatures are mostly still on the drawing boards of government ministries. The question often asked by Westerners—Why do Africans write in French?—assumes that a free and easy choice of among different literacies is available. But "literature" is for the moment synonymous with French-language literacy, both its cause and its effect.[5] Of course, in Africa, there is always the French canon to teach, and that is part of the problem.

The second consideration is the political and historical fact of colonialism that underlies any discussion of contemporary Africa. Literacy—and consequently literature as we define it—came to Africa at the end of a gun barrel; the cannon before the canon. The principal means of colonial inscription—which I discussed in the introduction as those processes which imposed European systems on Africa, what Said calls "manifest Orientalism"—was of course education. Through colonial schools, France

---

de Lévi-Strauss à Rousseau," 149–202; Walter Ong, *Interfaces of the Word: Studies in the Evolution of Consciousness and Culture* (Ithaca, N.Y.: Cornell University Press, 1977).

5. Walter Ong describes an analogous situation in Ireland, where the revival of Gaelic has had to contend with the absence of literature (what he calls "technologically processed speech") to teach (*Interfaces*, 42).

inculcated a new civics and a new means of expression, literature. The French canon of authors was taught and continues to be taught in the academies of francophone Africa, for some time ago "the legions withdrew and were replaced by schools."[6] The first text in the francophone African corpus of fiction was in fact a schoolbook, written in 1920 by a Senegalese who had only recently acquired literacy, designed to teach reading and loaded with an ideology of collaboration. *Les Trois Volontés de Malic* (Malic's three wishes), the first fiction written in French by a black African, is for obvious reasons not taught in Africa now.[7]

For the purpose of launching this inquiry into the conditions and effects of women entering what had been an all-male tradition, I am telescoping together a number of overlapping issues: literacy, literature, colonialism, and canonicity, all of which arrive in Africa simultaneously. Of these terms, canonicity is the most problematic. I will begin by using the slightly more straightforward term "corpus," by which I mean to indicate merely a body of texts, outside of the question of their reception and use by institutions. A corpus is simply what is published; a canon may be provisionally defined as that part of the corpus that is *taught.* Kwame Anthony Appiah writes: "One cannot too strongly stress the importance of the fact that what we discuss under the rubric of modern African writing is largely what is taught in high schools all around the continent."[8] To this I would add two considerations: what is taught in universities, and what is taught as African literature in the United States; these are questions to which I will return. Initially, I will address only the question of the corpus, in hopes of eventually dealing with the issue of canonicity. The first question at hand is therefore, What is the corpus of texts by women in francophone Africa, and how is its existence and condition to be understood? As we will see, the field of Africa logically narrows itself to a consideration of Senegal, for it is there that a literature by women first emerged and took root: Senegal "leads the way."[9]

The corpus of francophone African literary writing, beginning with *Les Trois Volontés de Malic* in 1920 and continuing through the colonial

---

6. John Guillory, paraphrasing R. R. Bolgar, in "Canonical and Non-Canonical: A Critique of the Current Debate," *ELH* 54, no. 3 (Fall 1987): 499. I have changed the tense of the quotation.

7. Ahmadou Mapaté Diagne, *Les Trois Volontés de Malic* (Nendeln: Kraus Reprint, 1973), first published in 1920. Kwame Anthony Appiah comments, "Colonial education, in short, produced a generation immersed in the literature of the colonizers, a literature that often reflected and transmitted the imperialist vision" (this is what I mean by *inscription*). "Out of Africa: Topologies of Nativism," *The Yale Journal of Criticism* 2, no. 1 (Fall 1988): 155.

8. "Out of Africa," 156.

9. Schipper, "Women and Literature," 48.

and postcolonial periods, was entirely male. This "silence" (as it is called) was broken in 1976 with the publication of Aminata Sow Fall's *Le Revenant* (autobiographies by women had appeared earlier, but these are rarely discussed).[10] Starting in 1976, then, a literature of one woman exists in Senegal, but it is not explicitly concerned with the particular condition of women; it is not "feminist." Only in 1979, with the publication (also in Senegal) of Mariama Bâ's *Une Si Longue Lettre,* do we see an explicit, self-conscious meditation on gender difference written by a woman in francophone sub-Saharan Africa.[11] My aim in this chapter is to uncover the conditions that governed this moment of emergence and to see how this meditation unfolds. I propose to address this in two ways: first, by reading the rhetoric of speech and silence that dominates this field; and second, by looking to historical, anthropological, and institutional factors that must be taken into account.

There is no question that the problem here is one of exclusion, nor that silence is the most powerful metaphor for exclusion from the literary mode of production. The currency of silence as an issue within Western feminist discourse hardly needs embellishing: many titles of books and articles use phrases that insist on the oppressivity of silence (out of silence; no time for silence; triumph over silence; rape, madness, and silence; silenced women; the barrenness of silence), while others find in silence itself a different kind of word to be listened to, perhaps a strategy of resistance (Adrienne Rich: "Silence can be a plan / . . . Do not confuse it / with any kind of absence").[12] Among the very few critics who have

10. Aoua Kéita, *Femme d'Afrique: La Vie d'Aoua Kéita racontée par elle-même* (Paris: Présence Africaine, 1975), and Nafissatou Diallo, *De Tilène au plateau: Une Enfance dakaroise* (Dakar: Nouvelles Editions Africaines, 1975). It is interesting to note that both of these women were midwives by profession, which is both symbolic of their role in literary history and a reflection of the class status of midwifery as the only Western profession open to African women for a long time. Another autobiography, Thérèse Kuoh Moukoury's *Rencontres essentielles* (n. p.: Adamawa, 1971), which is actually subtitled "roman," has not appeared in any study or bibliography. On autobiography see Mineke Schipper, " 'Who am I?': Fact and Fiction in African First-Person Narrative," *Research in African Literatures* 16, no. 1 (Spring 1985): 53–79. Mary Kay Miller, a doctoral candidate at Yale University, is working on a dissertation about the problematics of women's autobiography in France and Africa, including Diallo and *Une Si Longue Lettre* (which has been labelled by some as an autobiographical novel, against Mariama Bâ's wishes).

11. Fall's *Le Revenant,* the first novel by a woman, is a critical satire about social climbing in the Senegalese bourgeoisie; gender issues are very much at stake in this and in Fall's other works, but not in the programmatic and self-consciously political way that one finds in *Une Si Longue Lettre.* Fall's attitude toward the word "feminism" is indicative of her stance; see below, note 68. We will see that Bâ, on the other hand, has been associated with the word "feminism" while redefining it in her own terms.

12. Adrienne Rich, "Cartographies of Silence," in *The Dream of a Common Language* (New York: W. W. Norton, 1978): 17.

written on francophone African women writers, no one has yet considered their half-century of absence in anything but negative terms, as an exclusion from the privilege of literacy. It would be difficult to see it otherwise. However, these critics have not taken account of an opposing view that is articulated by feminist anthropologists of Africa, a point of view that destabilizes many assumptions of literary culture.

Mineke Schipper, a Dutch critic who has been one of the most active in opening the field, relies on the metaphors of voice and silence in her chapter on Africa in a volume she also edited, *Unheard Words: Women and Literature in Africa, the Arab World, Asia, the Caribbean and Latin America*. Note that in the title, hearing stands for the reception of literature, that is, for reading. Beginning with the Beti proverb that I used as an epigraph above, Schipper rapidly debunks any idealization of the position of women in precolonial Africa and goes on to describe patterns of restriction in colonial and postcolonial African society. What is missing from Schipper's analysis—which is of course only intended as an introduction—is a distinction between the oral and the written: literature is taken as a means of "speaking up" (54), of gaining "an equal voice" (38). This it undoubtedly is, in the sense that Schipper intends.

But to blur the crucial boundary between oral/precolonial and literate/colonial and postcolonial Africa, to let the metaphor of voice "speak" for written literature, is to risk imprecision. What may be lost is the specificity of a particular literacy like French interacting with a particular local culture, of which the African continent has many hundreds. Schipper begins with thirty proverbs gathered from all over Africa, all of which cast women in subordinate roles; the Beti proverb "women have no mouth" serves as the dominant metaphor for the condition of women's written literature throughout Africa (this proverb is reproduced prominently on the book's back cover). This is a necessary but insufficient step toward contextualizing the field: necessary because the global and continentwide patterns of oppression that Schipper refers to simply cannot be ignored; insufficient because "Africa" is a catchall term that groups together endless varieties of structures and patterns.[13] Thus the jarring effect of the second epigraph above, which comes from Camara Laye's introduction to his own Mande culture and its oral traditions. How can women have no mouth if speech is a female art? The answer is that these

---

13. My argument here runs parallel to one advanced in a critique of Maria Rosa Cutrufelli's *Women of Africa: The Roots of Oppression*, trans. Nicolas Romano (London: Zed Books, 1983), the critique by Chandra Talpade Mohanty, in "Under Western Eyes: Feminist Scholarship and Colonial Discourses," *Boundary 2* 12, no. 3/13, no. 1 (Spring/Fall 1984): 333–58. Mohanty complains about "homogenous groupings with little regard for historical specificities" (340).

two pronouncements emanate from two different cultures, separated by a thousand miles, different languages, and different histories. Terms such as "speech," "silence," and even "man" and "woman" cannot be assumed to be identical from culture to culture: each is a social construction demanding precise analysis; only in the presence of such analysis can the effects of literacy and literature be adequately assessed.[14]

Furthermore, in anticipation of attention I will give to Senegal presently, it should be noted that Camara Laye's statement about gender and speech is directly, anthropologically relevant to the country where African women began to write in French. Senegal is dominated culturally by the Wolof, whose history, social structure, and traditional cultural practices (such as the role of the griots within a caste system) are closely related to those of the neighboring Mande.[15] Francophone women's writings therefore emerged within a part of the general anthropological context that has dominated this study. The coincidence is a happy one, for the new light offered by women writers reflects back on the history of representing gender that we have already seen.

The metaphors of speech and silence in feminist literary criticism on Africa, while perhaps blurring a certain historical and sociological specificity, are nonetheless powerful rhetorical tools. Schipper writes else-

14. I have taken a lesson from Henrietta L. Moore's *Feminism and Anthropology* (Minneapolis: University of Minnesota Press, 1988), the main thesis of which is that feminism must come to terms with difference and form a "feminist anthropology based on difference" (11). She concludes that feminist anthropology "demonstrates that there can be no universal or unitary sociological category 'woman' " (189).

15. The resemblance is traceable to the domination the Wolof kingdom by the Mali Empire long ago. Isabelle Leymarie indicates that the function of the griot is the same within Wolof and Mande culture, and that the stratifications of these societies are so parallel that "inter-ethnic matrimonial and social alliances between professions of the same order tend to be more frequent than inter-class alliances within the same ethnic group" (in other words, it is easier for a Mande griot to marry a Wolof griot than a Mande noble); in addition, "the current griots [both Wolof and Mande] trace their historical origins to the reign of the Mandinka emperor Sunjata." Leymarie, "The Role and Functions of the Griots among the Wolof of Senegal," Ph.D. diss., Columbia University, 1979, 8–10. For further comparison of the Mande and the Wolof cultural organizations, see Patrick McNaughton, *The Mande Blacksmiths: Knowledge, Power, and Art in West Africa* (Bloomington: Indiana University Press, 1988): 158–60. Aside from the structural resemblance between Wolof and Mande, another essential element to the context here is the atmosphere of ethnic harmony that is characteristic of Senegal (the relations with Mauritanians being a tragic exception); Michael Crowder wrote: "In some ways Senegal from a racial and ethnic point of view represents the ideal West African state" (*Senegal: A Study of French Assimilation Policy* [London: Methuen, 1967]: 108). The intermarriage of ethnic groups in Senegal is such that it can be said that the Wolof are not an ethnic group at all because there are so few "pure" Wolof (Cheikh Aliou Ndao, interview, Dakar, January 15, 1987). For a full, recent ethnography of the Wolof, see Abdoulaye-Bara Diop, *La Société wolof: Tradition et changement* (Paris: Karthala, 1981).

where, "In African literature as a whole woman hardly has a mouth yet."[16] Anne Adams Graves, in her preface to the ground-breaking volume, *Ngambika: Studies of Women in African Literature*, refers first to the lack of *visibility* of francophone women writers but concludes: "There is hope, therefore, that the ranks will increase, thus raising the volume of the literary *voice* of the African woman."[17] Again, "voice" is the rhetorical tool of unity, homogenization, and empowerment; the metaphor is well taken, but its limitations and implications must also be recognized.

A nonliterary text by Awa Thiam (pronounced "Cham"), which has gained wide circulation as the prototypical African feminist sourcebook, provides the most compelling illustration of the voice metaphor in African women's studies. *La Parole aux Négresses*, translated as *Speak Out, Black Sisters*, juxtaposes essays by Thiam with her transcriptions and translations of testimonies by African women. Thiam introduces the group of personal testimonies with a meditation on women's exclusion from speech:

Prise, réappropriation ou restitution de la parole? Longtemps les Négresses se sont tues. N'est-il pas temps qu'elles (re)découvrent *leur voix*, qu'elles prennent ou reprennent la parole, ne serait-ce que pour dire qu'elles existent, qu'elles sont des êtres humains—ce qui n'est pas toujours évident—et, qu'en tant que tels, elles ont droit à la liberté, au respect, à la dignité?

Les Négresses ont-elles déjà pris la parole? Se sont-elles déjà fait entendre? Oui, quelquefois, mais toujours avec la bénédiction des mâles. *Leur parole* n'avait rien alors d'une parole de femme. Elle ne DISAIT pas la femme.

Black women have been silent for too long. Are they now beginning to find their voices? Are they claiming the right to speak for themselves? Is it not high time that they discovered their own *voices*, that—even if they are unused to speaking for themselves—they now take the floor, if only to say that they exist, they are human beings—something that is not always immediately obvious—and that, as such they have a right to liberty, respect and dignity?

Have Black women already spoken? Have they already made themselves heard? Yes, sometimes, but always with the blessing of the men. And then, *their voices* were not the voices of women. They did not EXPRESS the nature of woman.[18]

16. "Mother Africa on a Pedestal: The Male Heritage in African Literature and Criticism," in *Women in African Literature Today* (Trenton, N.J.: Africa World Press, 1987): 48.

17. Anne Adams Graves, preface to Carole Boyce Davies and Anne Adams Graves, eds., *Ngambika: Studies of Women in African Literature* (Trenton, N. J.: Africa World Press, 1986): x (emphasis mine).

18. *La Parole aux Négresses* (Paris: Denoël, 1978): 17; *Speak Out, Black Sisters: Feminism and Oppression in Black Africa* (London: Pluto Press, 1986): 15. The italics are mine (but not the capitals). It is interesting to note that the collective singular "voix" and "parole" in French become plural "voices" in English.

Is "speech" here metaphorical, as it was in other utterances we have seen? Certainly less so. Thiam's book is a vehicle by which actual speech acts are represented in print; real women tell their stories, which become available to the world market through Thiam's conversion of orality into literacy: "Their voices are reported here by way of interviews, of which I have selected the ones which I thought to be the most significant."[19] Thiam's position as mediator and as arbiter of significance is close to the position of the anthropologist, placed so as to allow for the redemption and salvage of a culture at risk (in this case, female African culture).[20]

Within this frame, *real* silence is *represented*: a thirty-year-old woman named Yacine, originally from Senegal, tells how she is taken by her husband to live in the Ivory Coast; pregnant for the third time in five years, she is dumbstruck when one night her husband comes home with a young woman and announces, "This is my new wife . . . You'll have to let us have the bed." Yacine's response is silence: "I chose to keep quiet and to submit. What else could I do? . . . put my own life and the life of my unborn child in danger? . . . As unbelievable as it may seem, I chose self-effacement."[21] But Yacine's story takes her beyond the status of mere silent victim, and it is here that Thiam's selection and editing serve a feminist cause. After the birth of her baby, Yacine resolves to leave her husband and takes steps to prepare her departure. The last step is the crucial one: she speaks to her husband and informs him of her decision:

"Je ne peux plus supporter ce mode de vie. Plutôt que de prendre une deuxième épouse, tu aurais mieux fait de trouver une solution aux différents problèmes de subsistence que je t'ai déjà posés. . . . Maintenant qu'il n'y plus rien entre nous, je veux regagner la maison de ma mère à Bamako." Pour toute réponse, il ricana. . . . Dès cet instant, j'ai estimé n'avoir plus rien à lui dire. (26)

"I can't put up with this kind of life any more. Rather than taking a second wife you'd have done better to try to find a solution to the problems of accommodation that the two of us already had with the children. . . . Now that there's nothing more between us, I want to go back to my mother in Bamako." His only reply was a snigger. . . . From that moment, I reckoned that I had nothing more to say to him. (18)

Here, then, is real silence leading to real words and a real act of liberation. *La Parole aux Négresses* allows the reader to "hear" both silence and words through the agency of Thiam's intervention.

19. *La Parole aux Négresses*, 22; *Speak Out*, 15, AT.

20. Thiam discusses her critical position and her reliance on Western theoretical borrowings in the preface to her study of "the ideolgy of blackness" in relation to women: "Les matériaux de conceptualisation que j'ai utilisés sont quasiment tous issus de la culture occidentale." *Continents noirs* (Paris: Tierce, 1987): 7.

21. *La Parole aux Négresses*, 24; *Speak Out*, 16–17, AT.

Thiam's intermediary role translates itself into narrative strategies that resemble the anthropological rhetoric of the francophone novelistic tradition. There are moments at which she seems to have inserted information needed by the non-African reader, information that an "informant" like Yacine seems unlikely to have provided spontaneously. For example, when Yacine tells about a friend of her husband's who comes looking for her in Bamako, she explains: "For, *in Black Africa*, when a woman has had a row with her husband . . . it is understood that he must come and fetch her. . . . He can also send a relative." [22] The phrase "in black Africa" and the whole anthropological explanation that follows would not need to be spoken (and I dare say probably was not spoken) between Yacine and her Senegalese interviewer, Awa Thiam. What is happening at this point is that Thiam's literacy is projecting itself onto Yacine's oral performance, interfiling information that the literate marketplace—that is, the largely Western readership—needs. At this moment, then, *La Parole aux Négresses* reverts to one of the oldest habits in the europhone African tradition, that of making one African character tell another information only the reader (and not either character) would need. We will see Mariama Bâ's interesting variation on this device in *Une Si Longue Lettre.*

The general pattern here, then, is for literate representations of silence and voice to erase the boundary between orality and literacy, thereby disguising their own secondary relation to the original object. My critique of that erasure should not be mistaken for a debunking of studies that focus on patterns of exclusion and silencing of women in Africa; rather I wish to reassert the essential boundary between orality and literacy as a political and economic fact that cannot long be ignored. Like most radical movements that attempt to bridge a gap between a motivated and educated elite on the one hand and the "illiterate" masses on the other, any African feminism is forced to come to terms with its own class base, and the border between literate and illiterate is the most accurate indicator of class in Africa. Therefore, to blur that borderline is to lose touch with an essential and unavoidable tool for analysis and action. [23]

As an ideology that originated in literate Western spheres, feminism enters Africa under a cloud of suspicion. It has a vexed relation to the masses of the population who do not read. People from among the non-literate majority of the population are discussed in European-language,

22. *La Parole aux Négresses*, 27; *Speak Out*, 18–19, emphasis mine.

23. It is important to bear in mind that literary writing is not the only locus of this borderline. Publications such as *Femmes et sociétés: Revue de la commission internationale pour l'abolition des mutilations sexuelles* provide another model. This journal has an office in Dakar, and publishes articles on specific aspects of women's culture in Senegal.

literate works and forums, but they do not contribute to them or participate in them. Any African feminism is eventually summoned by its critics,
enemies, and even supporters to defend itself against two charges: Eurocentrism and classism. As an ethical imperative, feminism sometimes
comes into conflict with localized exigencies and traditions. In some
cases, Western feminism is applied to African customs in an inflexible
discourse that leaves no room for local sensitivities; the feminist takes on
the role of missionary/ liberator/ colonizer, as the person who knows
better than the locals, even the local women.[24] On the other hand, the
claim of African cultural autonomy is sometimes used to fend off any
ethical inquiry into cultural practices, clitoridectomy and infibulation being the most notorious examples.[25] I will not attempt to explain or account for the ethical and political antinomies between feminism and the
African world in any general way, since to do so would lead us very far
afield. But I do need to point out that problems confronting African feminism are the very same problems that have affected the francophone literary tradition from the beginning: anyone who writes in Africa is an
"intellectual," potentially alienated from the masses.

Having called for greater specificity, I would like now to reframe the
question of silence, voice, and exclusion in terms of first, the literary history of francophone Africa, and second, the gender determinations of
voice and silence in the context that anthropology creates and imposes.

24. For example, Fran Hosken's *Hosken Report: Genital and Sexual Mutilation of Females*, 3d ed. (Lexington, Mass.: Women's International Network News, 1982), takes an
uncompromising, unrelativizing ethical position on excision and infibulation in Africa. This
produces a discourse of uncompromising neocolonialism in which traditional African belief
systems become primitive obstacles to moral progress. Thus Mali is described in the following manner: "Mali and much of the surrounding territory is inhabited by some of the most
traditional societies anywhere in the world. Many ethnic groups are still bound by a feudal
[*sic*] class system that has hardly changed for the past 800 years and is *quite incompatible
with any notions of development*" (201, emphasis mine). Hosken's moralism would only
be more effective in combatting these practices if it took into account the integrity of local
beliefs rather than dismissing them as primitive. At least one published African woman
gives a radically anti-Western viewpoint, which stands in marked contrast to Hosken's approach: Joséphine Guidy Wandja calls into question what she sees as a pleasure-based Western view of sexuality, which she considers an imperialistic imposition. For her, excision
is access to "respect and dignity" ("Excision? Mutilation sexuelle? Mythe ou réalité?"
Présence africaine 142 (1st Quarterly 1987): 57, 58. *Femmes et Sociétés*, mentioned above,
also provides contrast to the Hoskens approach. See also Benoîte Groult, "La haine du
c . . . ," in *Ainsi soit-elle* (Paris: Bernard Grasset, 1975): 93–118.

25. Cyprien Ekwensi, the Nigerian populist novelist, speaking at Yale University in October 1988, was asked about the role of women in his work and about the works of Flora
Nwapa, the Nigerian woman writer. Ekwensi dismissed Nwapa simply by pointing out that
"she drives a Mercedes;" that is, that her class status negates her claim to ethical authority
on the status of women in Nigeria.

These considerations must precede any discussion of the corpus or canon of women's writings.

Silence in Print

The representation of women in the male tradition of African writers has been analyzed in several studies; because of the asymmetrical number of texts by men, this subject sometimes seems to stand in the way of real attention to women writers. These "image" studies are necessary, and until the mid-1970s they were all there was to do, but they should not now outweigh careful readings of women's fictions. The organization of *Ngambika* reflects the state of Africanist literary studies of women in the mid-1980s: of its eighteen chapters, nine are devoted to male authors, five to female authors, and four to authors of both sexes; only two chapters are wholly concerned with a francophone woman writer (Mariama Bâ in both cases).[26] So in addition to the fifty-year lag in the emergence of women writers, there is a lag in critical attention. Curiously, several works about "women in African literature" published after 1976 ignore women writers: Arlette Chemain-Degrange, at the conclusion of her lengthy study of women's liberation in francophone male novels, limits her commentary on women writers to the following: "The silence [sic] of women in literature, until a recent date, is not a proof of their liberation" (*Emancipation féminine*, 352). And Mohamadou Kane, the dean of literary critics at Dakar, Senegal, wrote a long paper called "Le féminisme dans le roman africain de langue française," dated September 1978, in which male authors are treated as the sole liberating agents of their female characters; Kane does not even mention the possibility of women eventually writing for themselves, nor the fact that they had already begun.[27]

Moving back in history, I would like to invoke one representative moment of "silence" in the francophone literary tradition, through reading a text that is known to students in all of francophone Africa, a text that

26. See *Ngambika*; see also Arlette Chemain-Degrange, *Emancipation féminine et roman africain* (Dakar: Nouvelles Editions Africaines, 1980).

27. To be fair, it should be noted that the very few works by women that had been published before 1978 (the two autobiographies and Fall's *Le Revenant*) may not have been readily available to either Kane or Chemain-Degrange. It is nonetheless strange that Kane carefully and expertly traces the evolution of female characters from a state of passivity in early works, to a state of agency ("Elle cesse d'être un objet de libération, un être à libérer, pour devenir l'initiatrice de la libération africaine" [197]), without discussing the eventuality of women actually writing. "Feminism" in his essay remains totally a question between male authors and male critics. The noncanonicity of "non-literary" autobiographies may also play into the exclusion of Kéita and Diallo.

is therefore indisputably *canonical*. Léopold Sédar Senghor's "Femme noire" ("Black Woman"), published as part of the collection *Chants d'ombre* in 1945 and widely anthologized since then, eloquently promotes a vision of black female beauty. The ostensible agenda of the poem, its explicit "message" as agreed upon by critics, is the recuperation of black beauty, its redemption from the crushing effects of Western racism. Taken on these global political terms, the poem functions perfectly:

> Femme nue, femme noire
> Vêtue de ta couleur qui est vie, de ta forme qui est beauté!
> . . .
> . . . je te découvre . . .

Nude woman, black woman, / Clothed in your color which is life, in your shape which is beauty! / . . . / . . . I discover you . . . [28]

An analysis of gender roles in this poem can only be retrospective and impudent, but not impertinent. The woman is associated with beauty, obscurity, fruit, the savanna, a drum, an oil, and a gazelle. Meanwhile, a gendered division of labor is obvious from the moment the male speaker of the poem "discovers" her as a "promised land"; male and female both have a mouth, but one is subordinate to the other:

> Fruit mûr à la chair ferme, sombres extases du vin noir,
>   bouche qui fais lyrique ma bouche
> Savane aux horizons purs, savane qui frémis aux caresses
>   ferventes du Vent d'Est
> Tamtam sculpté, tamtam tendu qui grondes sous les doigts
>   du vainqueur
> Ta voix grave de contralto est le chant spirituel de l'Aimée.
> . . .
> Femme nue, femme noire
> Je chante ta beauté qui passe, forme que je fixe dans l'Eternel
> Avant que le Destin jaloux te réduise en cendres pour
>   nourrir les racines de la vie.

Ripe fruit with firm flesh, dark ecstasy of black wine, mouth that makes my mouth lyrical, / Savanna with pure horizons, savanna that trembles under the east wind's fervent caress / Carved tamtam, tamtam which rumbles under the conqueror's fingers / Your grave contralto voice is the spiritual chant of the Loved One. // . . . Nude woman, black woman / I sing of your fleeting beauty, a form that I affix in the Eternal / Before jealous Destiny reduces you to ashes / To feed the roots of life.

Her mouth is not for speaking directly; it is a condition of *his* lyricism. Her voice, which says nothing, is only the organ of a love-object, the

28. Léopold Sédar Senghor, "Femme noire," in *Poèmes* (Paris: Seuil, 1984): 16.

Loved One. The concluding gesture places the poet in the godlike position of promoting the woman to eternal status while at the same time
reducing her to fertilizer for future generations of poets. While the status
of "woman" here is full of ambiguity (she is elevated and debased at the
same time), there is no doubt about the fundamental inequality of the
sexes.[29]

The fact that Senghor was not thinking about gender equality—in a
poem that used the female figure to serve the end of racial equality—
confronts us with the reality of chronological history, of what came first.
As historical observation this is necessary, but as an ethical stance, the
"first things first" approach has been discredited. In the days of colonialism and anticolonialism, it was thought that certain forms of liberation
had to precede others: first racial liberation, then, eventually, perhaps,
gender liberation. Rarely stated explicitly, but highly influential, this thesis is often at work within the history of African literature.[30]

Here then is *literate* "silence": a woman who exists on paper and who
is spoken for rather than speaking. The silence of Senghor's woman is the
literary counterpart to the real silence that Awa Thiam's witnesses had to
overcome in real life. Senghor's "Black Woman" is a central figure in his
vision of Negritude, the global redemption of African culture as a unitary
force.[31] From the mid-1940s through the mid-1960s and beyond, Negritude was the dominant literary ideology in francophone Africa; Senghor
and Negritude remain virtually synonymous, due to his extensive and
continual elaborations of this ideology. While nuances are to be found
within Negritude poetry and essays, it is nonetheless fair to state that the

29. Camara Laye's poem "To My Mother," which serves as the epigraph and dedication
to *L'Enfant noir*, similarly glorifies the African woman but refrains from the excessive
allegorization of Senghor's poem. The woman in "To My Mother" is an agent and an
arbiter of *culture*, even if she is also associated with nature ("Femme des champs, femmes
des rivières . . ."). Camara Laye, *L'Enfant noir* (Paris: Plon, 1953): 9–10; the English
translation by James Kirkup and Ernest Jones, *The Dark Child* (New York: Farrar, Strauss
and Giroux, 1954), has only an abridged version of the poem, 5.

30. Schipper, introduction to *Unheard Words*, 10: "In African and Asia . . . , under the
motto 'first things first,' [female] emancipation is regularly passed off as a low-priority item,
born of Western influence."

31. On Senghor's Negritude, see Marcien Towa, *Léopold Sédar Senghor: négritude ou
servitude?* (Yaoundé, Cameroun: Editions CLE, 1971); Sylvia Washington Ba, *The Concept
of Negritude in the Poetry of Léopold Sédar Senghor* (Princeton, N.J.: Princeton University
Press, 1973); Irving Leonard Markovitz, *Léopold Sédar Senghor and the Politics of Negritude* (New York: Atheneum, 1969); see also Senghor's essays in the three volumes titled
Liberté (Paris: Seuil, 1964, 1971, and 1977). On Senghor and the mythification of women,
see Mona Mikhail, "Senghor, Women and the African Tradition," *Rackham Literary Studies* 1 (1971): 63–70; Mikhail writes, "More than any other poet of his generation of African writers using the French language, Senghor exalted and glorified woman, thus
continuing an ancient tradition of African poetry" (63).

movement as a whole reflected and participated in the exclusion of women. And it is reasonable to offer "Femme noire" as a representative example of the gender roles that were thinkable in this context. Negritude is nothing if not a creature of literacy; it was conceived and elaborated through reading and writing; "Femme noire" shows how francophone literacy constantly "talks" about women and depends on women for allegorical fuel but excludes women from the process of literate creation. The silence of Senghor's black woman—for us, with the advantage of hindsight—therefore stands as a figure of women's exclusion from francophone literacy. [32]

Silence in Anthropology

Anthropology has been the constant interlocutor in this study, and it has consistently proved to be part of both the problem and the solution in approaching African literature. As anthropologically-informed readers, we are constantly relying on sources that critical theory tells us to suspect. On the question of silence and gender in Africa, this will again be the case. The "experimental" anthropologists—reformers like James Clifford—describe dialogue as the condition to which anthropology must aspire; classical ethnographies tended to whittle polyvocality down to a manageable, authoritative monologue. The voices of "natives" were subsumed and silenced within the text; the polyvocality that underpins the ethnographic encounter was lost.[33] So a critique of silence and a valorization of voice are implied within the reform movement in anthropology (even if the reformers themselves have been accused of silencing women and gender as a question).[34]

32. To give Senghor his due, it must be acknowledged that in his capacity as president of Senegal he was largely responsible for the reforms in family laws enacted in 1972. These reforms began the process of granting equal status to women by abolishing certain forms of de jure discrimination. Of course, as acts of literacy, such changes in law have only a limited sphere of influence in Senegal; applying the law is "another kettle of fish" (Moriba Magassouba, L'Islam au Sénégal: Demain les mollahs? [Paris: Karthala, 1985]: 113). On more recent efforts to either undermine or strengthen the code, see T. K., "Yewwu-Yewwi en action," Amina 231 (July 1989): 8–12; and Fatou Sow, "Senegal: The Decade and Its Consequences," Issue: A Journal of Opinion (African Studies Association) 17, no. 2 (Summer 1989): 32–36. The latter provides a succinct overview of women's rights issues in Senegal.

33. See James Clifford, "On Ethnographic Authority," in The Predicament of Culture (Cambridge: Harvard University Press, 1988): 21–54.

34. See Micaele Di Leonardo, "Malinowski's Nephews," The Nation, March 13, 1989, 350–52. In a talk at the Whitney Humanities Center at Yale University (Fall 1987), Di Leonardo pointed to the elitism that was an organizing principle of the influential volume Writing Culture (ed. James Clifford and George E. Marcus [Berkeley: University of Califor-

An explicit attempt to think of anthropology and gender together seems to guarantee some attention to silence. Henrietta L. Moore's comprehensive treatment of this disciplinary intersection borrows Edwin Ardener's theory of "muted groups," in which women or other nondominant groups are excluded from the dominant means of expression. Women need not be actually silent, but "they remain 'muted' because their model of reality, their view of the world, cannot be realized or expressed using the terms of the dominant male model." [35] But here we must recognize a fork in the road: on the one hand, there is the question of women's silence within any given society, as described or analyzed by anthropology; on the other hand, there is the silencing of women and gender issues by the (largely) male ethnographic authorities.

I will offer one illustration of the latter problem, which has been amply documented.[36] It comes, as an exception that proves the rule, from a female anthropologist who worked among the "Bambara" of French West Africa in the 1950s. Viviana Paques's *Les Bambara* is a classical ethnography, a sweeping account of a culture in 119 pages. Within it Paques addresses "the position of woman" in a two-page section that is emblematic of the state of early anthropology of women. Paques describes the obstacles that confront anyone curious about the status of women:

> The society of women has remained much more impenetrable to European civilization. Women rarely go to French schools, and unlike the men, who at least during their military service are thrown into our system of civilization, women have few contacts with Whites and seem to be even more attached to custom than their husbands are. Few of them speak French, and all of these factors mean that their society has remained closed and very poorly known by Whites.[37]

Paques goes on to suggest that she will correct mistaken judgments that have been made about the inferior status of women in Bamana society, and in this she anticipates an important agenda within the feminist anthropology that will come much later: the debunking of "women-as-victim" studies. But Paques affirms that the Bamana woman is "always a minor from a legal standpoint." On speech and silence, she states, "A

nia Press, 1986]). The number of participants in the seminar was "strictly limited to ten" (vii), and Clifford, in his introduction, explains the exclusion of any feminist contribution from the volume by saying that "feminism had not contributed much to the theoretical analysis of ethnographies as texts" (20).

35. Moore, *Feminism and Anthropology*, 3.

36. See Moore, *Feminism and Anthropology*, and Margaret Strobel, "African Women: Review Article," *Signs* 8, no. 1 (Fall 1982): 109–31.

37. Viviana Paques, *Les Bambara* (Paris: Presses Universitaires de France, 1954): 74.

woman must not take part in any political discussion or demonstration," but may make her influence felt at the moment of succession and inheritance—in ways that conform to the muted groups theory (75). Paques at once critiques the problem of exclusion, points to its solution, and remains caught within its web. One of the most recent anthropological studies of the same area, Patrick McNaughton's *The Mande Blacksmith* reflects little or no advancement of knowledge about gender issues: in a lecture, McNaughton explained that ignorance of women's culture will continue to be the rule until women anthropologists go to the Mande, get initiated into women's secret societies, and publish their findings.[38] Thus the kind of source that would be the most useful here—a full-length ethnography of women within Mande or Wolof society—does not yet exist.[39]

The anthropological texts that I have relied on throughout the course of this study have had relatively little to say about gender, although we have seen that gender has been an important issue in the literary texts themselves. (It is only realistic to keep in mind that gender issues have come to the fore only in recent years; they are construed here in a way that comes from my own American academic environment.) In reading *L'Enfant noir* we saw the significance of Mande notions of "father-childness" and "mother-childness" as anthropological signposts (in both Mande and Wolof cultures, these gender associations are asymmetrical), between which the protagonist's understanding of his culture is formed.[40] In the case of *Les Soleils des indépendances*, Kourouma's treatment of Salimata opened the door to a skeptical critique of the traditional world that anthropology depicts and defends. I would like to look back briefly at a few of my sources now, in order to recast the question of gender as it pertains to silence and the emergence of women writers.

Sory Camara's *Gens de la parole*, on which I have relied for information and perspective on the role of Mande griots, contains a section on the "hierarchy of the sexes" that is of vital interest. Camara makes the following points: that before Islam, Mande religion was "men's business" only; that Islam only reinforced the assymetry of the sexes; that Mande culture discourages emotion in boys and tolerates it in girls; women be-

38. Patrick McNaughton, lecture at Yale University, Fall 1988.

39. There are however partial contributions that are of value, such as A. Raphaël Ndiaye's *La Place de la femme dans les rites du Sénégal* (Dakar: Nouvelles Editions Africaines, 1986).

40. See Leymarie, "The Role and Function of the Griots," 111: "asymmetry between the maternal lineage, which symbolizes affection, and the paternal lineage, which symbolizes strength and honor"; cf. McNaughton, *The Mande Blacksmiths*, 14.

come "an effective and silent support" for their men; and they "wind up having a muffled [*sourde*] and diffuse influence on the men which can totally escape the uninformed observer."[41] His depiction of the sexes as at odds with each other in Mande culture, and of the women as subordinated and muted ("a citizen who is an eternal minor"), is confirmed and expanded in his subsequent work *Paroles très anciennes*. In this ethnopsychoanalytic study of Mande culture, Camara interprets circumcision, hunting, agriculture, and polygamy as symbolic strategies by which the Mande male hero (acting under the flag of *fadenya*, father-childness) seeks to bypass the female and engender himself.[42]

In both studies, Camara affirms a point that is essential here: that griots are "neutral in regard to sexual identity, both socially and culturally"; in certain cases, this can provide them with "a veritable windfall," because they can "participate as women while remaining men" (*Paroles*, 182). In such a case, the griot represents liberation from the gender repression that society imposes; he fulfills the suppressed desire of all Mande men (the desires of women are not addressed by Camara). In *Gens de la parole*, Camara asserts that griots constitute a "connecting link" between the sexes; griots "due to their ambiguity, re-establish a continuity between these antithetical . . . categories" (57).[43]

The epigraph from Camara Laye begins to make sense in this context. If speech is "female," then griot women would be in a sense women "twice"; this can be surmised by looking at characterizations of griots' behavior, comparing them to women.[44] But actual griot women are

41. Sory Camara, *Gens de la parole* (Paris: Mouton, 1976): 51–55. Camara's use of the word *sourd* is interesting, since it confirms the notion of silence (*sourd* is "that which is hardly pronounced" [*peu prononcé*]—*Petit Robert*).

42. *Paroles très anciennes* (Grenoble: La Pensée sauvage, 1982), esp. 48–50, 72–75. Stephen Bulman writes: "In general, women are thought of by the Malinke to be dangerous to men, and . . . this danger come from those elements within them—emotionality, capriciousness, untrustworthiness, etc.—that are uncontrolled, unsocialised—*natural*. In contrast, all the official extra-domestic life of the village or state is exclusively the preserve of men—culture is male" ("The Buffalo-Woman Tale," in Karin Barber and P. F. de Moraes Farias, eds., *Discourse and its Disguises*, Birmingham University African Studies Series, no. 1 (Birmingham, England, 1989): 185.

43. As usual, the reference here is to male griots; almost nothing is stated about females.

44. In chapter 3, we saw allusions to the Mande construing of griots within the gender system. Mamby Sidibé wrote: "On compare couramment les *nyamakala* à des femmes et à des marabouts qui ont tendance à suivre ceux qui leur font de beaux cadeaux; c'est pourquoi tout en les traitant avec déférence, on s'en méfie" ("Les gens de caste ou nyamakala au Soudan français," *Notes africaines* 81 [1959]: 13–17). In the same vein, Innes quotes a Mande informant as saying "Griots are like women—they can never be completely trusted,

elided from discussions; when "griots" are compared to "women," the assumption is that the griot is male. The role and work of griot women have not been documented in any systematic way, and male griots are the only ones who have entered into collaborative relationships with historians and anthropologists.[45]

Camara Laye and the griot he is quoting and "novelizing" in *Le Maître de la parole* use gender as a wedge, to reaffirm the distinction between nobles' and griots' relation to speech:

La parole était un art femelle exclusivement réservée aux griots et aux femmes, le roi qui pratiquait un art mâle, l'art de gouverner un peuple, ne pouvait s'en emparer et ne devait hurler!—et le griot cria les décisions royales qu'il entendit et les commenta en les agrémentant. (56–57)

Speech was a female art reserved solely for griots and women. The king, who practiced a male art, the art of governing a people, could not appropriate that other art, and could not shout at the top of his voice! It was the griot who proclaimed the royal decrees he was allowed to hear, commenting on them and elaborating them. (54, AT)

This information about the symbolic gendering of speech in the Mande seems to work at cross-purposes with the initial framework of this chapter: in the realm of literacy, self-expression is male, and "silence" is female; in the traditional Mande according to these sources, speech is female, and silence (the silence of the king) is male. Sory Ca-

---

and they tend to go where the money is" (*Sunjata: Three Mandinka Versions* [London: School of Oriental and African Languages, 1974]: 105n, 130). In her autobiography, the midwife and political activist Aoua Kéita refers to women of caste as violent and provocative (*Femme d'Afrique*, 87): at a political meeting, "les femmes de caste qui pullulent dans ces régions se provoquèrent réciproquement. Les nôtres surtouts, étaient d'une violence rare, en gros mots." Similar characterizations can be found in the writings of early European explorers; Anne Raffenel (a man), described his encounter with female griots: "Un peu plus loin, le bruit du tamtam, des chants joyeux, et une grande clarté m'amenèrent sur une place où l'on dansait. C'étaient les griottes de l'almamy qui faisaient les frais de cette fête nègre. . . . Aussitôt que la conductrice du choeur m'eut aperçu, elle s'élança sur moi avec sa troupe, et toutes ensembles se livrèrent, à mon intention, à des chants d'une effrayante harmonie. . . . Les griottes, parvenues au paroxysme de leur exaltation, se ruaient convulsivement sur moi; elles ne riaient plus, elle grimaçaient. . . . Mes efforts pour échapper à cette légion de démons furent enfin aperçus. . . . Cela s'appelle *chanter* quelqu'un." (*Nouveau voyage dans le pays des nègres* [Paris: Imprimerie et Librairie Centrales des Chemins de Fer de Napoléon Chaix & Cie., 1856], 1: 46).

45. Mamadou Diawara confirms this situation and goes on to begin its rectification in "Women, Servitude, and History: The Oral Historical Traditions of Women of Servile Condition in the Kingdom of Jaara (Mali) from the Fifthteenth to the Mid-Nineteenth Century," in Barber and Moraes Farias, eds., *Discourse and its Disguises*, 109–37.

mara describes women's silence as a symptom of oppression, but this silence is real and not symbolically valorized like "noble" silence. This ambiguity of silence—as a sign of both oppression and power—is crucial, and it reflects an important topos in anthropology. We saw in chapter three how the griot Mamadou Kouyaté drew a line beyond which the secrets of the Mande would have to remain untouched, unbetrayed by speech and transliteration. His recourse to silence at that point is a defensive gesture and an act of power: "I have sworn to teach that which is to be taught and to hold silent [*taire*] that which is to be held silent." [46]

In the field of Mande ethnography, Dominique Zahan's *La Dialectique du verbe chez les Bambara* has the most to say about silence and secrecy in relation to speech. "These Sudanese," he writes in his slightly quaint way, "are certain that speech is only effective and can only be fully appreciated if it is enveloped in shadow"; [47] the truest word (*verbe*) is silence. Devices of veiling one's meaning—euphemism, double-entendre, symbolism—are prized, and secrecy is the organizing principle of the initiation societies. Silence both precedes and follows speech in the order of things. [48] Silence is synonymous with thought, although speech gives the appearance of thinking (154). Zahan ultimately associates silence with the sacredness of origins, finding in (oddly enough) the mother's fart "the symbol of the fiercest silence" (165). In *Le Coiffeur de Kouta*, Massa Makan Diabaté describes the mother's fart as "sacred." [49] So silence finally is feminized on the level of symbols, but only within the male experience that Zahan describes, and only as a question of symbolic gastric origins. His anthropology (and nearly everyone's in this area) pertains literally to *le* Bambara, the male only. [50]

Jean Jamin's *Les Lois du silence* provides a detailed anthropological interpretation of silence as a "plan" rather than an "absence." Arguing

46. Djibril Tamsir Niane, *Soundjata ou l'épopée mandingue* (Paris: Présence Africaine, 1960): 153.

47. Dominique Zahan, *La Dialectique du verbe chez les Bambara* (Paris: Mouton, 1963): 150.

48. A proverb that Zahan quotes strikes an echo with Sory Camara's thesis about self-engenderment. " 'Normalement, dit-on, c'est la mère qui met au monde l'enfant; dans le cas de la parole et du silence c'est, par contre, l'enfant [i. e. la parole] qui donne naissance à sa mère [i. e. au silence]' " (*Dialectique*, 153).

49. *Le Coiffeur de Kouta* (Paris: Hatier, 1980): 69. In *Les Soleils des indépendances*, Kourouma evoke the same cultural topos: " 'Mes dires ont donc sonné le silence comme le pet de la vieille grand-mère dans le cercle des petit-enfants respectueux' " (91).

50. Thus: "L'incident [le pet de la mère] impose le silence absolu *au fils* qui en serait témoin, en raison des idées associées à la mère et au pet" (*Dialectique*, 165, emphasis mine).

against those who would see in silence only a refusal of power (namely Pierre Clastres and his *La Société contre l'état*), Jamin shows it to be a strategy of masking, a ruse by which the powerful can "make you believe that the power is elsewhere."[51] Jamin's perspective is relevant to the problem I raised earlier, the predominant association of speech with power. He writes:

> If, to repeat Pierre Clastres' expression, the taking and exercise of power constitute a taking and exercise of speech, I would add that power is equally a function and fruit of silence, and that power can only be acquired and/or maintained by the *appropriation* and thus by the retention of speech. In primitive society, the chief is of course the master of words, but he is at the same time the master of silences and of secrets. . . . He is the one who knows how to impose silence and how to be silent [qui sait taire et se taire]. (59)

Referring to a study of Wolof children, Jamin maintains that learning to speak in certain African societies is synonymous with learning to be silent; zones of silence and speech are delimited at the same time (60). His general thesis has a good deal of relevance to the Mande and Wolof contexts, in which speech (which is vital but dangerous) is relegated to a marginal caste, the griots. Silence is therefore "noble." We could therefore get the impression that this valorization of silence provides an antidote to the "Western" view of silence as death, permitting us to understand and appreciate silence on its own terms.

But Jamin also makes it impossible to carry this appreciation too far, into a fetishization of silence. He shows the total dependency of silence on speech, and vice versa. This dependency marks the relation between the noble kings (the silent) and their griots (the speakers) in the traditional Mande.[52] The marginalized griots and other persons of caste in fact exercise great power by virtue of their very marginality: speech (and other *nyama*-inducing materials) marginalizes them but also empowers them.

The values encountered within anthropology (by which I mean both the Mande/Wolof world as we apprehend it through texts or contacts, and the interpretive machines of people like Zahan and Jamin) are thus

---

51. Jean Jamin, *Les Lois du silence: Essai sur la fonction sociale du secret* (Paris: Maspero, 1977): 63. One thinks here of the ruse used by the village authorities in *Les Soleils des indépendances*.

52. See Zahan, *Dialectique*, 147–48: " 'L'homme de caste, disent [les Bambara], est libre, parce qu'il est captif, comme le roi est captif parce qu'il est libre.' . . . A cause de leur métier qui les singularise, les castés deviennent des 'affranchis.' D'où cette liberté que ne peut avoir le 'noble', prisonnier qu'il est, lui, des règles de la société dont il participe. . . . En somme le griot possède un énorme pouvoir parce qu'il manipule la force la plus étonnante du monde, la parole."

at odds with those normally taken for granted in the West (the association of silence with oppression). There is an apparent watershed between the value attributed to speech (often metaphorically, meaning general self-expression) in literacy and the value attributed to silence in the anthropology of the Mande: it should not go unnoticed that in both cases, on both sides of this great divide, women wind up losing. Where silence is valorized (in Mande oral culture), speech is "female" but controlled by men; where speech is valorized (in literacy), women are "silent" (they don't write). Women are in fact silenced on both sides.

An incident that the midwife and political activist Aoua Kéita recounts in her autobiography provides some idea of how this actually happens and serves as a reminder of how all these issues may actually bear on people's lives. On the day of an important election in Mali, on the eve of independence, a village chief and French army veteran blocks Aoua Kéita's entry to the polling place, screaming in three languages:

Get out of my village, audacious woman! You must be not only audacious but also brazen, to try and measure yourself against men by taking the place of a man. . . . Get the hell out of here, woman with a honey-coated tongue! I don't give a damn about you or your words of the devil and Satan, or about your RDA [Rassemblement Démocratique Africain]. I have three wives like you who take turns scratching my back every night. Hold your tongue. If you continue to talk to me, I will have you beaten by the women. (389–90)

The chief uses imagery that evokes the traditional distrust of spoken words and their seductive power; he imposes silence. A veritable riot ensues, in which Kéita is attacked and insulted. Speech may be "female," but females are not at liberty to use it in any and all circumstances. Griots may be licensed to speak, but speech and power are not congruent because the nobles and chiefs control the more general scheme, in which speech is only one component.

If there is a lesson offered by this rapid look into the anthropology of gender and silence in West Africa, it is that the process of coming to speech cannot be wholly explained as an acquisition of power. Mande and Wolof ethnographies describe the power of speech as a mixed blessing, one that throws suspicion on the person using it. The relation of speech and silence does not permit any facile valorization of either. There is no simple dualism between the two, but rather a dialectic that demands attention to specific gains and losses, according to context. Aoua Kéita's life was the story of accession to one form of speech and empowerment, that of colonial and postcolonial politics; the passage above demonstrates how difficult that process must have been.

How, therefore, does the anthropology of speech and silence pertain to women's delayed entry into literature? This can only be answered by looking into the history of women's education.

The Ambiguous Adventure of Education

Nous refusions l'école pour demeurer nous-mêmes et pour conserver à Dieu sa place dans nos coeurs.
—Cheikh Hamidou Kane, *L'Aventure ambiguë* [53]

Fabrique de chômeurs?
—caption of cartoon depicting a school in Mali [54]

I have thus far touched on several modes of exclusion and moments of silence in francophone history. "Silence" has turned out, more often than not, to mean the absence of literacy or (in the case of Senghor's poem) the subordination of woman by literary means. Since Western literary and social criticism takes literacy as the norm, and its absence as a problem that must be explained, we cannot ignore the raw figures on literacy.

Schipper states that "illiteracy in Africa is four times as high among women as among men, and the higher the level of education, the lower the percentage of girls." [55] For most of the states of so-called francophone Africa, overall literacy is below forty percent of the adult population; in Senegal and Mali, the figure is below ten percent; in the Ivory Coast, as much as forty percent of the population may have some degree of literacy. In all cases, nearly twice as many boys as girls are enrolled in school. [56] In colonial times, neither colonizer nor colonized saw much point in sending girls to school: girls' education was largely thought to be vain. [57] Although a girl's school was opened in Senegal in 1826, in 1921 there were still only ten girls' primary schools in all of French West Africa. [58] An administrator writing in 1921 could say that colonial education reached only one person in five hundred, and that girls' education "hardly exists." [59] On the eve of World War II, only five to seven percent of students

53. *L'Aventure ambiguë* (Paris: Union Général d'Editions, 1961): 20

54. *Jamana* 9 (August 1986): 32.

55. "Women and Literature," 22.

56. Jocelyn Murray, ed., *Cultural Atlas of Africa* (New York: Facts on File, 1981): 98.

57. Kouamé Nguessan, "Femmes ivoiriennes: Acquis et incertitudes," *Présence Africaine* 141, no. 1 (1987): 104. René Dumont entitled one chapter of his classic *L'Afrique noire est mal partie* (Paris: Seuil, 1962) "Si ta soeur va à l'école, tu mangeras ton porte-plume."

58. Bernard Dadié, "Chronologie," in *Iles de tempête: Pièce en sept tableaux* (Paris: Présence Africaine,1973): 140; Bernard Dadié, "Misère de l'enseignement en A.O.F.", *Présence Africaine* 11 (December 1956-January 1957): 61.

59. J.-L. Monod, quoted in Dadié, "Misère de l'enseignement," 61.

finishing primary school in French Africa were girls; by 1960, there was some increase, followed by "stagnation."[60] The first institution of higher education for women, the Ecole Normale Supérieure of Rufisque, Senegal, opened in 1938, and, since Mariama Bâ was a student there, the existence of this school—turning out only thirty students per year—must be recognized as one very real material condition of the emergence of women's literature.[61] With the coming of independence, equality of access to education was widely recognized as a goal, but in most countries the idea is far from being implemented. In fact, while general literacy may be rising, the imbalance between the sexes seems to be worsening.[62]

The literature on the subject of girls' and women's education poses some troubling questions. Kouamé Nguessan identifies two factors that contribute to a continuing marginalization of women in the Ivory Coast: one is the plantation economy, the other is schooling.[63] School as a means of social promotion and empowerment presupposes that there is something to do with the skills one has acquired in school, such as literacy. But women in the Ivory Coast are vastly outnumbered by men (by four times, according to Nguessan's statistics) in public sector, literate jobs. Education may remove a woman from a sphere in which she has more freedom—that of the traditional market economy—and place her in either a pink collar ghetto or a bourgeois gilded cage. Education, modernization, and the supposed coming of egalitarian values have actually proved to be a mixed blessing to many African women, who may have had more control in traditional society. Claire Robertson states the problem straightforwardly: "Rather than leading the way to equality and greater opportunity, then, education for most women in Africa functions as an instrument of oppression to reinforce subordinate roles"; greater access to primary education "has become a disaster for women both by

60. Abdou Moumouni, *L'Education en Afrique* (Paris: Maspero, 1964): 118, 122.

61. In an autobiographical statement, Bâ attributed to a brilliant teacher of hers at Rufisque, a Mme Germaine Le Goff, tremendous powers of inspiration: she " 'taught me to know myself' . . . I cherish the memory of rich communions with her, which have made me a better person. Her discourse outlined the new Africa" ("Mariama Bâ on Her Life," *American Universities Field Staff Reports* 10 [1981], issue intitled "Africa Asserts its Identity": 7. Abdou Moumoumi reports that the students of the Ecole Normale of Rufisque were nicknamed "Mlles 'frigidaires,' 'femmes savantes,' 'précieuses ridicules' " (*L'Education en Afrique*, 123).

62. Claire Robertson, "Women's Education and Class Formation in Africa," in Claire Robertson and Iris Berger, eds., *Women and Class in Africa* (New York: African Publishing Co., 1986): 96. On the role of education in the construction of francophone culture, see Bernard Mouralis, *Littérature et développement* (Paris: Silex, 1984): 59–99.

63. "Femmes ivoiriennes," 103. See also Kamla Bhasin, "Literacy for Women, Why and How! Some Thoughts in the Indian Context," in Miranda Davies, ed., *Third World-Second Sex*, vol. 2 (London: Zed Books, 1983): 104–11.

reducing their labor force participation and by increasing their subordination to men."[64] A broad analogy can therefore be drawn between the
ethnography of speech and the sociology of education: speech is a means
of empowerment, but it marginalizes those who use it, placing them
within a suspect "caste"; education empowers but also marginalizes, by
subordinating women to new structures of confinement.

At the same time, Robertson seems to assume, curiously, that literacy
brings with it "awareness" and "self-confidence."[65] One assumes that
this would be a different institution of literacy from the one currently
available to women in francophone Africa. At least for the women described by Nguessan, literacy per se seems to be only part of a larger
pattern of marginalization. The problem is that literacy does bring with
it predetermined *awarenesses* (in the plural), ideologies, and influences.
So, again, the question becomes, Why would francophone women want
to join this tradition? What is to be gained?

Coming to Writing

Comment n'aurais-je pas eu le désir d'écrire? Alors que les livres me pren-
aient, me transportaient, me perçaient jusqu'aux entrailles, me donnaient à
sentir leur puissance désintéressée. . . .
     Tu peux désirer. Tu peux lire, adorer, être envahie. Mais écrire ne t'est
pas accordé. Ecrire était réservé aux élus. Cela devrait
se passer dans un espace inaccessible aux petits, aux humbles,
aux femmes.
,—Hélène Cixous, "La venue à l'écriture"[66]

The participation of women in literature overcomes an asymmetry, a dis-
juncture between class status and gender status. Writing of any sort in
Africa enjoys prestige; literary, published writing, as in the West, naturally is marked as the most esoteric and privileged. In turn, the novel
seems to exercise the most powerful "voice" among the literary genres.
In Africa as in the West, books are a synecdoche for the cult of progress

64. Claire Robertson, "Women's Education," 92, 110. Risa S. Ellovich asserts that "the
move to the city and often into the modern sector as well has reduced rather than increased
the status of Dioula women" ("Dioula Women in Town: A View of Intra-Ethnic Variation
[Ivory Coast]," in Erika Bourgignon, ed., *A World of Women: Anthropological Studies of
Women in the Societies of the World* [New York: Praeger, 1980]: 87).

65. "Most women are too desperately busy assuring the survival of themselves and their
families to spend time either on self-improvement or political action, and their illiteracy
may limit the awareness and self-confidence that would facilitate their involvement in either
activity" (112).

66. In Hélène Cixous, Madeleine Gagnon, Annie Leclerc, *La Venue à l'écriture* (Paris:
Union Générale d'Editions, 1977): 20–21.

through learning. The desire to overcome exclusion from this mode of expression is the desire to fill a vacuum.

I would like to examine the connotations and consequences of women's writing, through a consideration of certain texts and pronouncements. The question I would like to address is that of the relation of Senegalese women writers to the literary mode of production. This will entail an analysis of Mariama Bâ's positions and statements on writing. In the text of her first novel, *Une Si Longue Lettre*, and in other utterances, Bâ described and enacted a distinct philosophy of writing. The explicitness of her position on writing, and on women's issues as well, would appear to place her in the role of leader, and, posthumously, of prophet: she seems to speak and to write as the founder of a tradition that is to come. In light of the information provided by Koumé Nguessan and Claire Robertson, I would like to frame the question of women and the production of literature in the following manner: does literary writing enfranchise or marginalize? to what collectivity is the African woman writer accountable (ethnicity, gender, class, race)? I will look for answers to these questions by considering issues of material form, genre, publishing, and stylistic address.

I have already explored the first stage of African women's relation to the francophone literary mode of production, the stage of exclusion. Mariama Bâ summed up her views in what to my knowledge is her only published lecture, on "the political function of African literatures":

> Dans toutes les cultures, la femme qui revendique ou proteste est dévalorisée. Si *la parole qui s'envole marginalise la femme*, comment jugera-t-on celle qui ose fixer pour l'éternité sa pensée? C'est dire la réticence des femmes à devenir écrivain.

> In all cultures, the woman who demands or protests is devalued. If *the speech which flies away marginalizes women*, how will the woman who dares to put her thoughts down for eternity be judged? Hence the reluctance of women to become writers.[67]

Confirming the asymmetry of gender even within African orality, Bâ implies that things only get worse after the transition to literacy. She repeated this view and expanded on it in an interview printed in the Dutch translation of *Une Si Longue Lettre*:

> The woman writer in Africa has a special task. She has to present the position of women in Africa in all its aspects. . . . As women, we must work for our own future, we must overthrow the status quo which harms us and we must no longer

67. "La Fonction politique des littératures africaines écrites," *Ecriture française dans le monde* 3, no. 1 (May 1981): 6.

submit to it. *Like men, we must use literature as a non-violent but effective weapon. We no longer accept the nostalgic praise to the African Mother who, in his anxiety, man confuses with Mother Africa.*[68]

Any doubts as to a basic feminism among African writers should be dispelled by these remarks (although the conformity to any Western definition of feminism, as we shall see, is not absolute). African women writers have "a particular mission."[69] Mariama Bâ invokes the possibility of a new relation to the literary mode: militant but nonviolent, committed to difference. When she says, "Like men . . . ," Bâ is apparently comparing the current struggle of women to the anticolonial struggle of male writers; she implicitly acknowledges the historical reality of "first things first." But she also calls for a gender-specific mode of writing, a "special task" identified with the condition of women in Africa. One of the most interesting aspects of these remarks is the suggestion of an antiallegorical agenda: women writers would not follow Senghor in confusing African mothers with Mother Africa, for when the former becomes the latter, a rhetoric of exploitation seems to assert itself. Bâ thus addresses the question of women writing as a form of empowerment, of demarginalization and enfranchisement.

Her vision of literary literacy thus conforms to Claire Robertson's linkage of literacy to self-confidence and self-assertion. But she does not anticipate any of the negative consequences that Robertson and Nguessan attribute to education in general. Once literacy reaches the level of *literature*, it offers a promise to transcend its class origins and reach out to the whole of society. This impulse to re-enfranchise the illiterate within literary diegesis is basic to African literatures (it can also lead to a conversion from literature to film, as in the case of Ousmane Sembène). Like others before her, Bâ finds in francophone literacy the *promise* of selfhood, the assurance that writing redeems and uplifts groups that it represents, whether those groups are literate or illiterate. Her first novel, *Une Si Longue Lettre*, both sustains and subverts this thesis.

If Bâ is a "feminist,"[70] Aminata Sow Fall, who since Bâ's death in 1981

68. Quoted in Schipper, "Mother Africa," 46–47, emphasis mine. In "La fonction politique," Bâ writes: "Les chants nostalgiques dédiés à la mère africaine confondue dans les angoisses d'homme à la Mère Afrique ne nous suffisent plus" (7). Strangely, the text of the Dutch interview and that of the Bâ essay appear to be in part identical.

69. "Plus qu'ailleurs, le contexte social africain étant caractérisé par l'inégalité criante entre l'homme et la femme, par l'exploitation et l'oppression séculaires et barbares du sexe dit faible, la femme-écrivain a une mission particulière" ("La Fonction politique," 6).

70. Aminata Maïga Ka says that Bâ is a feminist, a "defender of women" ("Ramatoulaye, Aïssatou, Mireille et . . . Mariama Bâ," *Notre Librairie* 81 [October-December, 1985]: 134): "Le féminisme de l'auteur de fait aucun doute. Mariama Bâ à travers son oeuvre, est le défenseur de la femme, écrasée sous le poids des traditions et refoulée par la

has been the leading Senegalese woman writer, takes a cautious distance in regard to that term. Fall states that she is not a feminist "in the sense that people mean" (leaving open the possibility that she is a feminist in some other sense); that she is not a "feminist militant"; that she has "not been influenced by the feminist current"; and that the International Women's Year of 1975 had nothing to do with her coming to write.[71] At the same time, Fall affirms a general, positive value of writing, which she justifies as an act of "witnessing, a way of filtering the social reality of a certain moment."[72] For both Bâ and Fall, writing serves a positive social function, however it may be defined, whomever it may serve. The coming of women to writing in the mid-1970s is thus universally taken as a moment of "emergence" and self-assertion, the end of silence. Writing is "a powerful means of dissemination, of reaching the people with information; an effective tool for consciousness-raising [*conscientisation*]."[73]

In an autobiographical statement, Bâ describes her experience with French colonial education as a positive one, as a means of upward mobility for the first daughter of a civil servant to "do things differently." Two Frenchwomen had a particularly strong impact on her; of Mme Germaine Le Goff, Bâ says, "Her discourse outlined the new Africa." Her father was "a man of finance but also a man of letters"; "my father taught me to read. A flood of books accompanied his homecomings."[74] In this milieu, the book acquires a symbolic value far in excess of the messages it contains; the book stands for social mobility and promotion.

Mariama Bâ's *Une Si Longue Lettre* appears as somewhat of a manifesto and as an exemplification of this view of writing: what the novel has to say about writing gives the text an aura of prophecy, as the harbin-

---

modernité." Cf. Dorothy S. Blair: "*Une Si Longue Lettre* is the first truly feminist African novel" (*Senegalese Literature: A Critical History* [Boston: Twayne, 1984]: 139).

71. "Je n'ai pas été influencée par le courant du féminisme. Pour la bonne raison que moi, je ne suis pas féministe dans le sens où l'entendent les gens" (Interview in Kembe Milolo, *L'Image de la femme chez les romancières de l'Afrique noire francophone* [Saint-Paul Fribourg: Editions Universitaires Fribourg Suisse, 1986]: 293–94). Milolo emphasizes the Women's Year as a factor in the emergence of women writers (52), but Fall points out that her first novel, *Le Revenant*, was already completed and awaiting publication in 1972.

72. Sonia Lee, interview with Aminata Sow Fall, *African Literature Association Bulletin* 14, no. 4 (Fall 1988): 24.

73. Milolo, *L'Image de la femme*, 41.

74. "Mariama Bâ on Her Life," 7. On the subject of Bâ's biography, and in considering the belated entry of women in the literary tradition, it would be wrong to ignore the fact that Mariama Bâ had nine children and a career as a teacher before turning to novelwriting. In regard to her training in French schools, she wrote in "La Fonction politique": "Fruit de l'école coloniale et femme travailleuse, épouse et mère, je n'ai pu m'évader du carcan de formation hier imposé" (3).

ger of a general coming of women to writing (the production of a corpus) and perhaps even of a *canon* that is to come. This will be the reading of *Une Si Longue Lettre* that I will propose here. Adjourning for the moment the important questions of genre and address, I would like to examine the statements made about writing in this novel.

Ramatoulaye is the fictive author of *Une Si Longue Lettre*, an epistolary novel consisting of one letter addressed to a friend, Aïssatou, divorced and living in New York. In the middle of the novel, Ramatoulaye "reminds" Aïssatou (in fact, Bâ informs the reader) of Aïssatou's brave decision to leave her husband and reorganize her life by herself. The following passage links literacy and self-determination:

> Et tu partis. Tu eus le surprenant courage de t'assumer. Tu louas une maison et t'y installas. Et, au lieu de regarder en arrière, tu fixas l'avenir obstinément. Tu t'assignas un but difficile; et plus que ma présence, mes encouragements, *les livres te sauvèrent*. Devenus ton refuge, ils te soutinrent.
>
> Puissance des livres, invention merveilleuse de l'astucieuse intelligence humaine. Signes divers, associés en sons; sons différents qui moulent le mot. Agencement de mots d'où jaillit l'idée, la Pensée, l'Histoire, la Science, la Vie. Instrument unique de relation et de culture, *moyen inégalé de donner et de recevoir*. Les livres soudent des générations au même labeur continu qui fait progresser. Ils te permirent de te hisser. Ce que la société te refusait, ils te l'accordèrent: des examens passés avec succès te menèrent toi aussi, en France. L'Ecole d'Interprétariat, d'où tu sortis, permit ta nomination à l'Ambassade du Sénégal aux Etats-Unis.

> And you left. You had the surprising courage to take your life into your own hands. You rented a house and set up home there. And instead of looking backwards, you looked resolutely to the future. You set yourself a difficult task; and more than just my presence and my encouragement, *books saved you*. Having become your refuge, they sustained you.
>
> The power of books, this marvellous invention of astute human intelligence. Various signs associated with sound: different sounds that form the word. Juxtaposition of words from which springs the idea, Thought, History, Science, Life. Sole instrument of interrelationships and of culture, *unequaled means of giving and receiving*. Books knit generations together in the same continuing effort that leads to progress. They enabled you to better yourself [to raise yourself up]. What society refused you, they granted: examinations taken and passed brought you to France as well. The School of Interpreters, from which you graduated, led to your appointment into the Senegalese Embassy in the United States.[75]

75. Mariama Bâ, *Une Si Longue Lettre* (Dakar: Nouvelles Editions Africaines, 1976): 50–51; trans. Modupé Bodé-Thomas, *So Long a Letter* (London: Heinemann, 1981): 32, AT, emphasis mine. Further page references to the novel and its translation will appear in the text in that order.

Antilogocentrists may squirm. Once the word literacy is acknowledged to have a plural form, once the task is recognized to be the analysis of specific *literacies*,[76] the conditions of Senegalese women's lives can no longer be ignored in any reading of their views on writing. Bâ does not tell us what books Aïssatou is supposed to have read; it does not seem to matter. Books gave her access to the outside world, to a world outside the Senegalese institution of marriage, which, according to *Une Si Longue Lettre*, demands the submission and silence of women. It is of no pressing concern to Ramatoulaye—nor apparently to Bâ—that the outside is the West; that literacy is in French; that liberation came only through physical alienation from Africa. Aïssatou, as the fictive reader within the epistolary framework, stands in the place of the real reader of the novel; her place in the West and specifically in the United States makes of her an appropriate "double" for many readers of *So Long a Letter* (the translation). At the same time, the distance from Senegal to America is maintained by Aïssatou's absence from the text as a writer of letters. She is purely a reader who has not yet read.

The infatuation with writing in the quotation above seems to have two levels: first, a fascination with the power of writing to produce allegorical entities (Thought, History, Science, Life), and second, the implicit recognition of inequality ("unequaled means of giving and receiving"). If literacy is unequaled it is also *unequal*, asymmetrical in its ability to promote and "save"; it is unequaled by *orality*; the letter and the book "give and receive" best.[77] Some are more saved than others. Clearly, the straightforward praise of literacy is the conscious message of the text, while inequality resides in its "political unconscious."

If the good working order of the novel—and of Senegalese literate feminism in general—is to be maintained, women's self-assertion and self-promotion through literacy cannot fully escape this relation to the outside world. For someone engaged in a struggle, it is less important to know where the ethical imperative originated than how it is to be achieved. Furthermore, if Aïssatou is branded a cultural traitor for hav-

76. See Brian Street, *Literacy in Theory and Practice* (Cambridge: Cambridge University Press, 1984), and Christopher L. Miller, selection from the symposium, "Literacy, Reading and Power," *Yale Journal of Criticism* 2, no. 1 (Fall 1988): 225–30.

77. In the symposium excerpt referred to above, I misread the text of *Une Si Longue Lettre*, mistakenly quoting "moyen inégal" where the text is "moyen inégalé." The present interpretation attempts to correct that misreading. This passage from *Une Si Longue Lettre* finds an interesting reverberation in a text written by another Senegalese woman writer, Catherine N'Diaye: *Gens de sable* (Paris: P.O.L., 1984), in a chapter entitled "Le Livre-Objet:" "Avant de se définir d'une quelconque autre façon, le livre est un objet; un objet qui ouvre la voie au fétichisme le plus aigu, le plus exacerbé" (123).

ing left her husband and Senegal, and if literacy as Bâ describes it is taken
to be invalid as an African means of expression, then nothing can change.
Bâ's version of literacy does not shy away from its debt to French education or the French technology of the book; both Bâ and her characters
elaborately celebrate the value of education and writing. Mohamadou
Kane points out that (male) francophone writers unanimously subscribe
to the belief that education is "the surest means of women's emancipation."[78] Francophone literacy is a lever that Mariama Bâ uses to advance
the cause of the dispossessed, even if it is only one group of relatively
privileged women for whom she speaks.[79] It did not take long for anti-
feminist critics to accuse Mariama Bâ of Eurocentrism.[80]

Attention to the question of Europe, and specifically of the influence
of French feminism on francophone African women writers, is invited by
the resemblance between, on the one hand, Bâ's elegy to writing and
remarks on the repression of women who dare "fix their thoughts for
eternity," and on the other hand, the quotation from Cixous that is the
epigraph to this section. A full mapping of the "influence" or intercultural relations between French feminism and African women writers goes
beyond the scope of this chapter (and my competence), although such a
study is sorely needed. While I have no idea whether Bâ ever read "La
venue à l'écriture," I take the echo to be more than coincidental. According to Toril Moi's analysis, this passage in Cixous represents one of the
"metaphysical" moments of faith in "writing as voice, presence and
origin."[81] The fact that this reflects only one side of Cixous's continually shifting thought—the other side being "a Derridean emphasis
on textuality as difference"—says something about the luxury of self-
contradiction and *disponibilité* (see Moi, 125) that Cixous enjoys and Bâ
did not. Moi raises the issue of luxury with reference to Cixous's habit
of wearing ermine in her classroom appearances in Paris: "Ermine as
emancipation: it is odd that women of the Third World have been so
ludicrously slow to take up Cixous's sartorial strategy" (126). The intellectual emulation, if any, must of course be limited as well, and at the

78. Kane, "Le féminisme," 195.

79. Claire Robertson points out that "class" analysis and gender analysis in Africa do
not always obtain the same result: a husband and wife may have entirely different relations
to the mode of production and therefore belong, technically, to different "classes" ("Wom-
en's Education," 111).

80. See Femi Ojo-Ade, "Still a Victim? Mariama Bâ's *Une si longue lettre*," *African
Literature Today* 12 (1982): 71–87: "Ramatoulaye's middle-class origins are to her a
source of pride and her commitment as a pioneer is, first and foremost, to that class." See
commentary on Ojo-Ade in Schipper, "Women and Literature in Africa," 52–54.

81. Toril Moi, *Sexual/Textual Politics: Feminist Literary Theory* (London: Routledge,
1985): 119.

conclusion of this chapter I will return to the question of the limitations and strictures within which Bâ seems to operate.[82]

Epistolarity and Marginality

J'écris plus pour moi que pour vous, je ne cherche qu'à me soulager.
—*Lettres portugaises*, 88

The organization and generic status of *Une Si Longue Lettre* are at least as important as any explicit message it conveys. Mineke Schipper has pointed out that the epistolary novel is "little practiced in Africa," almost nonexistent in anglophone Africa, and rarely seen in the francophone tradition; Mbye Cham says that "Mariama Bâ's use of the letter form is unparalleled in its method and system in African literature."[83] *Une Si Longue Lettre*—consisting of one letter in twenty-seven chapters—thus represents an anomaly. Beyond the narratological questions that Bâ's epistolarity poses (which Schipper deals with), we have to look for the significance of Mariama Bâ's stance, the position that she was taking in relation to the rest of the francophone corpus. An informal but, I believe, fairly comprehensive survey of the corpus (not the canon) reveals a total of five epistolary novels, if by that term we mean simply those novels that present themselves as written in one or more letters. In fact, one of the five is called *Lettres de ma cambuse* (after Daudet), but does not use letter form at all;[84] two others were published after *Une Si Longue Lettre*.[85] Only two out of the five depict an actual exchange of letters: Lopes' *Sans tam-tam* (published after Bâ's novel) and a thirty-two-page

82. On the coming to writing of postcolonial women, see also Trinh T. Minh-ha, *Woman, Native, Other: Writing Postcoloniality and Feminism* (Bloomington: Indiana University Press, 1989), chapter 1, "Commitment from the Mirror-Writing Box," 5–44.

83. Mineke Schipper, " ' Who Am I?' Fact and Fiction in African First-Person Narrative," *Research in African Literatures* 16, no. 1 (Spring 1985): 53–79. Schipper surveys various first-person narratives in both fictional and nonfictional genres. Mbye Cham, "Contemporary Society and the Female Imagination: A Study of the Novels of Mariama Bâ," in Eldred Durosimi Jones, ed., *Women in African Literature Today* (Trenton, N.J.: Africa World Press, 1987): 100. I also benefitted from reading an anonymous unpublished manuscript, "Womanist Affinity and the Epistolary Novel: Mariama Bâ's *So Long a Letter* and Alice Walker's *The Color Purple*."

84. René Philombe, *Lettres de ma cambuse* (Yaoundé, Cameroun: Editions Abbia, 1964). The English translation of this work dispenses with the idea of letters altogether: *Tales from My Hut*, trans. Richard Bjornson (Yaoundé, Cameroun: Buma Kor, 1977).

85. Etoundi-M'Balla Patrice, *Lettre ouverte à Soeur Marie-Pierre* (Yaoundé, Cameroun: Editions CLE, 1978); this novel, like *Une si longue lettre*, consists of one letter; and Henri Lopes, *Sans tam-tam* (Yaoundé, Cameroun: Editions CLE, 1977).

pamphlet novel published by an obscure press in Zaïre, *Lettres kinoises (roman épistolaire)*.[86] This means that when Mariama Bâ was writing *Une Si Longue Lettre*, there were only two epistolary novels in the corpus before her: a fairly well-known classic by Bernard Dadié, *Un Nègre à Paris*,[87] and *Lettres kinoises*, which is virtually unknown. The only precursor with anything like canonical status, *Un Nègre à Paris*, is barely an epistolary novel: addressed to a vestigial reader who is not developed as a character, the novel reads like a journal addressed to a second person, until the writer signs "cordially yours" on the last page. Through a fitting irony, the French ancestor in the epistolary genre, *Lettres portugaises*, is the first exception to what will only later become the rule of exchange: Guilleragues' novel is also a one-way correspondence. The letter as a personal diary is, moreover, an ancient tradition.[88]

Une Si Longue Lettre, as its title indicates, uses the format of an epistolary novel that becomes more like a journal because there is no exchange of correspondence.[89] Bâ thus took a stance in regard to literary genre that placed her in a doubly marginal position: marginal in relation to the francophone corpus, which eschews epistolarity; and marginal in relation to the European epistolary genre, which normally represents an exchange of letters.

The significance of Bâ's stance in regard to genre cannot be appraised without a survey of the thematic concerns of *Une Si Longue Lettre*. Ramatoulaye is a middle-aged woman, the mother of twelve children, whose husband (Modou Fall) has just died. Confined to her house for the ritual four months and ten days of mourning required by Islam, Ramatoulaye opens a copybook (*cahier*) and begins the letter to Aïssatou as "a prop in my distress" ("point d'appui dans mon désarroi" [7; 1]). Writing is thus defined from the beginning as a process of self-reconstruction, compared to the daily exchange of messages between Ramatoulaye's and Aïssatou's grandmothers over the fence between their yards (and analogous

86. Nsimba Mumbamuna, *Lettres kinoises (roman épistolaire)* (Kinshasa, Zaïre: Centre Africain de Littérature, 1974).

87. Paris: Présence Africaine, 1959.

88. See Janet Gurking Altman, "The Letter Book as a Literary Institution 1539–1789: Toward a Cultural History of Published Correspondences in France," *Yale French Studies* 71 (1986): 47.

89. The journal or diary novel is relatively well known in the francophone tradition. The most famous example may be Ferdinand Oyono's classic anticolonial satire, *Une Vie de boy* (Paris: René Julliard, 1956); but what critics have not pointed out is the extent to which Oyono twists the journal format into a far more novelistic shape, allowing the boy who is supposed to be writing the journal to hold greater narratological authority than is "realistic." We will see that Mariama Bâ follows a similar pattern of deviation from a generic norm in *Une si longue lettre*. On journal novels, see Schipper, "'Who am I?'" 64–68.

to one theme of *Lettre portugaises*, as seen in the epigraph above). The first page of the novel therefore establishes a dialectic between exchange (the first words are: "Aïssatou, I've received your letter") and self-reflexivity ("I close my eyes. Ebb and tide of images").

Modou Fall died, interestingly, while dictating a letter to his secretary. Ramatoulaye relates the events surrounding his death and vents her resentment of Senegalese customs, which place the widow at the mercy of her in-laws. At the root of her feelings is the outrage that Modou Fall committed after twenty-five years of marriage: he took as a second wife the best friend of his own daughter, placing the mother of twelve out of his fifteen children in an untenable position.[90] Much of the text is devoted to remembering and working through the hurt caused by this offense.

Ramatoulaye's background is doubly privileged: she is from one of the great noble families, and she is a professional, a teacher, and therefore part of the literate elite. She drives a car, and her husband has enough money to buy an Alfa-Romeo and a villa (on credit) for Binetou, the second wife. Binetou is depicted as a spoiled brat and an *arriviste*, inferior in terms of class because her mother "was more concerned with putting the pot on the boil than with education" (72; 48). Not divorced but rather abandoned by her husband, Ramatoulaye begins a life that could come from one of the testimonies in Awa Thiam's *La Parole aux Négresses*: she lives alone and supports herself; she is often the only woman waiting in line to pay a bill; and as a "middle-aged lady without a partner" (76; 50), she is often stared at. She testifies to "the slender liberty granted to women." But she does not seek divorce, because she has "never conceived of happiness outside marriage" (82; 56), and she continues to look for the fault within herself. By the fortieth day, she has forgiven Modou; but when on that day Modou's brother proposes marriage, Ramatoulaye breaks "thirty years of silence" and refuses to be treated as "an object to be passed from hand to hand" (84; 58). She turns back a stream of other suitors, including Daouda Dieng, who is a nobleman, medical doctor, and member of the National Assembly. She refuses him because she does not really love him and because he already has a wife. Ramatoulaye ends her period of confinement with reflections on "the superiority of friendship over love," emphasizing the importance of the absent Aïssatou to the recuperation process (104; 22). As the last chapter closes, Ramatoulaye looks forward to meeting Aïssatou in person the next day and handing her the copybook that we are reading (which

90. The practice of a man marrying a woman of his own daughter's age is referred to as a problem in Solange Faladé's "Women of Dakar and the Surrounding Urban Area," in Denise Paulme, ed., *Women of Tropical Africa*, trans. H. M. Wright (Berkeley: University of California Press, 1963): 226.

complicates its status as "letter"). The tone of the ending is sharply different from the beginning: Ramatoulaye celebrates the liberation of women as an emergence "from the shadows" (129; 88), while at the same time she reaffirms the "inevitable and necessary complementarity of man and woman." Love between man and woman is "the natural link" that constitutes the family, which in turn is the building-block of "the Nation" (her use of the capital): "The success of a nation therefore depends inevitably on the family" (130; 89). The critical thrust of Ramatoulaye's thoughts lies in a limited critique of polygamy and of the exclusion of women from high government positions.[91]

Meanwhile, the story of Aïssatou's marriage runs parallel to the main narration. In chapters 8 through 12, Ramatoulaye "tells" Aïssatou her own story and reflects on it for the benefit of the real reader (as opposed to the fictive reader, Aïssatou). For the remainder of the novel, the two stories are interwoven. Aïssatou is different from Ramatoulaye in one important respect: she is a person of "caste," part of one endogamous subset of the Wolof *gnegno* (equivalent to the Mande *nyamakala*), respected and stigmatized for the powers they wield.[92] Aïssatou's marriage to a nobleman, Mawdo Bâ, is a scandalous form of miscegenation; Mawdo's mother, the princess Nabou, says so ("this cursed daughter of a goldsmith, worse than a *griot* woman" [42; 26]). Separated by the traditional barrier of caste, Ramatoulaye and Aïssatou are united by profession and class: both are part of an "army" marching to "plant everywhere the flag of knowledge and morality" (38; 22). By her marriage to a nobleman (*ger* in Wolof), Aïssatou associated herself with a higher station than that of her birth; by her participation in the education process—the march toward literacy—Aïssatou becomes "noble" in a new, reformed sense of

91. Bâ's position on polygamy is that it is "evil" as such, but that the "polygamous instinct" is "innate in every man" (quoted in interview with Barbara Arnhold, *Afrika* [Munich] 12 [1980]: 23). In an interview with Barbara E. Harrell-Bond, Bâ says, "I do not think that men *can* be sexually faithful. . . . All men. I believe in the fidelity of women as strongly as I am skeptical about the fidelity of men" ("An Interview with Mariama Bâ," *American Universities Field Staff Reports* 10 [1981], issue intitled "Africa Asserts its Identity": 10). See also Cyril Mokwenyé, "La polygamie et la révolte de la femme africaine moderne: Une lecture d'*Une Si Longue Lettre* de Mariama Bâ," *Peuples noirs, peuples africains* 6, no. 31 (January-February 1983): 86–94.

92. On the hierarchized system of "caste" relations (and cautions on the advisability of the term "caste"), see Leymarie, "The Role and Functions of the Griots," especially chapter 5, "The Griots' Position in the System of Social Stratification," 111–48; and Diop, *La société wolof*, 33–107. It should be understood that when Aïssatou is referred to as a *bijoutière* it does not refer to her profession (she is a teacher), but rather to her "caste" status. The word *bijoutière* could be considered a translation of the Wolof *tög*, designating males whose traditional métier is blacksmithing and jewelry making and females who are traditionally potters and hairdressers (Leymarie, 122).

the word.[93] For at least one Senegalese reader, Bâ's egalitarian views on caste are a very salient aspect of her work.[94]

Mawdo's mother, Nabou, schemes to subvert the marriage, which has already produced four children: seeking sameness of caste, so that "the blood" may "return to its source," she takes possession of her brother's daughter, also named Nabou, and curries her for marriage to Mawdo. (The oversameness—just short of incest—of this marriage to a first cousin has not been examined by any critic.) "Little Nabou" thus corresponds to Ramatoulaye's rival, Binetou, but Little Nabou distinguishes herself by entering the highly respected profession of midwifery. Mawdo reacts passively to his mother's initiatives and finds himself married to Nabou, living a double life. Aïssatou then does the unthinkable, she leaves her husband and begins the independent life in which literacy plays such an important role (it is at this point that the passage on books, quoted above, begins). Three years after this, Ramatoulaye's life is shattered by Modou's second marriage.

Along with the thematic structure of the novel, Bâ wrote herself into a singularly interesting position in regard to the epistolary genre. If, for purposes of argument, we take Janet Gurkin Altman's *Epistolarity: Approaches to a Form* as the description of a European formal code, *Une Si Longue Lettre* can be seen to represent a dialectic between borrowing from Europe and deviating from European norms. (The Europe/Africa opposition is inevitable here, since the epistolary genre is distinctly *not* African.) The most striking resonance of her choice of genre is its "gender." Epistolarity in Europe has not been a "woman's genre," but it has been described as a mode of writing that has played a privileged role in the history of writing by women.[95] Presently I will address the question of gender, genre, and the canon. But before that, I would like to describe how Bâ deviates from the epistolary "norm."

First of all, the absence of a real exchange of letters between Ramatoulaye and Aïssatou compromises what Altman calls "the epistolary pact," which is the relation to the other: "If there is no desire for exchange, the writing does not differ significantly from a journal" (*Epistolarity*, 89). This is precisely the case with *Une Si Longue Lettre*, although it would not appear to be the desire that is lacking, but the possibility. Ramatoulaye is confined and writes to create a simulacrum of contact with the outside world, with her friend. Exchange is blocked by the Islamic cus-

93. Teachers constitute "une armée *noble*" (38; 22, emphasis mine).
94. Aminata Maïga Ka, "Ramatoulaye, Aïssatou", 134.
95. See Ruth Perry, *Women, Letters, and the Novel* (New York: AMS Press, 1980); Patricia Meyer Spacks, "Female Resources: Epistles, Plot, and Power," *Persuasions* 9 (De-

tom of confinement of the widow, so Ramatoulaye constructs artificial exchanges, in which others speak and write through her recollections.

This produces a second kind of deviation, a general overextension of Ramatoulaye's knowledge and narrative authority, allowing her to quote conversations and letters that she "couldn't have known." In other words, verisimilitude is compromised. Ramatoulaye's consciousness reaches beyond the confines of her house and embraces anything necessary to advance the novel's progress. Altman refers to a technique found in *Les Liaisons dangereuses* (the Marquise de Merteuil's favorite trick) of quoting a correspondent's letters back to him; Bâ has Ramatoulaye quote (to Aïssatou) the letter that Aïssatou wrote to Mawdo to break off their marriage. Ramatoulaye says "I remember the exact words," and she quotes it in its entirety. Ramatoulaye often "reminds" Aïssatou of facts that would not need to be repeated between two friends, both Senegalese, who have shared a life together. This interlarding of information for the real reader's benefit reveals the compromise between epistolarity and narration that Bâ practices. The violation of the limited vision that epistolarity requires is plainly visible when Ramatoulaye tells the story of old Nabou's trip to the hinterlands to find Little Nabou; Ramatoulaye uses the supremely narrative technique of free indirect discourse to render old Nabou's inner thoughts as she travels alone (thoughts that Ramatoulaye "couldn't" know).[96] Epistolary discourse is further disrupted when Ramatoulaye begins a chapter by addressing her dead husband directly and without a pronoun antecedent ("Do you remember . . . ?" [24; 13]).

It would be all too easy to cast these deviations as "failures." Bâ could be said to have "failed" to adequately resolve the epistolary novelist's fundamental problem, that of reconciling "the exigencies of story (communication betweeen novelist and reader) with the exigencies of interpersonal discourse (communication between correspondents)."[97] However,

---

cember 1987): 88–98. On the French side, see Altman's analysis of published correspondences, in "The Letter Book"; see especially her attention to the first missive letter book, written by a woman to "defend and illustrate her sex" (27). Cf. Trinh: "The personal diary form . . . remains an effective means of self-expression for women to whom other avenues are often closed . . . but, looking at the diary exlusively as a means of self-expression is already a distortion and a confinement" (*Woman, Native, Other*, 35).

96. "Dans le car et sur la piste cahotante, avec émotion, elle [Nabou] se retranchait dans ses souvenirs. . . . Ton existence, Aïssatou, ne ternira jamais sa noble descendance, jura-t-elle" (43-45/27–28). The last sentence exhibits the doubling of address in *Une Si Longue Lettre*: direct address to Aïssatou as "tu," while at the same time narrating the inner thoughts of a third person as "live" thoughts, in the future tense (as in stream of consciousness). The English translation loses this double effect by changing the future tense to the future-in-the-past use of the conditional: "She swore that your existence, Aissatou, *would* never tarnish her noble descent" (emphasis mine).

97. Altman, *Epistolarity*, 210.

my question is not how well did Bâ adhere to a European standard but what is the significance both of her choice and of her departures from it.

It is important to note that these deviations operate in two registers at the same time. Thematically and culturally, they allow Ramatoulaye to better escape her confinement through writing, to embrace the world and Aïssatou, and to reconstruct a sense of selfhood (by which I mean that she describes herself as "emerging from the shadows"). Whether or not her confinement actually prevents her from mailing this letter and entering into an exchange of letters with Aïssatou, such an exchange would have to be minimal in the time allotted, so the one-letter format is the most plausible fiction. The liberties that Ramatoulaye takes permit her to transcend the format that is imposed on her by the situation. In terms of literary technique, these deviations alter the (European) epistolary norm and the demands of verisimilitude. Altman's complex description of the genre allows for its self-disruption, but within the polarities she analyzes, the genre remains "relatively codified."[98] *Une Si Longue Lettre* locates itself at the margins of that code by consistently breaking away from its logic and requirements. The two movements operate together and complement each other: European-language literacy and the European epistolary genre constitute a lever used against male domination (within the novel, domination of Ramatoulaye by a patriarchal culture, and outside the novel, domination of the francophone corpus by male authors). And deviations from European literary norms serve to strengthen Ramatoulaye's role as narrator, as someone in command of her own history. *Une Si Longue Lettre* is thus a peculiar hybrid, representing an original act of literary creativity, a brilliant departure.

It is dangerous to indulge in analogies between European and African cultural forms; the comparison often takes on an insidious life of its own. But the history of epistolarity in the West seems so relevant to this context that it cannot be ignored. Altman says that epistolarity "tends to flourish . . . at crisis moments," when writers begin to question writing (212). Others have pointed out the particular importance of the epistolary form for women writers; at certain points in European history, the letter novel is said to have allowed women to live vicariously, through "events of consciousness."[99] For Ruth Perry, the genre reflects women's

---

98. Altman, *Epistolarity*, 211. The polarities are 1) bridge/barrier (the mediatory property); 2) *confiance / non-confiance*; 3) writer/reader (the movement from private to public, evident in *Une Si Longue Lettre*); 4) I/You, here/there, now/then ("the impossible task of making present both events [through narration] and the addressee [through discursive address to a "you"])—this is the kind of conflict I pointed out in *Une Si Longue Lettre*; 5) closure/overture (the question of finality and ongoing dialogue); and 6) unit/unity, coherence/fragmentation (186–87).

99. *Women, Letters, and the Novel*, xii, 138.

alienation from the dominant means of production in seventeenth- and eighteenth-century English society (138). Discussing the African context, Carole Boyce Davies suggests that epistolarity may be part of "an overall female aesthetic." [100] But the most interesting bridge between commentaries on European, gender-based epistolarity and Mariama Bâ's original practice of it comes from Patricia Meyer Spacks, in her article on Jane Austen's *Lady Susan*. I will limit my comparison to the following phrases taken from Spacks:

> The conventional view of *Lady Susan* has it that Austen wrote awkwardly in the epistolary style. [The same could be said of *Une Si Longue Lettre*] . . . Yet by playing with epistolary convention in *Lady Susan*, I want to argue, Austen located herself in a female tradition, demonstrating subversive possibilities of a form that in previous uses by English women had reinforced literary and social restrictions on female enterprise. . . . *Lady Susan* realizes the possibility of a woman's exercising agency—partly by the act of writing letters. . . . Writing becomes a form of agency. (Spacks, "Female Resources," 89, 91)

One of points I have insisted on in this study is the dialectical ambiguity of literacy in various contexts. Here is a case in point. Disregarding all contextual differences, I would say that Mariama Bâ's practice in *Une Si Longue Lettre* bears a striking similarity to this interpretation of Austen. At a moment when the genre of the novel in Africa could hardly still be called a "European" form, Bâ took recourse to an anomalous subgenre, one which has a distinct history in Europe. By that act of borrowing, she set up a resonance with European women's epistolarity and aligned herself with a female tradition. Through the implications of her act and through Ramatoulaye's explicit statements in the novel, writing is associated with female agency and empowerment. So her choice of genre is implicitly subversive of the francophone African, all-male corpus (or canon).

But Bâ's work does not operate along gender lines alone. In addition, her manipulations of the genre and violations of its rules set her apart from the European tradition: by making an epistolary novel into a modified journal-novel, Bâ brings herself back into a dialogue with the francophone male tradition (which has a number of journal novels). The position that Mariama Bâ staked out for herself is unique, distinguishable from both the "European" female point of reference and the "African" male one. In effect, she has broken down that opposition between, on the one hand, "female" and "feminist" as uniquely European, and on the other hand, the francophone literary tradition as uniquely male. After *Une Si Longue Lettre*, it will be possible for the first time to think the terms "African," "woman," "francophone," "writer," and even "femi-

100. Carole Boyce Davies, introduction to *Ngambika*, 16.

nist" all together. Bâ showed us how to begin doing so, and that is why her writing is so important. She turned the double marginalization (by race and by gender) of her position as a writer into a doubly suggestive space for thinking. Mariama Bâ died in 1981 after completing her second novel (*Un Chant écarlate*),[101] but her contribution has already altered the course of francophone literature.

Projecting a Canon

"Femmes du Mandén, il ne nous reste plus qu'à réécrire notre histoire ou pourquoi pas, à être les véritables artisanes de l'histoire contemporaine africaine."
—*Le Tana de Soumangourou* [102]

I have discussed Mariama Bâ's practice in *Une Si Longue Lettre* as an alteration of the male corpus of francophone writings; by way of a conclusion, I would like to address the question of canonicity. I do not plan to resolve it or to translate into the African context all the questions that have been raised about canonicity in the United States. The debate is a peculiarly American one, and, as John Guillory's analysis reveals, it is one that is fraught with unexamined premises. The American debate on the canon presupposes an abundance of riches among which one might choose freely, a supermarket with thousands of products competing for attention. This includes widely dissimilar theoretical machines that are rolled out to support various positions. In Africa there is less numeric difference between the corpus (what is printed) and any canon, for the simple reason that the corpus is smaller by far; francophone literature has only been in production since 1920. Any consideration of the "canon" in Africa would have to begin with a survey of the material conditions governing publication and of the cultural and institutional criteria determining what is taught. There is no point in debating African canonicity unless one realizes how works are produced and what happens to them after they are printed.

It has already become apparent that books in Africa represent power and prestige. The literary subspecies—novels, plays, and poetry—represents an even more privileged mode. Mariama Bâ has given us one of the clearest explanations of this, showing exactly how writing and the book are esteemed, exactly how a nondominant group can use literacy to promote itself. If promotion is measured by commercial success, then

101. Dakar: Nouvelles Editions Africaines, 1981.
102. Ahmed-Tidjani Cissé, *Le Tana de Soumangourou* (Paris: Nubia, 1988): 47.

Une Si Longue Lettre, as a best-seller for Nouvelles Editions Africaines, promotes the collectivity of African women as it is sold.

But if books do what Ramatoulaye says they do, they nevertheless have other functions. By virtue of their mobility, books circulate in a wider economy and operate differently in new contexts. For francophone African literature, this means that the "outside" readership (non-Senegalese or non-African) is often larger than the local readership. Authors have known this from the beginning and have anticipated the needs of outside readers by adding explanatory remarks or notes. This is all known and acknowledged. But what is rarely alluded to, and what is most relevant here, is the importance of the translation and republication of francophone African fiction: the process by which these texts enter the American and anglophone market.

If Ngũgĩ wa Thiong'o writes in Gĩkũyũ and is published in Gĩkũyũ, it seems indisputable that he is working to "decolonise the mind."[103] But if his Gĩkũyũ-language texts are immediately translated into English and sold on a scale that dwarfs the original edition—especially if the original text is banned in Kenya, where Gĩkũyũ is spoken and read—then what has his writing become in its *material* dimensions? His anti-imperialist intention may be subverted by the forces of the market; the material text may be appropriated for mass consumption in English. This does not invalidate his project, it only raises questions about the fate of his work within the international marketplace: literature must be recognized to be a commodity; what cannot be bought cannot be read or "canonized." Ngũgĩ comes from one of the former British colonies, in which African-language literacy is far more developed and available to writers than in the francophone countries. Although Mariama Bâ wrote in a European language, there is an analogy to be drawn between the fate of Ngũgĩ's Gĩkũyũ texts and that of *Une Si Longue Lettre* in French. For Bâ was published by the newly-formed Nouvelles Editions Africaines, a consortium organized in 1973 by the Senegalese and Ivory Coast governments to promote African publication of African works (five French publishing houses nonetheless hold minority shares in the venture).[104] N.E.A. works to counter the centrality of Paris, which dominates the publishing of francophone African literature. But, as the beachhead of nationalized publishing in West Africa, N.E.A. faces tremendous problems: low levels of literacy, the low buying power of African readers, and the lack of book-

103. See Ngũgĩ wa Thiong'o, *Decolonising the Mind: The Politics of Language in African Literature* (London: James Currey, 1986).

104. See Adama Sow Dieye and Bernard Baritaud, "Autour du livre," *Notre Librairie* 81 (October-December 1985): 161.

stores outside a few major cities all make it difficult to bring works into print and keep them available.

However, certain texts, including *Une Si Longue Lettre,* even if they become unavailable in Africa, even if they fall out of print in French, meet another fate. They are immediately translated and republished for the worldwide English-language public, usually by Heinemann Educational Books in the tremendous African Writers Series (which constitutes "the pedagogical canon of anglophone Africa").[105] Whereas an average printing of a novel for N.E.A. runs to three thousand copies, Heinemann estimates that there are about twenty thousand copies of *So Long a Letter* in print, with "perhaps half of these in North America;" this does not include the copies in the British Virago edition.[106] One's chances of finding *Une Si Longue Lettre* on sale are far slimmer in Africa, France, and the United States than of finding *So Long a Letter.*[107] The American market for books exercises a certain power over African literature, a power that has not been analyzed. Just as the economic and political situation makes it nearly inevitable for scholars and writers like Maryse Condé, Edouard Glissant, V. Y. Mudimbe, and even Ngũgĩ to accept positions in American universities (thus constituting a real brain drain), the buying and reading power of the West and of the U.S. in particular tend to appropriate francophone texts. *Une Si Longue Lettre,* which was a "bestseller" for N.E.A., survives in the market as *So Long a Letter.*[108]

So the analysis of an African canon—particularly when done by an American critic—cannot ignore the forces of the market as they influence African literature. We face the distinct possibility that there are two "Af-

105. Appiah, "Out of Africa," 156.

106. The quotation is from a letter to me by John C. Watson, president of Heinemann Educational Books in Portsmouth, New Hampshire. I am grateful to Mr. Watson for providing this information. The information on print runs at Nouvelles Editions Africaines was given to me by Papa Gueye Ndiaye, president of the Senegalese branch of N. E. A., during an interview in January 1987, for which I am also grateful.

107. In the summer of 1989, I found only two copies of *Une Si Longue Lettre* in Paris, both in a specialized bookstore. The novel was never listed in *Les Livres disponibles,* the French *Books in Print.* Copies are nonetheless still in circulation and find their way into American classrooms.

108. The impact of economic conditions on literary texts shows up in Bâ's novel in a curious way. The original N.E.A. edition of *Une Si Longue Lettre* contains an editorial flaw: the chapters are misnumbered and go from 24 to 26, with no chapter 25. But in the Heinemann translation, the problem has disappeared. This is obviously a reflection of Heinemann's established and secure status as compared to N.E.A.'s tenuous foothold on the business. The translation "improved" the text but lost this sign of its material origins in the margins of francophone publishing. The misnumbering is a significant indicator, lost in translation.

rican" canons: one established and taught in Africa, the other in the United States (not to mention a third possible canon in France). Too often, American critics talk about the two as if they were the same. One of the differences between them would appear to be the importance given to women's writings: American instructors these days feel obliged to include women writers, whereas in Africa, gender issues and women writers are given less attention. Bernth Lindfors has surveyed the teaching of African literature in anglophone African universities and found that *Une Si Longue Lettre* (the only francophone woman's novel in the survey) was taught at six institutions in four countries.[109] But in spite of this impressive showing by Bâ, there is no doubt that women authors are not yet taught in proportion to their numbers; Christine Makward, presumably referring to what is taught in the West, states: "Literary francophone women do not exist in the canon."[110] My own experience and contacts in francophone Africa indicate that the teaching of any post-Independence African text is problematic, mostly for political reasons, and that women writers are hardly taught at all. As in the case of *Les Soleils des indépendances*, this will undoubtedly change as works like Mariama Bâ's grow older and lose their controversial edge.

A full account of what is canonical in Africa (or the United States) would require far more information about what is taught—more information than I have at my disposal. Lindfors finds that the African canon "is still in a state of creative gestation; hardly anything about it is fixed and immutable" (14). More surveys like his are necessary but would still not be sufficient, for one would then need to consider the uses of texts within pedagogical practices. Are African texts used as bearers of "values"—as some Americans say a canon must be used? I am not in a position to answer this question here, but by turning back to *Une Si Longue Lettre* I think we can see the kind of answer that Mariama Bâ herself may have suggested. (The fact that she did so in the context of a novel and not in a work of criticism only makes it more interesting.)

Une Si Longue Lettre espouses values unabashedly, unreservedly: Bâ is against silence, superstition, inequality, and dissoluteness; she is in favor of the advancement of women, friendship, and Morality (her capital

109. Bâ is one of six francophones in a list of thirty-five African authors. *So Long a Letter* is the twenty-second in a list of most-taught texts, of which only three are by women, but Bâ did not make it to a list of thirty-two "famous authors" from around the continent (Bernth Lindfors, "The Teaching of African Literature in Anglophone African Universities: A Preliminary Report," forthcoming. I am grateful to Bernth Lindfors for providing me with a copy of his text).

110. Christine Makward, with Odile Cazenave, "The Others' Others: Francophone Women's Writing," *Yale French Studies* 75 (1988): 190.

letter). Literacy is the vehicle that transmits these values, through education, and *Une Si Longue Lettre* is by implication an attempt to further their circulation. While it may be valid to claim on the theoretical level that the literary work is never a mere container of values (but rather the sign of their interrelationship),[111] it is equally imperative to recognize the need of suppressed groups to appropriate preexisting forms and use them. This means that Bâ's use of the novel as a container of values should be respected; to say that she should have been more radical—or to say that reform of the canon by teaching women writers like Bâ merely strengthens the resilience of the system—is to miss an essential point. Bâ makes her entrance into francophone literacy by changing only certain aspects of women's relation to the literary mode of production. She ends "silence" and exclusion; she borrows certain forms and twists them to her own needs. But her "radicalism" ends there: women's literature as she describes it will be a building-block of the family and the nation, beginning from a (re)construction of selfhood, an emergence from shadows. Women will write, but the values they espouse will pose no threat to the literary or economic system. Those who wish for something more radical will not find it among Senegalese women novelists, at least not yet.

Une Si Longue Lettre ends with the prefiguration of a moment of closure: in the last chapter of the letter, Ramatoulaye mentions that she will see Aïssatou the next day. One assumes that Aïssatou will be given the letter at that time, and that reading and talking will nearly coincide. That moment of closure remains outside the scope of the novel and cannot be represented. But the symbolic act of handing over this text to a friend seems to reinforce the positive image of literature that Bâ promotes: the text we are reading is a tangible sign of the link between the two women, and that link can lead to others. If enough links are made, if enough writing and reading brings people together under the sign of values, a kind of canon is formed. Books "knit [or weld] generations together in the same continuing effort that leads to progress" (51; 32). By asserting this, I would argue, Mariama Bâ is positing or projecting a tradition—and eventually, possibly, a canon. She is alluding to a reproduction of values through literature, the formation of a community of readers and writers.

Une Si Longue Lettre therefore prefigures a kind of canon and allows African women to think of bringing themselves together within the embrace of literacy. The novel wants us to believe in the closure that is supposed to take place after the book's end: in Aïssatou's sympathetic reading and even in the other readings that will take place and perhaps

---

111. See John Guillory, "Canonical and Non-Canonical," 487–88.

"knit generations together." The "wholesale reconsideration" of canonicity within the class system, which Cornel West calls for in the African-
American context, is therefore not what Mariama Bâ suggests.[112] Her
stance seems more analogous to that of Henry Louis Gates, who "borrows a leaf from the right, which is exemplarily aware of the role of
education in the reproduction of values."[113] Lillian Robinson describes
the choice confronting "the champions of women's literature" as an ex-
cruciating one, between "defending the quality of their discoveries" (that
is, women's writings), and "radically redefining literary quality itself";[114]
Bâ fits the former project more than the latter.

The intrinsic validity of either argument—the "radical" or the "liberal" one—is quite beside the point. The theoretical position that any
Western critic might take about "canonicity" (a theoretical issue involving the interrelation of innumerable literary works) is less important here
than what Mariama Bâ told us about women's literature in Senegal. I, for
example, find myself more compelled by Guillory's and West's arguments
than by Gates's, but only on the theoretical level. In the francophone
African context, the detachment necessary for a "wholesale reconsideration" seems an unlikely luxury—something of an ermine coat. "Radicalism" in regard to canonicity is the privilege of those with an abundance
of riches, available "wholesale."

What Mariama Bâ did was to *project*. As the first francophone woman
to address the question of women's writing—through her own writing—Bâ projected writing into a space that had been empty. Her confidence in the power of literature constitutes a faith in its healing and
redeeming powers, its ability to weld generations together. The performative, creative value of her work is in a way analogous to Ngũgĩ's nearly
single-handed creation of a Gĩkũyũ-language literature: working against
all odds, in the absence of a large readership, Ngũgĩ is laying the groundwork for a Gĩkũyũ corpus or canon that may follow. His act is all the
stronger because he ignores the irony of the marketplace I referred to
earlier; he ignores the hegemonic power of English and thereby makes it
thinkable to overcome that power in the future. Bâ and Ngũgĩ both position themselves as founders of traditions that they envision and prepare.

Various perspectives compete for the last word on Bâ's position. Cer-

112. Cornel West, "Minority Discourse and the Pitfalls of Canon Formation," *The Yale
Journal of Criticism* 1, no. 1 (Fall 1987): 197.
113. Henry Louis Gates, "Whose Canon Is It, Anyway?" *The New York Times Book
Review*, February 26, 1989: 45.
114. Lillian S. Robinson, "Treason Our Text: Feminist Challenges to the Literary
Canon," in Elaine Showalter, ed., *The New Feminist Criticism: Essays on Women, Literature, and Theory* (New York: Pantheon Books, 1985): 111.

tain American critical approaches suggest either that she was "wrong" about writing and values, or that one should look deeper to dig up the internal inconsistencies that may underly her argument. For example, by the fact that the act of closure cannot be represented inside *Une Si Longue Lettre* but must be projected beyond its ending, one could jump to the conclusion that closure is impossible within the language of literacy. This could then be extrapolated to the political level, to support a debunking of Bâ's faith in literacy: literacy in Africa never achieves closure with the masses. Robertson's social anthropology and Nguessan's insider's sociology invite skepticism about literacy, literature, and education; these studies cast a certain shadow over the optimism of *Une Si Longue Lettre* (Mariama Bâ belonged to a women's association called the Soeurs Optimistes Internationales).[115] They remind us of the precarious position of literature within the larger world: critics too often exaggerate the importance of literature, glossing over the difference between resolving a problem in print and resolving it in speech or politics. We like to think that we hear voices when we read. At the same time, we should recognize that Bâ sees literacy as providing the means to overcome the marginalization that education may cause: once one reaches a certain level of education—and that is the entire problem—books allow one to think one's way out of the margins, as Aïssatou did. Still, the sociologists make one wonder how many African women may find this to be helpful.

To assert the impossibility of closure is simply exceptional; it makes an essential point but misses much. *Une Si Longue Lettre*, like any novel, does have an "unconscious" level on which contradictions of this kind operate, lending complexity and nuance to the "conscious" message (while threatening to invalidate it). Closure does remain outside the grasp of language; speech is not recovered through writing; silence may not be overcome through books alone. Mariama Bâ seems deliberately to hold back from evoking any moment of closure, and her reluctance on this stands in interesting contrast to Alice Walker's epistolary novel, *The Color Purple*, with its vision of "(comm)unity."[116] For Bâ, closure remains hypothetical but eminently imaginable.

Une Si Longue Lettre operates within the frame of these conditions but also succeeds in pointing beyond them, to a (perhaps utopian) vision of communal progress. This is why I describe *Une Si Longue Lettre* as projective.

What has become of the project since Mariama Bâ's death? Writing by

115. Interview with Harrell-Bond, 11.

116. Michael Awkward, "*The Color Purple* and the Achievement of (Comm)unity," in his *Inspiriting Influences: Tradition, Revision and Afro-American Women's Novels* (New York: Columbia University Press, 1989): 135–64.

Fig. 4. Books on sale at the University of Abidjan, including Balzac, Hemingway, Simone de Beauvoir, John Kenneth Galbraith, and a "novelization" of "Dallas"; African works include Aké Loba's *L'Etudiant noir* and Mariama Bâ's *Une Si Longue Lettre*.

women has proliferated in the francophone sphere. A bibliography published in 1985 listed eight autobiographers, fifteen novelists, seven playwrights, and dozens of published poets and essayists.[117] The discursive field has widened to include many nations and a widening variety of styles. In relation to the male canon of francophone writers, the position of women's writing is still tenuous. In the university curricula of francophone Africa, the African male canon itself is still required to compete with the traditional French canon, which continues to inform students' approach to "literature" in general. Figure 4 illustrates the cultural dissonance of contemporary Africa: *Une Si Longue Lettre* and Sembène's novel *O Pays, mon beau peuple!* compete with a "novelization" of "Dallas" and study guides to the French canon in a kiosk at the University of Abidjan. African universities hesitate to fully "nationalize" their curricula, for fear of losing *équivalence* (recognition of their degrees by the French system).[118] In the United States, the faddishness of African literatures is both a boon and a danger. On both continents, and in between (in Europe), the francophone canon is still to some extent a "counterliterature."[119] At some point in the future, it may become possible to appraise the "success" or "failure" of Mariama Bâ's project, but for now such thinking would be premature and inappropriate. What is apparent now is the clear-sightedness with which Mariama Bâ faced the reality of exclusion and marginalization and the creativity and courage with which she projected a response.

117. Christine H. Guyonneau, "Francophone Writers from Sub-Saharan Africa: A Preliminary Bibliography," *Callaloo* 8, no. 24 (Spring-Summer 1985): 453–83.

118. En Afrique même, les universités qui sont organisées d'après le modèle du maître d'hier n'ont pas encore tout à fait intégré des enseignements sur la culture nationale/continentale. . . . On veille scrupuleusement à ce que la part réservée aux littératures nationales ou africaines ne dépasse pas le seuil tolérable pour ceux qui seront chargé de juger des équivalences" (Ambroise Kom, "Littérature francophone d'Afrique, parent pauvre des départments d'études françaises: récit d'une expérience," *Peuples noirs, peuples africains* 11, nos. 59–62 [September 1987-April 1988]: 166, 168).

119. See Bernard Mouralis, *Les Contre-littératures* (Paris: Presses Universitaires de France, 1975). I use Mouralis's term with less confidence about what he calls the "complete autonomy" (167) of black African literature, because it seems to me that anything defined as oppositional (like a counterliterature) must remain dependent in some way on its other.

Conclusion

It is appropriate that the last chapter of this study concluded with a discussion of *projection*. This term, with its connotations in psychoanalysis, literature, and politics, sums up a large number of the problems and solutions encountered in the course of this study. Projection is fundamental to both the object and the procedure of what I have done here.

In the introduction, I evoked a form of projection that has been revealed as illegitimate: the imposition of European or American standards and norms onto Africa. In literary theory, the critic who *inscribes* (that is, projects) an alien paradigm onto a text is setting up a situation of delusion; in political terms, such a critic allows Eurocentrism to command his or her discourse. The examples of Frobenius and Tempels served as cautionary tales about the pitfalls of interpreting Africa.

But if projection were always as easy to recognize and analyze as it was in those cases, the problem would not be so grave, or interesting. In the history of American literary theory and criticism, the reaction against projection and ethnocentrism—within which deconstruction is the most illustrious and seductive school—proved to be a double-edged sword. On the one hand, "theory" (as it came to be known) provoked strong critical thinking about the representation of cultures; it fed into the new trends in critical anthropology and opened dialogue with other disciplines.[1] Lessons taken from Derrida and others help us to debunk the ancient stereotypes of an ahistorical primitivism. But on the other hand, the impulse to

---

1. Simon P. X. Battestini, in his article entitled "Deconstruction and Decolonization of the Self" (*The American Journal of Semiotics* 6, no. 1 [1988–89]), is remarkably sanguine about the relationship between deconstruction and Africa. He interprets deconstruction as "the process of decolonizing the mind," which is plausible, even if he seems to make deconstruction into a form of self-help ("Each individual must deconstruct those mental provisional artifacts that help him or her face other such constructs . . . " [126]). But Battestini goes on to posit African culture globally as deconstructive in its very constitution (citing the example of "religious mobility" [125]). This reduces Africa as a whole to an illustration of a Western fashion, and deconstruction to a mere pluralism of attitude. See also Sunday O. Anozie, "Negritude, Structuralism, Deconstruction," in Henry Louis Gates, Jr., ed., *Black Literature and Literary Theory* (New York: Methuen, 1984): 105–25.

"theory" seems inevitably to block certain avenues of inquiry by encouraging a radical self-reflexivity that has little ethical ground to stand on. Theory maintains an inherent tendancy to universalism, which ineluctably erases differences. In academic circles, theory is power, and power is never easy to control.

Two important projects were bequeathed to us by the era of colonialism and totalization. The first project is the reading and critique of history. Within a historical understanding, the abstract and discredited trope of projection must be recognized as a fact that imposed itself on Africa. Through what I have been calling colonial inscription, the Africa of the European imagination was partially, violently, created and controlled. And from the moment that this process affected the reinvention of Africa within European modes of expression—from the moment that Senghor and Césaire took pieces of their new Africa from Frobenius—the problems of interpretation changed. "Africa" and "the West" ceased to be reified opposites; they entered a hall of mirrors in which cultural codes play off each other, corrupt each other, and enrich each other. This state of affairs has been reflected here in my dependency on both European and African sources of cultural information, and my inability simply to banish European theoretical concerns from this study.

Within this complex of conflicting codes, in which projections are rampant, how do we make distinctions? If the first project is the deciphering of colonial inscription, it engenders a second one, the thinking of ethical distinctions.

Within the field of this literature, the ethics of projection changes over time. There is a simple and fundamental difference between projecting for oneself or one's people and projecting for someone else or another people. This distinction—which is based on a recognition of borders, spheres, and agglomerations—is the armature of an ethics of representation. It demands a measure of "otherness," the recognition of something outside the self; it forces us to relativize. The history of African literature in French could be summed up as a progressive (if still incomplete) seizure of *the means of projection*, a transfer of the right to represent Africa in French, from French writers to Africans. This leaves Western readers on the outside, forced to come to terms with their difference.

The distinction between representing an other and representing oneself is thus the ethical underpinning of this literature: between Frobenius's act of projection and Mariama Bâ's there is a world of difference. But all is not solved by such a transfer of representational power. Ethical distinctions often become controversial because it is not clear where the borders of "self" and "other" are located. Too often critics adhere to simple and literalistic categories of race, gender, or class, while the literary text usually operates across borders as well as within them. Utopias of ethical "self"-representation are often illusory: the writer/leader claims to be possessed of the voice of the masses but speaks only for him/herself; the collapse into total self-representation and self-reflexivity, while perhaps constituting the fulfillment of ethics, also spells its end, its demise. We are left with partial, *relative* successes, framed by political considerations. If theory makes the recognition of a "self" problematic, political history makes it imperative to distinguish between Frobenius and Bâ, Baudelaire and Senghor, Delafosse and Sory Camara.

Projection, which was the means and end of colonialism, thus proved to be a weapon of decolonization. The ability to think oneself out of reality, into an *irreal* but *possible* sphere, is the trademark of authors like Ngūgī, Sembene, Camara Laye, and Mariama Bâ. The ability to project one's consciousness through refracted versions of other points of view particularly distinguishes Kourouma. The principal works studied here weave together utopian projections and critical realism. While they never "transcend" the conditions of their creation, they think their way toward a future that is different (even if that future, as in *L'Enfant noir* and many versions of the Sunjata epic, can only be conceived by reflecting on the past).

Any critic's position also depends on the tendency that he or she must guard against: while trying to avoid projection of personal and ethnocentric values onto the material in question, the critic must project him or herself into the world of the text, the context. The validity of what I have done in this study ultimately depends on the degree of success I have had in translating myself across various borders, projecting my attention into textual encounters with Africans. If there is no escape from projection, I hope that this particular act of projection will have been at least a step in the right direction.

September 19, 1989

Bibliography

A. B. [Alexandre Biyidi]. See Beti, Mongo.

Abastado, Claude. "La Communication littéraire dans *Les Soleils des indépendances* d'Ahmadou Kourouma." *Revue d'ethnopsychologie* 2–3 (1980): 145–49.

Achebe, Chinua. *Morning Yet on Creation Day*. London: Heinemann, 1975.

Achiriga, Jingiri J. *La Révolte des romanciers noirs de langue française*. Ottowa: Naaman, 1973.

Actes du Deuxième Colloque International de Bamako 10 février—22 février 1976. Paris: Fondation SCOA pour la Recherche Scientifique en Afrique Noire, 1976.

Adotevi, Stanislas. *Négritude et négrologues*. Paris: Union Générale d'Editions, 1972.

Africa Research Group. "Les études africaines en Amérique: la famille étendue." In *Anthropologie et impérialisme*, edited by Jean Copans. Paris: Maspero, 1975.

Aire, Victor. "Mariama Bâ, *Une si longue lettre*: compte rendu." *Canadian Journal of African Studies* 16, no. 3 (1982): 636–37.

Akmajian, Adrian, Richard A. Demers, Robert M. Harnish. *Linguistics: An Introduction to Language and Communication*. Cambridge, Mass.: MIT Press, 1984.

Allen, Philip M. "Francophonie Considered." *Africa Report* 13, no. 6 (June 1968): 6–11.

Altman, Janet Gurking. "The Letter Book as a Literary Institution 1539–1789: Toward a Cultural History of Published Correspondences in France." *Yale French Studies* 71 (1986): 17–62.

Amondji, Marcel. *Félix Houphouët et la Côte d'Ivoire: l'envers d'une légende*. Paris: Karthala, 1984.

Amselle, Jean-Loup. "Ethnies et espaces: Pour une anthropologie topologique." In *Au coeur de l'ethnie: Ethnies, tribalisme et état en Afrique*, edited by Jean-Loup Amselle and Elikia M'Bokolo. Paris: La Découverte, 1985.

Anderson, Benedict. *Imagined Communities: Reflections on the Origin and Spread of Nationalism*. London: Verso, 1983.

Anozie, Sunday O. "Negritude, Structuralism, Deconstruction." In *Black Literature and Literary Theory*, edited by Henry Louis Gates, Jr. New York: Methuen, 1984.

————. *Structural Models and African Poetics*. London: Routledge & Kegan Paul, 1981.

Appiah, Kwame Anthony. "Out of Africa: Topologies of Nativism." *Yale Journal of Criticism* 2, no. 1 (Fall 1988): 153–78.

————. "Strictures on Structures: The Prospects for a Structuralist Poetics of African Fiction." In *Black Literature and Literary Theory*, edited by Henry Louis Gates, Jr. New York: Methuen, 1984.

Armah, Ayi Kwei. "Masks and Marx: The Marxist Ethos vis-à-vis African Revolutionary Theory and Praxis." *Présence Africaine* 131, no. 3 (1984): 35–65.

Arnhold, Barbara. "The Long Road to Emancipation." Interview with Mariama Bâ. *Afrika* (Munich) 12 (1980): 23–24.

Asad, Talal, ed. *Anthropology and the Colonial Encounter*. New York: Humanities Press, 1973.

Autra, Ray. Preface to *Sikasso ou la dernière citadelle, suivi de Chaka* by Djibril Tamsir Niane. Honfleur: Pierre Jean Oswald, 1971.

Awkward, Michael. *Inspiriting Influences: Tradition, Revision and Afro-American Women's Novels*. New York: Columbia University Press, 1989.

Ba, Ahmadou Hampaté. "La Tradition vivante." In *Histoire générale de l'Afrique*, vol 1, *Méthodologie et préhistoire africaine*, edited by Joseph Ki-Zerbo. Paris: UNESCO, 1980.

Bâ, Mariama. "La fonction politique des littératures africaines écrites." *Ecriture française dans le monde* 3, no. 1 (May 1981): 3–7.

————. "Mariama Bâ on Her Life," *American Universities Field Staff Reports* 10 (1981): 7.

————. *Un Chant écarlate*. Dakar: Nouvelles Editions Africaines, 1981.

————. *Une Si Longue Lettre*. Dakar: Nouvelles Editions Africaines, 1976. English translation by Modupé Bodé-Thomas, *So Long a Letter*. London: Heinemann, 1981.

Ba, Sylvia Washington. *The Concept of Negritude in the Poetry of Léopold Sédar Senghor*. Princeton, N.J.: Princeton University Press, 1973.

Badday, Moncef S. "Ahmadou Kourouma, écrivain africain." Includes interview. *Afrique littéraire et artistique* 10 (1970): 2–8.

Bakhtin, Mikhail. *The Dialogic Imagination*, edited by Michael Holquist, trans. Caryl Emerson and Michael Holquist. Austin: University of Texas Press, 1981.

Banfield, Ann. "The Formal Coherence of Represented Speech and Thought." *PTL* 3, no. 2 (April 1978): 289–314.

————. "Narrative Style and Direct and Indirect Speech." *Foundations of Language* 10 (1973): 1–39.

Barber, Karin. "Yoruba *Oríkì* and Deconstructive Criticism." *Research in African Literatures* 19, no. 4 (1984): 497–518.

————, and Paulo Fernando de Moraes Farias, eds. *Discourse and its Disguises: The Interpretation of African Oral Texts*. Birmingham University African Studies Series, no. 1, Birmingham, England: Birmingham University African Studies Series, no. 1, 1989.

Battestini, Simon P. X. "Deconstruction and Decolonization of the Self." *The American Journal of Semiotics* 6, no. 1 (1988–89): 117–31.

Baudrillard, Jean. *L'Echange symbolique et la mort*. Paris: Gallimard, 1976.

Baulin, Jacques. *La Politique africaine d'Houphouët-Boigny*. Paris: Eurafor-Press: 1980.

Bazin, Jean. "A chacun son Bambara." In *Au coeur de l'ethnie*, edited by Jean-Loup Amselle and Elikia M'Bokolo. Paris: La Découverte, 1985.

Bénot, Yves. "Le 'Dialogue' avec l'Afrique du Sud, vu de Paris et vu de l'Afrique." *La Pensée* 160 (November–December 1971): 98–106.

———. *Idéologies des indépendances africaines*. Paris: Maspero, 1972.

Berman, Marshall. *All That is Solid Melts into Air*. New York: Simon and Schuster, 1982.

Bernard, Paul R. "Individuality and Collectivity: A Duality in Camara Laye's *L'Enfant noir*." *The French Review* 52, no. 2 (December 1978): 313–24.

Bernasconi, Robert. "Deconstruction and the Possibility of Ethics." In *Deconstruction and Philosophy: The Texts of Jacques Derrida*, edited by John Sallis. Chicago: University of Chicago Press, 1987.

Bessis, Sophie. "Qui a tué Amilcar Cabral?" *Jeune Afrique* 1193 (November 16, 1983): 53–61.

Beti, Mongo. "Afrique noire, littérature rose." *Présence Africaine*, n.s., nos. 1–2 (April–July 1955): 133–45.

———. "*L'Enfant noir*." *Présence Africaine* 16 (1954), issue intitled *Trois écrivains noirs*: 419–20.

———. "Seigneur, délivre-nous de la francophonie." *Peuples noirs, peuples africains* 11, nos. 59–62 (September 1987–April 1988): 105–106.

Bhasin, Kamla. "Literacy for Women, Why and How! Some Thoughts in the Indian Context." In *Third World-Second Sex*, vol. 2, edited by Miranda Davies. London: Zed Books, 1983.

Biarnès, Pierre. *L'Afrique aux Africains: Vingt ans d'indépendance en Afrique noire francophone*. Paris: Armand Colin, 1980.

Bird, Charles S. "Heroic Songs of the Mande Hunters." In *African Folklore*, edited by Richard M. Dorson. Bloomington: Indiana University Press, 1972.

———. "Oral Art in the Mande." In *Papers on the Mande*, edited by Carleton T. Hodge. Bloomington: Indiana University Press, 1971.

———. "Poetry in the Mande." *Poetics* 5 (1976): 89–100.

Bird, Charles S., and Martha Kendall. "The Mande Hero: Text and Context." In *Explorations in African Systems of Thought*, edited by Ivan Karp and Charles S. Bird. Bloomington: Indiana University Press, 1980.

Blair, Dorothy. *African Literature in French*. Cambridge: Cambridge University Press, 1976.

———. *Senegalese Literature: A Critical History*. Boston: Twayne, 1984.

Bloch, R. Howard. *Etymologies and Genealogies: A Literary Anthropology of the French Middle Ages*. Chicago: The University of Chicago Press, 1983.

Boahen, A. Adu, ed. *General History of Africa*, vol. 7, *Africa Under Colonial Domination 1880–1935*. London: Heinemann/UNESCO, 1985.

Boulaga, Fabien Eboussi. "Le Bantou problématique." *Présence Africaine* 66 (2d Quarterly, 1968): 3–40.

Bourgeacq, Jacques. "*L'Enfant noir*" de Camara Laye: sous le signe de l'éternel retour". Sherbrooke, Québec: Naaman, 1984.

Bravmann, René A. *Islam and Tribal Art in West Africa*. Cambridge: Cambridge University Press, 1974.

Brench, A. L. *The Novelists' Inheritance in French Africa*. Oxford: Oxford University Press, 1967.

Brière, Eloise A. "*L'Enfant noir* by Camara Laye: Strategies in Teaching an African Text." *The French Review* 55, no. 6 (May 1982): 804–10.

Brombert, Victor. *The Novels of Flaubert*. Princeton, N.J.: Princeton University Press, 1966.

Brunschwig, Henri. *Noirs et blancs dans l'Afrique noire française*. Paris: Flammarion, 1983.

Bu-Buakei, Jabbi. "Influence and Originality in African Writing." *African Literature Today* 10 (1979): 106–23.

Bulman, Stephen. "The Buffalo-Woman Tale: Political Imperatives and Narrative Constraints in the Sunjata Epic." In *Discourse and its Disguises*, edited by Barber and Moraes Farias. Birmingham, England: Birmingham University African Studies Series, no. 1, 1989.

Cabral, Amilcar. "National Liberation and Culture." *Transition* 45, vol. 9, ii (1974): 12–17.

Camara Laye. *L'Enfant noir*. Paris: Plon, 1953. English translation by James Kirkup and Ernest Jones, *The Dark Child*. New York: Farrar, Strauss and Giroux, 1954.

———. *Le Maître de la parole: Kouma Lafôlô Kouma*. Paris: Plon, 1978. English translation by James Kirkup, *The Guardian of the Word*. New York: Vintage Books, 1984.

———. *Le Regard du roi*. Paris: Plon, 1954.

Camara, Sory. *Gens de la parole: Essai sur la condition et le rôle des griots dans la société Malinké*. Paris: Mouton, 1976.

———. *Paroles très anciennes ou le mythe de l'accomplissment de l'homme*. Paris: La Pensée Sauvage, 1982.

Cashion, Gerald. "Hunters of the Mande: A Behavioral Code and Worldview Derived from the Study of their Folklore." Ph.D. diss., Indiana University, 1984.

Caute, David. *Frantz Fanon*. New York: Viking Press, 1970.

Césaire, Aimé. *Les Armes miraculeuses*. Paris: Gallimard, 1946.

———. *The Collected Poetry*, trans. Clayton Eshleman and Annette Smith. Berkeley: University of California Press, 1983.

———. *Discours sur le colonialisme*. Paris: Présence Africaine, 1955.

———. *Lettre à Maurice Thorez*. Paris: Présence Africaine, 1956.

———. *Une Saison au Congo*. Paris: Seuil, 1973.

Cham, Mbye. "Contemporary Society and the Female Imagination: A Study of the Novels of Mariama Bâ." In *Women in African Literature Today*, edited by Eldred Durosimi Jones and Eustace Palmer. London: James Currey, 1987.

Chemain-Degrange, Arlette. *Emancipation féminine et roman africain*. Dakar: Nouvelles Editions Africaines, 1980.

Chevrier, Jacques. "L'écrivain africain devant la langue française." *Notre Librairie* 53 (May–June 1980): 37–51.

———. *Littérature nègre*. Paris: Armand Colin, 1984.

Chinweizu. Review of *Art and Ideology in the African Novel* by Emmanuel Ngara. *Times Literary Supplement*, June 13, 1986.

———, Onwuchekwa Jemie, and Ihechukwu Madubuike. "The Leeds-Ibadan Connection: The Scandal of Modern African Literature." *Okike* 13 (January 1979): 37–46.

Cissé, Ahmed-Tidjani. *Le Tana de Soumangourou*. Paris: Nubia, 1988.

Cissé, Diango. *Structures des Malinkés de Kita: Contribution à une anthropologie sociale et politique du Mali*. Bamako: Editions Populaires du Mali, 1970.

Cixous, Hélène, Madeleine Gagnon, and Annie Leclerc. *La Venue à l'écriture*. Paris: Union Générale d'Editions, 1977.

Clark, Katerina, and Michael Holquist. *Mikhail Bakhtin*. Cambridge: Harvard University Press, 1984.

Clément, Pierre. "Le Forgeron en Afrique Noire: quelques attitudes du groupe à son égard." *Revue de géographie humaine et d'ethnologie* (April–June, 1948): 35–58.

Clifford, James. *The Predicament of Culture: Twentieth-Century Ethnography, Literature, and Art*. Cambridge: Harvard University Press, 1988.

———, and George E. Marcus, eds. *Writing Culture: The Poetics and Politics of Ethnography*. Berkeley: University of California Press, 1986.

Cochin, Jacques. Review of *Gens de la parole* by Sory Camara. *Notre Librairie* 88/89 (July-September 1987): 183.

Comte, Auguste. *Oeuvres choisis*. Paris: Editions Montaigne, n. d. English translation by Paul Descours and H. Gordon Jones, *The Fundamental Principles of the Positive Philosophy*. London: Watts & Co., 1905.

Condé, Alpha. "Les Sociétés traditionnelles mandingues." Typescript without place or date, but probably published around 1972.

Condé, Maryse. "Anglophones et francophones: les frontières littéraires existent-elles?" *Notre Librairie* 65 (July–September 1982): 27–32.

Cornevin, Robert. *Littératures d'Afrique noire de langue française*. Paris: Presses Universitaires de France, 1976.

Crapanzano, Vincent. *Tuhami: Portrait of a Moroccan*. Chicago: University of Chicago Press, 1980.

———. "Waiting." *The New Yorker*, March 18, 1985, 50–99.

Cri des nègres [Le]: Organe mensuel des travailleurs nègres. Appeared in Paris, 1931–34.

Crowder, Michael. "Indirect Rule—French and British Style." *Africa* 34, no. 3 (July 1964): 197–205.

———. *Senegal: A Study of French Assimilation Policy*. London: Methuen, 1967.

———. "'Us' and 'Them': The International African Institute and the Current Crisis of Identity in African Studies." *Africa* 57, no. 1 (1987): 109–22.

Curtin, Philip D. "Africa in World History." In *Africa and the West*, edited by Isaac Mowoe and Richard Bjornson. New York: Greenwood Press, 1986.

Cutrufelli, Maria Rosa. *Women of Africa: The Roots of Oppression*, trans. Nicolas Romano. London: Zed Books, 1983.

Dabla, J.-J. Séwanou. *Nouvelles écritures africaines: romanciers de la seconde génération*. Paris: L'Harmattan, 1986.

Dadié, Bernard. *Iles de tempête: Pièce en sept tableaux*. Paris: Présence Africaine, 1973.

———. "Misère de l'enseignement en A.O.F." *Présence Africaine* 11 (December 1956–January 1957): 57–70.

———. *Un Nègre à Paris*. Paris: Présence Africaine, 1959.

Dalby, David. "Distribution and Nomenclature of the Manding People and Their Language." In *Papers on the Manding,* edited by Carleton T. Hodge. Bloomington: Indiana University Press, 1971.

Davidson, Basil. *Let Freedom Come: Africa in Modern History*. Boston: Little, Brown, 1978.

Davies, Carole Boyce, and Anne Adams Graves, eds. *Ngambika: Studies of Women in African Literature*. Trenton, N.J.: Africa World Press, 1986.

Delafosse, Charles. "Des soi-disant clans totémiques de l'Afrique Occidentale." *Revue d'ethnographie et des traditions populaires* 1, no. 2 (1920): 87–109.

———. "Souffle vital et esprit dynamique chez les populations indigènes du Soudan Occidental." *Compte rendu de l'Institut français d'anthropologie* 1912: 89–94.

Delas, Daniel. *Léopold Sédar Senghor: Lecture blanche d'un texte noir ("L'Absente")*. Paris: Temps Actuels, 1982.

De Man, Paul. *Allegories of Reading*. New Haven: Yale University Press, 1979.

———. "The Rhetoric of Temporality." In *On Interpretation,* edited by Charles S. Singleton. Baltimore: Johns Hopkins University Press, 1969.

Deniau, Xavier. "La Dimension francophone dans la politique française." *France-Eurafrique* 247 (May–June 1974): 4–5.

———. *La francophonie*. "Que Sais-Je?" Paris: Presses Universitaires de France, 1983.

Dépêche africaine [La]: grand organe républicain indépendant de correspondance entre les Noirs et d'études des questions politiques et économiques coloniales. Appeared in Paris, 1928–32.

Depestre, René. *Alléluia pour une femme-jardin*. Ottowa: Leméac, 1973.

———. *Bonjour et adieu à la négritude*. Paris: Robert Laffont, 1980.

Derrida, Jacques. *De la grammatologie*. Paris: Minuit, 1967.

———. *La Voix et le phénomène*. Paris: Presses Universitaires de France, 1967.

Désalmand, Paul. *Sciences humaines et philosophie en Afrique: La différence culturelle*. Paris: Hatier, 1978.

Deschamps, Hubert. "Et Maintenant, Lord Lugard?" *Africa* 33, no. 4 (October 1963): 293–306.

Diabaté, Massa Makan. *L'Aigle et l'épervier ou la geste de Sunjata*. Paris: Pierre Jean Oswald, 1975.

———. *L'Assemblée des djinns*. Paris: Présence Africaine, 1985.

———. *Le Coiffeur de Kouta*. Paris: Hatier, 1980.

———. *Kala Jata*. Bamako: Editions Populaires, 1970.

———. *Le Lieutenant de Kouta*. Paris: Hatier, 1983.

———. *Le Lion à l'arc*. Paris: Hatier, 1986.

Diagne, Ahmadou Mapaté. *Les Trois Volontés de Malic*. Nendeln: Kraus Reprints, 1973 [first published in 1920].

Diakité, Claude Abou. *Guinée enchaînée ou le livre noir de Sékou Touré*. Paris: D.A.C., 1972.

Diallo, Bakary. *Force-Bonté*. Nendeln: Kraus Reprints, 1973 [first published in 1926].

Diallo, Nafissatou. *De Tilène au plateau: Une Enfance dakaroise*. Dakar: Nouvelles Editions Africaines, 1975.

Diarra, Sékou Oumar, and Massa Makan Diabaté [not the same as Diabaté listed above]. *Etude comparée de trois versions de l'épopée mandingue*. Mémoire de fin d'études, Ecole Normale Supérieure, Bamako, 1982–83.

Diawara, Mamadou. "Les Recherches en histoire orales menées par un autochtone, ou l'inconvénient d'être du cru." *Cahiers d'études africaines* 97, no. 1 (1985): 5–19.

———. "Women, Servitude, and History: The Oral Historical Traditions of Women of Servile Condition in the Kingdom of Jaara (Mali) from the Fifteenth to the Mid-Nineteenth Century." In *Discourse and its Disguises*, edited by Barber and Moraes Farias. Birmingham, England: Birmingham University African Studies Series, no. 1, 1989.

Diawara, Manthia. "Popular Culture and Oral Traditions in African Film." *Film Quarterly* 41, no. 3 (Spring 1988): 6–14.

Dieng, Amady Aly. *Hegel, Marx, Engels et les problèmes de l'Afrique noire*. Dakar: Sankoré, 1978.

Dieterlen, Germaine. *Essai sur la religion bambara*. Paris: Presses Universitaires de France, 1951.

———. "The Mande Creation Myth." *Africa* 27, no. 1 (January 1957): 124–40.

Dieye, Adama Sow, and Bernard Baritaud. "Autour du livre." *Notre Librairie* 81 (October–December 1985): 161–66.

Di Leonardo, Micaele. "Malinowski's Nephews." *The Nation*, March 13, 1989, 350–52.

Diop, Abdoulaye-Bara. *La Société wolof: Tradition et changement*. Paris: Karthala, 1981.

Diop, Majhemout. *Histoire des classes sociales dans l'Afrique de l'ouest*, vol. 1, *Le Mali*. Paris: Maspero, 1971.

Diop, Mamadou Traoré. "Colonial Spasms: The Martyrs of Thiaroye." *West Africa* 3546 (August 12, 1985): 1647.

Dogbé, Yves-Emmanuel. *Réflexions sur la promotion du livre africain*. Le-Mée-sur-Seine: Editions Akpagnon, 1984.

Duchet, Michèle. *Anthropologie et histoire au siècle des lumières*. Paris: Maspero, 1971.

Dumont, René. *L'Afrique noire est mal partie*. Paris: Seuil, 1962.

Ellovich, Risa S. "Dioula Women in Town: A View of Intra-Ethnic Variation (Ivory Coast)." In *A World of Women: Anthropological Studies of Women in the Societies of the World*, edited by Erika Bourguignon. New York: Praeger, 1980.

Encyclopedia of Islam. London: Luzac & Co., 1936.

Erickson, John D. *Nommo: African Fiction in French South of the Sahara*. York, S.C., French Literature Publications Co., 1979.

Etoundi-M'Balla, Patrice. *Lettre ouverte à Soeur Marie-Pierre*. Yaoundé, Cameroun: Editions CLE, 1978.

Faladé, Solange. "Women of Dakar and the Surrounding Urban Area." In *Women of Tropical Africa*, edited by Denise Paulme, translated by H. M. Wright. Berkeley: University of California Press, 1963.

Fall, Aminata Sow. *Le Revenant*. Dakar: Nouvelles Editions Africaines, 1976.

Fanon, Frantz. *Les Damnés de la terre*. Paris: Maspero, 1978 [first published in 1961]. English translation by Constance Farrington, *The Wretched of the Earth*. New York: Grove Press, 1963.

———. *Pour la révolution africaine*. Paris: Maspero, 1964. English translation by Haakon Chevalier, *Toward the African Revolution*. New York: Grove Press, 1967.

Femmes et sociétés: revue de la commission internationale pour l'abolition des mutilations sexuelles 1 (1983).

Fernandez, James. "Filial Piety and Power: Psychosocial Dynamics in the Legends of Shaka and Sundiata." *Science and Psychoanalysis* 14 (1969): 47–60.

———. *Persuasions and Performances: The Play of Tropes in Culture*. Bloomington: Indiana University Press, 1986.

Finnegan, Ruth. *Oral Literature in Africa*. Nairobi: Oxford University Press, 1976.

Fish, Stanley. "Being Interdisciplinary Is So Very Hard to Do." *Profession* 89 (1989): 15–22.

Flaubert, Gustave. "Un coeur simple." In *Trois contes*. Paris: Garnier-Flammarion, 1965.

Fodéba, Kéita. *Aube africaine*. Paris: Pierre Seghers, 1965.

———. "La Danse africaine et la scène." *Présence Africaine* 14–15 (June–September 1957): 202–9.

———. *Le Maître d'école, suivi de Minuit*. Paris: Pierre Seghers, 1953.

———. *Poèmes africains*. Paris: Pierre Seghers, 1950.

———. Preface to *Les Hommes de la danse* by Michel Huet. Lausanne: La Guilde du Livre, 1954: 7–11.

Fontenot, Chester J. *Frantz Fanon: Language as the God Gone Astray in the Flesh*. University of Nebraska Studies, n.s., no. 60. Lincoln: University of Nebraska Press, 1979.

Fortes, Meyer. *Oedipus and Job in West African Religion*. With an essay by Robin Horton. Cambridge: Cambridge University Press, 1983.

Fox, Robin. "*Totem and Taboo* Reconsidered." In *The Structural Study of Myth and Totemism*, edited by Edmund Leach. London: Tavistock Publications, 1967.

Freud, Sigmund. *Totem and Taboo*, trans. James Strachey. New York: W. W. Norton, 1950.

Frobenius, Leo. "Die Kunst Afrikas." *Der Erdball* No. 3 (1931): 85–114.

Gallais, Jean. "Signification du groupe ethnique au Mali." *L'Homme* 2, no. 2 (May–August 1962): 106–129.

Gassama, Makhily. *Kuma: Interrogation sur la littérature nègre de langue française*. Dakar: Nouvelles Editions Africaines, 1978.

Gates, Henry Louis, Jr. *The Signifying Monkey: A Theory of Afro-American Literary Criticism.* New York: Oxford University Press, 1988.
——. "Whose Canon Is It, Anyway?" *The New York Times Book Review,* February 26, 1989, 1–45.
——, ed. *Black Literature and Literary Theory.* New York: Methuen, 1984.
Geertz, Clifford. *The Interpretation of Cultures.* New York: Basic Books, 1973.
——. *Local Knowledge.* New York: Basic Books, 1983.
——. "Thinking as a Moral Act: Ethical Dimensions of Anthropological Fieldwork in the New States." *Antioch Review* 28, no. 2 (1968): 139–158.
Gendzier, Irene. *Frantz Fanon: A Critical Study.* New York: Pantheon Books, 1973.
Gérard, Albert. *Etudes de littérature africaine francophone.* Dakar: Nouvelles Editions Africaines, 1977.
Glissant, Edouard. *Le Discours antillais.* Paris: Seuil, 1981.
Goody, Jack. *The Domestication of the Savage Mind.* Cambridge: Cambridge University Press, 1977.
——, and Ian Watt. "The Consequences of Literacy." In *Literacy in Traditional Societies,* edited by Jack Goody. Cambridge: Cambridge University Press, 1968.
Grant, Stephen H. "Léopold Sédar Senghor: Former President of Senegal." Interview. *Africa Report* 28, no. 6 (November–December 1983): 61–64.
Greenberg, Joseph H. "Anthropology: The Field." In *International Encyclopedia of the Social Sciences.* New York: Free Press, 1968.
Groult, Benoîte. *Ainsi soit-elle.* Paris: Bernard Grasset, 1975.
Gugelberger, Georg M., ed. *Marxism and African Literature.* Trenton, N.J.: Africa World Press, 1985.
Guidy Wandja, Joséphine. "Excision? Mutilation sexuelle? Mythe ou réalité?" *Présence africaine* 142 (1st quarterly 1987): 53–58.
Guilleragues, Sieur de [Gabriel de Lavergne]. *Lettres portugaises.* In *Lettres portugaises, lettres d'une Péruvienne et autres romans d'amour par lettres,* edited by Bernard Bray and Isabelle Landy-Houillon. Paris: Flammarion, 1983.
Guillory, John. "Canonical and Non-Canonical: A Critique of the Current Debate." *ELH* 54, no. 3 (Fall 1987): 483–527.
Guyonneau, Christine H. "Francophone Writers from Sub-Saharan Africa: A Preliminary Bibliography." *Callaloo* 8, no. 24 (Spring–Summer 1985): 453–83.
Haberland, E. *Leo Frobenius: An Anthology.* Wiesbaden: Franz Steiner, 1973.
Hansen, Emmanuel. *Frantz Fanon: Social and Political Thought.* Nairobi: Oxford University Press, 1978.
Harrell-Bond, Barbara E. "An Interview with Mariama Bâ." *American University Field Staff Reports* 10 (1981): 5–12.
Harris, Marvin. *The Rise of Anthropological Theory.* New York: Columbia University Press, 1968.
Hazoumé, Paul. *Doguicimi.* Paris: Larose, 1938.
Hebga, Meinrad P. "Eloge de l'"ethnophilosophie.'" *Présence Africaine* 123 (3d quarterly, 1982): 20–41.

Hegel, G. W. F. *Phänomenolgie des Geistes*. Frankfurt/M: Ullstein Verlag, 1970.
———. *The Philosophy of History*, trans. J. Sibree. New York: Dover, 1956.
Herdeck, Donald E., et al. *African Authors: A Companion to Black African Writing*. Washington, D.C.: Black Orpheus Press, 1973.
Herskovits, Melville J. *Dahomey: An Ancient West African Kingdom*. Evanston, Ill.: Northwestern University Press, 1967.
———, and Frances S. Herskovits. "Sibling Rivalry, the Oedipus Complex and Myth." *Journal of American Folklore* 71, no. 279 (1958): 1–15.
Hirschkop, Ken. "A Response to the Forum on Mikhail Bakhtin." *Critical Inquiry* 11, no. 4 (June 1985): 672–86.
Hobsbawm, Eric, and Terence Ranger, eds. *The Invention of Tradition*. Cambridge: Cambridge University Press, 1983.
Hodge, Carleton T. *Papers on the Mande*. Bloomington: Indiana University Press, 1971.
Hollier, Denis. *The Politics of Prose*, trans. Jeffrey Mehlman. Minneapolis: University of Minnesota Press, 1986.
Holquist, Michael. Glossary in *The Dialogic Imagination*, by Mikhail M. Bakhtin. Austin: University of Texas Press, 1981.
Hopkins, Nicolas S. "Maninka Social Organization." In *Papers on the Manding*, edited by Carleton T. Hodge. Bloomington: Indiana University Press, 1971.
———. *Popular Government in an African Town: Kita, Mali*. Chicago: University of Chicago Press, 1972.
Hosken, Fran. *The Hosken Report: Genital and Sexual Mutilation of Females*. 3d ed. Lexington, Mass.: Women's International Network News, 1982.
Huannou, Adrien. *La Littérature béninoise de langue française*. Paris: Karthala and ACCT, 1984.
Hountondji, Paulin. "Reprendre." In *The Surreptitious Speech: "Présence Africaine" and the Politics of Otherness 1947–1987*, edited by V. Y. Mudimbe. Forthcoming.
———. *Sur la "philosophie africaine."* Paris: Maspero, 1977.
Houphouët-Boigny, Félix. *Le Président Houphouët-Boigny et la nation ivoirienne*. Abidjan: Nouvelles Editions Africaines, 1975.
———. *Propos sur la culture: Extraits de discours 1959–1980*. Abidjan: Ministère des Affaires Culturelles, 1980.
Hymans, Jacques Louis. *Léopold Sédar Senghor: An Intellectual Biography*. Edinburgh: Edinburgh University Press, 1971.
Hymes, Dell, ed. *Reinventing Anthropology*. New York: Pantheon, 1972.
Innes, Gordon. *Sunjata: Three Mandinka Versions*. London: School of Oriental and African Studies, 1974.
Irele, Abiola. *The African Experience in Literature and Ideology*. London: Heinemann, 1981.
Jackson, Michael. *Allegories of the Wilderness: Ethics and Ambiguity in Kuranko Narratives*. Bloomington: Indiana University Press, 1982.
Jahn, Janheinz, Ulla Schild, and Almut Nordman. *Who's Who in African Literature*. Tübingen: Horst Erdmann Verlag, 1972.
Jameson, Fredric. *Marxism and Form*. Princeton, N.J.: Princeton University Press, 1971.

————. *The Political Unconscious: Narrative as a Socially Symbolic Act.* Ithaca, N.Y.: Cornell University Press, 1981.

Jamin, Jean. *Les Lois du silence: Essai sur la fonction sociale du secret.* Paris: Maspero, 1977.

Johnson, Barbara. "Gender Theory and the Yale School." In *Rhetoric and Form: Deconstruction at Yale,* edited by Robert Con Davis and Ronald Schleifer. Norman: University of Oklahoma Press, 1985.

Johnson, John William. "Yes, Virginia, There is an Epic in Africa." *Research in African Literatures* 11, no. 3 (Fall 1980): 308–326.

Johnson, John William, with Fa-Digi Sisòkò. *The Epic of Son-Jara: A West African Tradition.* Bloomington: Indiana University Press, 1986.

Jones, Eldred Durosimi, and Eustace Palmer, eds. *Women in African Literature Today.* London: James Currey, 1987.

Joseph, George. "Free Indirect Discourses in *Les Soleils des indépendances.*" *The American Journal of Semiotics* 6, no. 1 (1988–89): 69–84.

July, Robert. *The Origins of Modern African Thought.* London: Faber & Faber, 1968.

Ka, Aminata Maïga. "Ramatoulaye, Aïssatou, Mireille et . . . Mariama Bâ." *Notre Librairie* 81 (October–December, 1985): 129–34.

————. *La Voie du salut suivi de Le Miroir de la vie.* Paris: Présence Africaine, 1985.

Kaba, Lansiné. "The Cultural Revolution, Artistic Creativity, and Freedom of Expression in Guinea." *The Journal of Modern African Studies* 14, no. 2 (June 1976): 201–218.

Kane, Cheikh Hamidou. *L'Aventure ambiguë.* Paris: Union Générale d'Editions, 1961. English translation by Katherine Woods, *Ambiguous Adventure.* New York: Walker and Co., 1963.

Kane, Mohamadou. "Le Féminisme dans le roman africain." *Annales de la Faculté des Lettres et Sciences Humaines de Dakar* (University of Cheikh Anta Diop) 10 (1980): 141–200.

————. *Roman africain et tradition.* Dakar: Nouvelles Editions Africaines, 1982.

Katz, Stephen. *Marxism, Africa and Social Class: A Critique of Relevant Theories.* Montreal: McGill University Centre for Developing-Area Studies, 1980.

Kéita, Aoua. *Femme d'Afrique: La vie d'Aoua Kéita racontée par elle-même.* Paris: Présence Africaine, 1975.

Kesteloot, Lilyan. *Black Writers in French: A Literary History of Negritude,* trans. Ellen Conroy Kennedy. Philadelphia: Temple University Press, 1974.

————. "De Baro à Boiro: Djibril Tamsir Niane." *Notre Librairie* 88/89 (July–September 1987): 97–99.

King, Adele. "Camara Laye." In *A Celebration of Black and African Writing,* edited by B. King and K. Ogungbesan. London: Oxford University Press, 1975.

————. *The Writings of Camara Laye.* London: Heinemann, 1980.

Knapp, Steven, and Walter Benn Michaels. "Against Theory." In *Against Theory: Literary Studies and the New Pragmatism,* edited by W. J. T. Mitchell. Chicago: University of Chicago Press, 1985.

Kodjo Léonard. "Noms de rues, noms de maîtres." Paper presented at the colloquium, Noms et Appellations en Afrique, at the University of Abidjan, January
1987.

Kom, Ambroise, ed. *Dictionnaire des oeuvres littéraires négro-africaines de langue française*, Sherbrooke, Quebec: Naaman, 1983.

———. "Littérature francophone d'Afrique, parent pauvre des départments
d'études françaises: récit d'une expérience." *Peuples noirs, peuples africains*
11, nos. 59–62 (September 1987–April 1988): 165–69.

Konaké, Sory. *Le Grand Destin de Soundjata*. Paris: ORTF-DAEC, 1973.

Kotchy, Barthélémy N'Guessan. "Signification de l'oeuvre." In *Essai sur "Les
Soleils des indépendances,"* edited by Joseph M'lanhoro. Abidjan: Nouvelles
Editions Africaines, 1977.

Koudou Gbagbo Laurent. *Soundjata le lion du Manding*. Abidjan: CEDA, 1979.

Koula Lucien. "Fraternité." *Fraternité-Matin*. March 3, 1987.

Kuoh Moukoury, Thérèse. *Rencontres essentielles*. N. p.: Adamawa, 1971.

Kourouma, Ahmadou. *Les Soleils des indépendances*. Paris: Seuil, 1970. English
translation by Adrian Adams, *The Suns of Independence*. New York: Africana, 1981.

Kunene, Daniel P. Introduction to *Chaka*, by Thomas Mofolo. London: Heinemann, 1981.

Labouret, Henri. *Les Mandings et leur langue*. Paris: Larose, 1934.

Launay, Robert. *Traders without Trade: Responses to Change in Two Dyula
Communities*. Cambridge: Cambridge University Press, 1982.

Layoun, Mary N. "Fictional Formations and Deformations of National Culture."
The South Atlantic Quarterly 87, no. 1 (Winter 1988): 53–73.

Lazarus, Neil. "Great Expectations and After: The Politics of Postcolonialism in
African Fiction." *Social Text* 13/14 (Winter/Spring 1986): 49–63.

Leach, Edmund, ed. *The Structural Study of Myth and Totemism*. London: Tavistock Publications, 1967.

Leclerc, Gérard. *Anthropologie et colonialisme: essai sur l'histoire de l'africanisme*. Paris: Fayard, 1972.

Lee, Sonia. *Camara Laye*. Boston: Twayne, 1984.

———. "Entretiens avec Aminata Sow Fall (Dakar, 1987)." *African Literature
Association Bulletin* 14, no. 4 (Fall 1988): 23–26.

Leiner, Jacqueline. "Interview avec Camara Laye." *Présence francophone* 10
(Spring 1975): 153–67.

LeVine, Victor T. "Cameroon, Togo, and the States of Formerly French West
Africa." In *Politics and Government in African States 1960–1985*, edited by
Peter Duignan and Robert H. Jackson. Stanford, Calif.: Hoover Institution
Press, 1986.

Leymarie, Isabelle. "The Role and Function of the Griots among the Wolof of
Senegal." Ph.D. diss., Columbia University, 1979.

Leynaud, Emile, and Youssouf Cissé. *Paysans Malinké du Haut Niger*. Bamako:
Imprimerie Populaire du Mali, 1978.

Lévi-Strauss, Claude. "Introduction à l'oeuvre de Marcel Mauss." In *Sociologie et anthropologie* by Marcel Mauss. Paris: Presses Universitaires de France, 1950.

————. *Totemism,* trans. Rodney Needham. Boston: Beacon Press, 1963.

Lexique du français du Sénégal. With a preface by Léopold Sédar Senghor. Dakar: Nouvelles Editions Africaines, 1979.

Lezou, Gérard Dago. *La Création romanesque devant les transformations actuelles en Côte d'Ivoire.* Abidjan: Nouvelles Editions Africaines, 1977.

————. "Temps et espace." In *Essai sur "Les Soleils des indépendances,"* edited by Joseph M'lanhoro. Abidjan: Nouvelles Editions Africaines, 1977.

Lindfors, Bernth. "The Teaching of African Literature in Anglophone African Universities: A Preliminary Report." Forthcoming.

Lopes, Henri. *Sans tam-tam.* Yaoundé, Cameroun: Editions CLE, 1977.

Lord, Albert. *The Singer of Tales.* Cambridge: Harvard University Press, 1960.

Luc, Jean-Claude. "Les Chances de l'agence de coopération culturelle et technique des pays francophones." *Revue française d'études politiques africaines* 57 (September 1970): 62–81.

Lugard, Lord Frederick. *The Dual Mandate in British Tropical Africa.* London: Frank Cass, 1965.

McHale, Brian. "Free Indirect Discourse: A Survey of Recent Accounts." *PTL* 3 (1978): 249–87.

McNaughton, Patrick. *The Mande Blacksmiths: Knowledge, Power, and Art in West Africa.* Bloomington: Indiana University Press, 1988.

Macquet, Jacques. "Les Bambara." In *Contes bambara du Mali,* edited by Veronica Görög. Paris: Institut National des Langues et Civilisations Orientales, 1979.

Magassouba, Moriba. *L'Islam au Sénégal: Demain les mollahs?* Paris: Karthala, 1985.

Magnier, Bernard. "Les Soleils des indépendances." In *Dictionnaire des oeuvres littéraires négro-africaines de langue française,* edited by Ambroise Kom. Sherbrooke, Quebec: Naaman, 1983.

Makarius, Laura. "Observations sur la légende des griots malinké." *Cahiers d'études africaines* 36, no. 9 (1969): 626–40.

Makouta-M'Boukou, Jean-Pierre. *Les Exilés de la forêt vierge.* Paris: L'Harmattan, 1974.

————. *Le Français en Afrique noire.* Paris: Bordas, 1973.

————. *Introduction à l'étude du roman négro-africain de langue française.* Abidjan: Nouvelles Editions Africaines, 1980.

Makward, Christine, with Odile Cazenave. "The Others' Others: Francophone Women's Writing." *Yale French Studies* 75 (1988): 190–207.

Malinowski, Bronislaw. *Sex and Repression in Savage Society.* New York: Harcourt, Brace & Co., 1927.

————. *Sex, Culture, and Myth.* New York: Harcourt, Brace & World, 1962.

Manning, Patrick. *Francophone Sub-Saharan Africa 1880–1985.* Cambridge: Cambridge University Press, 1988.

Maran, René. *Batouala: Véritable roman nègre.* Paris: Albin Michel, 1965 [first published in 1921].

————. *Djouma, chien de brousse*. Paris: Albin Michel, 1927.

Marcus, George E., and Michael M. J. Fischer. *Anthropology as Cultural Critique: An Experimental Moment in the Human Sciences*. Chicago: University of Chicago Press, 1986.

Markovitz, Irving Leonard. *Léopold Sédar Senghor and the Politics of Negritude*. New York: Atheneum, 1969.

Marnham, Patrick. *Fantastic Invasion: Notes on Contemporary Africa*. New York: Harcourt, Brace, Jovanovich, 1979.

Mateso, Locha. *La Littérature africaine et sa critique*. Paris: ACCT/Karthala, 1986.

Mauss, Marcel. *Oeuvres*, vol. 1, *Les Fonctions sociales du sacré*. Paris: Minuit, 1968.

Mazrui, Ali. "Cultural Forces in African Politics: In Search of a Synthesis." In *Africa and the West: Legacies of Empire*, edited by Isaac James Mowoe and Richard Bjornson. New York: Greenwood Press, 1986.

Mbongo, Nsame. "Problèmes théoriques de la question nationale en Afrique." *Présence Africaine* 136, no. 4 (1985): 31–67.

Medjigbodo, Nicole. "Quelques réflexions sur la responsabilité de l'écrivain en Afrique colonisée et néo-colonisée: le cas de Camara Laye." *Présence francophone* 19 (Fall 1979): 59–87.

Meillassoux, Claude. *L'Anthropologie économique des Gouro de Côte d'Ivoire*. Paris: Mouton, 1964.

————. "Les Cérémonies septennales du Kamablo de Kaaba (Mali)" *Journal de la société des africanistes* 38, no. 2 (1968): 173–83.

Memel-Fotê, Harris. "La Bâtardise." In *Essai sur "Les Soleils des indépendances,"* edited by Joseph M'lanhoro. Abidjan: Nouvelles Editions Africaines, 1977.

Mfizi, Christophe. "Qui a tué Batouala?" *Afrique littéraire et artistique* 46 (1977): 78–88.

Michaud, Guy. "Représentations culturelles dans *Les Soleils des indépendances* d'Ahmadou Kourouma." *Revue d'Ethnopsychologie* 2–3 (1980): 137–44.

Michelman, Frederic. "Independence and Disillusion in *Les Soleils des indépendances*: A New Approach." In *Design and Intent in African Literature*, edited by David Dorsey, et al. Washington, D.C.: Three Continents Press, 1982.

Mikhail, Mona. "Senghor, Women and the African Tradition." *Rackham Literary Studies* 1 (1971): 63–70.

Midiohouan, Guy Ossito. "Exotique? Coloniale? Ou quand la littérature africaine était la littérature des Français d'Afrique." *Peuples noirs, peuples africains* 29 (1982): 119–26.

————. *L'Idéologie dans la littérature négro-africaine d'expression française*. Paris: L'Harmattan, 1986.

————. "Le Sottisier francophone." *Peuples noirs, peuples africains* 11, nos. 59–62 (September 1987–April 1988): 175–85.

Miller, Christopher L. *Blank Darkness: Africanist Discourse in French*. Chicago: University of Chicago Press, 1985.

————. Selection from the Symposium on "Literacy, Reading and Power." *Yale Journal of Criticism* 2, no. 1 (Fall 1988): 225–30.

————. "Trait d'union: Injunction and Dismemberment in Yambo Ouologuem's *Le Devoir de violence.*" *L'Esprit créateur* 23, no. 4 (Winter 1983): 62–73.

————. "Unfinished Business: Colonialism in Sub-Saharan Africa and the Ideals of the French Revolution." Forthcoming.

Miller, J. Hillis. *The Ethics of Reading.* New York: Columbia University Press, 1987.

Milolo, Kembe. *L'Image de la femme chez les romancières de l'Afrique noire.* Saint-Paul Fribourg: Editions Universitaires Fribourg Suisse: 1986.

M'lanhoro, Joseph, ed. *Essai sur "Les Soleils des indépendances."* Abidjan: Nouvelles Editions Africaines, 1977.

Mohanty, Chandra Talpade. "Under Western Eyes: Feminist Scholarship and Colonial Discourses." *Boundary 2* 12, no. 3/13, no. 1 (Spring/Fall 1984): 333–58.

Moi, Toril. *Sexual/Textual Politics: Feminist Literary Theory.* London: Routledge, 1985.

Mokwenyé, Cyril. "La Polygamie et la révolte de la femme africaine moderne: une lecture d'*Une si longue lettre* de Mariama Bâ." *Peuples noirs, peuples africains* 6, no. 31 (January–February 1983): 86–94.

Monteil, Charles. *Les Bambara du Ségou et du Kaarta.* Paris: Emile Larose, 1924.

Monteil, Vincent. *L'Islâm noir: Une Religion à la conquête de l'Afrique.* Paris: Seuil, 1980.

————. "Le Problème linguistique en Afrique noire." *Esprit* 311 (November 1962): 796–809.

Moore, Henrietta L. *Feminism and Anthropology.* Minneapolis: University of Minnesota Press, 1988.

Moreau, René Luc. *Africains musulmans: Des Communautés en mouvement.* Paris: Présence Africaine, 1982.

Morson, Gary Saul. "Dialogue, Monologue, and the Social: A Reply to Ken Hirschkop." *Critical Inquiry* 11, no. 4 (June 1985): 672–86.

Mouloungui, Jean-Félix. Editorial. *Francophonie Magazine* 2 (June 1989): 3.

Moumouni, Abdou. *L'Education en Afrique.* Paris: Maspero, 1964.

Mouralis, Bernard. *Les Contre-littératures.* Paris: Presses Universitaires de France, 1975.

————. *Littérature et développement: Essai sur le statut, la fonction et la représentation de la littérature négro-africaine d'expression française.* Paris: Silex/ACCT, 1984.

————. "Sékou Touré et l'écriture: Réflexions sur un cas de scribomanie." *Notre Librairie* 88–89 (July–September 1987): 76–85.

Mowoe, Isaac James, and Richard Bjornson, eds. *Africa and the West: Legacies of Empire.* New York: Greenwood Press, 1986.

Mudimbe, V. Y. *L'Autre face du royaume: Une Introduction à la critique des langages en folie.* N. p.: L'Age d'homme, 1973.

————. *The Invention of Africa: Gnosis, Philosophy and the Order of Knowledge.* Bloomington: Indiana University Press, 1988.

————. *L'Odeur du père: Essai sur les limites de la science et de la vie en Afrique noire.* Paris: Présence Africaine, 1982.

Murray, Jocelyn, ed. *Cultural Atlas of Africa.* New York: Facts on File, 1981.

Nadeau, Maurice. "La Langue appartient à ceux qui l'utilisent." *La Quinzaine littéraire* 436 (March 16–31, 1985): 3–4.

Ndiaye, A. Raphaël. *La Place de la femme dans les rites du Sénégal.* Dakar: Nouvelles Editions Africaines, 1986.

N'Diaye, Bokar. *Les Castes au Mali.* Bamako: Editions Populaires, 1970.

N'Diaye, Catherine. *Gens de sable.* Paris: P.O.L., 1984.

Nerval, Gérard de. *Voyage en Orient.* In *Oeuvres*, vol. 2. Bibliothèque de la Pléiade. Paris: Gallimard, 1961.

Ngara, Emmanuel. *Art and Ideology in the African Novel: A Study of the Influence of Marxism on African Writing.* London: Heinemann, 1985.

Nguessan, Kouamé. "Femmes ivoiriennes: Acquis et incertitudes." *Présence Africaine* 141, no. 1 (1987): 103–13.

Ngùgì wa Thiong'o. *Decolonising the Mind: The Politics of Language in African Literature.* London: James Currey, 1986.

———. *Writers in Politics.* London: Heinemann, 1981.

Ngate, Jonathon. *Francophone African Literature: Reading a Literary Tradition.* Trenton, N.J.: Africa World Press, 1988.

Nguyen Nghe. "Frantz Fanon et les problèmes de l'indépendance." *La Pensée* 107 (January–February, 1963): 23–36.

Niane, Djibril Tamsir. "Mythes, légendes, et sources orales dans l'oeuvre de Mahmoud Kati." *Recherches africaines* 1–4 (1964): 36–42.

———. "Le Problème de Soundjata." *Notes Africaines* 88 (October 1960): 123–26.

———. *Recherches sur l'Empire du Mali au Moyen Age.* République de Guinée, Ministère de l'Information et du Tourisme: Mémoires de l'Institut National de Recherches et de Documentation, no. 2, 1962.

———. *Sikasso ou la dernière citadelle, suivi de Chaka.* Honfleur: Pierre Jean Oswald, 1971.

———. *Soundjata ou l'épopée mandingue.* Paris: Présence Africaine, 1960. English translation by G. D. Pickett, *Sundiata: An Epic of Old Mali.* London: Longman, 1965.

Nkashama, Pius Ngandu. "L'Edition et le livre en Afrique." *La Quinzaine littéraire* 435 (March 16–31, 1985): 8–9.

———. *Kourouma et le mythe.* Paris: Silex, 1985.

Nordman, Daniel, and Jean-Pierre Raison, eds. *Sciences de l'homme et conquête coloniale: constitution et usages des sciences humaines en Afrique.* Paris: Presses de l'Ecole Normale Supérieure, 1980.

Norris, Christopher. "Deconstruction Against Itself: Derrida and Nietzsche." *Diacritics* 16, No. 4 (Winter 1986): 61–69.

Notre Librairie. Series of special issues on national literatures in Africa: 83 (April–June 1986), 84 (July–September 1986): and 85 (October–December 1986).

Nsimba Mumbamuna. *Lettres kinoises: Roman épistolaire.* Kinshasa: Centre Africain de Littérature, 1974.

Nwoga, Donatus Ibe. "The Limitations of Universal Critical Criteria." In *Exile and Tradition: Studies in African and Caribbean Literature*, edited by Rowland Smith. New York: African Publishing Co., 1976.

———. "Plagiarism and Authentic Creativity in West Africa." *Research in African Literature* 6, no. 1 (1975): 32–39.

N'Wozan, Simeon Aka. "Sublime dialogue." *Fraternité-Matin.* March 3, 1987.

Ojo-Ade, Femi. "Still a Victim? Mariama Bâ's *Une si longue lettre.*" *African Literature Today* 12 (1982): 71–87.

Okeh, Peter Igbonekwu. "Two Ways of Explaining Africa: An Insight into Camara Laye's *L'Enfant noir* and Ferdinand Oyono's *Le Vieux Nègre et la médaille.*" In *Exile and Tradition*, edited by Rowland Smith. New York: Africana Publishing Co., 1976.

Okilie, M. A. E. "Nostalgia and Creative Secret: The Case of Camara Laye." *Okike* 23 (February 1983): 8–15.

Okpewho, Isidore. *The Epic in Africa: Towards a Poetics of the Oral Performance.* New York: Columbia University Press, 1975.

Ong, Walter. *Interfaces of the Word: Studies in the Evolution of Consciousness and Culture.* Ithaca, N.Y.: Cornell University Press, 1977.

———. "Orality-Literacy Studies and the Unity of the Human Race." *Oral Tradition* 2, no. 1 (January 1987): 371–82.

Onoge, Omafume F. "The Crisis of Consciousness in Modern African Literature." In *Marxism and African Literature*, edited by Georg M. Gugelberger. Trenton, N.J.: Africa World Press, 1985.

Ortigues, Marie-Cécile and Edmond. *Oedipe africain.* Paris: Union Générale d'Editions, 1973.

Ortova, Jarmila. "Les femmes dans l'oeuvre littéraire d'Ousmane Sembène." *Présence Africaine* 71, no. 3 (1969): 69–77.

Oyono, Ferdinand. *Une Vie de boy.* Paris: René Julliard, 1956.

Palmer, Eustace. *An Introduction to the African Novel.* New York: Africana Publishing Co., 1972.

Paques, Viviana. *Les Bambara.* Paris: Presses Universitaires de France, 1954.

Parin, Paul, Fritz Morgenthaler, and Goldy Parin-Matthèy. *Fear Thy Neighbor as Thyself*, trans. Patricia Klamerth. Chicago: The University of Chicago Press, 1980.

Pascal, Roy. *The Dual Voice.* Manchester: Manchester University Press, 1977.

Perruchot, Claude. "Le style indirect libre et la question du sujet." In *La Production du sens chez Flaubert: Colloque de Cerisy*, edited by Claudine Gothot-Mersch. Paris: Union Générale d'Editions, 1975.

Perry, Ruth. *Women, Letters, and the Novel.* New York: AMS Press, 1980.

Person, Yves. "Samori and Islam." In *Studies in West African Islamic History*, vol. 1, *The Cultivators of Islam*, edited by John Ralph Willis. London: Frank Cass, 1979.

———. *Samori: Une Révolution dyula.* 3 vols. Paris: IFAN, 1968–75.

———. *Samori: La Renaissance de l'empire Mandingue.* Dakar: Nouvelles Editions Africaines, 1976.

———. "Tradition orale et chronologie." *Cahiers d'études africaines* 7, no. 2 (1962): 462–76.

Peuples noirs, peuples africains 11, nos. 59–62 (September 1987–April 1988). Special issue, "La Francophonie contre la liberté des peuples africains."

Peyrega, Catherine. *Sékou Touré est-il marxiste?* Bordeaux: Publications d'Etudes et de Recherches Socio-Economiques, 1977.

Philipson, Robert. "Literature and Ethnography: Two Views of Manding Initiation Rites." In *Interdisciplinary Dimensions of African Literature*, edited by Kofi Anyidoho. Annual Selected Papers of the African Literature Association, no. 8. 1982. Washington, D.C.: Three Continents, 1985.

Philombe, René. *Lettres de ma cambuse.* Yaoundé, Cameroun: Editions Abbia, 1964. English translation by Richard Bjornson, *Tales from My Hut.* Yaoundé: Buma Kor, 1977.

Pointer, Fritz H. "Laye, Lamming, and Wright: Mother and Son." *African Literature Today* 14 (1984): 19–33.

Preiswerk, Roy, and Dominique Perrot. *Ethnocentrisme et histoire: L'Afrique, l'Amérique indienne et l'Asie dans les manuelles occidentales.* Paris: Anthropos, 1975.

Quinzaine littéraire 436 (March 16–31, 1985) and 437 (April 1–15, 1985). Series of articles on francophonie.

Raffenel, Anne. *Nouveau voyage dans le pays des nègres, suivi d'études sur la colonie du Sénégal et de documents historiques, géographiques et scientifiques.* Paris: Napoléon Chaix, 1856.

Ranger, Terence. "The Invention of Tradition in Colonial Africa." In *The Invention of Tradition,* edited by Eric Hobsbawm and Terence Ranger. Cambridge: Cambridge University Press, 1983.

Rich, Adrienne. *The Dream of a Common Language.* New York: W. W. Norton, 1978.

Rivière, Claude. "La difficile émergence d'un artisanat casté." *Cahiers d'études africaines* 36, no. 9 (1969): 600–625.

———. *Guinea: The Mobilization of a People,* trans. Virginia Thompson and Richard Adloff. Ithaca, N.Y.: Cornell University Press, 1977.

Roberts, T. D., et al. *Area Handbook for Ivory Coast.* 2d ed. Washington, D.C.: United States Government Printing Office, 1973.

Robertson, Claire. "Women's Education and Class Formation in Africa." In *Women and Class in Africa,* edited by Claire Robertson and Iris Berger. New York: Africana Publishing Co., 1986.

Robinson, Lillian S. "Treason Our Text: Feminist Challenges to the Literary Canon." In *The New Feminist Criticism: Essays on Women, Literature, and Theory,* edited by Elaine Showalter. New York: Pantheon Books, 1985.

Rouget, G. "La Musique: Les Ballets africains de Kéita Fodéba," *Présence africaine* 7 (April–May, 1956): 138–40.

Rousseau, Jean-Jacques. "Discours sur l'origine de l'inégalité." In *The Political Writings of Jean-Jacques Rousseau.* New York: John Wiley & Sons, 1962.

Said, Edward W. *Orientalism.* New York: Random House, 1979.

———. *The World, the Text and the Critic.* Cambridge: Harvard University Press, 1983.

Sall, Abdoulaye. *Epopée et actualité à la lumière de "Kala Jata" de Massa Makan Diabaté et de l'épopée mandingue de Djibril Tamsir Niane.* Mémoire de fin d'études, Ecole Normale Supérieure, Bamako, May 1977.

Sartre, Jean-Paul. "Orphée noir." Preface to *Anthologie de la nouvelle poésie nègre et malgache de langue française*, edited by Léopold Sédar Senghor. Paris: Presses Universitaires de France, 1948.

Schikora, Rosemary G. "Narrative Voice in Kourouma's *Les Soleils des indépendances*." *The French Review* 55, no. 6 (May 1980): 811–17.

Schipper, Mineke. "Mother Africa on a Pedestal: The Male Heritage in African Literature and Criticism." In *Women in "African Literature Today"*, edited by Eldred Durosimi Jones and Eustace Palmer.

———. " 'Who am I?': Fact and Fiction in African First-Person Narrative." *Research in African Literatures* 16, no. 1 (Spring 1985): 53–79.

———, ed. *Unheard Words: Women and Literature in Africa, the Arab World, Asia, the Caribbean and Latin America*, trans. Barbara Potter Fasting. London and New York: Allison & Busby, 1985.

Schwartz, Alf. *Colonialistes, africanistes et Africains*. N. p.: Nouvelle Optique, 1979.

Scribner, Sylvia, and Michael Cole. *The Psychology of Literacy*. Cambridge: Harvard University Press, 1981.

Sékou Touré. London: Panaf Books, 1978.

Sellin, Eric. "Alienation in the Novels of Camara Laye." *Pan-African Journal* 4, no. 4 (Fall 1971): 455–72.

Sembène Ousmane. *Les Bouts de bois de Dieu*. Paris: Presses Pocket, 1960.

———. *Le Dernier de l'Empire*. 2 vols. Paris: L'Harmattan, 1981.

———. *Man is Culture/L'Homme est culture*. The Sixth Annual Hans Wolff Memorial Lecture. Bloomington: African Studies Program, Indiana University, 1979.

———. *O pays, mon beau peuple!* Paris: Presses Pocket, 1957.

Senghor, Léopold Sédar. *Ce que je crois: Négritude, francité et civilisation de l'universel*. Paris: Bernard Grasset, 1988.

———. "Les Leçons de Leo Frobenius." In *Leo Frobenius 1873/1973: Une Anthologie*, edited by Eike Haberland. Wiesbaden: Franz Steiner Verlag, 1973.

———. "Les Leçons de Léo Frobenius." *Présence Africaine* 111, no. 3 (1978): 147–48. (Not the same article as above.)

———. *Liberté*, vol. 1, *Négritude et humanisme*. Paris: Seuil, 1964.

———. *Liberté*, vol. 3, *Négritude et civilisation de l'universel*. Paris: Seuil, 1977.

———. *Poèmes*. Paris: Seuil, 1984.

———, ed. *Anthologie de la nouvelle poésie nègre et malgache de langue française*. With a preface by Jean-Paul Sartre. Paris: Presses Universitaires de France, 1948.

Shelton, Austin J. "The Problem of Griot Interpretation and the Actual Causes of War in Sondjata." *Présence Africaine* 66, no. 2 (1968): 145–52.

Sidibé, Mamby. "Les Gens de caste au Soudan français." *Notes africaines* 81 (1959): 13–17.

Siebers, Tobin. *The Ethics of Criticism*. Ithaca, N.Y.: Cornell University Press, 1988.

Sine Babacar. *Le Marxisme devant les sociétés africaines contemporaines*. Paris: Présence Africaine, 1983.

Siriex, Paul-Henri. *Houphouët-Boigny ou la sagesse africaine*. Abidjan: Nouvelles Editions Africaines, 1986.

Smith, Michael G. "The Social Functions and Meaning of Hausa Praise-Singing." *Africa* 27 (1957): 26–45.

Soleils et francophonie 1 (June 1989).

Sollors, Werner. *Beyond Ethnicity: Consent and Descent in American Culture*. New York: Oxford University Press, 1986.

Sonfo, Alphamoye. "La Mère dans la littérature romanesque de la Guinée, du Mali et du Sénégal." *Revue ouest-africaine des langues vivantes* 2 (1976): 95–107.

Sony Labou Tansi. *Les Sept Solitudes de Lorsa Lopes*. Paris: Seuil, 1985.

Sow, Fatou. "Senegal: The Decade and Its Consequences." *Issue: A Journal of Opinion* (African Studies Association) 17, no. 2 (Summer 1989): 32–36.

Soyinka, Wole. "From a Common Back Cloth: A Reassessment of the African Literary Image." *The American Scholar* 32, no. 3 (Summer 1963): 387–96.

———. *Myth, Literature and the African World*. Cambridge: Cambridge University Press, 1976.

Spacks, Patricia Meyer. "Female Resources: Epistles, Plot, and Power." *Persuasions* 9 (December 1987): 88–98.

Sperber, Dan. "L'Interprétation en anthropologie." *L'Homme* 21, no. 1 (January-March 1981): 69–92.

———. *Le Savoir des anthropologues*. Paris: Hermann, 1982.

Spiro, Melford E. *Oedipus in the Trobriands*. Chicago: University of Chicago Press, 1982.

Statistics of Educational Attainment and Illiteracy. Paris: UNESCO, 1977.

Stocking, George W., Jr. *The History of Anthropology*, vol. 2, *Functionalism Historicized: Essays on British Social Anthropology*. Madison: University of Wisconsin Press, 1984.

Street, Brian V. *Literacy in Theory and Practice*. Cambridge: Cambridge University Press, 1984.

Strobel, Margaret. "African Women: Review Article." *Signs* 8, no. 1 (Fall 1982): 109–31.

T. K. "Yewwu-Yewwi en action." *Amina* 231 (July 1989): 8–12.

Tallon, Brigitte. "Le Français de Moussa." *Autrement* 9 (October 1984): 148–154.

Taylor, Patrick. *The Narrative of Liberation: Perspectives on Afro-Caribbean Literature, Popular Culture, and Politics*. Ithaca, N.Y.: Cornell University Press, 1989.

Tempels, Placide. *Bantu Philosophy*, trans. Colin King. Paris: Présence Africaine, 1959.

Terray, Emmanuel. *Marxism and "Primitive" Societies*, trans. Mary Klopper. New York: Monthly Review Press, 1972.

Tétu, Michel. *La Francophonie: Histoire, problématique et perspectives*. With a preface by Léopold Sédar Senghor. Montreal: Guérin Littérature, 1987.

Thiam, Awa. *Continents noirs*. N. p.: Tierce, 1987.

———. *La Parole aux Négresses*. Paris: Denoël, 1978. English translation by Dorothy S. Blair, *Speak Out, Black Sisters: Feminism and Oppression in Black Africa*. London: Pluto Press, 1986.

Thomas, P. "L'Alphabétisation en Côte d'Ivoire: Situation actuelle." *Cahiers Ivoiriens de Recherche Linguisitique* 1 (1977): 51–86.

Thompson, Robert Farris. *The Flash of the Spirit*. New York: Random House, 1983.

Thornton, Robert. "Narrative Ethnography in Africa, 1850–1920: The Creation and Capture of an Appropriate Domain for Anthropology." *Man*, n. s. 18, no. 3 (September 1983): 502–20.

Tine, Alioune. *Etude pragmatique et sémiotique des effets du bilinguisme dans les oeuvres romanesques de Ousmane Sembene*. Dissertation (Thèse de 3e cycle), University of Lyon II, 1981.

———. "Wolof ou français, le choix de Sembene." *Notre Librairie* 81 (1985): 43–50.

Todorov, Tsvetan. *Mikhail Bakhtin: The Dialogical Principle*. Minneapolis: University of Minnesota Press, 1984.

Tougas, Gérard. *La Francophonie en péril*. Montreal: Le Cercle du Livre de France, 1967.

Touré, Abdou. *La Civilisation quotidienne en Côte d'Ivoire*. Paris: Karthala, 1981.

Touré, Ahmed Sékou, et al. *Révolution démocratique africaine*, no. 38, *Le Complot permanent*. Conakry, Guinea: Imprimerie Nationale Patrice Lumumba, 1970.

Toutain, Dr. "Notes sur les castes chez les Mandingues et en particulier chez les Banmanas." *Revue d'ethnographie* 3 (1885): 343–52.

Towa, Marcien. *Essai sur la problématique philosophique dans l'Afrique actuelle*. Yaoundé, Cameroun: Editions CLE, 1971.

———. *L'Idée d'une philosophie négro-africaine*. Yaoundé, Cameroun: Editions CLE, 1979.

———. *Léopold Sédar Senghor: négritude ou servitude?* Yaoundé, Cameroun: Editions CLE, 1971.

Traoré, Ismaila Samba. *Les Ruchers de la capitale*. Paris: L'Harmattan, 1982.

Trinh T. Minh-ha. *Woman, Native, Other: Writing Postcoloniality and Feminism*. Bloomington: Indiana University Press, 1989.

Turner, Bryan S. *Marx and the End of Orientalism*. London: George Allen & Unwin, 1978.

Turner, Victor. *The Forest of Symbols*. Ithaca, N.Y.: Cornell University Press, 1967.

Tyler, Stephen A. "Post-Modern Ethnography: From Document of the Occult to Occult Document." In *Writing Culture*, edited by James Clifford and George E. Marcus. Berkeley: University of California Press, 1986.

Vachon, G.-André. "La 'Francité.'" *Etudes françaises* 4, no. 2 (May 1968): 117–18.

Valente, Joseph. "Hall of Mirrors: Baudrillard on Marx." *Diacritics* 15, no. 2 (Summer 1985): 54–65.

Vallières, Pierre. *Nègres blancs d'Amérique: Autobiographie précoce d'un "terroriste" québecois*. Paris: Maspero, 1969.

Van Gennep, Arnold. *Tabou et totémisme à Madagascar: Etude descriptive et théorique*. Paris: E. Leroux, 1904.

Wâ Kamissoko. *L'Empire du Mali. Un récit de Wâ Kamissoko de Krina, enregistré, transcrit, traduit et annoté par Youssouf Tata Cissé*. Second International Collouium of Bamako, February 16–22, 1976. Paris: Fondation SCOA pour la Recherche Scientifique en Afrique Noire, 1976.

Wali, Obiajunwa. "The Dead End of African Literature?" *Transition* 3, no. 10 (September 1963): 13–15.

Wallace, Edwin R., IV. *Freud and Anthropology: A History and Reappraisal*. New York: International Universities Press, 1983.

Wallace, Karen Smyley. "*Les Bouts de bois de Dieu* and *Xala*: A Comparative Analysis of Female Roles in Sembene's Novels." *Papers in Romance Studies* 5, no. 3 (Autumn 1983): 89–96.

———. "Women and Alienation: Analysis of the Works of Two Francophone African Novelists." In *Ngambika*, edited by Carole Boyce Davies and Anne Adams Graves. Trenton, N.J.: Africa World Press, 1986.

Wauthier, Claude. *L'Afrique des Africains: Inventaire de la négritude*. Paris: Seuil, 1964.

Webster, Steven. "Dialogue and Fiction in Ethnography." *Dialectical Anthropology* 7 (1982): 91–114.

Weiskel, Timothy C. *French Colonial Rule and the Baule Peoples: Resistance and Collaboration, 1889–1911*. Oxford: Clarendon Press, 1980.

West, Cornel. "Minority Discourse and the Pitfalls of Canon Formation." *The Yale Journal of Criticism* 1, no. 1 (Fall 1987): 193–201.

Wiredu, Kwasi. *Philosophy and an African Culture*. Cambridge: Cambridge University Press, 1980.

Woddis, Jack. *New Theories of Revolution: A Commentary on the Views of Frantz Fanon, Régis Debray and Herbert Marcuse*. London: Lawrence and Wishart, 1972.

Wondji, Ch.-G. "Le Contexte historique." In *Essai sur "Les Soleils des indépendances,"* edited by Joseph M'lanhoro. Abidjan: Nouvelles Editions Africaines, 1977.

Worsley, Peter. "Groote Eylandt Totemism and *Le Totémisme aujourd'hui*." In *The Structural Study of Myth and Totemism*, edited by Edmund Leach. London: Tavistock Publications, 1967.

Wright, Donald R. *Oral Traditions from the Gambia*, vol. 1: *Mandinka Griots*. Papers in International Studies, no. 37. Columbus: Ohio University Center for International Studies, 1979.

Yannopoulos, Tatiana, and Denis Martin. "De la question au dialogue . . . A propos des enquêtes en Afrique noire." *Cahiers d'études africaines* 71, no. 18 (1978): 421–42.

Young, Crawford. "Patterns of Social Conflict: State, Class, and Ethnicity." *Dædalus* 111, no. 2 (Spring 1982): 71–98.

Zahan, Dominque. *La Dialectique du verbe chez les Bambara.* Paris: Mouton, 1963.

Zemp, Hugo. "La légende des griots malinké." *Cahiers d'études africaines* 24, no. 6 (1966): 611–42.

Zolberg, Aristide R. *One-Party Government in the Ivory Coast.* Rev. ed. Princeton, N.J.: Princeton University Press, 1969.

Index

Achebe, Chinua, 2
Adotevi, Stanislas, 19–20, 103
Algeria, 49
Altman, Janet Gurkin, 281–82, 283
Amondji, Marcel, 242
Amselle, Jean-Loup, 20, 34–35
Anderson, Benedict, 15 n
Anglophone Africa, 196–97. *See also* Indirect rule
Anozie, Sunday, 5 n
Anthropology: and collective wholes, 156–57, 160–62; defined, 10–11; defined by Lévi-Strauss, 161; and dialogism, 25–29; dual role of, 139; Freud's, 151; Frobenius's, 17–18, 19; and gender, 265; and *Les Soleils des indépendances*, 204–9, 213–24; and literary criticism, 4–6, 11, 24, 156; and Marxism, 32, 41; and Negritude, 10–21; new critical, 20, 25–29, 34, 66, 260; and polyvocality, 260; and reading of African literature, 21; "reciprocal," 216–17; resistance to, 31; and rhetoric, 6; and silence, 260–68; and sociology, 11; of totemism, 144–57
Apartheid, 13
Appiah, Kwame Anthony, 5 n, 6 n, 249, 287
Armah, Ayi Kwei, 38 n
Assimilation, 12; and Fanon, 47; and indirect rule, 183, 193, 196, 198 n; and Senghor, 19
Authenticity, 26, 34, 45; in *L'Enfant noir*, 179
Autobiography, 127, 250
Awkward, Michael, 291 n

Ba, A. Hampaté, 86
Bâ, Mariama, 247, 250, 257, 297; her

education, 269; and epistolarity, 277, 281–85; philosophy of writing, 271–77; on polygamy, 280 n; death of, 285. *See also Une Si Longue Lettre*
Badenya, 131–32, 262
Bakhtin, Mikhail, 26–28, 219, 223, 237–38
Bamako (Mali), 82
Bamana, 69, 74, 261–62
Bazin, Jean, 20
Bergson, Henri, 155
Béti, Mongo, 47, 167, 179; on *L'Enfant noir*, 122–23; on francophonie, 197
Biarnès, Pierre, 242
Bird, Charles, 80 n
Blair, Dorothy, 39, 121
Boulaga, Fabien Eboussi, 13 n
Bourgeacq, Jacques, 4 n, 132 n
Brunschwig, Henri, 15 n

Cabral, Amilcar, 44, 46–47
Camara (clan), 135, 141
Camara, Sory, 77–81, 108–9, 262–63
Camara Laye, 199, 259 n, 297; on gender and speech, 251–52, 264; name, 116–17; and Sékou Touré, 62. See also *Enfant noir; Maître de la parole*
Canon, canonicity, 248–49, 285–93; and corpus, 249; and *L'Enfant noir*, 125; and education, 248–49
Caste, 77–78; in the novel, 110–13; in *O pays, mon beau peuple!* 43; and the Wolof, 280 n. See also *Nyamakala*
Caute, David, 48
Censorship, 27, 240, 243
Césaire, Aimé, 13, 16, 24, 39, 188, 296
Cham, Mbye, 277
Chemain-Degrange, Arlette, 257

323